RETHINKING UKRAINIAN HISTORY

Edited by Ivan L. Rudnytsky

With the assistance of John-Paul Himka

The Canadian Institute of Ukrainian Studies
The University of Alberta
Edmonton 1981

Canadian Cataloguing in Publication Data

Rethinking Ukrainian History

(The Canadian library in Ukrainian studies)

Papers and discussion from the Ukrainian Historical Conference held at the University of Western Ontario, London, in May 1978.

ISBN 0-920862-12-8 (bound).
ISBN 0-920862-14-4 (pbk.).

1. Ukraine - History - Congresses. I. Lysiak-Rudnytskyi, Ivan. II. Himka, John-Paul, 1949- III. Ukrainian Historical Conference (1978: University of Western Ontario). IV. Canadian Institute of Ukrainian Studies. V. Series.
DK 508.5.R48 947.71 C81–091218–X

Cover: Peter Matilainen

Printed in Canada by Printing Services, University of Alberta
Distributed by the University of Toronto Press
5201 Dufferin St.
Downsview, Ontario
Canada M3H 5T8

Contents

Contributors

Ivan L. Rudnytsky	Professor of History University of Alberta
John-Paul Himka	Visiting Assistant Professor Canadian Institute of Ukrainian Studies University of Alberta
Steven L. Guthier	Analyst U.S. Department of Defence
Patricia Herlihy	Visiting Associate Professor of History Brown University, Research Associate Harvard Ukrainian Research Institute
Zenon E. Kohut	Editor American Bibliography of Russian and East European Studies
Omeljan Pritsak	Mykhailo Hrushevsky Professor of History Harvard University, Director Harvard Ukrainian Research Institute
George Y. Shevelov	Professor Emeritus Columbia University
Orest Subtelny	Associate Professor of History Hamilton College, New York, Associate Harvard Ukrainian Research Institute
Frank Sysyn	Assistant Professor of History, Research Fellow, Russian Research Center Harvard University, Research Fellow Harvard Ukrainian Research Institute
Roman Szporluk	Professor of History University of Michigan
Peter Woroby	Professor of Economics University of Regina

Publisher's Preface

This book has been produced using MTS Textform, an advanced computer word-processing system especially designed to improve editorial control over the text through consistent page-formating, pagination, and the correction of errors prior to typesetting by the high-speed computerized APS-5 system. The system allows for quick reproduction of updated editions. Special thanks are due to Mr. David Holberton and the Textform Group and to Mr. Peter Buttuls of Integrated Graphics, Computing Services, University of Alberta, for their invaluable assistance in the publication of this book.

Introduction

This volume contains presentations to the Ukrainian Historical Conference at the University of Western Ontario, London, Ontario, on 29–31 May 1978. The conference, which took place within the framework of the annual meeting of the Canadian Association of Slavists, was organized jointly by the Canadian Institute of Ukrainian Studies, the Harvard Ukrainian Research Institute and the Ukrainian Historical Association. The Canadian Institute of Ukrainian Studies sponsored the conference and was responsible for the technical preparatory work. The conference committee consisted of Ivan L. Rudnytsky (CIUS), Frank E. Sysyn (HURI) and Lubomyr R. Wynar (UHA).

The programme of the conference comprised six topical sessions: "Historiography," "Ukraine and the Muslim World," "The Historical legacy of Kievan Rus'," "Ukrainian Elites," "Ukraine and the Russian Revolution," "The Role of the City in Ukrainian History" and a Round Table discussion on "Problems of Terminology and Periodication in the Teaching of Ukrainian History." The guest speaker at the conference banquet, held jointly with the Canadian Association of Slavists, was Professor George Y. Shevelov who presented the "Reflections of a Linguist on Ukrainian History."

This collection does not contain the entire conference proceedings, since limitations of space necessitated the exclusion of papers on historiography and Ukraine and the Russian Revolution. Moreover, there already exist several excellent English-language studies of the revolutionary period (1917–21) in Ukraine, and the highly specialized nature and complexity of the subject of historiography warrants more extensive treatment in a separate publication. Of the sessions, only "The Role of the City in Ukrainian History" is fully represented in this volume, as some papers of the other sessions were not made available to the editor. The included papers have not only been revised by the authors, but their sequence has been rearranged for chronological and substantive reasons.

On the panel of the Round Table discussion were six professors, all teachers of Ukrainian history courses in North American universities. The panel was chaired by Professor Omeljan Pritsak, the Mykhailo Hrushevsky Professor of Ukrainian History at Harvard University and Director of the Harvard Ukrainian Research Institute. The discussion was transcribed from the tapes and then edited. Despite minor changes, it is hoped that the printed record retains the original flavour of a spontaneous and lively scholarly debate.

Professor Shevelov's after-dinner address has appeared in the *Journal of Ukrainian Graduate Studies* 6 (Spring 1979): 62–9. At Professor Shevelov's request, it was superseded in this volume by his earlier article "L'ukrainien littéraire," published originally in *Revue des études slaves* 33 (1956): 68–83 and reprinted in G. Y. Shevelov, *Teasers and Appeasers: Essays and Studies on Themes of Slavic Philology* (Munich: Wilhelm Fink Verlag, 1971), 245–60. An English translation was prepared for *The Slavic Literary Languages: Formation and Development*, edited by Alexander M. Schenker and Edward Stankiewicz, a forthcoming volume in the Yale and East European Publications series. It is reproduced here with permission and with minor stylistic changes. By focusing on questions of continuity and discontinuity in the development of the Ukrainian literary language, the paper suggests illuminating parallels for scholars engaged in rethinking Ukrainian history.

—

While responsibility for the factual statements and interpretations advanced in the papers of this collection rests, as usual, with the individual contributors, the planning of the Ukrainian Historical Conference was based on certain general guidelines which are reflected in the present publication. The organizers were faced with a choice between a "conference of Ukrainian historians" or a "Ukrainian historical conference." In opting for the latter, the organizers wished to ensure the highest professional and academic standards for the conference, and to avoid any suggestion that it was just a gathering of émigré notables. Similarly, the decision to conduct the conference entirely in English was designed to bring Ukrainian history visibly into the mainstream of North American historical scholarship. While it is expected that the study of Ukrainian history will appeal to scholars who are themselves Ukrainian, it does not follow that only persons of Ukrainian background will work in the field. In fact, the future of Ukrainian historical studies in the West may well depend on the number of non-Ukrainian specialists which such studies attract. The conference was attended by several non-Ukrainian scholars, and it is hoped that their participation will set a trend for the future.

The lamentable condition of historical studies in the Ukrainian SSR is of great concern to scholars in the West. The low level of Soviet historiography results mostly from the imposition of a stifling official ideology, in which an ossified Marxism-Leninism is amalgamated with a rigidly Russocentric vision of Ukrainian and general East Slavic history, which tolerates no topics, methods and interpretations that cannot be pressed into its straitjacket.

How should Western students of Ukrainian history respond to this distressing situation? Many in the Ukrainian diaspora community believe that Soviet ideological orthodoxy ought to be met with an equally rigid and militant "patriotic" orthodoxy. In the conference organizers' view, such an approach would be self-defeating. What is needed is the application of free, critical thought, untrammelled by dogmas of any kind, whether Marxist or nationalist. The test of critical thought is the readiness to face unpleasant facts and painful issues and to scrutinize the preconceptions, biases and favourite myths even of one's own community.

Among the ills which afflict Soviet Ukrainian historiography none perhaps is more debilitating than its enforced isolation from the outside world. Soviet Ukrainian historians do not publish in foreign journals, hardly ever travel abroad for reasons of research and rarely attend international scholarly conferences and symposia. When they do, it is usually as supernumerary members of general Soviet delegations. Even their access to foreign scholarly literature appears to be seriously limited. The result—intended by the regime—is the impoverishment, stultification and increased provincialism of the Ukrainian nation's cultural life in general and of the historical science in particular.

Western scholars can help to remedy these deformations, provided they themselves study Ukrainian history in a universal context. This does not mean that the existing links between the Ukrainian and Russian historical processes should be played down; they should merely be reduced to their proper dimension, with due attention to reciprocal relations between

Ukraine and such other countries and civilizations as the Mediterranean world, Central Europe and the Eurasian sphere. Focusing on this complex network of relationships and influences will bring to light Ukraine's unique historical identity; it will also contribute to a better understanding of the history of Eastern Europe as a whole. One can always hope that the labours of Western scholars might induce positive changes in Soviet Ukrainian historiography and ease the strictures which handicap it at present. However, the prerequisite is that Western specialists in Ukrainian history learn how to approach their subject in a consistently non-parochial spirit. Thomas G. Masaryk used to admonish his fellow Czech intellectuals to study the Czech problem as a world problem. This advice is equally valuable in the Ukrainian case.

Such were the basic guidelines for the 1978 Ukrainian Historical Conference. Readers may judge for themselves how well they have been realized.

The assistance of the following persons and institutions is gratefully acknowledged: the executive of the Canadian Association of Slavists and its former president, Professor Peter J. Potichnyj, McMaster University, for accommodating the Ukrainian Historical Conference within the programme of the association's 1978 annual meeting; the Humanities and Social Sciences Research Council of Canada for its financial assistance; Professor Eva S. Balogh, Russian and East European Studies, Yale University, for making available the English translation of Professor Shevelov's paper; Mr. Brent Kostyniuk for undertaking the difficult task of transcribing the taped text of the Round Table discussion; and the editorial staff of the Canadian Institute of Ukrainian Studies.

I would like to express special thanks to my colleague, Professor John-Paul Himka, whose help in preparing the conference and in editing the papers was invaluable.

Ivan L. Rudnytsky
University of Alberta
May 1981

Omeljan Pritsak

Kievan Rus' and Sixteenth-Seventeenth-Century Ukraine

I

Before addressing my specific topic of "Kievan Rus' and Sixteenth-Seventeenth-Century Ukraine," I feel obliged to elaborate on the question of what Kievan Rus' actually was. Finding a suitable answer is not an easy task, especially if one needs a general but workable definition which does not go too much into details. However, one element of the answer is certain; contrary to the prevailing view in Ukrainian historiography, Kievan Rus' was *not* one constant political structure existing from the tenth to the thirteenth centuries.

The term "Kievan (or Rus') empire," which one finds so often in scholarly literature, can be applied only to the reign of Iaroslav the Wise, beginning with his victory over the Pechenegs in Kiev in 1036 up to his death in 1054. Iaroslav apparently followed the example of other "sedentary" rulers in destroying a "nomadic" empire which challenged him, as Charlemagne had done with the Avars (ca. 800) and Otto I with the nomadic predecessor of the Hungarian realm (955). It seems fairly certain that Iaroslav patterned his imperial order, centred spiritually on St. Sophia, after the political structure of the Byzantine empire, which had a patrimonial system of rule of a neo-Hellenistic type.[1]

Of course, the Slavic character of Kievan Rus' must play a weighty role in our discussion. Therefore, let us turn again to the epoch of Iaroslav, since it was he who, having come from Novgorod, brought to Kiev the

Slavonic rite[2] with its ready corpus of ecclesiastic, edificational and juridical literature, written in the foreign, artificial, so-called Church Slavonic language.[3]

Iaroslav apparently had no faith in the wisdom of leaving his empire in the care of his immediate offspring, as the Byzantine system of succession required. He may have been influenced by the experience of the Byzantine empire itself, which after the death of the valiant emperor Basil II, in 1025, was ruled by incompetent women and their favourites. As the successor to the Khazar *kagan* traditions,[4] Iaroslav opted for the steppe system of succession, whose primary goal was to keep the empire together. In the Rus' sources this system is known as *lestvichnoe voskhozhdenie* or "ascendance by steps."[5]

In order for the system to function successfully, it was necessary to establish three ruling branches of the dynasty. Each received a permanent hereditary domain (in Rus'ian, *volost*), also called a patrimony (in Rus'ian, *otchina*), which was its own possession. This domain or patrimony was distinct from a "political" state seat (throne) and the connecting territories (annexes) which were only temporarily at the disposal of the dynasty's ruling members.

There were two types of succession: a) the private—the succession to the *otchina*; obligatory here was the regulation recorded in the *Ruskaia pravda*: "The father's household as a whole always (passes) to the youngest son" (article 100);[6] b) the political—the succession to five thrones (one supreme and four subordinated) within the system of *lestvichnoe voskhozhdenie*; obligatory here was the principle of seniority, so that the senior members of each of the three ruling branches had, on a rotating basis between the branches, the opportunity to ascend to the highest ranking central throne. The system was designed to avoid separatism among the ruling branches and to prevent violent attempts to acquire the supreme throne.[7]

Two senior members of each branch had the right to succession. After all the members of one generation had taken their place in the system, they were followed by the same assortment of members from the next generation. Members of the dynasty whose fathers, because of death or other circumstances, did not reach one of the three highest political thrones were to leave the system to become non-ruling (non-political) landowners or "knights of fortune" (Old Rus' *izgoi*, Turkic *kazak*).

In Iaroslav's variant of *lestvichnoe voskhozhdenie*, the supreme throne in Kiev was reserved for the senior members of the entire dynasty, and the four thrones available to other rulers were, in descending rank order: Chernihiv, Pereiaslav, Smolensk and Volodymyr-in-Volhynia. The thrones of Chernihiv and Pereiaslav were superior, since they were reserved for two heirs-apparent, while the thrones of Smolensk and Volodymyr were fully subordinate. Through this system of five thrones there came into being a college of three triumvirs and two assistants.

The thrones of the triumvirs were situated on territory where Iaroslav's retinue had settled permanently. Only the lands of Kiev, Chernihiv and Pereiaslav had acquired this special recognition as the "land of Rus'" par excellence (*rus'skaia zemlia*).[8] Three main trading and "maritime" centres were attached to the two superior thrones: to Kiev, Great Novgorod and Oleshe at the two extremities of the Dnieper route; and to Chernihiv, Tmutorokan. The annexes of the Kievan throne were the former Derevlianian land (Volhynia), Pohoryna, Berestia and Galicia. The annexes of the Chernihiv throne were the land of the Siverians and the "towns of the Viatichians." The annexes of the Pereiaslav throne were Posemia and Kursk. The lower thrones did not possess annexes, and were themselves under the direct control of the college of triumvirs.

The three branches of Iaroslav's progeny were supposed to develop into three separate dynasties, which, in turn, were to guarantee the uninterrupted functioning of the system of *lestvichnoe voskhozhdenie*. The patrimonies which the three elder sons of Iaroslav received as subsistence for their dynasties were Turov-Pinsk in Polissia (Iziaslav's dynasty), Murom in the Oka basin (Sviatoslav's dynasty) and Rostov in the middle Volga basin (Vsevolod's dynasty).

The system of *lestvichnoe voskhozhdenie* did not develop fully in Rus'. The immediate cause, although only one of several, was that not the two eldest, but the two youngest sons of Iaroslav were the first to die.[9] Their sons were ineligible for succession because the fathers had not attained a throne of the triumvirate; these sons then became founders of the *izgoi* dynasties, of which the most important was the Rostislavichi dynasty in Galicia (ca. 1080–1199). At first, the triumvir, Vsevolod, disposed of his two brothers and peopled all the thrones with members of his own branch.

I cannot dwell here on the reasons behind the non-functioning of the original *lestvichnoe voskhozhdenie*. It must suffice to say that the outcome was a "revised" edition of the system which resulted in political separatism. The dynasty of Iziaslav was permanently removed from the system (Iaroslav had previously excluded the Polotsk branch of the Riurikids; the *izgoi* dynasty of Rostislavichi were here considered to be included into the system). They became local rulers of Polissia (Turov-Pinsk) and did not participate in the political life of Kievan Rus' in the twelfth-thirteenth centuries. The two remaining dynasties—that of Sviatoslav (originally Murom-based) and of Vsevolod (Rostov-based)—each created their own system of two superior thrones, and then began to compete for the supreme Kievan throne. In 1125 Murom had separated from Chernihiv, the former superior political throne. Chernihiv had gradually become an independent political body that combined political rule with elements of patrimony (Putyvl).

Shortly after the death of Mstislav Monomakhovich, the great grandson of Iaroslav, while the Chernihiv dynasty was holding the Kievan throne, 1139–46, the older branch of the Monomakh dynasty turned Volhynia, hitherto the annex of the supreme Kievan throne, into their patrimony. The Rostov patrimony remained the undisputed possession of the younger branch of the Monomakhovichi and became a political body.

In the meantime, events of international importance had taken place. In 1070–1 both the army and the fleet of the Byzantine empire suffered resounding defeats—the army by the Turkic Seldjuks at Mazikert in East Anatolia, and the fleet at Bari in Italy.[10] As a result, Byzantium-Constantinople-Tsargrad lost its dominant position in international economic and political life. The Byzantine international trade now moved to the Italian cities of Venice and Genoa. These cities were interested in the Crimean, Central Asian and Near Eastern, especially Persian, markets.[11]

Some decades later, we witness the commercial emancipation of the North. The German cities, predecessors of the Hanse, gradually made the Baltic Sea their internal lake. By the beginning of the thirteenth century they had established themselves both in Riga/Reval and Danzig (Gdańsk).[12] The famous artery from the Varangians to the Greeks, the Dnieper route, which had once given rise to the Rus' Kievan state, had entered a period of decline. Now new economic centres were established around the Baltic Sea, the Azov Sea and the Crimean peninsula, and the old Volga trade route was resurrected as the basic link between the two poles.[13]

The first signs of the new epoch were the loss of Tmutorokan and the proclamation of independence by Great Novgorod (1136).[14] The glory of Kiev was fading and its economic and political importance was shifting to two hitherto marginal territories: Galicia-Volhynia, with its access, via the Dniester-San or the Western Bug rivers, to the Baltic Sea; and the Rostov land with its centres of Suzdal, Rostov and Vladimir-on-the-Kliazma, located within the basin of the Volga, the main highway of the Caspian, Azov-Crimean and Persian trade. The non-Slavic Lithuanians were also entering into the picture, partly because of German invaders, but also because of the attraction of the new commercial "bonanza" itself; the Polotsk *zemlia*, outside the system of the *lestvichnoe voskhozhdenie*, proved to be easy for the Lithuanians to penetrate.[15]

One hundred years after Iaroslav's death, Kiev finally lost its standing as the supreme political throne. Its economic supremacy had waned and the *lestvichnoe voskhozhdenie* became bankrupt. The two destructions of Kiev—one provoked by the Volga ruler Andrei Bogoliubsky in 1169 and the other carried out by the Mongols in 1240—were to some measure coups de grâce for the past giant.

Great Novgorod has already been mentioned. That commercial centre best preserved a system of governing that apparently went back to times long before the Riurikids ascended to power. The system was a variation on the classical and Hellenistic *polis* with an oligarchic system of government, although sovereignty theoretically rested with the city assembly (*veche*). Another very important trading town with a similar oligarchic system was Halych which, incidentally, had always maintained close ties with Great Novgorod (e.g., the *izgoi* Rostislavichi dynasty was of Novgorodian origin).

Now let us return to the question posed at the outset of this discussion: what was Kievan Rus'? Aside from Iaroslav's twenty-year reign as *tsesar*, "emperor" of Rus', Kievan Rus' was a conglomerate of constantly emerging local states called *zemli*, having different and fluctuating degrees of independence. They were ruled either by a hereditary ruler or by an oligarchic clique with an elected prince functioning as a magistrate engaged by the town, and existed within or outside a superstructure of several variants of the steppe's unifying system of *lestvichnoe voskhozhdenie*.

All these states, however, were distinguished by four common elements which can be called characteristics of the pre-political cultural sphere. The first, and one could say the primary, element was the (originally foreign) Orthodox religion in the "revised" Slavonic rite. In the course of the twelfth century, the original Slavonic rite, which was neutral in the struggle between the papacy and Byzantium, had been replaced by its Byzantine version. In the crucial thirteenth-fourteenth centuries, in Latin Europe (especially Poland and Hungary), as a result of the "nationalization" of the Catholic churches, a secular awareness of a national past developed. It, in turn, brought about a sense of national consciousness and a peculiarly national political culture.[16]

The greatest achievement of the contemporary Byzantine mind was the spiritual movement called hesychasm. Centred in the monastic republic of Mount Athos, it propagated the belief that the only purpose of human life was to achieve divine tranquility (Greek *hesychia*) through the contemplation of God in uninterrupted prayer.[17] One outcome was that in Kievan Rus' the spontaneous "barbaric" interest in history, which had produced such gems as the *Pověst' vremennykh lět*, the "Kievan Chronicle" and the "Galician-Volhynian Chronicle" in the eleventh-thirteenth centuries, was subsequently replaced by the "Lives" of saints and the "Patericon."[18] The only literary products of Kievan intellectuals in the fifteenth century were two hesychastic redactions of the Patericon of saints of the Kievan Caves Monastery (*Pecherskii paterik*), the two so-called Kassian versions.[19] The first Kievan "historical" work to be published was notably the Polish translation of the "Patericon" by Sylvester Kosov in Kiev in 1635. In consequence, secular literature had no place in the territories of the former Rus' in the fourteenth-sixteenth centuries. The interest in the political past of the territory and its people was now almost completely lost.

The second element common to the states was the dynastic-cultural sphere called "Rus'." This term, which is of disputed origin, first referred to the dynasty and its retinue, as well as to the territories possessed by the dynasty in opposition to the territories ruled by other dynasties. Iaroslav's attempt to nationalize his Rus', specifically in the nucleus of his empire, i.e., in the lands of Kiev-Chernihiv-Pereiaslav, had, practically speaking, failed. In the thirteenth to fifteenth centuries, the name "Rus'" was adopted to refer to other parts of the Riurikids' possessions, the former annexes, or non-political patrimonies, which were now politically "loaded," especially by Galicia and Volhynia. Now several parallel Rus'es had come into being. The name "Rus'" in relation to Kiev—[Chernihiv]-Pereiaslav—was paradoxically enough gradually falling out of use and was soon to be replaced by another designation, Ukraina, with the result that—as one contemporary seventeenth-century author remarked—"na Rusi nie stało Rusi," i.e., "no Rus' had remained in Rus'."[20]

However, the name Rus' never lost its application in the religious identification of all territories that were part of the Kievan metropolitan see. (Attempts to divide this disproportionately vast ecclesiastical province were unsuccessful until the second half of the fifteenth century (1457).) The Slavonic rite in Eastern Europe had become identified with the "Rus'ian religion." Its corpus of religious and edifying literature (now in hesychastic re-working) was named "Rus'ian script," and the foreign, artificial Church Slavonic language was regarded as the native Slavo-Rus'ian literary language, and the "indigenous" written vehicle for communication was the Rus' chancery language ("die West-Russische Kanzleisprache").[21] Also paradoxically, the universal, pre-secular church in Eastern Europe received a "national" and "secular" label.

The third element unifying the states of Kievan Rus' was the patrimonial state structure. I agree with Richard Pipes that Max Weber's concept of patrimonial system applies here, namely, a political system where "the rights of sovereignty and those of ownership blend to the point of becoming indistinguishable, and political power is exercised in the same manner as economic power."[22] The ruler (a person or group) holds a monopoly of political, economic and legal power. There is no political authority other than the ruler, and therefore it is impossible to form or develop an elite.[23] Undoubtedly, this was a new phenomenon introduced by the Rus' dynasty, which after it became a part of the Orthodox world (since 1054 separated from the "progressive" Catholic world) had no option in choosing a pattern of governing other than to accept the only two political systems known in Eastern Europe, both ultimately of Hellenistic origin—those of the Bosporan Kingdom (later Tmutorokan) and the Byzantine empire.

The pre-Rus' East European society was, one may speculate, a community of at least two "classes" of free peasants and merchants, and bound slaves (including artisans). The legal documents of the Rus' imperial period (1036–54), as well as those from the eleventh and twelfth centuries, distinguish clearly between four strata, each having their specific *wergeld*:[24]

1) *muzhi*, or the originally foreign upper class, the ruling dynasty and the ruling oligarchy;

2) *liudi*, the pre-Rus' basic yeomen society, now the middle class of free men;

3) *smerdy*, freemen of somewhat limited status;

4) *cheliad*, half-free strata (artisans), freedmen and slaves.

During the thirteenth-sixteenth centuries, society was polarized between free oligarchic clans and bound serfs. The middle strata had two possibilities: either to move upward and become a part of the oligarchy (very few, of course, could attain such a goal) or to fall to the status of a serf. Since the majority of the populace of the former Kievan Rus' did belong to these middle strata, they could hardly be satisfied with the existing options and looked outside of the Rus' cultural sphere for guidance and salvation.

The fourth element, a result of the previous three, was the fact that there was no basis for the development of a system of estates in Rus' which could produce an elite able and ready to become involved in political and state affairs alongside the ruler. In Western Europe the emergence of an estate society was conditioned by the charters (immunities) granted from the twelfth century on by political rulers to the church following the outcome of the struggle for investiture. Gradually, the secular strata followed the path of ecclesiastics and were able to obtain similar charters for themselves. Their common struggle brought about an "estate solidarity" and an interest in public affairs. In this way an elite emerged that replaced the primitive oligarchic cliques.[25] "Estate solidarity" and involvement in public affairs bound the elite to the territory and to its past, which normally leads to the development of the feeling of separateness and uniqueness that is the foundation of national consciousness.[26]

The Eastern church was totally subordinated to the patrimonial political power. Considering this and the hesychastic view of life which prevailed there in the thirteenth to sixteenth centuries, one can readily understand why the Ukrainian church had no interest whatsoever in public affairs until the sixteenth century. Members of the secular strata knew only two virtues: service to the ruler and acquisition of fame in such service. There was no idea of a "national" ruler. Every master who controlled a territory and who was gracious to his servitors was recognized as suzerain.

In the fifteenth and sixteenth centuries the Ukrainian upper strata were proud that they could serve the Polish kings with the same devotion as their ancestors had served the rulers of Rus'.[27]

During the period between the eleventh and fourteenth centuries "Kievan Rus'" was not suited to produce a concept of a "political Rus'," in contrast to the emerging Polish state in the thirteenth-fourteenth centuries, which, on the basis of its Western-type estate state system, created the notion of a "political Pole" irrespective of ethnic or religious origin.

II

In contrast to Kievan Rus', which—as stated above—was basically patterned after the Khazar and Byzantine system, Galician-Volhynian Rus' was strongly, if indirectly, exposed to developments in the West. For over two centuries the "West" (i.e., the Catholic West) was represented there by Hungary, for a long time the only kingdom in Central Europe. After 1320 Western influences were represented by the newly emerged Kingdom of Poland.

Because both Hungary and Poland had had no real feudal law, their transition to an estate society had some peculiarities. Military service (*ius militari*)—basic for land tenure—brought about a very numerous nobility (in Hungary about 5 per cent and in Poland about 10 per cent of the entire population). There were some differences between the two kingdoms: in Hungary of the twelfth-thirteenth centuries (as well as in Little Poland) the nobility was divided into two strata. The upper stratum, comprised of several hundred magnate families called *barones*, concentrated all wealth, power and status in their hands. The barons, who were the early members of the king's council, also ruled the country *de jure*, often to their own benefit. In contrast to the English Magna Carta, which the English barons extracted from King John, the Hungarian Golden Bull (1222) resulted from pressure by the lower stratum of free men "directed more against the barons than against the King."[28]

In Poland the Košice pact (1374) assured the middle class of legal equality with the magnates; the new estate, now generally known as *szlachta*, was freed from all taxes and was independent of the royal judiciary; in addition, it received jurisdiction over the peasants on its own territory. It soon took almost total control over the emerging parliamentary institutions, thus preventing the involvement of two other estates—the clergy and the burghers—in the process.[29]

After the first local dynasty died out, the Galician boyars often invited members of the Hungarian (Árpád) dynasty to be their princes (Andrew—1189, Koloman—1214–21, Andrew—1227–30, 1232–3). Sometimes new Western knightly customs reached Volhynia and Galicia even earlier. In 1149 the "Kievan Chronicle" noted that the Great Prince of Cracow, Bolesław IV (1146–73), a relative of Iziaslav II (1146–54) of Volhynia and Kiev, had, during a stay in Lutske, knighted sons of many local boyars by giving each the requisite ceremonial blow on the neck.[30] According to the "Galician-Volhynian Chronicle," Galician and Volhynian princes fenced in the Western style (1230)[31] and sometimes held tournaments outside a city "to pass the time of the siege" (1245).[32]

The documents of Iurii II (1325–40) show that two classes of nobles existed in his realm: *barones sive milites*, the higher stratum; and *nobiles*, the lower stratum.[33] The *barones*, called *boiary* in Rus'ian, were of heterogeneous origin: among them were grandsons of priests and sons of *smerdy* (free peasants).[34] As during the Kievan period, these individuals acquired nobility by serving in the retinue (*druzhina*). On five occasions they committed crimes on a scale previously unknown in princely Rus': they burned at the stake the common-law wife of Prince Iaroslav Osmomysl in 1173, because she belonged to a newcomer noble clan, and later, in 1188, they poisoned her and Iaroslav's son Oleg; in 1211 the boyars hanged two princes of the Chernihiv branch of the dynasty (Roman and Sviatoslav), whom they had previously invited to rule over Halych; the last Galician-Volhynian ruler, Iurii II, was also a victim of poisoning, but this time in Volodymyr-in-Volhynia. In 1214 one of the boyars, Volodislav Kormilchich (son of the major-domo), made himself the ruling prince of Halych (the only case in the history of princely Rus' where a boyar usurped princely power).

The Galician boyars were divided into several factions, usually in an ad hoc arrangement designed to assure a given clique political power based on the patrimonial "charisma" of a minor or incapable prince. It seemed to be the boyars' "political" ideal never to develop group solidarity; therefore they were unable to become a legal estate.

Whereas in Galicia the barons were the dominant figures in politics, after 1250 in commercially oriented Volhynia townsmen seemed to play the pre-eminent political role. There were two types of towns in Volhynia-Galicia: the "Oriental," where local traders resided side by side with the Armenians and Jews (the Sudak/Surozh—Kaffa-centred Black Sea trade was in their hands), and the newly emerged urban patriciate in the cities under Magdeburg law. The latter had been settled by German colonists around 1250 and had close links to the Hanse cities and the Baltic trade.

The "Galician-Volhynian Chronicle" describes Mstislav's ascendancy to the throne of Volhynia (1288) in the following way:

> Upon his arrival [in Volodymyr-in-Volhynia], Mstislav entered the cathedral—the Church of the Blessed Mother—and summoned: [a] his brother's boyars of [the city of] Volodymyr and [b] the Rus'ian *městichě* (townsmen) and the German *městichě*. [Then] he ordered his brother's document dealing with the bequeathal of the land and all the cities [including] the capital city of Volodymyr [in Volhynia] to be read before everyone, and they all listened, both the humble and the great ones (*vsi ot mala i do velika*).[35]

Unfortunately, we do not know how these two very different kinds of citizens co-existed side-by-side in everyday life. It seems, however, that the German urban patricians had the greater role: for instance, during the deliberations between the Galician-Volhynian princes and the Lithuanians in 1268, a German urban patrician from Volodymyr-in-Volhynia, Markholt, invited the princes to deliberate at his home and the proposal was gladly accepted.[36] In other ways the social structure seemed to remain without great change. The *smerdy* retained their free status as yeomen; the *church people* remained under the jurisdiction of the clergy; the *slaves* and *indentured labourers* continued to exist and *serfdom* was still unknown.

The superficial co-existence of the Western-type and Eastern-type social structures had a catastrophic end. When the patrimonial dynasty ended, the Galician-Volhynian state fell (1349), even though at the height of its development, and it did so without leaving any trace.

The Galician boyars (and Volhynian townsmen) educated in the system of Orthodox patrimonial culture were not prepared politically to form the legal estates that were given in somewhat limited form to their Polish and Hungarian contemporaries through the Western-based system of feudalism, which trained them in Roman inheritance law and taught them about the separation of clerical and secular fields. Therefore the boyars, attracted to Polish estate privileges, threw over their patrimonial state in return for privileges.[37] The Orthodox church leaders, having lost their protectors, emigrated to the North (Smolensk, Moscow) or gave up their estates. The Old Ruthenian (Ukrainian) inheritance did not die as a result of the fall of the Galician-Volhynian state in 1349. In fact, it did some forty years earlier, when it appeared to be at its highest point of development. The fall arose from the failure of the ruling strata (the patrimonial prince, the boyars, church strata, "local" and foreign burghers) to resolve internal conflicts at a time when they faced an immediate confrontation between the old Orthodox patrimonial, apolitical thought and the new Catholic political thought and legal system.

III

One myth still dominates Ukrainian and East European historiography. This is the idea of a Mongolian "chasm" in 1223–40, allegedly responsible for the political and cultural decline of Ukraine (and/or Russia) and for the break of tradition between the thirteenth and sixteenth centuries. According to the nineteenth-century Russian historian Mikhail Pogodin, the Mongol catastrophe caused the migration of the alleged Great Russians of Kiev to the North; their place was then gradually taken up by the ancestors of the Ukrainians, coming from Galicia and Volhynia. Ukrainian historians, from Pogodin's friend Mykhailo Maksymovych to Mykhailo Hrushevsky, were obliged to invest much of their time and effort in combatting this artificial intellectual construction.[38]

The major point here, however, is that there was *no* Mongolian chasm. Of course, the Mongols did invade Eastern Europe and caused destruction on a large scale, although still within a framework typical of any foreign military invasion of that day. But the Mongols did not excel in destroying cultural or religious life. The fact that I am an Orientalist, involved in Turkic and Mongolian studies, does not make me the devil's advocate on this issue. On the contrary, knowledge of Mongolian history and culture (strangely enough, the Mongols *did* possess their own culture!) provides a perspective necessary if one is to view their East European activities impartially.

Let me add that the "*Pax Mongolica*" prevailed not only in Eastern Europe, but also in Transcaucasia, Iran, Central Asia and even China. In every case, Mongolian rule fostered a very productive cultural life: for example, Persian poetry, both lyric and epic, reached its apex at that time, and Chinese literature, scholarship and visual arts bloomed in freedom from its isolation, and was now able to draw on the rich Iranian culture.[39] Also, it was under Mongolian rule, during the second half of the thirteenth century, that the most advanced work of Ukrainian medieval historical prose was written, namely the famous "Galician-Volhynian Chronicle."

Not the Mongols, but the Lithuanians created a chasm in Ukrainian historical development. This statement will certainly be received by many with amazement and perhaps even outrage. For more than 150 years, Ukrainians have had a concept of a Lithuanian-Rus'ian/Ukrainian period in their history. Nevertheless, the truth is that neither the Mongols nor the Poles are responsible for the disruption of the Ukrainian historical and institutional process. Responsibility lies with the Ukrainians' alleged alter ego, the Lithuanians. Now let me elaborate on this statement, weighty in its consequences.

In the first decade of the thirteenth century, the territory of the former Kievan Rus' consisted of three differentiated zones of cultural Rus' (as defined above), each of which was a system of patrimonial hereditary principalities and/or oligarchic cliques. Located in the South, in the interconnected basins of the middle and lower Dnieper, the Dniester and the Prypiat rivers, were three sets of hereditary principalities: Volhynia-Galicia, Turov-Pinsk and Chernihiv-Putyvl-Briansk. Each had the same origin: they were the former patrimony-dynasties, first conceived by Iaroslav (as discussed above). Outside that system there co-existed several oligarchic realms, among which the Kievan and Podillian were most significant. In the northwest, in the basins of the Upper Dnieper and of the Western Dvina, four political entities had developed: the set of the principalities Polotsk (estranged during the Kievan period) and Vitebsk, the principality of Smolensk and the two oligarchic ("ochlocratic") "republics" of Novgorod and Pskov.

The principality of Smolensk deserves special attention. Originally it was one of the two lower seats in the system of *lestvichnoe voskhozhdenie*. But with Kiev's decline and with its own proximity to the Baltic Sea (there was a portage system from the Upper Dnieper to the Western Dvina), Smolensk gradually took over Kiev's dominant position on the Dnieper trade route, now reduced in importance. Rostislav Mstislavich, a grandson of Monomakh and himself for a time prince of Kiev (d. 1167), had established there a vigorous dynasty of the older Monomakhovichi, which for a time also ruled over Kiev (1180–1234). The other division of the older branch of the Monomakhovichi became rooted in Volhynia; this was the dynasty of Roman and King Danylo. In the thirteenth century Smolensk maintained close ties with the German Hanse merchant republics and therefore experienced a comparatively strong influence from Western Europe.[40]

In the fourteenth and fifteenth centuries contemporaries viewed Smolensk as the successor to Kiev. When the Lithuanian ruler Vitovt (d. 1430) decided, at the beginning of the fourteenth century, to have the chronicle of the Lithuanian princes written down, he had a copy made of the "Galician-Volhynian Chronicle," then preserved in Pinsk (with the successors of Danylo's dynasty), but he also commissioned some literati of Smolensk to write down the Lithuanian historical memories. This marked the beginning of the so-called "Lithuanian-Rus'ian chronicles."[41]

The third set of Rus' principalities was Rostov-Vladimir-Moscow, located in the Volga basin and directly connected with the political centre of the Mongolian empire of the Golden Horde, which it was to succeed at the end of the fifteenth century.[42] This area exported grain to Great Novgorod, which despite its commercial connections was never able to be self-sufficent in its food supply.[43] In consequence, Novgorod had to maintain close political ties with the Northeastern Rus', later Moscow, with the result that it finally became incorporated into the Moscow state, although culturally and economically it belonged to the Northwestern Rus' and to the Baltic economic and cultural sphere. (Incidentally, the three zones discussed here are identical with the three East Slavic nationalities—Ukrainian, Belorussian and Russian.)

In the first decades of the fourteenth century, the Lithuanian princes and their oligarchic ruling strata decided that Rus' should become their hunting ground. The classic formulation of this expansionist programme was Olgerd's (d. 1377), statement (in 1358): "Omnis Russia ad Letwinos deberet simpliciter pertinere," i.e., "All of Rus' simply must belong to the Lithuanians."[44] The fact that the still-pagan Lithuanians did not form their own higher "national" culture, but chose to create along the fringes of the Rus'ian lands (Novgorod of Lithuania, Grodno) a Lithuanian variant of the Rus' culture which used both Rus' languages, the chancery and the ecclesiastical (as did the Romance Moldavians after 1340 in the basins of the Lower Dniester and Pruth), made their advance an easy task. Intermarriage with members of the Rus'ian dynasties also contributed positively to the realization of the Lithuanian task.

Lulling the local populace with the slogan "we shall keep the tradition and not introduce novelties,"[45] the Lithuanians used every opportunity to fill vacant thrones and leadership positions in the oligarchic realms with members of their own dynasty. As a result, by the middle of the fourteenth century, all Ukrainian territories (with the exception of Galicia) had Lithuanian rulers. True, most of the new rulers accepted Orthodox Christianity or became culturally Rus'ian. The responsible Lithuanian policy-makers were, however, displeased with the prospect of de-nationalization. All they had wanted was to possess the Rus' territories and the labour of their inhabitants. Realizing that they were numerically inferior to the masses of Rus'ians, the Lithuanians decided to exchange Orthodoxy for Catholicism thus separating themselves from the Rus', and to enter into a political union with Poland. Both states had a common foe—the Teutonic Order.[46]

It was Prince Jagiełło, who in 1385–6 had the Lithuanians baptized in the Catholic rite, and Vitovt, his co-ruler, who began the process of destroying the Ukrainian local political structures. The principalities of Kiev, Lutske (Volhynia) and Podillia were liquidated as political bodies and absorbed into the now centralized Lithuanian system. Throughout their lives Jagiełło and Vitovt competed for power in Lithuania; but on their general policy of destroying the vestiges of Rus'ian/Ukrainian separatism and humiliating Orthodoxy, they were in full agreement. (It was again Jagiełło, who, as king of Poland, finally introduced the Polish administrative system into Galicia and liquidated the Orthodox hierarchy there.)

Internal difficulties induced the Lithuanian government to restore the Kievan and other Rus' principalities for a time in the 1440s. But thirty years later, when the situation stabilized, the long-range policy had its final execution: in 1470, despite the protest of the local population, the Kievan prince (a member of the Lithuanian dynasty) had to make way for a Lithuanian *voevoda*. The same situation took place in the other princely seats.

We can now see clearly that the Lithuanians and not the Mongols are to blame for the interruption of the institutional and historical tradition in Ukraine. In such circumstances, it is small wonder that the Ukrainians (especially the middle nobility) pleaded for secession from the Lithuanian grand duchy and for incorporation into the Polish kingdom–the Lublin Union of 1569.

There are three periods in the economic (and socio-economic) history of Old Lithuania: the first lasted until the middle of the fourteenth century, i.e., until the Lithuanians obtained the Rus' territories; the second lasted until the unions with Poland (end of the fourteenth century to the beginning of the fifteenth century); the third followed thereafter.[47]

One can say that Lithuania owes its existence as a nation to the fact that its forests and meadows were rich in such products as hides, timber, wood ashes, wax and honey, which were all very desirable to the merchants of the German city of Riga, built (in 1201) at the mouth of the river Dvina. Riga was a "colony" (*Tochtergründung*) of Lübeck, later centre of the Hanse. Hanse merchants soon established themselves in the only major Lithuanian town, Kaunas. Throughout the thirteenth century and up to the middle of the fourteenth century, the merchants of Riga, its archbishop, and the Franciscans and Dominicans, did their best to tutor the inexperienced, newly emerged political entity and to protect it against the expansionist attempts of the Teutonic Order. The social structure of Lithuania at that time consisted almost entirely of free yeomen and slaves (the latter were former prisoners of war). The greater part of the cultivated land was divided into independent peasant farms, cleared by very primitive burning techniques.

After coming into contact with the more highly organized Rus' system of ownership, the grand prince claimed possession of all uncultivated and uninhabited lands, and also those which were économically very productive, regardless of ownership. Soon the prince started to grant lands to his helpers—to village leaders (*seniores, potentiores*) and to the ever-growing number of warriors (*homines militares*). The first endowment of land occurred in 1387 when the Latin bishopric of Vilnius was erected. In the course of the fourteenth century, many great estates were granted to the numerous members of the dynasty and to other important people. In this way a privileged class of the rich nobility (*barones, magnates*, in Slavic, *pany*) was legally recognized. The recipients of smaller estates received the status of gentry (equal to the Polish *szlachta*) in 1386; they possessed manors comprising no more than thirty-two undivided farms. Many of the gentry, having no tenants, had to cultivate the soil themselves.

In 1434 the grand prince exempted his subjects from payments in kind directly for his own benefit, and in 1447 he resigned his claim to permanent money payments and labour from private-estate peasants. The Lithuanian boyars (*barones, milites*) were legally recognized as having equal rights with the Polish *szlachta*: they were now freed from all taxes, were independent of the royal judiciary and, in addition, had jurisdiction over peasants on their own territory. But there was a basic difference between the Lithuanian and Polish systems: whereas in Lithuania the *barones* were able to legally establish themselves as a dominant class, there was legally only one gentry class in Poland.

The fifteenth century witnessed a new development in Lithuania which followed a Polish example: a considerable number of peasants became liable to *corvée* on the lord's demesne. This development was tantamount to the so-called European second serfdom. The estates were organized in a more productive way patterned on the German *Vorwerk* (> *folvarok*). The *voloka* (about twenty-one hectares) was introduced as a unit of measurement. The third Lithuanian Statute (1588) abolished slavery as an institution, since the *voloki* charter (1557) had already established serfdom as a legal institution. The Polish influence became decisive after the fall of Novgorod and the closing of the Hanseatic *Kontore* (trading post) there in 1494. The Lithuanian economy had at that time to make a shift from the north to the south and southwest.

Originally (until 1434), only Catholic Lithuanians obtained *szlachta* privileges. Orthodox Ukrainians under the Lithuanian regime had two options: to move upward by becoming Catholics and members of the class of *barones*, which was possible only in exceptional cases; or to be downgraded to the position of serfs, certainly an unattractive choice.

The prospect of receiving Polish political rights on their own was tempting to the Ukrainian middle nobility of the Lithuanian grand duchy. Therefore, they opted for the Lublin Union, especially since it did not oblige them to change their religion in order to become a member of the *szlachta* estate. Soon, as we know, Polish religious tolerance ended and the Catholic Counter Reformation forced many a "political Pole" to renounce Orthodoxy in order to make a career in the commonwealth. But this outcome does not diminish the significance of the new development: for the first time, the Ukrainian territory had produced a political elite, conscious both of its political rights, privileges and duties, and of its estate solidarity rooted in the territorial principle. This concept was entirely secular; not religion or language, but estate solidarity was the decisive factor for this new political body. In this fashion, a Rus' *patria* came into being, a political *novum* in the newly created palatinates of Kiev, Volhynia, Bratslav and (later) Chernihiv, that is, in practically all of Ukraine except Galicia. The formation of a new type of elite[48] had a great attraction for other strata of the Ukrainian population.

By the end of the sixteenth century, a mirror image of the Ukrainian territorial *szlachta* had emerged, the "anti-*szlachta*," in the form of the Ukrainian "registered" Cossacks. Their merger would later lead this newly created elite to attempt actively the restoration of the Rus' historical past through the creation (in Hadiach in 1658) of the Grand Duchy of Rus' as an equal political partner of the Kingdom of Poland and Grand Duchy of Lithuania.

IV

The second half of the fifteenth century had become critical for Kiev and Rus' proper. As already stressed, in 1470 the Kievan great principality was once and for all abolished by the Lithuanians, so that the term "Rus'" lost its political meaning in Kiev. A decade earlier, in 1458, occurred the definite partition of the former Kievan Orthodox metropolitanate. The two new successors were Moscow and Vilnius. Rus' proper now became a religious *tabula rasa*, without even a bishop's see.

The rivalry between Lithuania and Muscovy over Great Novgorod and Pskov and Lithuanian military weakness led to a coalition between Muscovy and the Crimean Khanate (which had come into being only three decades earlier as a Lithuanian creation). Thus in the spring of 1482, inspired by promises of gifts from Ivan III of Muscovy, the Crimean Khan Mengli Girey (1465–1515) captured and decisively destroyed Kiev, plundered the Caves Monastery and the cathedral of St. Sophia, and triumphantly sent Ivan III a golden chalice robbed from the latter. Kiev, the former centre of the Rus' empire and of East European Christianity, gradually turned into a ghost town.

By the end of the century, one part of the Kievan principality proper became known as Ukraine, or the frontier of the civilized world, and the other received the name of wilderness, called in Polish "*dzikie pole.*" This turbulent frontier attracted adventurous frontiersmen, who dared to occupy the steppes in spite of the danger of the Tatar sword, and to fight for the sake of freedom without a landlord.

Every spring emigrants from Kievan Polissia, northern Volhynia and even from Galicia (very often peasants or poverty-ridden townsmen) moved to unoccupied country where they lived by fishing, hunting and bee keeping. As they increased in number, they began to organize themselves into armed bands and in the early spring went on expeditions (*ukhody*) into the steppes, staying there until early winter and coming back to their permanent residences with great supplies of hides, cattle, fish and honey. The more daring did not return for the winter at all, but remained in the steppes. Constantly on guard against Tatar attacks, these Ukrainian pioneers attacked the Tatars whenever they felt strong enough. In time they turned into freebooters of the Turkic *qazaq* type; they also became mercenaries hired by the governors of the Lithuanian frontier towns both as guards and for use in expeditions against Tatar forts.

Many members of the settled new Polish-Ukrainian nobility joined the "romantic" Cossack way of life. Their physical presence, intellectual influence and the very existence of the *szlachta* on the Ukrainian territories gave the Cossacks a model for their aspirations. One of them, Prince Dmytro Vyshnevetsky, was to play the decisive role in the organization of the Cossacks as a military force. About 1550 he built a strong permanent fortress (*sich*) on the Dnieper rapids; this territory was at that time the safest location for the Cossacks, since on the one hand, it was out of reach of the officials of far-off Lithuania or Poland and on the other, dense forest, whirlpools and water rapids prevented heavy Ottoman galleys from coming up the river. Shortly, the Cossacks from this fortress below the Dnieper rapids ("the Zaporogians") established themselves as a kind of naval academy and also a military order of knightly condottieri (*rytsari*). They developed their characteristic ideology of a class equal to the Polish *szlachta* with claims of equal rights and privileges in exchange for their military service. The years 1600–20 marked the heroic era when the Cossacks in their light boats called "seagulls" (*chaiky*) cruised unhampered on the Black Sea, inflicting defeats upon the Crimea and Ottoman porte at a time when all Europe was trembling in fear of the Turks.

The first attempt of the Polish government to control the rising Zaporogian Cossack power was made soon after the Poles acquired Ukraine from Lithuania (1569). In 1570 a Cossack detachment of three hundred men was enrolled in a register. These Cossacks were excluded from the jurisdiction of the local administration and served directly under the Polish crown hetman or military commander-in-chief. In 1578 Stephen Báthory, preparing for war with Muscovy, compiled a new register of five hundred Cossacks with a Polish noble as their elder. The centre (and the hospital) of the registered Cossacks was the town of Trakhtemyriv to the south of Pereiaslav. The Polish government made similar attempts later (a register was compiled in 1583, 1588, 1597 and subsequently) and increased the number of registered Cossacks initially to six hundred, and eventually to over three thousand.

But the Polish government was not in a position to put all Ukrainian Cossacks under its control. Their actual number was much greater than that determined by the register. (Internally, the introduction of registers caused the differentiation of the Cossacks and the growth of class consciousness among the registered Cossacks, distinct from the Cossacks not admitted to the register, the actual Zaporogian Cossacks.) In dealing with the Cossacks the Polish government met a contradiction which it could not resolve. The Cossacks were needed dearly to combat the many Tatar attacks and to implement each variant of the anti-Ottoman and/or anti-Muscovite policies of the Polish kings, since they were the only professional military force available and equipped for such undertakings.

However, once the conflict was over, it was inconvenient for the Polish government to have Cossacks in large numbers within their frontiers. First, the Polish king had neither the authority nor the strength to keep the Cossacks under control and to prevent them from making sea expeditions that led to threats of war from the Ottoman porte. Second, the Polish magnates, and especially the *szlachta*, feared the Cossacks' demands for special privileges, since their fulfillment would make the Cossacks their rivals for power in Ukraine, viewed by the *szlachta* as its personal hunting preserve and private area for exploitation.

Although the majority of the Ukrainian Cossacks were probably of local ethnic Ukrainian origin, there was no racial or religious discrimination toward those who wished to join their bands. The sources show clearly that among the Ukrainian Cossacks were not only ethnic Poles and West Europeans but also Turks, Tatars, Armenians, Jews and others. Originally, the Ukrainian Cossacks had only their corporative interests in mind; national, ethnic or religious matters were completely irrelevant to them. They also, until 1615 (as will be shown later), had no knowledge or interest in the historical and cultural traditions of Kievan Rus'.

V

But what of the members of the former Rus' dynasty, living in the Lithuanian (and later Polish-Lithuanian) state? Of the three basic centres of Rus' proper, Kiev and Pereiaslav never managed to create a dynasty of their own, primarily because of the role both cities played as decisive steps in the mobile system of *lestvichnoe voskhozhdenie.* Only Chernihiv possessed a dynasty of its own; but its main lines were destroyed by the conquering Lithuanians: the Chernihiv line in 1372 and the Putyvl line (at that time ruling also in Kiev) a decade earlier in 1363. The very numerous and multi-branched Novhorod-Siversk line of the old Chernihiv dynasty, the Princes Karachevsky, Novosilsky, Obolensky, Tarussky, Volkonsky and others had opted by 1500—as did many members of the Lithuanian dynasty—for allegiance to the Orthodox Riurikids of Moscow, for reasons described so convincingly by Oswald P. Backus in his study of the *Motives of West Russian Nobles in Deserting Lithuania for Moscow, 1377–1514.*[49] The only princely dynasty of landowners in Rus' proper to survive Lithuanian rule were the Princes Rozhynovsky-Polovtsi (with their domains in the basins of the Kamianka, Rostovets and Skvyra rivers to the south of Kiev) who claimed that their ancestor was the Kuman-Polovtsian ruler Tugor-ta[r]kan (d. 1096), the father-in-law of the Kievan king, Sviatopolk II (1093–1113); their residence was in Velykopolovetske near Skvyra.[50] In

Volhynia several princely families claimed as their origin the Turovo-Pinsk branch of the Riurikids, the ancestor of which was the above-mentioned Sviatopolk II. They were the Dolsky, Horodelsky, Nesvytsky, Sokolsky and Sviatopolk-Chetvertynsky families. Roman Mstislavich's (d. 1205) branch of the Rus' dynasty, ruling a century and a half in the kingdom of Galicia and the great principality of Volhynia (1199–1349) was never very numerous. No single member of it survived in Galicia proper; the last ruling member of the dynasty, Iurii prince of Kholm (Chełm), died one year after his son passed away (in 1377), thus leaving his land to the Polish dynasty. Only one non-ruling side-branch survived in Volhynia: the Princes Ostrozhsky, the magnates who in the fifteenth and sixteenth centuries owned about one third of Volhynia.

In the patrimonial Rus' system (which later was also taken over by the Lithuanians) the actual ruler held a monopoly on political, legal and economic power, thus the non-ruling members of the dynasty never developed civic instinct and interest in political life. They were either military commanders loyally serving their masters, or landowners concentrating their attention on financial and family affairs. After 1470 they all recognized as their only master the Lithuanian grand prince residing in Vilnius (or Cracow, if he were also king of Poland).

VI

The second half of the sixteenth century brought a twofold transformation of the highest social stratum of Rus' origin in the great principality of Lithuania. By 1550 the majority of these individuals had joined the Reformation, but since they were Orthodox, not Catholic, they did not have the basis and intellectual strength to create their own Rus' version of the Reformation. Therefore the stratum became a component of the Polish reformational movement and by 1600 was wholly absorbed by the Jesuit Counter Reformation, as was the Reformation in Poland proper. In this way, members of the Rus' Orthodox princely families and the highest stratum of formerly Orthodox Rus' became religiously and culturally integrated into the Catholic and Polish body politic.[51]

But before that class disappeared from Rus', it provided the first impetus for its own rebirth. In the 1570s Prince Vasyl Konstiantyn Ostrozhsky (1527–1608) followed the example of his Lithuanian colleagues who had fostered Protestant schools and founded at his residence at Ostrih in Volhynia the first Ukrainian intellectual centre since the fall of Kiev.[52] The educational complex consisted of a school of higher learning (or academy), a printing shop and an assembly of secular and religious textologists. In keeping with the spirit of the epoch, they set as their main task the creation of a Church Slavonic text of the entire Bible.[53] The majority of the scholars invited to Ostrih were members of the middle or petty Orthodox nobility or townsmen. While searching in the forgotten book repositories, they, among others, rediscovered the texts of the Old Rus' Kievan and Galician-Volhynian chronicles (of the type of the Hypatian Collection) and put them in circulation.

By the time of Danylo Romanovych's coronation (1253), a concept of Halych as the second Kiev, and Galicia as Rus' par excellence had developed in Galicia (but not in Volhynia).[54] The idea was so strong that the Poles continued to call Galicia Rus', even after they had occupied it and began to govern. In the official terminology the land was referred to as "the palatinate of Rus'." This fact deserves special attention, for of all Rus'-Ukrainian territories included in the Polish-Lithuanian Commonwealth, only Galicia, a land which during the epoch of Kievan Rus' (tenth to thirteenth centuries) was never understood to be Rus', became associated with its name and, indeed, was considered to constitute Rus'. What social force lay behind this phenomenon?

It has already been mentioned that during the period 1387 to 1434, the Galician *barones* became, politically, Poles. This they did in order to keep their dominant position in the realm. But the local middle and petty nobility had no reason to give up their religion and their allegiance to Rus', especially since only they were eligible for higher offices in the Orthodox hierarchy. Several bishoprics and monasteries existed, some with considerable lands. So this lower and middle Rus'ian nobility was in a position to defend its rights successfully.

Like their Polish colleagues and competitors, the Rus'ian nobles possessed coats of arms, which at that time was the only unquestionable proof of their aristocratic origin. Heraldry, which rapidly took root throughout Western Christendom between the second and third Crusades (1147–92), became an essential part of the feudal system there during the fourteenth and fifteenth centuries which now gave rise to a closed and hereditary society.[55] Approximately one hundred Galician Orthodox families, mostly from the Sambir and Zhydachiv districts, as well as from Kholm, managed, under circumstances still not entirely clear, to obtain entry into the "Polish genealogical tribe" and to bear their own heraldic symbols.[56] Most possessed either the *Sas* or the *Korchak* coat of arms, both of which were held by old genealogical tradition to be of Hungarian origin.[57] But some were part of the "genealogical tribe" of the *Pobóg* and others of the *Abdank*. Being a component part of the new social system, capable of preserving its peculiarities, the class of Rus' middle and petty nobles used every opportunity and all channels of influence to guard the Kievan Rus' historical traditions, once they had rediscovered and appropriated them at the end of the sixteenth century. The emergence of this small but very tightly-knit stratum had tremendous importance for the moulding of Rus' sentiments which took place in the seventeenth century, and thus for the formation of the modern Ukrainian nation.

Another stratum existed which cannot always be separated from the heraldic nobility. It comprised the Orthodox townsmen of the cities under Germanic law in Galicia (Rus') and Volhynia. Because they were not Catholics, on their own territory they were treated as second-class citizens, forced to fight for the very right to exist. The climate was conducive to organized collaboration between them and the Rus' lower and middle nobility. This gave rise to the emergence of a sense of allegiance and the institution of Rus' fraternal organizations (*bratstva*) during the sixteenth century.[58] Their activities included the publication of books and maintenance of schools. Prince Vasyl Ostrozhsky lost interest in the Ostrih Academy and that institution lost its protector, but cultural establishments of the Lviv Stavropigian Brotherhood emerged to take its place.

The first quarter of the seventeenth century witnessed the emergence of a Ukrainian historical consciousness, based on the re-adaptation of the accomplishments of the Orthodox Kievan Rus'. "Nationalized" Rus' Galicians, such as Pletenetsky, Kopystensky, Boretsky, Zyzanii, Berynda, Kalnofoisky and others, went to Kiev—as did the Polish *szlachta* after 1569—and took the leadership of intellectual affairs into their own hands. In a very short period they transformed Kiev from a forgotten frontier town into a leading cultural centre of Eastern Europe. The printing house, the school and the brotherhood became the cornerstones for a new educational system. It was symbolic that in 1615, when the first Kievan brotherhood was established, the hetman of the Zaporogian Cossacks together with his entire army declared themselves its members and protectors. Hetman at the time was Petro Konashevych-Sahaidachny (d. 1622), who epitomized the new development. He himself was a Galician of heraldic petty nobility (with the *Pobôg* coat of arms) who had studied at the Ostrih Academy and had connections with the Lviv brotherhood.[59]

After the Union of Brest, the Polish government outlawed the Orthodox church. By 1620 not a single Orthodox bishop remained. The reaction was an unusual solidarity of all Ukrainian social and political groups (led by the Galicians). The Kievan burghers invited Theophanes, patriarch of Jerusalem, to visit Ukraine; the Zaporogian host, headed by the Galician nobleman Sahaidachny, and only recently displaying an interest in religious matters, provided security for the visit. The scion of the Riurikid dynasty, Prince Stepan Sviatopolk-Chetvertynsky, fulfilled the role of the host at his residence in Zhyvotiv (in the Bratslav palatinate) and the Galician-born Rus' literati regarded the visit as a suitable occasion to present the prince with a copy of the Kiev-Galician-Volhynian chronicle about Old Rus'.[60]

The patrimonial system of Kievan Rus' could not have given rise to a concept of legal estates. The Lithuanians cut short the development of the institutional and historical traditions on the territory that had been Kievan Rus' proper. These two factors, not the so-called Mongolian chasm, are responsible for the interruption of the Ukrainian historical process.

The re-establishment of the Old Rus' traditions in Ukraine was mainly the work of the Galician petty Orthodox (heraldic) nobility and the second-class citizens of the Galician towns under Magdeburg law. They were attempting to retain the former loyalty of the descendants of the Old Rus' princely elite to the Rus' traditions. But the inspiration for their outlook and activity came ultimately from Western humanism, and especially its Reformation and Counter Reformation.

In their struggle for the Rus' faith the Orthodox Rus' nobility of Galicia succeeded in co-opting the new military power in Eastern Europe, the Zaporogian Cossacks. The nobles even secured for themselves the commanding posts in the host. But for this they had to pay a very high price: focus soon shifted from the new Western concept of the Rus' body politic to the "Oriental" mercenary Cossack idea of Ukraine as a frontierland. The clock was set back.

Notes

1. At that time, the experience and means (structure) to perpetuate an empire after the death of its founder had not yet been developed. See, for example, the fate of Charlemagne's empire. Concerning the term "patrimonial," see Max Weber, *The Theory of Social and Economic Organizations*, trans. and ed. T. Parsons (New York, 1964), 346–51.
2. See the entry 6545/1037 in the *Pověst vremennykh lět*, ed. D. S. Likhachev, (Moscow-Leningrad, 1956), 1: 102–3. Here Iaroslav clearly had followed the pattern established by the Bulgarian Tsar Simeon (873–927). On the other hand, Volodymyr of Kiev, like the Bulgarian Boris I (852–89) before him, seems to have been baptized in the Greek (and not the Slavonic!) rite.
3. On the foreign character (from the point of view of the Eastern Slavs) of the Church Slavonic language, see the thought expressed by the late

A. V. Isatschenko: *Mythen und Tatsachen über die Entstehung der russischen Literatursprache (Sitzungsberichte der Österreichischen Akademie der Wissenschaften* 298) (Vienna, 1975), 5. See also H. G. Lunt, "On the Language of Old Rus: Some Questions and Suggestions," *Russian Linguistics* 2 (1975): 269–81.

4. See *Slovo o zakoně i blagodati* by Ilarion (about 1050): "Pokhvalim zhe i my, po silě nashei, malymi pokhvalami—velikaa i divnaa sŭtvorshago nashego uchitelia i nastavnika, velikago kagana nashea zemlia, Vladimera, vnuka starago Igoria, syna zhe slavnago Sviatoslava .... " L. Müller, ed., *Das Metropoliten Ilarion Lobrede auf Vladimir den Heiligen und Glaubensbekenntnis* (Wiesbaden, 1962), 100.
5. The term appears first in the Nikon Chronicle in the entry 6704/1196. The senior of the Chernihiv branch, Iaroslav Vsevolodovich, refused to give up his (and his branch's) rights to Kiev, arguing as follows: "Ne budi mně otluchitisia velikogo stola i glavy i slavy vsea Rusi Kieva, no iakozhe i ot praděd nashikh lestvitseiu kozhdo voskhozhashe na velikoe kniazhenie Kievskoe, sitse zhe i nam i vam, vozliublennaia i dragaia bratia, lestvichnym voskhozhdeniem komu ashche Gospod' Bog dast' vzyti na velikoe kniazhenie velikago Kieva, sego bratie ne razariaite, ne presetsaite, da ne Bozhii gněv na sebe privletsete, khotiashche ediny vo vsei Rusi gospodstvovati." *Polnoe sobranie russkikh letopisei* [PSRL] 10 (SPb., 1885; repr. Moscow, 1965), 26.
6. *Pravda russkaia*, 2: *Kommentarii*, ed. B. D. Grekov (Moscow-Leningrad, 1947), 665–7: "A dvor bez děla oten' vsiak men'shemu synovi."
7. As to the way the steppe-succession system operated, see my description of the situation in the Hunnic Hsiung-nu realm in: "Die 24 Ta-ch'ên. Studie zur Geschichte des Verwaltungsaufbaus der Hsiung-nu Reiche," *Oriens Extremus*, no. 1 (Hamburg, 1954): 178–202.
8. On the concept of "Rus'skaia zemlia," see A. N. Nasonov, *"Russkaia zemlia" i obrazovanie territorii drevnerusskogo gosudarstva* (Moscow, 1951).
9. Viacheslav (b. 1034) in 1057, and his immediate senior Igor, in 1060.
10. On Manzikert, see C. Cahen, "La Campagne de Mantzikert d'après les sources musulmanes," *Byzantion* 9 (1934): 613–42; C. Cahen, "La première pénétration turque en Asie Mineure (seconde moitié du XIe siècle)," *Byzantion* 18 (1948): 5–67. On Bari, see I. Gay, *L'Italie méridionale et l'empire byzantin depuis l'avenèment le Basile Ier jusqu'à la prise de Bari par les Normands, 867–1071* (Paris, 1904).
11. See R. S. Lopez, *The Commercial Revolution of the Middle Ages, 950–1350* (Cambridge, 1976), and W. Heyd, *Histoire du commerce du Levant au Moyen-Age*, ed. F. Raynaud, 2 vols. (Leipzig, 1885–6; repr. Amsterdam, 1967).
12. F. Rörig, *Wirtschaftskräfte im Mittelalter. Abhandlungen zur Stadt- und Wirtschaftsgeschichte* (Weimar, 1959); Fritz Rörig, *Die europäische Stadt und die Kultur des Bürgertums im Mittelalter*, 4th ed. (Göttingen, 1964).

13. See A. P. Kazhdan, "Vizantiiskii podatnoi sborshchik na beregakh Kimmeriiskogo Bospora v kontse XII v.," *Problemy obshches tvenno-politicheskoi istorii Rossii i slavianskikh stran* (Festschrift M. N. Tikhomirov) (Moscow, 1963), 93–101; G. G. Litavrin and A. P. Kazhdan, "Ekonomicheskie i politicheskie otnosheniia Drevnei Rusi i Vizantii v XI - pervoi polovine XIII v.," *Proceedings of the 13th International Congress of Byzantine Studies* (Oxford, 1967), 69–81.
14. See V. L. Yanin, *Novgorodskie posadniki* (Moscow, 1962), 94–106.
15. L. V. Alekseev, *Polotskaia zemlia* (Moscow, 1966), 287–8; N. de Baumgarten, "Polotzk et la Lithuanie," *Orientalia Christiana Periodica* 2, 1–2 (Rome, 1936): 223–53.
16. See Marc Bloch, "Transformation of the Nobility into a Legal Class," *Feudal Society*, 2 vols. (Chicago, 1964), 2: 320–31; E. Lederer, "La structure de la société hongroise du debut du moyen-âge," *Études historiques publiêes par la Commission nationale des historiens hongrois* 1 (Budapest, 1960), 195–218; Z. Wojciechowski, "La condition des nobles et le problème de la féodalité en Pologne au Moyen-Âge," *Revue historique du droît français et êtranger* 15-16 (Paris, 1936–7). See also O. Ranum, ed., *National Consciousness, History, and Political Culture in Early Modern Europe* (Baltimore, 1975), and Walter Ullmann, *A History of Political Thought: The Middle Ages* (Hammondsworth, 1965).
17. J. Meyendorff, *Introduction à l'êtude de Grêgoire Palamas* (Paris, 1950); T. A. Hart, "Nicephorus Gregoras: Historian of the Hesychast Controversy," *Journal of Ecclesiastical History* 2 (London, 1951): 169–80.
18. See M. Hrushevsky, *Istoriia ukrainskoi literatury*, 5 volumes (Kiev-Lviv, 1923–7), 5, part 1: 3–25.
19. Cf. M. Hrushevsky, *Istoriia Ukrainy-Rusy* (Lviv-Kiev, 1907), 6: 348.
20. See "Supplikatia do przeoświeconego i jaśnie wielmożnego przezacnej korony polskiej i w.x. litewskiego obojego stanu duchownego i świeckiego senatu, w roku tym teraźniejszym 1623 do Warszawy na sejm wolny przybyłego," in W. Lipiński [V. Lypynsky] ed., *Z dziejôw Ukrainy* (Kiev, 1912), 99–111.
21. See C. S. Stang, *Die westrussische Kanzleisprache des Grossfürstentums Litauen* (Oslo, 1935).
22. Richard E. Pipes, *Russia under the Old Regime* (New York, 1974), 22–3.
23. On Hellenistic patrimonialism, see J. Kaerst, *Geschichte des Hellenismus*, 2d ed. (Leipzig, 1926), 2: 335.
24. See, e.g., George Vernadsky, *Kievan Russia*, 7th printing (New Haven, 1973), 130–72.
25. See D. W. Hanson, *From Kingdom to Commonwealth: the Development of Civic Consciousness in English Political Thought* (Cambridge, Mass., 1970); Hans Roos, "Ständewesen und parlamentarische Verfassung in Polen (1505–1772)," in *Ständische Vertretungen in Europa im 17. und 18. Jahrhundert*, ed. D. Gerhard (Göttingen, 1969), 368–97.
26. See J. Tazbir, *Rzeczpospolita i świat. Studia z dziejôw kultury XVII wieku* (Wrocław, 1971).

27. See note 20.
28. D. Sinor, *History of Hungary* (London, 1959), 62.
29. J. Maciszewski, *Szlachta polska i jej państwo* (Warsaw, 1960).
30. *PSRL*, ed. A. A. Shakhmatov, 2d ed. (St. Petersburg, 1908), 2: col. 386: "I tu [in Lutske] pasashe Boleslav syny boiarsky mechem mnogy."
31. *PSRL*, 2d ed., 2: col. 762: "I obnazhivshu mech' svoi igraia na slugu koroleva, inomu pokhvativshi shchit igraiushchi."
32. *PSRL*, 2d ed., 2: col. 801: [Rostislav Mikhailovich] "gordiashchu zhe sia emu i s"tvori igru pred gradom." The Hungarian troops which in 1150 came to the support of Iziaslav Mstislavich were invited to perform their knightly tournaments in Kiev: "I tu obědav s nimi [Iziaslav with the Hungarians] na velitsem dvorě na Iaroslavli i prebysha u velitsě vesel'i; togda zhe Ugre na farekh i na skokokh igrakhut' na Iaroslavli dvorě mnogoe mnozhestvo. Kyiane zhe diviakhutsia Ugrom mnozhestvu i kmet'stva ikh i komonem ikh." (*Ibid.*, col. 416).
33. See the collection edited by E. Kunik, *Boleslav Iurii II* (St. Petersburg, 1907), 153–5 (the charters from 1334 and 1335).
34. See *PSRL*, 2d ed., 2: cols. 789–90 (s.a. 1240): "Dobroslav zhe vokniazhilsia bě i Sud'ich' popov vnuk i grabiashe vsiu zemliu .... Lazor' Domazhirets' i Ivor Molibozhich' dva bezakon'nika ot plemeni smerd'ia."
35. *Ibid.*, col. 905.
36. *Ibid.*, col. 868.
37. Cf. Hrushevsky, *Istoriia Ukrainy-Rusy*, 2d ed. (Kiev-Lviv, 1907), 4: 221–2; (Lviv, 1905), 5: 82–9.
38. On the Pogodin hypothesis and its history, see Hrushevsky *Istoriia Ukrainy-Rusy*, 3d ed. (Kiev, 1913), 1: 551–6; M. I. Marchenko, *Ukrainska istoriohrafiia* (Kiev, 1959), [1]: 203–14.
39. One can add that in China during the Mongolian rule and under its influence there appeared the popular novel (unknown in China previously) and popular theatre, alongside new developments in the exact sciences, especially in mathematics and astronomy. Last but not least, it was as a result of the impact of the Mongolian universal rule that the Jewish physician and politician Rashid ad-Din (d. 1318) created at the court of the Iranian Mongols the first truly universal history, *Jāmi at-tawārīkh*, in which he used, side by side, Persian, Latin, Frankish, Turkic, Chinese, Indian and other original sources.

    See L. Kwanten, "Cultural Life under the Mongols," in *A History of Central Asia, 500–1500* (Philadelphia, 1979), 221–4; Ch'en Yüan, *Westerners and Central Asians in China under the Mongols*, trans. Ch'ien Hsing-hai and L. Carrington Goodrich (Los Angeles, 1966). See also O. Franke, *Geschichte des chinesischen Reiches* (Berlin, 1948), 4: 579–95; W. Eberhard, *Chinas Geschichte* (Bern, 1948), 271–4; C. T. Hsia, *The Classical Chinese Novel, a Critical Introduction* (New York, 1968), 34–114; U. Librecht, *Chinese Mathematics in the Thirteenth Century: The*

Shu-shu chiu-chang of Ch'in Chiu-shao (Cambridge, Mass., 1973); E. G. Browne, *A Literary History of Persia*, 3: *The Tartar Dominion (1265–1502)* (Cambridge, 1920; repr. 1951); "Rashid ad-Din," in Ch. A. Stori, *Persidskaia Literatura. Bio-bibliograficheskii obzor*, trans. Iu. E. Bregel (Moscow, 1972), 1: 301–20, and 3: 1,394–5; K. Jahn, *Wissenschaftliche Kontakte zwischen Iran und China in der Mongolenzeit*, Abhandlungen der Österreichischen Akademie der Wissenschaften 108, no. 8 (Vienna, 1971).

40. See T. A. Sumnikova and V. V. Lopatin, *Smolenskie gramoty XIII–XIV vekov*, ed. R. I. Avanesov (Moscow, 1963).
41. M. Hrushevsky, *Istoriia ukrainskoi literatury*, 5, part 1: 162–73.
42. Of the enormous specialized literature, one can mention for the purpose of this paper the following items: A. N. Nasonov, *Mongoly i Rus' (Istoriia tatarskoi politiki na Rusi)* (Moscow-Leningrad, 1940); A. E. Presniakov, *Obrazovanie velikorusskogo gosudarstva. Ocherki po istorii XIII–XV stoletii* (Petrograd, 1918); L. V. Cherepnin, *Obrazovanie russkogo tsentralizovannogo gosudarstva v XIV–XV vekakh* (Moscow, 1960).
43. Especially when the harvest was poor: see N. L. Podvigina, *Ocherki sotsialno-ekonomicheskoi i politicheskoi istorii Novgoroda Velikogo v XII–XIII vv.* (Moscow, 1976), 62; L. V. Danilova, *Ocherki po istorii zemlevladeniia i khoziaistva v Novgorodskoi zemle v XIV–XV vv.* (Moscow, 1955), 22–3; A. P. Pronshtein, *Velikii Novgorod v XVI veke* (Kharkiv, 1957), 114–15.
44. See *Scriptores Rerum Prussicarum*, ed. F. Hirsch et al. (Leipzig, 1863), 2: 80.
45. See M. Hrushevsky, *Istoriia Ukrainy-Rusy*, 2d ed. (Kiev-Lviv, 1907), 4: 99.
46. On the early history of Lithuania, see H. Łowmiański, *Studia nad początkami społeczeństwa i państwa litewskiego*, 2 vols. (Vilnius, 1930–2); J. Ochmański, "Uwagi o litewskim państwie wczesnofeudalnym," *Roczniki Historyczne* 27 (1961): 143–60; J. Ochmański, *Historia Litwy* (Wrocław-Warsaw-Cracow, 1964), and V. T. Pashuto, *Obrazovanie litovskogo gosudarstva* (Moscow, 1959).
47. On Lithuanian socio-economic history, see K. Avizonis, *Die Entstehung und Entwicklung des litauischen Adels bis zur litauisch-polnischen Union 1385* (Berlin, 1932); M. Krasauskaité, *Die Litauischen Adelsprivilegien bis zum Ende des XV Jahrhunderts* (Leipzig, 1927); O. Backus, "Die Rechtsstellung der litauischen Bojaren 1387–1506," *Jahrbücher für Geschichte Osteuropas* 6 (1958): 1–32; J. Ochmański, *Powstanie i rozwój latyfundium biskupstwa wileńskiego (1387–1550). Ze studiów nad rozwojem wielkiej własności na Litwie i Białorusi w średniowieczu* (Poznań, 1963); W. Peltz, "Ród Giedygołda i jego majętności. Z dziejów tworzenia się wielkiej własności ziemskiej w Wielkim Księstwie Litewskim w XV wieku," *Zeszyty Naukowe Uniwersytetu im. Adama Mickiewicza: Historia*, zeszyt 11 (Poznań, 1971): 23–44; P. Dąbkowski, *Dobra rodowe i nabyte w prawie litewskim od XIV do XVI wieku* (Lviv, 1916); S. Kasperczak, *Rozwój gospodarki folwarczej*

na Litwie i Białorusi do połowy XVI wieku (Poznań, 1965); Z. Ivinskis, *Geschichte des Bauernstandes in Litauen von der ältesten Zeit bis zum Anfang des 16. Jhs.* (Berlin, 1933); D. L. Pokhylevych, *Krestiane Belorussii i Litvy v XVI–XVIII vv.* (Lviv, 1957). Cf. also W. Kamieniecki, *Społeczeństwo litewskie w XV wieku* (Warsaw, 1947).

48. The basic relevant literature is R. Grodecki, *Początki immunitetu w Polsce* (Lviv, 1930); M. Szczaniecki, *Nadania ziemi na rzecz rycerzy w Polsce do końca XIII w.* (Poznań, 1938); J. Matuszewski, *Immunitet ekonomiczny w dobrach kościoła w Polsce do roku 1381* (Poznań, 1936); W. Korta, "Rozwój terytorialny wielkiej świeckiej własności feudalnej w Polsce do połowy XIII wieku," *Sobótka* 16 (Wrocław, 1961): 528–66.

49. (Lawrence, Kansas, 1957). See also S. M. Kuczyński, *Ziemie czernihowsko-siewierskie pod rządami Litwy* (Warsaw, 1936).

50. A. Jabłonowski, *Polska XVI wieku pod względem statystycznym* 11: *Ziemie ruskie. Ukraina* (Warsaw, 1897), 579–80; *Istoriia mist i sil Ukrainskoi RSR. Kyivska oblast* (Kiev, 1971), 577.

51. G. H. Williams, "Protestants in the Ukraine during the Period of the Polish-Lithuanian Commonwealth," *Harvard Ukrainian Studies* 2 (1978): 41–72, 184–210. See also M. Hrushevsky, *Kulturno-natsionalnyi rukh na Ukraini v XVI–XVII vitsi* (Lviv, 1912).

52. O. Terletsky, *Vasyl Kostantyn Kniaz Ostrozky* (Ternopil, 1909).

53. "Ostrozka akademiia," in Hrushevsky, *Istoriia Ukrainy-Rusy*, 6: 479–98; Ia. Isaievych, *Dzherela z istorii ukrainskoi kultury doby feodalizmu* (Kiev, 1972).

54. A. I. Hensorsky, *Halytsko-volynskyi litopys* (Kiev, 1958), 84–95.

55. D. L. Galbreath, *Handbüchlein der Heraldik*, 2d ed. (Lausanne, 1948); S. W. H. St. John Hope, *A Grammar of English Heraldry*, 2d ed. (Cambridge, 1953).

56. See J. Szymański, *Nauki pomocnicze historii* (Warsaw, 1972), 328.

57. See the stories in B. Paprocki's *Herby rycerstwa polskiego* [first published in 1584], 2d ed. (Cracow, 1858), 677–92 (Korczak) and 695–7 (Sas). In this connection see notes 30–2 above on the adoption of Western knightly customs in Galicia.

58. See Ia. Isaievych, *Bratstva ta ikh rol v rozvytku ukrainskoi kultury XVI–XVIII st.* (Kiev, 1966).

59. See K. Sakovych's "Virshi na zhalosnyi pohreb zatsnoho rytsera Petra Konashevycha Sahaidachnoho" (Kiev, 1622), reprinted in V. P. Kolosova and V. I. Krekoten, *Ukrainska poezia. Kinets XVI - pochatok XVII st.* (Kiev, 1978), 322–38.

60. See O. Pritsak, "The Hypatian Chronicle and Its Role in the Restoration of Ukrainian Historical Consciousness," in *Chomu katedry ukrainoznavstva v Harvardi?* (Cambridge, Mass., 1973), 54–60; also 42–53.

Frank Sysyn

The Problem of Nobilities in the Ukrainian Past: The Polish Period, 1569–1648

Where now is that priceless stone which like a candelabra spread its rays, the carbuncle that was among other pearls as a sun among stars, that I wore as a crown on my head—the house of the princes Ostrozky, which with the shimmer of the light of its ancient faith shone more strongly than all others? Where are the other precious and also priceless stones of that crown—the glorious houses of Ruthenian princes, the precious sapphires and priceless diamonds, the princes Slutsky, Zaslavsky, Zbarazky, Vyshnevetsky, Sangushko, Chartorysky, Pronsky, Ruzhynsky, Solomyretsky, Holovchynsky, Kroshynsky, Masalsky, Horsky, Sokolynsky, Lukomsky, Puzyna and others without number? It would be a lengthy affair to count them individually! Where are those who surrounded them, the other of my precious jewels, I say—the well-born, glorious, brave, strong and ancient houses of the Ruthenian nation who were renowned throughout the world for their high repute, power and bravery—Khodkevych, Hlibovych, Kyshka, Sapiha, Dorohostaisky, Voina, Volovych, Zenovych, Pats, Khaletsky, Tyshkevych, Korsak, Khrebtovych, Tryzna, Hornoastai, Bokiia, Myshka, Hoisky, Semashko, Hulevych, Iarmolynsky, Cholhansky, Kalynovsky, Kyrdei, Zahorovsky, Meleshko, Bohovytyn, Pavlovych, Sosnovsky, Skumyna, Potii and others? I do not mention here that ample and costly robe of mine, strewn with countless pearls and multicolored stones, with which I was adorned—the principalities and counties in the boundaries of the Ruthenian land.

Meletii Smotrytsky [Teophil Ortolog], **Threnos—to jest lament św. Powszechney Apostolskiej Wschodniej Cerkwie ...** (Vilnius, 1610)[1]

In 1610 Meletii Smotrytsky expressed the anguish of the Orthodox church over the desertion of so many of her children among the Ruthenian aristocrats, through conversions that reflected more than private decisions about faith or a widespread conviction of the truth of Roman Catholicism. For the men of the early seventeenth century, the Orthodox Rus' church was the core of the institutional structure of the Ruthenian historical tradition and national community. The church leaders had good cause to be concerned about the defections. By 1631, when Prince Iarema Vyshnevetsky (Jeremi Wiśniowiecki) "from a Ruthenian became a Liakh" through his conversion, the Orthodox metropolitan's emotional call for him to return to his ancestral faith included a response to allegations that Orthodoxy was a peasants' faith.[2] In the "Republic of the Nobles," Poland-Lithuania, the loss of so many nobles confronted the Orthodox church and the Ruthenian community with a threat to their very existence.

Research on the Ukrainian Nobility

The laments of Smotrytsky and his contemporaries deeply influenced Ukrainian historical thought in the nineteenth and twentieth centuries. In the intervening two centuries, Khmelnytsky's revolt had swept away the old social order in the central Ukrainian lands. A new nobility of Cossack officers (*starshyna-shliakhta*) formed in the Hetmanate, but in the eighteenth century was in its turn absorbed into the Russian imperial nobility (*dvoriansto*). Although some of the descendants of the old and the new Ukrainian nobilities displayed regional loyalties and contributed both intellectually and financially to the Ukrainian national reawakening of the nineteenth century, most of the descendants of the old nobility identified with Polish culture and the Polish national movement, and most of the new nobility chose Russian imperial culture and the "all-Russian" nation. Deprived of the support of a traditional elite, many historians active in the Ukrainian national movement condemned the nobility, past and present, for betraying its people, and directed their efforts to the common folk. These populist historians lavished their attention and affection on the history of peasants and Cossacks and studied the nobility only reluctantly and unsympathetically. At the beginning of the twentieth century, a few Ukrainian historians broke with the populist school and began to revise attitudes toward the nobility, but their work was cut short by the Soviet triumph in most of the Ukrainian territories. Soviet Ukrainian historians have combined the old populist distaste for the nobility with new Marxist clichés. Russian and Polish historians, in general, have been less reluctant to study the nobles of Ukraine, but have often viewed them as fully integrated into the Russian or Polish nobilities, and not as a distinct group.[3]

Nineteenth- and early twentieth-century scholars, Ukrainians, Russians and Poles alike, published a wealth of source material and pursued fundamental studies of specialized topics on the Ukrainian nobility.[4] All too often, however, the questions that they posed were determined by their own political and national preoccupations. That after more than a half century their approaches to the study of the Ukrainian nobility are in need of revision should, of course, be expected. What is troubling is that their studies included few theoretical works on the question of nobilities in Ukrainian history or comprehensive studies on the development of the Ukrainian nobility.[5] This gap has not been filled by Soviet Ukrainian historians; since the 1930s they have simply condemned all nobles as economic oppressors and national traitors and have not even continued to publish source materials or studies on specialized topics about the nobility. This paper will consider some of the general problems in writing the history of the Ukrainian nobility as they affect the study of the period from 1569 to 1648 and propose a framework for incorporating prior research and for organizing new studies.

Problems of Ukrainian Social History and the Study of the Nobility

The paucity of synthetic studies and comprehensive works on the nobility can only be partially attributed to the ideological stances of Ukrainian, Polish and Russian historians in the past two centuries. Writing histories of the Ukrainian nobility poses a number of difficulties inherent in the field of Ukrainian "national" history. The criteria of territory, political structure, culture, historical tradition and ethnicity that are used to define a national history are rarely precise and incontestable. National histories are often created by projecting the present onto the past and by rigidly organizing events and phenomena according to a national category. Yet in studying "German," "Italian," "French" or "Ukrainian" history, the historian is in effect proposing that the organization of political, social, cultural and economic factors over a long period in a national category provides one type of fundamental understanding of the past, but of course not the only one.

The historian of the Ukrainian past, and particularly the social historian, must rigorously question his categories and presumptions. The three major challenges to any Ukrainian social history are posed by the frequent disunity of the Ukrainian territories, by discontinuities in the formation of social strata and by the absorption of Ukrainian social groups into those of neighbouring societies.

First, the Ukrainian lands frequently have neither formed a single administrative unit nor shared common institutions. Whenever they were divided among a number of states or administered as unrelated units within one state, the ties uniting the nobilities and elite groups were weakened. For each period, the historian must consider whether the elements of disunity allow the study of the Ukrainian nobility across state and regional boundaries.

Second, social strata have evolved with discontinuities; not only have states and administrations risen and disappeared in the Ukrainian lands, but whole territories have been settled, depopulated and recolonized in recent times. Few institutions and social groups have endured intact through the tumultuous Ukrainian past. A historian of the Ukrainian nobility would be hard put to postulate a clearly evolutionary pattern from the *druzhyna* of the Kievan princes; through the boyars of Galicia-Volhynia; the princes, *pany*, and boyars of the Grand Duchy of Lithuania; the *szlachta* of the Polish period; the Cossack officer-nobles of the Hetmanate; to the diversified nobility of the Ukrainian lands of the nineteenth century. Continuities, in descent and tradition, do exist, but often the type, political culture and even constituency of the nobility of one period are drastically different from those that came before and after. Even the use of the term "nobility" to describe all these elite groups must be carefully scrutinized.

A third major challenge in Ukrainian social history derives from the impact on Ukrainian social groups of societies and cultures based outside the Ukrainian territories and drawing their values and traditions from radically different sources. In the early modern period annexations of the Ukrainian lands to the Polish and the Muscovite-Russian states were accompanied by cultural and intellectual changes and by a restructuring of the social order. The impact of neighbouring societies and states has been particularly important in determining the development of elite groups and the historian must carefully consider whether in some periods integration into the Polish or Russian nobility had not proceeded so far as to preclude the existence of a distinct "Ukrainian" nobility.

A Characterization of the Nobility in Ukraine, 1569–1648

The writing of histories of the Ukrainian nobility for discrete periods poses fewer methodological problems than does a study over a longer time span. The years 1569 to 1648 form a clearly distinct period in Ukrainian political and social history. Politically, it begins with the inclusion of almost all Ukrainian lands into the Kingdom of Poland and ends with the Khmelnytsky uprising that terminated Polish rule in the eastern Ukrainian territories. Socially, it begins with the transformation of all Ukrainian elite orders into a Polish-type nobility or *szlachta*, and ends with the destruction of the nobility's political and economic position in the eastern Ukrainian lands. Although the *szlachta* order survived in the western Ukrainian territories, the mid-century wars and their consequences substantially altered the composition and the political, economic and cultural configuration of the nobility.

Exponents of comparative history have used the term "noble" to describe hereditary traditional elite groups throughout the world. In their call for comparative studies of nobilities, Marc Bloch and Lucien Febvre define the idea of a nobility as embodying three elements: "l'hérédité, le prestige, et quelque chose de commun et de caractéristique dans le genre de vie des individus."[6] Thus, just as the concept of "feudalism" has been used to describe political, social and economic systems far removed in time and place from its European prototype, so "nobility" has been used in a broader context. It has, however, retained a narrower identification with the West European elites that evolved from the high feudal lords, knights and landed notables of the Middle Ages. In the broad sense, Ukrainian nobilities existed from the formation of the Kievan polity in the tenth century. But in discussing the nobility of the period from 1569 to 1648, it is necessary to discuss the nobilities of Western and Central Europe that served as models for elites in the Ukrainian lands during the late medieval and early modern periods.

The mores and laws of the evolving feudal elites (coats of arms, feudal law, military ethos) transcended realms and spread far beyond Northwestern Europe. What constituted living a noble life might vary from region to region, but the perception of a family of kindred European nobilities was deeply embedded in the societies of medieval and early modern Europe. The division of populations into corporate orders among which nobles enjoyed considerable political and economic privileges and rights, often embodied in regional representative institutions, was a distinctive characteristic of West European development. The definition of the noble corporate order differed from realm to realm, particularly over the relationship of great titled lords to petty knights. In countries as diverse as France, Spain and Hungary, the nobility was viewed as including both the great lord and the impoverished descendant of medieval knights, although the stratification of the nobility was reflected in differing privileges. Because of the unique development of English society, there is frequent confusion and inconsistency in applying the terms "noble" and "gentry" to discuss the French *noblesse*, the Polish *szlachta* or the German *Adel*. These can usually be resolved only by defining whether "nobility" is being used for the entire group, as it is in this study, or merely for an upper stratum.[7]

Although the nobilities of Europe had very different political and economic positions in various European polities in the early modern period, they still constituted a pan-European family from Madrid to Vilnius, from Stockholm to Rome. The common heritage and symbols of this otherwise extremely variegated family of nobilities made them perceive the wealthy and powerful of the Ottoman empire, Japan or Muscovy as outside the family, although they realized that these elites often fulfilled military and political roles similar to their own. The existence of this important, albeit amorphous, European noble heritage was confirmed most strikingly when it was imitated.

The Muscovite case is particularly important for the study of nobilities in Ukraine, because it represents a model that came to have great impact on Ukrainian elite groups. In seventeenth-century Muscovy, the literary works, coats of arms and, finally, name of the Polish *szlachta* spread to the Muscovite elite strata of *boiare* and *dvoriane*. In the eighteenth century, Russian rulers from Peter to Catherine created the imperial nobility or *dvorianstvo* by adopting and transforming the institutions and cultures of European nobilities for Russia's service elite. Although the old *boiare* and *dvoriane* certainly had qualified as "nobles" under the broad interpretation of Bloch's and Febvre's definition, the process of selecting and adopting from the social orders and noble cultures of societies to the west indicated that the Muscovite elite was outside the European family. The adaptation of Swedish and French models created a new nobility, but could not substitute for the stages of development in which the Muscovite elite had not participated. The elites of Muscovy had never functioned as a corporate order with guaranteed rights and privileges, representative institutions and regional ties deriving from stable landholding patterns. In the age of absolutism, the newly Westernized Russian nobility of St. Petersburg was very similar to the nobility at Versailles, but the Russian noble and Russian society still bore the imprint of the Muscovite past.[8]

Viewing the nobility in a narrow sense, as a European corporate order that possessed a core of common culture and traditions, is particularly important for studying early modern East Central European societies. The term "European" has often been endowed with almost mystical significance by East Central European historians, who have often felt unsure of their place in a revered European community and have sought to bolster their national egos in the face of successful Russian and Ottoman domination. While avoiding the controversies about the boundaries and essence of European civilization, one must recognize that the extension of Latin

Christian cultural, religious and political institutions to the peoples of East Central Europe in the ninth and tenth centuries stamped their entire subsequent development. The East Central European peoples entered a long-term tutelage as the recipients of ideas and institutions evolving in very different societies west of them. Hence in conjunction with West European peoples, they evolved into societies of well-defined corporate orders.[9]

In the societies divided into corporate orders that evolved throughout most of Europe in the early modern period, the nobilities and their institutions occupied a prominent position in administration and rule. Nowhere was the nobility's position so strong in relation to other strata of the population and to the sovereigns as in East Central Europe. The great historian of European society and institutions, Otto Hintze, has attributed that dominant role to the transfer of West European institutions to a backward territory that had not experienced West European political feudalism.[10] In Poland and Hungary, as in the other borderland of Europe, Spain, a relatively large percentage of the population succeeded in attaining noble status. In order to study the nobles of Ukraine between 1569 and 1648, it is necessary to discuss the Polish model that shaped the evolution of Ukrainian elites in the late medieval and early modern periods.

The Polish state of the sixteenth century has been called the *Rzeczpospolita szlachecka* or "Republic of the Nobles," an apt designation, since during that time distinctions between the institutions of the noble order or estate and the institutions of the state almost disappeared.[11] Although the Polish king reigned, the state functioned as a virtual republic of the "citizen nobles." After the extinction of the Jagiellonian dynasty in 1572, the monarchy was fully elective and successful candidates were bound by election contracts and oaths. In law, the king became one of the political estates that composed the Diet. He continued, however, to retain great power not only because of the authority of the office of king, but also because he distributed offices. No monarch was reconciled to his lot; each sought to transform the kingship into a hereditary office and to obtain a position comparable to other monarchs of the age. The political history of the commonwealth frequently revolved around the king's plans to change the constitution and the nobles' vigilant resistance to the slightest increments in royal power.

The major characteristics of the Polish nobility were embodied in its attachment to the concepts of liberty and equality. "Liberty" signified the sweeping political and economic freedoms enjoyed by each member of the nobility; it was assured by numerous royal charters and by systems of elective legislatures and courts. The systems of administration and government were cumbersome, but they did guarantee the nobles' rights. The concept of liberty even extended to religious toleration. Liberty was a monopoly of the nobles, however, and they increasingly curtailed the rights of the rest of the population. By the end of the sixteenth century, the nobility had used the Diet to place strict limitations on entrance to its corporate order.

"Equality" referred to the absence of legal distinctions or titles within the noble order. Its numerous members, estimated at 8–10 per cent of the population, varied greatly in wealth and power but not in inherited titles, rights and privileges. Offices in the Senate were held for life, but were not hereditary, and were theoretically open to all nobles. The "execution-of-the-laws movement" in the mid-sixteenth century prevented the great nobles from accumulating royal offices and lands. Although great magnates continued to acquire tremendous power and influence, none ever attempted to abolish the principle of equality.

Wealth derived from property and the right to exploit the peasantry attached to it. Allodial ownership of land was the prerogative of the nobility. The king's court attracted many, both great and small, but it never supplanted the family estate as the noble's primary residence. Although the greatest magnates could exercise power throughout the realm, most nobles exerted influence at a local level as men of standing in their palatinates. Each palatinate functioned as a mini-republic ever jealous in defence of local privilege.

The maintenance of the entire system demanded a high degree of loyalty and civic responsibility among the nobles. The sixteenth century, an age of particular prosperity for large segments of the Polish nobility, owing partially to the grain trade, was the apogee of Polish "noble democracy," in which the "middle" nobles exerted great influence on all aspects of Polish politics and culture. Relative peace and weak neighbours assured success in foreign affairs. The outdated levy of the nobility did not have to be called frequently, since the small standing army and mercenaries were sufficient for Poland's defence. Prosperity served as the basis for a flowering of the arts, education and literature, including the development of a vibrant Polish vernacular. These achievements remained very largely a noble preserve. Knowledge of the classics strengthened dedication to republican virtues. The success of the nobility and its state led to an increasing estrangement from the rest of the population. At first the nobles simply justified their privileges on the grounds that they were the descendants of the knights who had traditionally defended the realm. Eventually, however, they came to see themselves as a different breed;

unlike the commoners, they were descended from the ancient warrior Sarmatians. Sarmatism or the Sarmatian myth offered an explanation as to why all nobles, despite differences in language and descent, were closely related. It also served to emphasize the differences between nobles and commoners.

In sum, the Polish noble system that spread to Ukraine was based on the recognition of broad individual rights for each noble, on the affirmation of legal equality for a numerous, but economically diverse noble order, on the exclusion of other strata of the population from government, on the diminution of the rights of the monarch, on regionalism and decentralization, on the substitution of the nobility's corporate institutions for those of the state and on the creation of a noble republican ideology based on the Sarmatian myth.

The Polish *szlachta* order of the fourteenth to sixteenth centuries appealed to the elites in the surrounding territories, and its political and cultural influence was felt from Prussia to Moldavia. Its greatest impact was in the vast domains of the Grand Duchy of Lithuania, especially after the union of Poland and Lithuania in 1386. The elite and service orders of the grand duchy, which had hitherto varied not only in wealth and power, but also in titles and privilege, gradually began to assume the characteristics of the Polish *szlachta*. The lower strata of the elite had to struggle to free themselves from onerous obligations to rulers and great lords and, for some time, service obligations for landholdings remained in force. Initially, the Orthodox elite were not permitted to attain full noble status (e.g., coats of arms) and offices. Yet although the economy, military situation, and ethnic and religious composition of the grand duchy remained markedly different from those of Poland, the elite of the grand duchy adopted the ideology of the Polish *szlachta*. The Union of Lublin of 1569 was not so much a unification of the two states, as a recognition of the merger of their respective nobilities.[12]

The "Commonwealth of the Two Nations" that resulted from the Union embodied the unity of the nobility in the new joint Diet. Union did not bring total fusion; the administrative structures of the two states remained separate, and in neither case did loyalty to the commonwealth supersede particularism. In practice, the nobles of the grand duchy jealously guarded the integrity of their fatherland against infringements by their brother nobles.

The expansion of the "Republic of the Nobles" eastward was not limited to Polish influence on the institutions and inhabitants of the grand duchy; it had its effects on the Polish state and its nobility as well. Lithuania's hostilities against Muscovy taxed the finances and institutions of the hitherto more secure Polish nobility. The princes and magnates of the territories of the grand duchy, who far surpassed in wealth and power the magnates of the Polish lands, formed an oligarchy of almost independent territorial rulers and made a sham of the principle of noble equality. Finally, the transfer of the Volhynian and Kievan lands to the Kingdom of Poland directly involved the Polish state and nobility in the turbulent problems of the Ukrainian frontier.

In the period from 1569 to 1648, the elite of the Ukrainian lands belonged fully to the pan-European family of nobilities in its Polish variant. This period marked the high point of the process of Central European and Latin Christian influence in the Ukrainian territories. As with the transfer of so many West European institutions (for example, the Magdeburg city law), that of the institutions and traditions of Central European nobilities to Orthodox East Slavic territory involved both contradictions and frictions. Yet, however much the Ukrainian population resisted, adopted and then transformed these influences, from the thirteenth to the sixteenth century the legal norms and social structures of the Latin West took hold in the Ukrainian lands. With these came the formation of a clearly defined noble order, with its corporate institutions, duties and privileges. The fact that Muscovite society did not undergo a similar process created a fundamental difference between political cultures and social orders of the East Slavic peoples that had far-reaching consequences for Ukraine after the middle of the seventeenth century.[13]

The Nobility of 1569–1648 and the Problems of Ukrainian Social History

Before discussing specific problems for the study of the nobility of the Ukrainian lands between 1569 and 1648, we must confront the questions raised earlier, of political unity, historical continuity and outside penetration. In fact, these questions cannot always be sharply demarcated since they pertain to related events and phenomena.

A certain political unity for Ukraine was assured by the Union of Lublin, which brought almost all Ukrainian ethnic territories under the Kingdom of Poland by uniting the formerly Lithuanian lands of Volhynia and Kiev (after 1569 constituted as the palatinates of Kiev, Volhynia and Bratslav) and of Podlachia[14] with the former Polish palatinates of Ruthenia, Podillia and Belz. The new state borders both united the Lviv and Kiev regions and separated the Kiev region from the ethnic Belorussian lands. Political unity was accompanied by increasing uniformity of noble privileges and institutions for all nobles in the Ukrainian territories, but this did not result in a well-integrated distinct noble elite within a Ukrainian administrative unit. The commonwealth was a diune, not a triune, state: the Rus'-Ukrainian lands had nothing like the status of either the grand duchy or the kingdom. No common administrative institutions existed for the Ukrainian lands. The palatinates formed from the newly annexed Volhynian and Kievan lands were appended to the kingdom as part of the administrative division of Little Poland and were legally no more closely associated with the palatinates of Ruthenia and Podillia than with those of Cracow or Lublin. The period between 1569 and 1648 had brought almost all the Ukrainian nobles into one political entity, but the lack of any common Ukrainian administration or institutions prevented a common territorial loyalty for the nobles of pre-1569 Lithuania and Poland.

Despite the inclusion of most Ukrainian lands in one political entity, the decision to select the nobles of Ukraine as a subject of historical inquiry is not self-evident. Scholars agree on the importance of studying the decentralized commonwealth region by region. The palatinate, as the centre of the nobility's political life, is the basic unit for local study, though larger units can be combined to examine regional patterns. The eastern Ukrainian palatinates, with their distinct history and shared administrative practices, form a coherent unit. Yet although similar privileges furthered the political integration of the elite of the four eastern Ukrainian palatinates (Volhynia, Kiev, Bratslav and Chernihiv), even they had few offices or institutions in common. Combining the western and eastern Ukrainian lands for study is not as clearcut a choice. In particular, the greater integration of the western Ukrainian lands into the Kingdom of Poland must always be kept in mind. Including all the Ukrainian lands together may be partly explained on territorial grounds. Certainly they shared the sixteenth-century steppe frontier that extended as far as Lviv and Kamianets-Podilskyi.

A more basic reason for this grouping is the cultural-religious bond of many nobles in these territories. Although Polish influence had resulted in a greater proportion of Roman Catholics and immigrants from Polish territories in the western lands, a considerable segment of nobles in that area still adhered to the Orthodox church and Ruthenian culture, making them part of the Rus' community. It is true that in the period from 1569 to 1648, more and more Rus' nobles forsook their ancestral faith and tongue. However, it may be argued that the dynamics of this cultural process, and in particular the opposition of some of the nobles in both west and east, who defended traditional ways, make the combination of the two regions desirable. All these factors speak for considering the Ukrainian lands as a unit when studying the nobility. This should not, however, exclude studies of other geographic divisions such as the eastern Ukrainian lands; all Rus' lands, including Belorussia; and the old lands of the kingdom (including the Ruthenian palatinate).

The problem of continuity comprises three separate aspects that require examination: the origins and predecessors of the nobility; the changes in the noble order from 1569 to 1648; and the relationship of the pre-1648 nobility to nobilities after 1648.

In all regions of Ukraine, the nobility evolved out of elite groups of Kievan Rus', with frequent infusions of immigrants. The nobility of 1569 in all Ukrainian lands included descendants of both native elites and immigrants. The varying composition of the nobility reflected the different political fates of the western and eastern Ukrainian territories.

The westernmost Ukrainian population had been influenced by Polish and Hungarian society even before its annexation to Poland in the fourteenth and fifteenth centuries. From the fourteenth century western Ukrainian elites had taken part in the formation of the Polish nobility. The boyar families of Galicia had been joined by immigrants from the Polish territories and from Western Europe. In the steppe land of Podillia, the proportion of immigrants was particularly high. *Szlachta* privileges were granted to large numbers of defenders of the realm, and the western lands contained a numerous petty nobility. Along the Carpathian belt of the Ruthenian palatinate, large clans of Orthodox Ukrainian nobles, some of Ruthenian and some of Moldavian extraction, shared a limited number of coats of arms (e.g., Sas, Korchak). Although Podlachia was part of the grand duchy in the early sixteenth century, its close historic association with Masovia linked its development with that of the other western Ukrainian territories. While it contained a large number of petty Ruthenian Orthodox nobles, they had been overwhelmed by colonists from Masovia, thus making Podlachia the home of the largest number of Roman Catholic ethnic Polish nobles in the Ukrainian-Belorussian lands.[15]

The nobility of the palatinates of Volhynia, Bratslav and Kiev had followed a course of development similar to that of the other nobilities of the Grand Duchy of Lithuania. The decentralized structure of the Lithuanian state and the great distances from Vilnius had assured the distinctiveness of the nobles of the Ukrainian lands. Although the descendants of the Riurikid and Gedimid princes had lost their status as independent rulers, they had retained economic and political influence. In Volhynia, less subject to devastations from the steppe than the Kiev and Bratslav palatinates, a particularly large number of princely families, ranging from the fabulously wealthy to small property holders, controlled the life of the palatinate. Descendants of the great local non-princely families also played a major role in the life of the territories. By the sixteenth century the *ziemiane*, *pany* and boyars of the grand duchy had wrested numerous privileges from the grand dukes. The process involved imitation of Polish social and administrative models, and culminated in the 1560s with the final creation of a *szlachta* order in the grand duchy. The adaptation of the Polish model imposed the noble-commoner distinction throughout the population of the grand duchy. Some of the lower elements of the old elite, such as the boyars of Ovruch, were not admitted to the new *szlachta*. In 1569 the nobility of the eastern Ukrainian palatinates was largely indigenous or long resident, Orthodox in faith, and Ruthenian in culture.[16]

Between 1569 and 1648 no major legal changes affected the position of the nobility, but factors such as migration, cultural and religious assimilation, intra-order relations and landholding patterns did alter its composition, especially in the newly annexed lands. The question of how similar the nobility of 1648 was to that of 1569 has not yet been resolved. In particular, we must ask whether the adoption of the Polish model was merely superficial in the eastern lands, or whether the elite order was transformed in basic ways. The most important political act of the period was the annexation of the Chernihiv lands from Muscovy in 1618. With the formation of the Chernihiv palatinate in 1635 the institutions of the nobility were fully established in this area, which was granted the same privileges as the palatinates of Kiev, Volhynia and Bratslav.[17]

For the post-1648 period the problem of the survival of the old nobility is essential to any study of continuity of Ukrainian noble orders. Most nineteenth-century scholars believed that the Khmelnytsky uprising had driven the nobility from the lands in which the Cossacks triumphed. Through painstaking research in the early twentieth century, Viacheslav Lypynsky established that there were in fact thousands of nobles among the Cossack forces and that both through their presence and through their influence the old nobility shaped the new Ukraine.[18] But how many old noble families were present in the Cossack *starshyna-shliakhta* of the late seventeenth and early eighteenth century we do not yet know. Particularly important is the transferral of the political and social views of the old nobility to the new elite and the impact of the seventeenth-century revolution on the nobility in the lands retained by Poland.

The problem of influence and penetration must be examined to determine whether integration into the Polish, or rather all-commonwealth, nobility in the period 1569–1648 had gone so far as to preclude study of a "Ukrainian" nobility altogether. Indeed, the transformation of elite groups in Ukraine into a Polish-type *szlachta* before 1569 and the further integration of this nobility into the *szlachta* of the entire commonwealth between 1569 and 1648 are the two dominant themes of the nobility's development in Ukraine. The nobles of the Grand Duchy of Lithuania underwent a similar course of development after 1569 even though they retained a political structure that differentiated them from the nobles of the kingdom. It is clear that loyalty to the concept of a pan-commonwealth Sarmatian nobility advanced more quickly than homogenization of customs, adoption of the Polish language or conversion to Roman Catholicism. Most studies of the Polish nobility take a long-term perspective, and in so doing pay little attention to stages and tempos over shorter periods. This practice is particularly questionable for the Ukrainian lands, where the Khmelnytsky uprising drastically changed the composition of the nobility and the context of its political and cultural integration.

Though integration into the commonwealth's nobility and Poland's culture had advanced very far by 1648, the nobles of the Ukrainian lands remained sufficiently distinct and cohesive to justify regarding them as a separate group. This was particularly true for the nobles of the newly annexed lands, who were guaranteed a number of privileges that differentiated them from the nobles of Poland. Princes were allowed to retain their titles; the "execution-of-the-laws" statute was not enforced; Ruthenian was the language of administration; the Second Lithuanian Statute of 1566 remained the law of the land; and the Orthodox nobles had special charters affirming full equality with Roman Catholics. Even the nobles in the Ukrainian territories that did not possess legal and administrative institutions markedly different from those of the Polish territory remained distinct. The economic and military affairs of the Ukrainian frontier and the Black Sea basin created an environment very different from that of Masovia or Great Poland. Religion continued to differentiate the nobles of the Ukrainian lands from those of Polish lands since even immigrants from ethnic Poland or converts to Roman Catholicism and Protestantism lived among the numerous faithful of the Eastern church. Although Rus' was not an administrative unit, it was perceived as a geographic entity that had its own history and traditions and as the homeland of the Ruthenian people. Hence the nobles of Ruthenian-Ukrainian descent served to mark Ukraine off from the Polish territories. Just how distinct the nobles of Ukraine were can only be determined by comparing them with their contemporaries in the Polish territories.

Proposals for Research on the Ukrainian Nobility, 1569–1648

Any work on the "Ukrainian" nobility for the period from 1569 to 1648 must investigate all nobles who inhabited the Ukrainian territories. But although a territorial principle should be followed, special attention should be paid to the nobles who by descent, culture and religion belonged to the Ruthenian-Ukrainian tradition. The lines cannot be sharply drawn for a time of interpenetration of populations, cultures and identities, but by studying all the nobles of the Ukrainian lands we will better understand the native Ruthenian element and the process of its transformation under Polish rule. The nobles of Ukraine must be investigated in the context of the nobility of the entire commonwealth. This will allow us to take advantage of the major achievements of Polish scholars of the last thirty years, while at the same time it may provide insights into the Ukrainian dimension so frequently absent in their works. Their writings on the commonwealth cannot be viewed as satisfactory as long as their findings are based on research only on the Polish lands of the commonwealth.

The discussion that follows poses questions and proposes hypotheses on various aspects of the Ukrainian nobility. Much of it challenges assumptions in scholarly literature and is offered in the spirit of sharing preliminary findings and views from research in progress, even though they are not backed up by conclusive evidence. It is the author's hope that other students of Ukrainian social history will put these hypotheses to the test while carrying on their own research.

Two problems should be kept in mind. First, the Ukrainian lands encompass a large territory and generalizations are difficult to make before sufficient regional research has been undertaken. Second, the acceptance of the juridical-legal category "noble" as a subject of study produces a large and disparate group. Differences within the group were tremendous and intensive study of the various strata of the noble order is necessary. For many problems the acceptance of seventeenth-century divisions of men may seem to becloud an understanding of economic, social and political processes. Certainly study of the commonwealth's inhabitants through other criteria is necessary (economic position, religious belief, relation to political power). Yet as unwieldy a group as the nobility is for study, it constituted a self-conscious grouping that shared rights, privileges and responsibilities in early modern Ukraine, and an understanding of it as a totality is necessary to comprehend the period.

The Composition and Economic Position of the Nobility

Any study of the Ukrainian nobility must confront the problem of numbers. The estimate that in the seventeenth century the commonwealth's nobility constituted 8 to 10 per cent of a total population of eight to ten million is based on eighteenth-century statistics projected backward and on scattered landholding and military registers.[19] Yet even these rough figures are not available for the Ukrainian territories. Estimates of Ukraine's population range from Jabłonowski's figure of a million and a quarter to a million and a half for the late sixteenth century to Baranovych's reckoning of five million for the early seventeenth century.[20] No attempt has been made to estimate the number of nobles in the Ukrainian territories. The number of families owning peasant-populated lands could be ascertained relatively accurately from published tax records, but the computation of petty nobles without peasant-populated lands and landless nobles could only be estimated by an extensive study of court records, military registers and epistolary and narrative sources.[21]

Although the numbers of the Ukrainian nobility have not been computed, all evidence points to a lower percentage of nobles in the general population than was the case in Polish territories. While Podlachia may have surpassed even Masovia in the percentage of nobles, the other western Ukrainian lands seem to have been well below the average in the commonwealth. The eastern Ukrainian lands, with their concentration of large holdings in a few great magnates' hands, appear to have contained a very thin layer of nobles at the time of their annexation to the kingdom.[22]

Only more thorough study of the size of the noble order in Ukraine will provide an understanding of the political and cultural processes of the period. If indeed the nobles were a smaller percentage of the population in most Ukrainian lands than in the Polish areas, the causes of the tensions of Polish rule in Ukraine will become clearer. A political system that works well when 8 to 10 per cent of its population are privileged would not necessarily function as well if only 2 or 3 per cent have that status. Differences in the size of the noble order would explain migration patterns. The small size of the indigenous elite would encourage migration into Ukraine since the political-cultural system would also be undermanned. Thus, for example, petty Masovian nobles probably found service at the courts of the great magnates because few native petty nobles were available for those positions. Hence study of the number of nobles must pay particular attention to migratory patterns and social origins. Also a study of the eastward migration of nobles is needed in order to answer questions about the homogenization of the nobles of the commonwealth and about the integration of the nobles within the Ukrainian territories. An examination of the origins of the nobility of the Ukrainian lands throughout the period will provide some explanation of religious and cultural trends. If the native Ukrainian nobles were relatively few in number, it becomes apparent why they were not more resistant to linguistic assimilation and religious conversion.

Despite considerable research, we do not know enough about the nobles' role in the Ukrainian economy and, in particular, about the organization of nobles' estates. More intensive cultivation, husbandry and exploitation of natural resources (particularly forest products) in sixteenth-century Ukraine has been explained as being in part the result of an expanding population and active economy in the Vistula basin. Conversion of noble lands into manorial estates, increased demand for peasant labour, and specialization in grain for West European markets were the dominant trends in the Polish economy of the sixteenth century. The growing demand for foodstuffs has been seen as the major impetus behind the colonization of Ukraine. But the extent of the colonization and population increase is in dispute and the method of colonization is not fully understood. One school of historians claims that the nobility organized the settlement of new lands; another asserts that the peasants pioneered the settlements, only to be followed by the nobles.[23]

The most important unresolved problem centres on the organization of agricultural production. The western Ukrainian lands and Volhynia had the advantage of the Vistula river basin, but the Ukrainian territories further east had no access to the Baltic. This makes it unwise to assume large-scale export of grain from those territories. In addition, we do not really know how widespread manorial agriculture based on labour services had become in this territory, since the regulations increasing labour obligations for the peasantry may have preceded actual practice. At least in the frontier regions, payments in cash and kind seem to have predominated over labour services. In studying nobles' estates, comparisons should be made of techniques and productivity of small estates, large holdings and leased properties. The effects of temporary transfers of property as collateral for debts and the management of lands by stewards and retainers must be examined. Until we know more about the Ukrainian economy, it will be difficult to evaluate the role of the nobility in it. The major obstacle to that study is the scarcity of nobles' estate records.[24]

Study of the nobility's economic activities must be based on examination of landholding patterns. Throughout the commonwealth, the late sixteenth century and early seventeenth century was a period of land redistribution in favour of large holders, with a corresponding growth in numbers of very small landholders and landless nobles. It is not yet known whether the Ruthenian and Belz palatinates followed this trend. Even before 1569 the Podillian and Volhynian palatinates were overwhelmingly in the possession of large holders, and their possessions may have increased further after that date. The Kiev, Bratslav and Chernihiv palatinates followed a different course because of their rapid colonization between 1569 and 1648. The statutes of 1590, which declared any land for which no ownership charters existed to be vacant, led to a distribution that ended with the concentration of vast tracts of land in relatively few hands. The large holdings of royal land (*starostwa*) in these territories were administered by the great magnates. The colonization of the Dnieper basin afforded opportunities for nobles such as Jeremi Wiśniowiecki and Stanisław Koniecpolski to create virtually autonomous domains.[25]

A number of questions about landholding in the 1569 to 1648 period must be posed. Were large landholdings created at the expense of middle and small holdings throughout Ukraine or were all segments of the nobility increasing their holdings in hitherto underpopulated areas of the Dnieper basin? Did the proportion of land owned by nobles increase in relation to royal and church lands between 1569 and 1648? How rapid was the redistribution of lands among the nobles through marriage, purchase and leasing and how frequently were great holdings assembled and lost? What proportion of the nobles' lands was administered by stewards? How much Ukrainian territory passed to new immigrants from Poland or to families resident in Polish territories? Past discussions of Polish nobles' penetration of the lands annexed at the Union of Lublin have been based on impressionist data. Only comprehensive studies of the change in landholding patterns over the entire period for all strata of the nobility will prove whether seventeenth-century assertions of an increasing Polish presence were justified.

Landholding patterns reflected the internal structure of the noble order, in particular the dominant position of the magnates. The existence of powerful magnates in the eastern Ukrainian territories before 1569 and the formation of virtually independent magnate domains in the Dnieper basin between 1569 and 1648 have been viewed as deforming influences on the Polish political system of "noble democracy." The eastern Ukrainian lands contained a magnate stratum that possessed not only wealth and power, but also traditions of dominance and, in some cases, princely titles. Although it has long been recognized that the magnates from Ukraine exercised a decisive influence on the political and social structure of the entire commonwealth, no systematic study of the stratum has been undertaken.

The problem has been partly one of definition. Unlike "noble," "magnate" was not a juridically determined status, and it is a merely descriptive term for powerful or important nobles. Thus there are no clear guidelines as to who belonged to the magnate stratum. Even those historians who ascribe magnate status merely on the criterion of landholding admit that regional differences must be taken into account, since, for example, the large holdings of Belz would be swallowed up in the vast eastern Ukrainian domains. One must also consider attributes of power and influence. For example, it is possible that a prince Chetvertynsky surpassed a much richer new immigrant from the Polish lands in power and influence because of the authority he derived from local connections and historical traditions.

Once general criteria are established for defining the magnate stratum, attention must be paid to changes in its composition. How many new families from Poland entered it? How many old families died out? How frequently did local families rise to magnate status and how many magnate families became impoverished? The evidence is readily available, but hitherto historians have dealt with examples and impressions.

The relationship of the magnates to other strata of the nobility must be investigated more thoroughly. It is clear that legal rights did not immediately eradicate obligations of service by the lower to the higher elite strata. In certain cases (e.g., creation of the legally entailed domain or *ordynacja* of the Ostrozky family), recognition of the special relation of a magnate to his domain and servitors was legislated. Certainly, the new noble servitors who immigrated into Ukraine to serve the magnates were not "equal brother" nobles in practice. The retention and development of subinfeudation in Ukrainian noble society must be more fully treated.[26]

Although the middle nobility has been viewed as the backbone of the "Republic of the Nobles," little attention has been paid to this stratum in the Ukrainian territories. It has been presumed that this group was overshadowed by the magnates. Yet while middle nobles may have been less significant than in the Polish territories, they had been an important factor in the decision to unite with Poland in 1569. The western Ukrainian territories and Volhynia had networks of well-established middle noble families who should be carefully studied before generalizations about the overriding importance of the magnates in Ukraine are accepted. Endowed with *szlachta* privileges, the middle nobles had considerable opportunity to obtain wealth and education. Hence, they had the tools to make their voices heard in the dietines and courts of Ukraine. In addition, as more magnates abandoned the Orthodox church, positions of church leadership opened up to the middle nobles, who led the movement for the defence of

Orthodoxy in the early seventeenth century.[27]

The petty nobles formed a large and variable group. There were small landholders who owned a few plots of land worked by peasant serfs. Some worked their land with hired labourers or with only the labour of their families. Others were landless, living on the fringes of rural society, working in free professions or serving the households of magnates or middle nobles. In regions such as Podlachia, the Carpathian crests of the Ruthenian palatinate and the Ovruch area of the Kievan palatinate, large numbers of nobles sharing a surname and a coat of arms existed in villages. The most important differentiation in noble society was between landed and landless, for political right was seen as derived from ownership of land in a region and the participation of *non possessionati* in the dietines of the palatinates was frequently challenged. Studies on the petty nobles in Ukraine will probably confirm that except in Podlachia, they were much less numerous and hence less influential than in the Polish territories. There is evidence that on a regional basis they were major political actors, as in the Przemyśl land, where they conducted a campaign against a Uniate bishop that embroiled the region in turmoil for decades. The links of the indigenous petty nobility to the Orthodox church appear to have been strong and their role in providing cadres for the church and Ukrainian cultural institutions must be examined. Since the power of magnates depended on their retainers, the careers of petty nobles as servitors in the magnates' military and financial affairs must be studied. It would appear that in general, the positions were filled not by the less numerous petty nobles of the Ukrainian lands but by immigrants from Polish territories. The much touted noble equality must be carefully measured against the great disparities of wealth and power within the noble order of Ukraine.[28]

Nobles and Other Strata of the Population

In the world view of the nobles of the commonwealth, the fundamental distinction between men was that between nobles and commoners. To be on the noble side of the divide was a much sought after status. The divide ran through the old elite groups of Ukraine with gross inconsistencies, reflecting historical development and sheer chance. Thus numerous military frontiersmen and servitors in the Carpathians entered the nobility, while more prominent eastern Ukrainian boyars were denied noble status. In particular, the existence of boyars in the Ukrainian lands after 1569 impeded any clear-cut division of society into nobles and commoners, although boyars without noble status were increasingly deprived of their privileges as members of a military elite stratum. Once recognized as noble, one passed the status on to all descendants, and only by committing treason or taking up the life-style of a burgher or a Cossack could one place one's status in jeopardy. One was a noble because one's ancestors had been nobles, but the records were often scarce and claims to noble status were often difficult to prove or disprove.

Although the Polish-Lithuanian nobility had become a self-regulating corporate order that allowed few ennoblements after the end of the sixteenth century, numerous commoners gained entry through bribery and a variety of other tricks, including adoption by noble families and false testimony purchased from noble witnesses. It seems likely that such practices were widespread in Ukraine, where record-keeping began late and destruction of documents was frequent. Migration to a new area was a useful expedient for the determined social climber, and eastern Ukraine must have been an ideal place for the newly minted noble to start again. It is not known how many of the "petty nobles" immigrating to eastern Ukraine assumed noble status as they travelled to a new land. The immigrant was at an advantage over local boyars, burghers and Cossacks in asserting claims to be a noble, since local men of substance aspiring to take up the noble life were too well-known to succeed in chicanery. The frustration of powerful Cossack officers and wealthy Kievan burghers in yielding precedence to penurious nobles from Masovia must have increased if they doubted the noble origins of the newcomers. Only future research can determine the validity of these suppositions.[29]

As for relations of the nobles to other orders of the population, a number of generalizations that have been posited for the entire Polish-Lithuanian Commonwealth must be scrutinized with data from the Ukrainian territories. It has generally been assumed that the nobility became more estranged from other social strata and played an increasingly important role in all aspects of political, economic and cultural life throughout the commonwealth from 1569 to 1648. Certain peculiarities of the Ukrainian territories point to significant divergences from this pattern. In particular, eastern Ukraine was an area of frontier conditions and new settlements, where rigid distinctions between corporate orders were difficult to enforce, a situation that surely affected the nobility and the relations of the nobles with the rest of the population.

Although the nobles of Ukraine enjoyed the same sweeping rights over their lands and the peasants inhabiting them as the nobles in the rest of the commonwealth, relative underpopulation, abundance of lands and unstable conditions gave the Ukrainian peasantry significant advantages in resisting noble dominance. In the late sixteenth and early seventeenth century, new agricultural settlements were formed throughout the

Ukrainian territories, and the noble had to attract peasants to his lands. The peasantry of the Carpathians and the Dnieper basin had not been fully subjected to a noble landowning class, and in the Dnieper basin frontier conditions allowed for a rough-and-ready democracy that at times blurred the practical distinction between orders. Tatar raids assured that the peasants learned martial arts. The peasants also had a wide variety of outlets for expressing their dissatisfaction. In a newly colonized, underpopulated land, they could move on to another landlord who would be less demanding. The newness of settlements and land titles also made changing orders possible; one simply moved to any of the numerous settlements governed by urban law that had sprung up throughout the area. Then, too, the Cossack life beckoned, and new lands awaited the adventuresome beyond the Muscovite border. Finally, the numerous Cossack revolts (1590s, 1625, 1630, 1635–8) also provided the peasants with ample opportunity to challenge the nobles' regime. Spurred on by the desire to increase revenue and to exercise the prerogatives enjoyed by nobles in Masovia or Great Poland, the nobles of Ukraine conducted a relentless struggle to subjugate the peasants. Their success was much greater in the West than in the East.[30]

The relationship of the nobles to the burghers, the diverse inhabitants of the cities, must also have differed substantially from that in the western territories of the commonwealth. After the formation of the nobles' commonwealth, the cities and burghers played a minor role in the state's political life. The one great city of the land, Gdańsk, was almost cut off from the commonwealth's body politic and its largely German partriciate chose to seek greater autonomy from Warsaw rather than a greater role in the government. Except for the Baltic littoral, above all Royal Prussia, cities were weakly developed in the commonwealth, and their political and economic positions relative to that of the nobles declined in the period from 1569 to 1648. The upper stratum of the burghers failed to produce a culture that could compete with that of the nobles and instead sought to mimic the latter.

Until the mid-sixteenth century, the Ukrainian lands could be described as an extreme example of the weakness of cities and the burgher groups throughout the commonwealth. Cities were small in size and few in numbers and the great nobles dominated most aspects of urban life. But the economic boom and population growth in the Ukrainian lands enhanced the development of cities and burgher communities and created some divergences from the general pattern of noble-burgher relations.

Lviv remained the largest city on Ukrainian territory and continued to thrive. Other, smaller cities in the West also showed signs of vitality. The period was one of urban rebirth in the Dnieper basin; ancient cities grew and numerous new towns were founded. Kiev expanded rapidly, almost surpassing Lviv, and the old capital of the Rus' princes thrived as its political and cultural elite rebuilt the city's ruins and re-established its position as an Orthodox ecclesiastical and cultural centre. Royal and private settlements under urban law multiplied, particularly in the Kievan palatinate where half the population lived in settlements under urban law. True, most of these settlements were urban in name only; the full rights of the West European burghers were withheld from them and private cities were dominated by magnate owners. Many were merely fortified agricultural settlements. But this large-scale granting of urban rights still resulted in a population in Dnieper Ukraine markedly different from that of western Ukraine and most of the Polish territories. The nobles accepted the existence of a large population that could exercise significant, albeit limited, urban privileges. This is not to say that the burghers challenged the nobles' rule in Ukraine or that the nobles did not frequently infringe on the few privileges granted to burghers in private cities. But whether in great royal cities or in private farming towns, the burghers formed a significant group that was not fully subjugated to the nobles. Settlements similar to the eastern Ukrainian agricultural towns were serf villages in the Polish territories. In much of Ukraine, self-interest and recognition of local conditions induced the nobles to accept a social structure very different from that of the western territories of the commonwealth. While the detrimental effects of the nobles' policies and exactions on the burghers and cities of Ukraine have been well documented, the influence of the proportionally numerous burgher order in areas of Ukraine has not been explored.[31]

Noble-burgher relations in Ukraine also reflected the religious and ethnic heterogeneity of the Ukrainian cities. Ukrainian cities not only had a large Jewish population, which, as in Polish cities, was excluded from urban rights and jurisdiction and existed under its own law and royal privileges, but also influential Armenian communities living under separate jurisdiction. The existence of these groups, who were often in competition with the burghers under the city magistrate, afforded the nobles an opportunity to play one urban faction off against another. The burgher order proper was divided into Catholic and Orthodox segments, though in many cities only Catholics enjoyed full burgher privileges. Although weight of numbers negated restrictions against the Orthodox in many areas of the Dnieper basin, the persecution of Orthodox burghers by Catholic patriciates and guilds made the cities centres of religious and national tensions even before the rise of intolerance during the Counter

Reformation and the controversies over the Union of Brest.

The conflict between largely Polish, Catholic burghers and largely Ukrainian, Orthodox burghers in the Ukrainian cities gave noble-burgher relations an aspect absent in the Polish territories. Communal tensions in the Ukrainian cities gave the Ruthenian-Ukrainian burghers a stimulus to adopt cultural tendencies emanating from the West to defend and reform the Ruthenian Orthodox Church. The role of the burghers of Lviv and their *bratstvo* (brotherhood) in Ukrainian ecclesiastical affairs, printing and education is the outstanding example. Yet although the Lviv Brotherhood was primarily an organization of burghers, it later enrolled Ukrainian nobles, including magnates. Brotherhoods in Lutske, Kiev and other cities similarly included nobles, Cossacks and clerics, along with burghers. The existence of important civic, cultural urban institutions that included both nobles and commoners indicates that the Ruthenian Orthodox nobles' relation to the Ruthenian burghers differed significantly from that of their Polish counterparts. The Ruthenian burghers' influence went beyond mere intellectual and cultural contacts. They not only exhorted the nobles to remain firm in Orthodoxy and to render them aid, but also provided the noble adherents of Orthodoxy with financial assistance. The Lviv Brotherhood was even able indirectly to influence the Diet through Orthodox planning sessions on tactics that the Orthodox noble delegates were to follow. The initial intellectual and cultural unpreparedness of the Ukrainian Orthodox nobility for challenges from Protestants and Catholics, followed by the conversion of many nobles to those faiths, increased the importance of the burghers in the Ukrainian Orthodox community. The nobles still controlled the church and the community, but the failings in their leadership ensured close co-operation with the burghers.[32]

The nobles of the eastern Ukrainian lands had to deal with a stratum in the population that did not exist elsewhere in the commonwealth—that is, with the Cossacks. Though the government and the nobles depended on the Cossacks in times of war, as the nobles extended their landholding south and east the insubordinate Cossack population became a major irritant. The nobles of the Ukrainian lands, like those of the commonwealth as a whole, rejected Cossack demands for political and economic rights. Denied the privileges of every petty Masovian noble, the Cossacks attempted to retain and expand their de facto rights through foreign adventures and rebellions. As a result, the landowning nobles of the Ukrainian areas were adamant in asserting the need to subjugate them.

Relations between the nobles and Cossacks, however, were not entirely hostile and rancorous. In practice, the magnates who dealt summarily with the Cossacks did the same with small noble landowners, which may well have bred some feeling of alliance between the two latter groups. Nobles played an important role in the Cossack Host; in the mid-sixteenth century great lords were frequently Cossack leaders and by the late sixteenth and early seventeenth century numerous petty nobles had joined the Cossack Host, whether in an effort to escape their old lives or tempted by the economic opportunities the Cossack life presented. In doing so they placed their status as nobles in jeopardy, and as a result became vociferous proponents of full recognition of the Cossacks as a privileged order.

In practice, Orthodox nobles also co-operated with the Cossacks in other ways, which, in the 1610s and 1620s, allowed the Cossacks to assume a major role in Orthodox religious and cultural affairs. Hetman Petro Konashevych-Sahaidachny, who appears to have descended from a noble family of the Sambir region, endowed a chair in Greek studies in the Lviv Brotherhood's school and enrolled the Host in the Kiev Brotherhood. Devout Orthodox nobles enlisted the support of the Cossack hetman in restoring the Orthodox hierarchy in 1620. Although the Orthodox nobles might be opposed to Cossack demands and turbulence, they had still to rely on the Cossacks if they were to achieve political and religious goals. However anti-Cossack the nobles were as a group, many individual nobles still had good reason to support Cossack actions and demands.[33]

The Cossacks were not a monolithic group in the period from 1569 to 1648. Registered Cossacks, never more than eight thousand in number in times of peace, were a recognized social grouping. Behind them stood the tens of thousands of men who followed the Cossack way of life and swelled the armies of the commonwealth in time of danger. The Ukrainian frontier had afforded an opportunity for a new social order to emerge from the inhabitants of the commonwealth. But the Cossacks, particularly those not in the register, were just the most salient of a large number of men who remained outside the stable categories of noble, peasant, burgher and clergyman. Everywhere there were rootless men—adventurers, paupers, bandits and vagabonds who had broken their ties with the traditional orders. These elements posed a problem for the authorities throughout the commonwealth, but it was only in the Ukrainian frontier that they could find a relatively secure haven, particularly among the unregistered Cossacks. The nobles of Ukraine, like their fellows throughout the commonwealth, railed against the "stray men," but without finding a solution to the Cossack problem there was no hope of putting an end to the "stray men" in Ukraine.[34]

The relation of three other segments of Ukraine's population to the nobility must be discussed: the clergy, the legally-defined religious-national minorities (Jews and Armenians) and the military. In the first and third groups, nobles provided the leadership. The second group was enmeshed in the nobles' economic and social system.

Excluding the clergy, the traditional first estate, from Ukraine's major corporate orders may seem questionable since clergymen were a well-defined corporate group that enjoyed juridical and financial privileges. Yet the clergymen of the commonwealth differed from the nobles, peasants, burghers and Cossacks in that they straddled the divide between nobles and commoners. The clergy functioned as a group parallel to the laity, with important churchmen drawn from the nobles and lower clergymen from the commoners. Service in the churches did not negate noble status, and the noble-bishop or noble-abbot often identified more strongly with his brother-nobles than with his fellow-clergymen. This phenomenon can be seen in both the Roman Catholic and the Eastern Orthodox Churches.

The composition of the clergy as a mirror image of lay society stemmed from the laity's rights to patronage. In the fifteenth century the Polish kings gained the right to select Roman Catholic bishops, while the nobles exercised patronage over country livings. Since Roman Catholic bishops were senators of the commonwealth and most high church offices conveyed substantial benefices, the nobles legislated that candidates must be chosen from their own ranks. Although the reforms of the Catholic church of the late sixteenth century intensified religious convictions and loyalty to Rome among the clergymen, the Roman church never challenged the imposition of the commonwealth's social structure on the clerical order.[35] In the Orthodox church, royal and lay rights to patronage were even more sweeping. While the Catholic kings of Poland had to deal respectfully with the wishes of Rome, they could treat the Orthodox patriarchs of Constantinople, the subjects of the Ottoman porte, with less deference. In the sixteenth century the kings selected their supporters to fill positions in the bishoprics and the major monasteries, while the nobles expanded their rights of patronage over parish churches and smaller monasteries. Although Orthodox, and later Uniate, bishoprics did not convey senatorial chairs, the positions did confer wealth and power. As in the Catholic church, the nobles reserved all major posts for themselves.[36]

In examining the relations of the nobles of the Ukrainian lands to the clergymen and churches, one must take into account the difference in the religious composition of these areas from other lands in the commonwealth and the drastic changes in religious affairs between 1569 and 1648. The Polish-Lithuanian Commonwealth differed from most of Europe in its religious toleration, a policy derived from the persistent presence of a powerful Orthodox minority and based on the guarantee of religious toleration issued at the Confederation of Warsaw in 1573. In practice, however, religious freedom was chiefly the prerogative of the nobility. Throughout the commonwealth, Catholicism recuperated its losses in the late sixteenth and early seventeenth centuries.

In the Ukrainian lands, with the possible exception of the far-western territories, most inhabitants, including nobles, were Orthodox in 1569. Roman Catholic bishoprics were few and a network of Catholic parishes hardly existed in the eastern territories, where lands belonging to the Catholic church formed a small part of total landholdings. Between 1569 and 1648 the Roman Catholic Church made great strides in numbers and wealth, owing mainly to conversions among the nobles. Even so, a large proportion remained adherents of the Eastern church. The king's distribution of Orthodox church offices as benefices to supporters brought the Orthodox church to its moral nadir in the sixteenth century, but in the 1570s an active reform movement restored its authority. Still, numerous conversions of nobles from Orthodoxy continued, with a large share going to the Calvinists. From the 1620s to the 1640s nobles in the Volhynian and Kievan palatinates constituted a major segment of the radical Socinian church, but by this time the Catholic church was making headway against the Protestants. After 1596 the Orthodox church had to compete with the Uniate church for believers. After some initial hesitation most of the nobles opted for Orthodoxy over Uniatism, and chose the Latin rite if they converted to Catholicism. From 1596 to 1632 nobles loyal to Orthodoxy found themselves adherents of a church not officially recognized or tolerated. These nobles played a dominant role in sustaining the church and challenged the laws of the "Republic of the Nobles." The respect for nobles' liberties and the weak executive power of the commonwealth assured considerable successes for the intransigent Orthodox, but the hostilities aroused over the struggle opened fissures in the unity of Ukraine's noble order.[37]

Although the outlines of the religious situation emerge from commentaries of the time and scattered evidence, there has been no systematic study of the changes in the nobility's religious allegiances. A number of studies have attempted to establish when the great families abandoned Orthodoxy, but there is insufficient evidence to allow for generalizations about middle and petty nobles and about regional variations.[38] Nothing has been done to correlate career advancement, property holdings and leasings, educational experience and marriage choices with religious preferences.

The nobles' relations with the clergymen and the churches must be examined on three levels: their attitudes toward the clergy, their relations with the churches as institutions, and their religious beliefs and personal piety. Religious pluralism complicates any study because conditions differed within the various religious denominations and because a noble inevitably viewed other faiths, churches and clergymen differently from his own. Still, shared attitudes by the nobles about the place of their own order in society created common views that transcended religious allegiances.

The attitudes of the nobles toward individual clergymen were determined by the given clergyman's social status. Catholic bishops were powerful senators and were often scions of the first families of the land. They commanded respect and deference, and occasionally were influential far beyond church affairs (e.g., Paweł Piasecki and Józef Wereszczyński).[39] Respect declined with lower social origin and office, although the position of the Roman Catholic Church as a favoured minority faith centred mainly in towns and near great nobles' residences precluded the existence of a large number of humble village priests in the Ukrainian lands. Protestant clerics were a much more plebeian group. The very nobles who saw the abolition of high church dignitaries as a positive reform were little inclined to send their sons to serve the new "cheap" church. Immigrants from Polish and German cities seemed to have filled the pulpits of Ukraine.[40]

The nobles' attitudes toward the Orthodox clergy were as varied as the clergy's social origins. Without senatorial status or huge "latifundia," the Orthodox bishoprics were not sought after by the greatest magnate families. In one instance, however, a member of a ruling family, Petro Mohyla, son of the hospodar of Moldavia, who was related to the greatest magnate families of the commonwealth, served as archimandrite of the Kievan Caves Monastery and metropolitan of Kiev. His election as metropolitan was part of an accommodation between the king and the Orthodox nobles to end the "rebel" status of Orthodoxy after the Union of Brest, and his presence and views assured both greater respect for his church and Orthodox loyalty to the "Republic of the Nobles."

Most of the sixteenth-century bishops appear to have been nobles of substance (many of whom gave up lay offices and wives to accept holy orders and be consecrated as hierarchs), but the "illegal" status of the church after 1596 decreased the attractiveness of bishoprics, at least until 1632. In general, the defections of the great nobles from Orthodoxy opened up more and more positions to lesser nobles. At the other end of the spectrum were village priests, who at times were taxed and treated as peasants. Not enough is known, however, to make definite statements about the lower clergy's origins, and the position of a priest in a city or in a village inhabited mainly by nobles was undoubtedly different from that on a magnate's estate. It seems likely that in many instances the petty nobles actively sought the position of priest, a practice well-documented for later periods in the Carpathian zone. As for the Uniate clergy, the promise that union would elevate their status was not fulfilled; the bishops did not receive seats in the Senate and the clergymen were not viewed as equals of their Latin-rite co-religionists. With a small pool of noble supporters in Ukraine and with scanty church lands, the Uniate church was hard put to attract the vocations of great nobles. It would appear that nobles from the Belorussian territories were the main source of Uniate hierarchs, but that in general the pattern was similar to that of the Orthodox church.[41] All current discussions of the clergy's origins and nobles' attitudes must be based on impressions rather than statistical studies.

Although the nobles had successfully penetrated the clerical estate, the clergy retained sufficient autonomy and group solidarity to confound the nobility's wishes. The guaranteed senatorial chairs of the Roman Catholic bishops gave them an unassailable position in political affairs. Thus successes of the Protestant denominations in converting nobles could never culminate in an all-Protestant Senate. The Catholic bishops could frustrate Orthodox demands even though the majority in the House of Delegates and Senate was in favour of compromise. The nobles whittled away the rights of the clerical courts, but the latter continued to exist. The commonwealth demanded "voluntary" contributions for the military, but the clergymen defended their tax-exempt status. The struggle was, of course, muted by the stake that so many noble families had in church offices. The nobles appreciated the services of clergymen who were, with a few exceptions such as the Socinians, more than willing to preach a Gospel that justified the existing social and political order. The great Jesuit Piotr Skarga quickly abandoned the pro-absolutist tendencies of his West European colleagues and the Orthodox monk-polemicists glorified the princely families of Rus'.[42]

An important area of noble-clerical friction was over the governance of the churches. The king and nobles had made inroads on the clergy's dominance of the Roman Catholic Church by appropriating rights to make clerical appointments and by diminishing the clergy's juridical and financial privileges, but the clergymen still had the weight of tradition, charters and support from Rome to maintain their dominant role in defining the faith and administering the church. Dissatisfaction with this situation led many nobles to convert to Protestantism, but the Catholic church endured intact through a period of uncertainty and revived with even more clerical control after the reforms of the Council of Trent took hold. Increasingly effective clerical influence on education reconciled the nobility to this situation, and antagonism to foreign "heretic" states (Sweden and Muscovy) strengthened loyalty to the Catholic church. The Catholic nobles settled for monopolization of high church offices instead of corporate noble rights within the church.[43]

The Protestant denominations represented the opposite extreme. Lay nobles dominated the synods of the churches and took an active role in the formulation of dogmas. As faiths of the nobles, rather than the bourgeoisie, Calvinism and Socinianism in Ukraine reflected the noble-dominated social structure. Although elements of the religious and social radicalism of Anti-Trinitarianism influenced the Socinian nobles of the Volhynian and Kiev palatinates, even inducing the liberation of serfs, the noble constituency tended to modify the radical aspects of the faith.[44]

Clergy-laity relations were most profoundly transformed in the Orthodox church as the noble-dominated social order imprinted itself on a church that derived its canons and traditions from a very different political-social order. The Orthodox church in Ukraine was in the difficult position of inheriting concepts of church-state relations from Byzantium that were incongruous in a state ruled by a Catholic king. The exercise of patronage rights by the kings of Poland and grand dukes of Lithuania in the fifteenth and early sixteenth centuries had converted high church offices into royal appointments and limited the powers of the patriarch of Constantinople. The low calibre of bishops diminished the hierarchy's authority. The church turned to the great Orthodox nobles for support, although their patronage was often a mixed blessing as it converted village clergy to the thralls of local lords and allowed the lords to challenge the authority of the bishops. When combined with the assault on the bishop's authority by the urban reform brotherhoods, this challenge was threatening enough to drive some of the bishops toward union with Rome.

Opposition to the Union of Brest further strengthened the position of the nobles in the church, since it was based on the denial of the right of the hierarchs to represent the entire church and on the assertion of Orthodox rights deriving from the guarantees of freedom of religion to the nobility. During the negotiations for the restoration of the Orthodox hierarchy in 1620 and even more strikingly for the legalization of the Orthodox church in 1632, the nobles spoke for the entire church. In the church councils, the lay house, composed overwhelmingly of nobles, often played a leading role and the clergymen frequently expressed their inability to come to decisions without the consent of the nobility. Metropolitan Mohyla used his great personal authority to increase the power of the hierarchs, but even he did not dare deny the nobles a significant role in governing the church. He was still dependent on their support in confrontations with the Uniates, as for example in the Przemyśl diocese, where the numerous petty nobility kept the Uniate bishop from exercising authority. At the parish level, nobles continued to select clergy, and an Orthodox noble interested in church affairs might prove more difficult to deal with than an indifferent Catholic or Protestant landowner. The nobles' position in the church contained an element of instability for Orthodoxy because just as the church's difficult position increased the role of the nobles, more and more nobles were abandoning their faith. The major thrust of noble-clerical relations between 1569 and 1648 was the evolution of an Orthodox church far different in structure and governance from its mother church in Constantinople and its sister church in Muscovy. This triumph of the nobility reinforced traditions of an active laity in Ukrainian Orthodoxy that remain vital to the present day.[45]

The bishops who embarked on the Union did so to augment their own authority, as well as that of the Eastern church. Denied seats in the Senate, the Uniate bishops never obtained their hoped-for equality with the Roman Catholic bishops. They did, however, create a church in which bishops and clergy exerted primary influence, though their success in this sphere was largely a result of their failure to win widespread support for the Union. After a short period of hesitation, most Orthodox nobles in Ukraine came out against the Union, thus the governance of the church was placed firmly in the hands of hierarchs, who were deeply influenced by policies emanating from Rome. These dedicated bishops and monks could seldom depend on consistent support even from Roman Catholic nobles, many of whom looked on the Uniate church with derision. But in failing to win the nobles' support for the Union, the Uniate clergymen avoided the friction over the laity's position in the church that would have been inevitable had the entire Orthodox population of Ukraine adhered to the Union of Brest.[46]

The nobles' relations with the churches as institutions were often contradictory. Diets and dietines legislated against donations of noble lands to ecclesiastical institutions largely because so many individual nobles wished to make donations. Devout Catholic nobles condemned the Catholic church's obstructionist tactics against the commonwealth's accommodation with the Orthodox prior to the Smolensk War. Good Orthodox nobles bristled at the contacts of their hierarchs with Moscow and Constantinople. The nobles may have permeated the churches with their cadres and ideology, but the churches remained distinct institutions with international connections and their own ideological traditions. Faced with the defection of the nobles, the Orthodox polemicist Ivan Vyshensky turned to the Christian message of exaltation of the poor and the humble.[47] Reinforced by orders from Rome, Catholic bishops ground the wheels of state to a halt. The Union of Brest was not a plot by the nobility to Polonize Rus' and increase control over the peasants as some scholars have portrayed it. Indeed many nobles thought that it caused unnecessary friction, but were prevented from rectifying the matter by a small group of Uniate and Catholic zealots and the wishes of Rome. In general, the nobles of Ukraine, and the commonwealth as a whole, were able to integrate the churches well into their "Republic of the Nobles," but the integration was far from complete and the churches at times presented difficult problems to the noble corporate order.

The key to noble relations with the clergy and churches was the religious conviction of each noble. There have been no studies on the religious views of the nobles of Ukraine between 1569 and 1648.[48] It would appear that the period was one of regeneration of religious faith and that more and more nobles ceased to regard religion as an ascriptive designation and began viewing it as a personal commitment. Protestant calls for individual decision produced an educated and articulate following among the nobles of the Volhynian and Kievan palatinates, including the major Ukrainian religious and political thinker Iurii Nemyrych, who ultimately returned to the Orthodox faith of his ancestors.[49] Catholic devotionalism spread with Jesuit education, and Albrycht Stanisław Radziwiłł, who had holdings in Volhynia, wrote memoirs that embody the new Catholic convictions.[50] Although their numbers were decreasing, the Orthodox nobles left numerous testimonies to their faith in the foundation charters of new monasteries.[51] Anyone who has read the tribulations of Metropolitan Iosyf Rutsky must be impressed by the depth of faith that inspired those nobles who did serve the Uniate church.[52] With this new piety came a decline in tolerance and grave consequences for the religious pluralism that had thrived in the sixteenth-century commonwealth, including Ukraine. However, this new piety should not blind us to the views of numerous nobles who continued to view religion as merely an ancestral inheritance or a beneficial affiliation. Moreover, it is clear that some nobles were influenced by secular ideas and remained indifferent to Christian denominational divisions. The influence of Socinians, who saw many possible paths to salvation, went beyond their own circle. As with so many aspects of the nobility of Ukraine, there exist indications but no conclusive evidence about changes in religious beliefs.[53]

The Jews and Armenians, religious-national groups organized as legally separate communities under royal charters and protection, occupied important positions in the nobles' economic and even political affairs. Communal divisions and hatreds between Jewish and Armenian merchants and craftsmen and their Orthodox and Catholic peers allowed nobles to play one group off against the other. Denied access to many of the professions of the Christian community, Jews turned their attention to commercial and artisan trades. The colonization of Ukraine offered Jews an opportunity to escape the overcrowded ghettos of western Poland and the nobles were not slow in enlisting their skills, most significantly for tax-farming, revenue collection, estate management and banking. The symbiotic relations of great lords and Jews aroused hatreds in other strata of the population that were a combination of the anti-Semitism endemic throughout Europe and socio-economic grievances against the noble order in Ukraine. In rebellions culminating in 1648, the Jews, including the urban poor who had little to do with the nobility, were to be the major victims of the wrath against the nobles' social order.

The emotion-laden issue of the Jewish position in Ukraine has thus far been explored almost exclusively by specialists in Jewish history. In recent years Soviet historians have been so infected by the anti-Semitic line of their government that they even avoid mention of the slaughter of Jews in 1648.[54] Thanks to the researches of Shmuel Ettinger, Salo Baron and Bernard Weinryb, we have a good picture of Jewish colonization, community life and economic activities that can serve as a basis for an examination of Jewish-noble relations.[55] For the Ruthenian palatinate, Maurycy Horn has written a study on the Jewish community that includes discussion of its economic relations with nobles.[56] Further study is needed on Jewish attitudes toward the nobles and contemporary Jewish evaluations of the activities of their community in Ukraine's socio-political affairs. Conversely, studies on the nobles' attitudes toward Jews must be pursued, including noble anti-Semitism in a context in which nobles needed and protected Jews. Particular attention should be paid to the differences in attitude of various strata of the nobility, since petty nobles derived little benefit from the Jewish communities, and nobles serving magnates must have viewed Jews as competitors for tax-farms and estate stewardships. Finally, exploration of everyday contacts is needed. Baron has described eastern Ukraine as a land in which a new type of Jew evolved, different in socio-economic and cultural make-up from his co-religionists in the western lands of the commonwealth, and he has pointed out instances of more open Gentile-Jewish relations. Just how this situation affected noble-Jewish relations is not known. Although Baron views the laws granting converted Jews noble status as dead letters, the frontier eastern Ukrainian lands would be a likely area to look for instances of Jews entering the noble order, by legal means or by the subterfuges that Gentiles used.[57]

The small, but economically powerful, Armenian community controlled the eastern trade that supplied the nobles with the luxury goods and the cultural models for Sarmatian noble life. Over the past thirty years the Soviet Ukrainian scholar Iaroslav Dashkevych has carefully studied all aspects of the community's activities. He has shown that while the Armenian patricians provided the nobles with loans and aspired to, and occasionally succeeded in obtaining, noble status, the poorer Armenian artisans and craftsmen became increasingly estranged from the "Republic of the Nobles," particularly because of attempts to unite the Armenian Apostolic diocese of Lviv with Rome. As in the case of the Jewish community, the Armenians' contacts with the nobles and their religious estrangement from the Orthodox and Catholic masses made them targets for the enemies of the noble-dominated socio-economic order.[58]

The nobles cultivated a military ethos that was becoming increasingly anachronistic. However much they prided themselves on being the traditional warriors of the land, most had been transformed from knights into provincial landowners and the mass levy of the nobility had become an unwieldy and ineffective army. The nobles' inability to field a modern force did not prompt them to raise taxes for a large professional army. The perilous state of the commonwealth's military between 1569 and 1648 was not revealed only because of the weakness of neighbours and the limited warfare of the period. The commonwealth took no part in the sixteenth-century wars of religion, nor was it engaged directly in the Thirty Years' War. The nobles were content with their borders and were careful to avoid a situation in which the Polish king leading a victorious army could strengthen his power. The "Republic of the Nobles" was a pacifist state: even the intervention in the Muscovite Time of Troubles was a result more of the collapse of Muscovy and the adventurism of individual magnates than of an aggressive policy by the Diet. After 1648 the defects in the commonwealth's military order were to bring disaster after disaster.[59]

Wars, arms and violence affected the nobles in three ways: service in the army provided them with a profession and a means of advancement and enrichment; the army as an institution drew off revenue and constituted a political force; and possession of private troops and arms gave nobles power that could be used internally and in foreign affairs.

As elsewhere in Europe, the sons of Ukraine's noble houses joined the military, since it constituted one of the major avenues for occupational and social advancement. Although many nobles made brilliant careers and achieved magnate status through service in the forces of the commonwealth, the small size of the standing army limited the number engaged in long-term military service. Only during the periods of major hostilities could large numbers of nobles obtain rewards through military service in the commonwealth's army. The relatively successful wars against Muscovy and less successful confrontations with Sweden and the Ottoman Turks gave the commonwealth's nobles the opportunity for advancement in military campaigns, but did not make war the dominant occupation for the entire nobility. In contrast to the turbulent period after 1648, the majority of the nobles were not at this time constantly engaged in battle. A solitary mass levy of the nobility was called in 1620–1 to resist an Ottoman offensive. For the poor or adventurous, foreign service remained an outlet and foreign powers recruited in the commonwealth during the Thirty Years' War.[60]

The nobles of Ukraine were, however, much closer to the ideal of knights than were their fellow nobles in Poznań and Samogitia. Tatar attacks and peasant and Cossack rebellions ensured that the local nobles frequently were called to service. There is no evidence that the nobles of the Ukrainian lands were more likely to pursue careers in the standing army or enlist for short-term stints than the nobles of other areas of the commonwealth, but this assumption would seem likely because of the more widespread militarization of the inhabitants of the Ukrainian lands and the quartering of the standing army in Ukraine. In any event, rewards for military service were likely to be distributed in the eastern Ukrainian lands, thus steadily increasing the numbers of local nobles who rose through military ranks.[61]

The quartering of the standing army in Ukraine made the army loom much greater in the lives of local nobles than in those of nobles in other areas of the commonwealth. It would appear that the Ukrainian nobles were more willing to raise taxes for the army than the nobles of core Poland since they benefited directly from its services in defence of their estates. The army's leaders could influence local politics. The hetmans of the Polish army were usually magnates in the Ukrainian lands who expanded their private holdings through the influence of their office. Yet however grateful the local nobility may have been to the standing troops in times of danger, their presence in times of peace inevitably evoked tensions with the local population. The frequent mutinies and military confederations in the kingdom's armies provided an element of instability in noble affairs. At times the nobles joined these confederations to thwart royal power, such as during the Zebrzydowski rebellion of 1606–9.[62]

The most salient difference between most of the Ukrainian territories and the other lands of the commonwealth was the higher level of instability, violence and use of private arms. The banditry and violence within the noble order that marked noble life throughout Europe seems to have been even more widespread in the undergoverned commonwealth with its cumbersome system of justice and legal enforcement. If the commonwealth nobles suffered less than their Central European brethren in the first half of the seventeenth century, it was because their society was spared the upheaval of the Thirty Years' War. Although the Masovian and Great Polish nobles were part of this pattern of internal violence, the Ukrainian nobles lived in an environment in which the opportunities and means for internal warfare were considerably greater. Frequent Tatar raids and Cossack and peasant rebellions that reached the city walls of Lviv assured that the nobles of Ukraine were in a state of military preparedness. Frontier conditions and contested land grants guaranteed that military force often resolved disputes. The existence of magnates' armies far surpassing in numbers the retainers of any grandee of the Płock area and equal to the private armies of the great Lithuanian magnates, provided the means for bloody and prolonged conflicts between nobles. Petty nobles found employment in these private armies. The picture that Łoziński drew of a violent noble society in his extensive study of the western Ukrainian palatinate of Ruthenia can be seen as an indication of what transpired in the less settled lands to the east. Just how pervasive violence was in Ukrainian noble life must be examined, but the task is not an easy one since placid life and peaceful negotiations of disputes tended to go unrecorded, while violence was reflected in protests and litigation.[63]

While levels of violence are difficult to estimate, use of arms to embark on foreign adventures is easier to quantify. Control of foreign relations by central governments was limited everywhere in early modern Europe, but nowhere more than in the Polish-Lithuanian Commonwealth. Nobles in Ukraine were particularly apt to conduct their own foreign policies, including the waging of war: they had the necessary resources at their disposal; the actions of the Crimean Tatars, Ottomans and Muscovites affected them and their estates directly; and the central government responded too slowly to continual threats of immediate attack. The interventions in Muscovy and Moldavia are good examples of great Ukrainian lords conducting their own policy by armed incursions outside the commonwealth.[64] The private armies that assembled for these enterprises probably contained a disproportionate number of Ukrainian nobles. In addition, the hetmans of the Polish army often treated independently with the Crimean Tatars and intervened in their affairs. The tradition of Zaporozhian activity in foreign affairs that the nobility found so troublesome in the seventeenth century had been initiated by great nobles who led the Host in the sixteenth century. Hence opportunities were abundant for the nobles of Ukraine to embark on foreign ventures.[65]

The Private and Public Life of the Nobles

The most valuable contributions nineteenth- and early twentieth-century historians made to the study of the Ukrainian nobility were their descriptions of the life, culture and attitudes among that group. The voluminous records of noble courts offered a treasure of colourful figures and incidents, which provided material for these descriptions that were often as close to belles-lettres as to scholarship. The finest example is Władysław Łoziński's controversial *Prawem i lewem*, which describes life among the nobles in the Ruthenian palatinate. The works of Orest Levytsky, Antoni Rolle, Kazimierz and Julian Bartoszewicz and numerous others provide information ranging from the status of women to the practice of martial arts.[66] A few aspects of noble life in Ukraine are still studied by Soviet Ukrainian scholars, who have provided works on art history, portraiture and regional ethnography.[67] A systematization of materials must be undertaken so that the nutrition, families, households and vital statistics of the nobles can be examined. Also nineteenth-century studies can serve as a starting point for modern works examining the *mentalité* of the nobles.

Studies on the nobles of the entire commonwealth have increased our understanding of the Ukrainian nobility as well, but have generally under-emphasized or ignored a number of problems particularly pertinent to Ukraine.[68] In the sixteenth century the relatively moribund Byzantine-influenced cultural patterns among the nobles unraveled under influences from the West.[69] Western impact on the customs, patronage, tastes and views of the Ukrainian nobility must be studied further, for to date, aside from some work done in art history, only one small study on the influence of the West on the Ukrainian nobility has been published.[70] More abundant sources and more Western forms of expression make biographical studies possible. Late sixteenth-century nobles, in stark contrast to the shadowy figures of the pre-1569 Ukrainian elite,[71] expressed their opinions in terms similar to those of their West European contemporaries.

But the increasing influence of the West should not cause us to ignore an almost as powerful Eastern impact on the Ukrainian elite. Life on the eastern frontier was very different from that in the western lands. It was there that Christian and Muslim, agriculturalist and nomad, came up against each other. Scholars have paid insufficient attention to the impact of Islam and nomadic societies on the life, taste and possibly the attitudes of the nobles of Ukraine.[72] The orientalized magnates of Ukraine influenced the Baroque culture of the commonwealth.

High culture in Ukraine, although expressed frequently in religious terms, was to a considerable extent noble culture. The contributions of the more humble burghers and non-noble clerics were not negligible, however, and the delineation of the nobles' role in education, publishing, art patronage and literature should be made with care. The rapid spread of formal education and the founding of numerous schools (the brotherhood schools of Lviv and Lutske, the Uniate school of Volodymyr, the Jesuit academies, the Zamość Academy and the Kievan Collegium) changed Ukraine's intellectual climate. Yet, although we have a preliminary study on the attendance of Ukrainian nobles in West European schools, we have no similar studies for schools in the commonwealth. The changes in attitude of the nobles of Ukraine toward education and learning, the spread of literacy amongst them and their preferences in language have yet to be examined.[73]

For all aspects of the culture of sixteenth- and seventeenth-century Ukraine, the role of the nobles as producers, patrons and consumers must be analysed. This is essential for an understanding of the divergent tendencies of traditionalism and modernism, religious and secular culture, Byzantine and Latin culture, Ruthenian-Slavonic and Polish culture among the nobles. In any examination of life, culture and attitudes, particular attention must be paid to the tremendous difference among the great magnates, the middle-size holders and the often poverty-stricken petty nobles as well as to the question of common characteristics within this culturally diverse corporate order.

In contrast to the daily life and culture of the nobles of Ukraine, their political institutions have been little studied. The basic institution of noble political life was the dietine of the palatinate or land, which sent delegates to the Diet of the commonwealth. Political relations were also reflected in the allocation of local elective and appointed offices. Except for the Ruthenian palatinate, local politics have not been examined.[74]

The dietines left few official records other than their instructions to the delegates of the Diet. Thus an extensive archival search will be needed to uncover the rare materials describing the functioning of these dietines, the way they reached decisions and the distribution of power within them. The questions to be resolved are numerous. What influence did the magnates wield? What was the role of long-resident families as opposed to newcomers? Is it true, as it appears, that in palatinates such as Volhynia and Kiev, the older families maintained their control despite the influx of new landholders and petty nobles from the west?

The delegates' instructions, many of which have been published, already enable us to determine the composition of the delegations, including what strata they came from and how often certain individuals or families monopolized the post of delegate.[75] In conjunction with a study of the office-holding patterns in each palatinate (palatine, castellan, court positions and honorific posts), the patterns of local power and influence might then emerge. A detailed study of the contents of the instructions, particularly for the four eastern lands, could shed light on three major issues concerning the nobility in Ukraine: taxation and defence, the struggle over the Union of Brest and relations with Cossacks. The proportion of the taxes of the commonwealth paid by the inhabitants of the Ukrainian lands and the taxation policies of the nobles of Ukraine must be examined.

Until the extant diaries of the Diets of the commonwealth have been collected, edited and published, it will be difficult to study the activities and roles of the delegates from the Ukrainian lands.[76] At present, the only exhaustive study has been on the noble defenders of the Orthodox church.[77] An examination of the laws enacted by the Diet that affected the Ukrainian lands can easily be undertaken. These laws are included in the *Volumina legum*, which again has only been used in a major study for its bearing on the Orthodox church issue.[78] A particularly fruitful undertaking would be to investigate the special legislation enacted to administer the lands annexed at the Union of Lublin.[79]

An examination of decrees of central government chanceries affecting the nobles of Ukraine should be undertaken in conjunction with the study of their activities in the Diet. The king usually conferred vacant offices of church and state during sessions of the Diet and the grants were registered in the chancery books of the Kingdom of Poland and the Grand Duchy of Lithuania. For the king, these conferrals were a means to gain support for his programme, and many a noble's politics can be explained by the hope of receiving a *starostwo* or a bishopric. Studies of office-holding should include an examination of how often the nobles from Ukraine held central posts (chancellors, hetmans, etc.) and their influence on commonwealth policies, as well as the correlation of conferrals of local offices and lands with the recipients' politics.[80] While the central registry books of the Kingdom of Poland, the Crown Metrica, have long been accessible to researchers in Warsaw, the special books the central government kept for the eastern Ukrainian lands, the Ruthenian or Volhynian Metrica, have been retained in Moscow, and over the past fifty years have seldom been cited, even by Soviet scholars. Until this source becomes available, study of the political culture of the nobles of Ukraine will be severely hampered.[81]

The nobles were extremely litigious, and legal statutes and court records are excellent sources not only for describing the economic and social aspects of their life, but also for documenting their political activities and views. The retention of the Second Lithuanian Statute of 1566 made the legal code of the lands annexed at the Union of Lublin different from that of other territories of the kingdom. Indeed, after the adoption of the Third Lithuanian Statute in the grand duchy in 1588, the Second Statute became a uniquely Ukrainian code that influenced legal and political relations in Ukraine until the beginning of the nineteenth century. While the statute dealt with public law and with other orders of the population, it was primarily a code of the rights and duties of the nobility. Its theory and practice have yet to be examined for their influence on the institutions and political thought of the nobles.[82]

At the Union of Lublin the nobles of the annexed lands were guaranteed a separate court tribunal at Lutske, but after the 1580s, this tribunal lapsed and all cases for the Ukrainian lands and many for the Polish territories were heard at Lublin.[83] However, the retention of the Lithuanian Statute of 1566 and the Ruthenian tongue assured that cases from the annexed lands had to be heard separately. Just as Warsaw was the centre for the delegates from the dietines, who gathered with monarch and senators to legislate, Lublin became the centre of litigants and of judges elected by the dietines, who gathered to hear the cases. Here too assembled the nobles from the western Ukrainian territories, who were subject to the law codes in use throughout the kingdom. The destruction of the Lublin Tribunal records by the Nazis during the Second World War remains the greatest single loss to the history of the Ukrainian nobility, and we must make do with the numerous citations from the tribunal records in nineteenth-century heraldry books and a published volume of indices of tribunal records for the Kiev and Bratslav palatinates.[84]

The centre of the public life of a noble was the local court. The court system at the palatine or county level epitomized the blurring of distinctions between the institutions and functions of the king, the state and the noble order. Just as the king's powers of ultimate appeal were progressively usurped by a system of elected judges in the Lublin Tribunal, so the authority of the king's local judges was diminished by the increasing rights of the local nobilities. The royal-appointed palatines, castellans and *starostas* kept certain rights of adjudication over non-nobles, but the local courts that affected the nobility were converted into courts of the noble order for which local elections became more and more important in the appointment procedure. As the distinctions of the courts of the land and the courts of the castle disappeared, the records of the courts were converted into registry archives for the local nobility. It is from the thousands of volumes of these court records, preserved almost intact for the western

Ukrainian lands and in large numbers for the eastern Ukrainian territories, that most of the nineteenth-century source publications drew their materials.[85] In recent decades Soviet scholars have only occasionally cited these sources, which are essential for an understanding of Ukrainian history in the early modern period.[86]

The study of the nobility's legislatures, administration and courts provides only the structure of political life, not the contents of the political process. What were the mechanisms of power relations and practical politics among Ukraine's nobles? Careful distinctions must be drawn between our perceptions of how the system worked and those of its participants. The essential problem, which has been dealt with frequently in this essay, is whether emphasis should be placed on the theories and institutions that marked the commonwealth as the joint property of the entire nobility or on the de facto power of an amorphous group of magnates. Polish historians have described the pre-1648 Kingdom of Poland and commonwealth as a state governed by nobles or a "gentry democracy," and the post-1648 system as the "oligarchy of the magnates."[87] They would, of course, be the first to admit that even the cataclysmic year of 1648 should not be seen as a definite divide and that they are in fact describing a continuum of political change in a society that did not recognize that it had altered its form of government. Many students of the Polish nobility and state see the tremendous de facto inequality in the eastern lands and the existence of a small circle of extremely wealthy aristocrats originating in a society far different from that of ethnic Poland as a major factor in the change of the political and social structure over the entire commonwealth. The student of the Ukrainian nobility must examine to what degree the Ukrainian lands were dominated politically and economically by a group of magnates between 1569 and 1648. In such a study, attention must be paid to whether nobles in Ukraine perceived the political structure of their lands as different from that of the Polish territories.

Any study of the nobles of Ukraine must deal not only with institutions and political practices, but also with political theories and consciousness. Since the publication of Lypynsky's works before the First World War, no major studies of the political culture of the Ukrainian nobility have appeared. As the nobility was the "political nation" of the commonwealth, the presence or absence of a specific Ukrainian-Ruthenian political culture and of a perception of belonging to a historical-cultural community among some segments of the nobles is the most significant indication of the distinctiveness of the Ukrainian nobility. I have shown elsewhere that to a limited degree a Ukrainian political culture and national consciousness existed, and I propose merely to summarize my findings here as they relate to the nobility.[88]

Although adherence to the political values and loyalties of all the nobles of the commonwealth, in general, and of the Kingdom of Poland, in particular, prevailed among the nobles of Ukraine, a countervailing, though not always antagonistic, Ukrainian-Ruthenian noble political culture was also discernible between 1569 and 1648. In 1569 the nobles of Ukraine seemed unlikely to resist full assimilation into the nobility of the Kingdom of Poland. Even the indigenous Ruthenian nobles in the sixteenth century had little awareness of their history or of the former polities of Kievan Rus' and the Galician-Volhynian principality; therefore they did not act as bearers of a separate political tradition, and this enabled the Polish political tradition and Sarmatism to make rapid progress among them. Nevertheless, the existence of the Orthodox church, an institution rooted in the Rus' past and in Ruthenian-Slavonic culture, did provide a separate Ruthenian (Ukrainian-Belorussian) tradition, and the very weakness of this institution and Ruthenian culture before an advancing Polish Roman Catholic society elicited the reaction through which a new Ukrainian political culture was born. Orthodox polemicists renewed interest in Kievan Rus'; Ruthenian writers dedicated books to Ruthenian nobles which included genealogies that traced their ancestry back to eleventh-century figures from the chronicles. Kiev was extolled as a holy city, a second Jerusalem and the former capital of a once great Ruthenian state. As the ancient seat of the princes rose from ruins, Orthodox churchmen assiduously ordered frescos to be made depicting the princes of Kiev together with their sixteenth- and seventeenth-century descendants. Thus Ruthenian consciousness was intensified among segments of the nobility at the very time that many nobles were losing the religious and cultural affiliations that made them part of the Rus' community.

While religious patriotic historical sentiment could only take hold among Ruthenian nobles of Orthodox faith, all nobles in the lands annexed at the Union of Lublin were open to expressions of regional particularism. Common laws and customs led the nobles of the palatinates of Volhynia, Kiev, Bratslav and Chernihiv to call their lands the "four Ruthenian palatinates" and to act as a bloc at the Diet. Attacks on regional traditions, such as the use of princely titles, were resisted. This regional solidarity extended to all noble inhabitants of these lands, whatever their faith or origin. But while the Roman Catholics and Poles were seen as full members of the regional noble bloc, the lands and nobilities were still perceived as organically linked to the Ruthenian historical tradition, culture and people.

The mix of Ruthenian consciousness and regionalism made the nobles of the lands annexed at the Union of Lublin the political nation of a Rus' *patria*. Some of these nobles became defenders of the Orthodox church, and usually based their defence on the Union of Lublin, which they regarded as a kind of constitution and a free union between the nobles of Rus' and the nobles of Poland. The fact that this was a distortion of the past did not diminish its potency: there are even indications that, combined with political regionalism and historical cultural patriotism, the constitutional theory of the Union of Lublin produced a Ruthenian Sarmatism. In sum, economic and cultural vitality in Ukraine appears to have been accompanied by a new Ukrainian political culture among certain segments of the nobility.

The intellectual and political significance of these tendencies can only be determined by a thorough examination of seventeenth-century books and manuscripts. Political tracts and opinions are often preserved in *silvae rerum*, or copy books of nobles, which are particularly difficult to locate, but the impressive work of Lypynsky in the archives of Cracow indicates that the material exists, although regrettably access to the most important archives, those of Kiev and Lviv, is difficult. But however numerous expressions of these tendencies prove to be, it should always be remembered that they were less important than the trends that were integrating the nobles of Ukraine into the commonwealth, the Kingdom of Poland, and the belief in the brotherhood of the Sarmatian nobility. The latter trends were all-pervasive and influenced even the exponents of Ukrainian political culture—who were in any case a minority expressing a rather weakly developed regionalism and Ruthenian consciousness. They were enthusiastically adopted by many nobles along with the Polish language, Roman Catholicism and Polish identity. The expressions of regionalist sentiment and Ruthenian patriotism among the nobility should never be confused with modern national consciousness or nationalism. They should, nonetheless, be seen as an important link in the development of Ukrainian historical consciousness and political thought, particularly through the influence they had over the Cossack Hetmanate.[89]

Conclusions

In the tenth century the rulers and elite groups of Kievan Rus' were attracted to the Byzantine world and brought the Rus' polity, society and culture into its orbit. Subsequent generations of Ukrainian historians have, with the benefit of hindsight, debated the wisdom of their decision. Some have pointed to the rapid cultural and political achievements of Kievan

Rus', while others have lamented that the young polity was cut off from the Latin West, the civilization to which the future belonged. The Ukrainian elites of the fourteenth to sixteenth centuries were far less independent as historical actors. Still, it is clear that from the boyars of fourteenth-century Halych to the middle nobles at the Union of Lublin, Ukrainian elite groups were strongly attracted to the Kingdom of Poland. The core of that attraction was the wish to gain the privileges of the Polish *szlachta.* Modern historians have also differed on the consequences of these actions for the evolution of the Ukrainian people and culture. Some have emphasized the benefits of the Westernization of society and culture, while others have decried the alienation of the elite and the importation of social, political and cultural models that were to prove sterile and ineffective in the seventeenth and eighteenth centuries.

Leaving such broad evaluative questions aside, we should instead examine the role of the nobles in bringing on 1648. The nobles of Ukraine were one of the few seventeenth-century elites to witness a lasting change in the political and social order. Weaknesses and fissures within the noble order and the failure of the nobles to control and lead the inhabitants of the Ukrainian lands constituted the central problems of the breakdown of the commonwealth's administration in Ukraine. On the other hand, inherent strengths and cohesiveness within the nobility stirred most nobles to a tenacious, and partially successful, struggle to restore the old order. Only through careful study of the nobility can we understand the causes and development of a major turning-point in Ukrainian history, the revolt of 1648 and the formation of the Cossack Hetmanate.

In dealing with the role of the nobility in the breakdown of the commonwealth's rule in Ukraine, we must address the questions that Smotrytsky posed, albeit in a different manner. Once we have established a composite picture of the nobles of the Ukrainian lands between 1569 and 1648, we can turn to an examination of the processes and consequences of the integration of the Ruthenian-Ukrainian elite into the commonwealth's "Polish" nobility. In 1610 Smotrytsky could hardly have foreseen 1643; but he did draw attention to a process that was estranging many Ukrainian nobles from the other orders of the Ukrainian population. In order to understand the process that Smotrytsky lamented, we must examine anew the transformation of the Ukrainian nobility from the Union of Lublin to the Khmelnytsky uprising.

Notes

1. The translation is from a Ukrainian translation of excerpts from Smotrytsky's work in O. I. Biletsky, ed., *Khrestomatiia davnoi ukrainskoi literatury (do kintsia XVIII st.)*, 3d ed. (Kiev, 1967), 167–8.
2. Metropolitan Isaia Kopynsky's letter is published by Viacheslav Lypynsky as document 8 of "Echa przeszłości," in Wacław Lipiński, ed., *Z dziejôw Ukrainy. Księga pamiątkowa ku czci Włodzimierza Antonowicza, Paulina Święcickiego i Tadeusza Rylskiego* (Kiev [Cracow], 1912), 131–3.
3. Of nineteenth-century Ukrainian historians, only Mykhailo Maksymovych stressed the positive aspects of the nobility's role in Ukrainian history. Mykola Kostomarov, Volodymyr Antonovych and Mykhailo Hrushevsky belonged to the *narodnytska shkola* (populist school) that sympathized with the masses' strivings for freedom and condemned ruling classes and states. In Antonovych's case, political and national views combined to prompt his "betrayal" of his Polish Roman Catholic noble peers and his espousal of the positions of the peasantry, the Ukrainian national movement and Orthodoxy.

   Political and intellectual changes in the Ukrainian national movement were reflected among Ukrainian historians in the early twentieth century. The shift from work to improve the cultural, social and economic position of the Ukrainian masses to political and military activity to form a Ukrainian state was accompanied by the formation of a new historical movement, the *derzhavnytska shkola* (statist school). Emerging with the publication of Viacheslav Lypynsky's *Z dziejôw Ukrainy* in 1912, the statist school dominated Ukrainian historical work in Western Ukraine between the wars and even influenced Soviet Ukrainian historians during the relatively liberal 1920s. Renouncing the values of the populists, Viacheslav Lypynsky, Stepan Tomashivsky, Ivan Krypiakevych, Myron Korduba, Dmytro Doroshenko and many others argued that elites and states had frequently acted in the "interests" of the Ukrainian nation. Yet although Lypynsky's *Z dziejôw Ukrainy* was devoted to the Ukrainian nobility, most of the "statist" historians focused their attention on the Cossack Hetmanate's administration and foreign policy. For discussions of Ukrainian historiography, see Dmytro Doroshenko, "A Survey of Ukrainian Historiography," and Oleksander Ohloblyn, "Ukrainian Historiography, 1917–1956," in *Annals of the Ukrainian Academy of Arts and Sciences in the United States* 5–6, nos. 4 (18) – 1–2 (19–20) (1957); B. Krupnytsky, *Istorioznavchi problemy istorii Ukrainy (Zbirnyk stattei)* (Munich, 1959); and M. I. Marchenko, *Ukrainska istoriohrafiia (Z davnikh chasiv do seredyny XIX st.)* (Kiev, 1959).

   Contemporary political and national considerations explain the general neglect and the sporadic interest of Ukrainian historians in the nobility. Lypynsky's fundamental work, *Z dziejôw Ukrainy*, begins with a preface calling on the Polish-language work's readers to return to their proper place as leaders of the Ukrainian nation (v–xi). Russian and Polish historians have been just as strongly interested in contemporary political considerations. Only the social and political revolutions after the Second World War finally removed the nobility as an active political factor in the Ukrainian lands and ended the need to use history to win the support of the noble social groupings. Two examples from the 1860s and the 1930s will suffice to demonstrate how often political considerations have inspired historians' studies.

In the 1850s and 1860s Russian publicists, some of whom were "Little Russians," challenged the view that Right-Bank Ukraine was Polish territory. Governmental support was given to a Kievan archeographic commission to publish documents that would undermine Polish claims. A volume of instructions of dietines to delegates to Polish-Lithuanian Diets appeared in 1861 with anti-Polish introductions by M. Iuzefovich and N. Ivanishev. *Arkhiv Iugo-Zapadnoi Rossii izdavaemyi Vremennoiu kommissieiu dlia razbora drevnikh aktov*, 35 volumes, 8 parts (Kiev, 1859–1914), 1, part 2 (hereafter *Arkhiv Iugo-Zapadnoi Rossii*). Iuzefovich emphasized the political goals of the publication by stating: "For some time, articles have appeared in foreign Polish journals that have the clear aim of convincing public opinion in Europe that the West Russian land along the Dnieper is a Polish land and that the name *Rusin* does not denote a Russian person, but that it is a provincial name for a Pole, like Masovian, Cracovian or Great Polanian. This theory, as is well-known, was first devised in Galicia, from where it was transferred here, as support for unbridled Polish patriotism, which feels, here as there, the weakness of the ground for the realization of its claims." (v) With a dangerously egalitarian tone for tsarist Russia, Iuzefovich went on: "Is it possible in our nineteenth century that one can still seriously think not only to assert, but no less to strive to realize, the thought that dominance among the nobility gives the right to rule?" (xiii) Disclaimers to the contrary, Russian authorities and patriots were deeply troubled by the predominance of Polish patriots among the Right-Bank nobles and sought to undermine it. Hence, N. Ivanishev stressed the non-Polish composition of the area's nobility in the sixteenth and seventeenth centuries and the elements of Rus' patriotism and devotion to the Rus' language in the instructions. Within a few years, Iuzefovich prefaced a volume of documents entitled "Acts about the Origins of Noble Families in South-West Russia" with a chart documenting when families had abandoned Orthodoxy. He asserted that only one-tenth of the area's nobles were of Polish descent and that he had established the "Rus' " origins of over seven hundred families. *Arkhiv Iugo-Zapadnoi Rossii*, (Kiev, 1867), 1, part 4: i–xiii.

The commission's activities raised such a furor among the nobles of the region that it was forced to justify its choice of materials for publication. *Otvet Kievskoi Kommissii dlia razbora drevnikh aktov na obvineniia nekotorykh gazet i zhurnalov po povodu vykhoda v svet II-i chasti "Arkhiva Iugozapadnoi Rossii"* (Kiev, 1861). Already by the 1860s, however, the government began to see some unexpected negative results from its campaign. Historians such as Volodymyr Antonovych were pleased to accept government subsidies and even the government's assertion that the lands were not originally Polish. Yet Antonovych and his colleagues rejected the contention that *Rusin* denoted a Russian person, and saw the documents as proof of Ruthenian-Ukrainian national distinctiveness.

As late as the 1930s, studies of the nobility could still be undertaken largely in response to government campaigns and subsidies. On this occasion a Polish government tried to convince Ukrainian-speaking, Greek Catholic petty nobles in Eastern Galicia that their ancestors had been Poles. Subsidies were made available to form associations of these nobles, "threatened by Ukrainianization," to put out popular literature and to publish scholarly works. Needless to say, the parallel with the Russian policies of the 1860s seemed to go unnoticed even by reputable scholars. As in the 1860s, valuable documents and studies were published, along with tendentious tracts.

For an account of the campaign, see Władysław Pobóg-Malinowski, *Najnowsza historia polityczna Polski*, 2d ed., (London, 1967), 2: 823–5. As an example of a work that combines useful research with political agitation, see Władysław Pulnarowicz, *Rycerstwo polskie Podkarpacia. Dawne dzieje i obecne obowiązki szlachty zagrodowej na Podkarpaciu*, 2d printing (Przemyśl, 1937). These provincial popular publications rarely reached North American or West European libraries, but are essential for study of the western Ukrainian petty nobility. Many are noted in the bibliography to Maria Biernacka's *Wsie drobnoszlacheckie na Mazowszu i Podlasiu. Tradycje historyczne a współczesne przemiany* (WrocławWarsaw-Cracow, 1966).

4. The lack of a Ukrainian historical bibliography hampers all work on Ukrainian history and is only partially compensated by the standard Polish and Russian historical bibliographies. No greater failing can be attributed to Soviet Ukrainian historiography, particularly since Soviet Belorussian historians put out a historical bibliography a decade ago: *Bibliiahrafiia pa historyi Belarusi. Feadalizm i kapitalizm*, ed. M. Krekane and A. Sakolchyk (Minsk, 1969). Incomplete as this work is, it can be used with profit by historians of Belorussia and Ukraine. The historiographic essays by Doroshenko and Ohloblyn (see note 3) are almost all that exists for Ukrainian history. Compiling bibliographies on the Ukrainian nobility is the necessary first step toward advancing study of the topic. The task is particularly difficult because numerous sketches and documents appeared in nineteenth-century newspapers and popular journals. Often the materials that they are based on have been destroyed, thereby rendering them the only source of information on persons, families and genealogies. In this essay, only the most important relevant works will be cited under specific topics. For published sources on the period, most of which deal with the nobility, see the studies by N. P. Kovalsky, *Istochnikovedenie istorii*

Ukrainy (XVI-pervaia polovina XVII veka), part 1: *Analiz sovetskikh arkheograficheskikh publikatsii dokumentalnykh istochnikov. Uchebnoe posobie* (Dnipropetrovske, 1977); *Istochnikovedenie i arkheografiia istorii Ukrainy XVI-pervoi poloviny XVII v.*, part 2: *Analiz dorevoliutsionnykh otechestvennykh publikatsii istochnikov. Uchebnoe posobie po spetskursu* (Dnipropetrovske, 1978); *Istochnikovedenie istorii Ukrainy XVI-pervoi poloviny XVII veka*, part 3: *Kharakteristika publikatsii istochnikov na inostrannykh iazykakh. Uchebnoe posobie* (Dnipropetrovske, 1978). Because his rather bizarre system of classification precludes treating Ukrainian publications issued outside of the "Fatherland" (i.e., the Russian empire or the Soviet Union), Kovalsky refers the reader to his article "Istochniki po istorii Ukrainy XVI-pervoi poloviny XVII v. vo lvovskikh arkheograficheskikh izdaniiakh XIX-nachala XX v.," in *Analiz publikatsii istochnikov po otechestvennoi istorii* (Dnipropetrovske, 1978), 20–48. He fails to mention the largest publication of sources in recent decades, Section 3 of Series 2 of *Analecta OSBM*. Since 1953, the Basilian Fathers in Rome have published eleven volumes of documents exclusively on the period from 1569 to 1648, and seven containing some documents. He also omits the pertinent volumes (1, 2, 9–10) of the St. Clement Catholic University's *Monumenta Ucrainae Historica*, 10 vols. (Rome, 1964–71). On published sources, also see I. P. Krypiakevych, *Dzherela z istorii Halychyny periodu feodalizmu (do 1772 r.). Ohliad publikatsii* (Kiev, 1962).

The problem of secondary works is more difficult to resolve. Extensive bibliographical notes, including some on the nobles of the Ukrainian lands, are found in Hans Roos, "Ständewesen und parlamentarische Verfassung in Polen (1505–1772)," in Dietrich Gerhard, ed., *Ständische Vertretungen in Europa in 17. und 18. Jahrhundert* (Göttingen, 1967) (Veröffentlichungen des Max-Planck-Instituts für Geschichte 27 and Studies Presented to the International Commission for the History of Representative and Parliamentary Institutions 37), 310–68. For coats of arms and genealogies, in addition to the standard Polish heraldic works, consult Kazimierz Pułaski, *Kronika polskich rodôw szlacheckich Podola, Wołynia i Ukrainy* (Brody, 1911); Józef Wolff, *Kniaziowie litewsko-ruscy od końca czternastego wieku* (Warsaw, 1895); Adam Boniecki, *Poczet rodôw w Wielkiem Ksiestwie Litewskim w XVI i XVII wieku* (Warsaw, 1887); and S. Golubev, "Opisanie i istolkovanie dvorianskikh gerbov iuzhnorusskikh familii v proizvedeniiakh dukhovnykh pisatelei XVII veka," *Trudy Kievskoi dukhovnoi akademii*, no. 10 (1872): 259–382.

The problem of family histories is especially difficult, since these volumes were often issued in small editions. They are often particularly valuable because of their inclusion of extracts and summaries of documents. While some family histories are frequently mentioned in the scholarly literature and available in major libraries (e.g., Z. L. Radzimiński, ed., *Monografiia XX. Sanguszków oraz innych potomków Lubarta-Fedora Olgerdowicza X. Ratneńskiego*, 3 vols. [Lviv, 1906–11]), many are rarely cited and only a few copies are in existence. Two noble families from Western Ukraine issued their family histories in 200 copies with warnings that they were "published in 200 numbered copies as a manuscript" and "issued in 200 copies as a publication of the family for its own use." The second part of Jan Hr. Drohojowski, *Kronika Drohojowskich na podstawie badań archiwalnych*, 2 parts (Cracow, 1904) contains summaries of 1,139 documents, while Maurycy Dzieduszycki, *Kronika domowa Dzieduszyckich* (Lviv, 1865) contains a valuable addendum of documents. The existence of these "private" publications makes the need for thorough bibliographic work on the nobility even more urgent. Numerous family histories appeared in the *Rocznik Towarzystwa Heraldycznego we Lwowie*, 11 vols. (1908–9—1931–2), and the *Miesięcznik Heraldyczny*, 18 vols. (1908–39), both of which were founded in Lviv.

Although there is no adequate work on the nobility of Ukraine between 1569 and 1648, a number of fundamental studies provide substantial information. The works of Aleksander Jabłonowski describe the nobility by regions at the end of the sixteenth century (the early seventeenth century for the Kiev and Bratslav palatinates). He wrote his studies as introductory essays to the sources on demography that he published in *Źrôdła dziejowe*, published by the Towarzystwo Naukowe Warszawskie, Wydział II: Nauk antropologicznych, społecznych, historyi i filozofii, Komisya historyczna, 24 vols. (Warsaw, 1876–1915), 5–6, 17–22. These were reprinted in his collected works: *Pisma*, 7 vols. (Warsaw, 1910–13).

The most comprehensive discussion of the position of the nobility in Ukrainian history in this period is found in Mykhailo Hrushevsky, *Istoriia Ukrainy-Rusy*, reprint, 10 vols. (New York, 1954–8). The essays and documents in *Z dziejów Ukrainy* are the most useful sources on the Ruthenian nobility's political activities and thought. The major Soviet history of the period by Oleksander Baranovych (Aleksandr Baranovich) contains useful observations and statistics: *Ukraina nakanune osvoboditelnoi voiny serediny XVII v. (Sotsialno-ekonomicheskie predposylki voiny)* (Moscow, 1959).

5. Viacheslav Lypynsky [Wacław Lipiński], *Szlachta na Ukrainie*, 1: *Udział jej w życiu narodu ukraińskiego na tle jego dziejów* (Cracow, 1909) contains interesting observations on the nobility's role in Ukrainian history, but the short work (eighty-eight pages) was intended as a political statement to the Polish-speaking nobles of Right-Bank Ukraine. Z. L. Radzimiński and W. Rulikowski, *Kniaziowie i szlachta między Sanem, Wieprzem, Bugiem, Prypecią, Siniuchą, Dniestrem i północnymi stokami Karpat osiedleni. Opowiadania historycne, heraldyczno-genealogiczne i obyczajowe ...* Cracow, 1880), 1, parts 1 and 2, is the most comprehensive study of nobles in the Ukrainian lands from the period of Kievan Rus' to the eighteenth century. Written by Polish nobles who loved their native Ukraine, the book is a mixture of well-informed commentary based on a wide reading of the sources and of

propagation of political and cultural theories (e.g., the confrontation of Germano-Christian and Greco-Christian ideas, the importance of Viking blood in the formation of East European elites, Gobineau's race theories). The authors revealed their internal struggles in their tortuous demonstrations that the assimilation of Ruthenian nobles to Polish identity was a natural and desirable process and in their ambiguous attitude toward the Cossacks. The book contains 816 pages, but the second half (431–816), which deals with the period after Kievan Rus', was destroyed by the authors. This section is extant in only four copies. Maryan Gorzkowski, *O rusińskiej i rosyjskiej szlachcie* (Cracow, 1876) is a popular work, chiefly of interest to students of Polish attitudes toward Ukrainians and Russians. For works on specific periods, see note 12 for the Lithuanian period and Kohut's essay in this volume for the Hetmanate.

6. Marc Bloch and Lucien Febvre, "Les noblesses I. Reconnaissance générale du terrain," *Annales d'Histoire economique et sociale* 8 (no. 39) (May 1936): 239.

7. For recent comparative studies on European nobilities, see Jean Meyer, *Noblesses et pouvoirs dans l'Europe d'Ancien Régime* ([Paris], 1973) Jean-Pierre Labatut, *Les noblesses europëenes de la fin du XVe siècle à la fin du XVIIIe siècle* (Paris, 1978), Franç Billacois, "La crise de la noblesse européenne (1550–1650)," *Revue d'Histoire moderne et contemporaine* 23 (April-June 1976): 258–77, W. H. Zaniewicki, *La noblesse "populaire" en Espagne et en Pologne* (Lyon, 1967) and the review article by Carlo Capra, "La nobilita europea prima della rivoluzione," *Studi storici*, no. 1 (1977): 118–38. Problems of definition and terminology are encountered in the volume of essays edited by A. Goodwin, *The European Nobility in the Eighteenth Century: Studies of the Nobilities of the Major European States in the Pre-Reform Era* (London, 1953). In his essay "England," H. J. Habakkuk maintains (page 1): "In the continental countries nobility was usually a status. The rights attaching to it varied from country to country, but it was reasonably clear in any particular country what the rights of a noble were and who was entitled to enjoy them. The outlines of class were clear and distinct .... In England there was no nobility in this strict sense." He proceeds to combine the English gentrymen and nobles in order to compare the English "nobility" with its European counterparts. C. A. Macartney on "Hungary" and A. Bruce Boswell on "Poland" deal with similar problems and come to opposed terminological decisions. Macartney uses "magnate" and "gentry" to describe layers of the Hungarian "nobility" while Boswell asserts: "The absence of a peerage, together with the number of its class, make it appropriate to translate szlachta as gentry rather than nobility, which for non-Polish readers has the implication of a small peerage or an oligarchy grouped around a strong monarchy" (160). Although Boswell's assertion is fundamentally correct, his terminological decision is out of keeping with the title of the volume and with the essays of J. McManners, "France"; Raymond Carr, "Spain";

H. G. Schenck, "Austria"; and C. A. Macartney "Hungary." Describing, for example, Prince Konstantyn Ostrozky, the owner of scores of cities and hundreds of villages, as a member of the "gentry" would also be disconcerting to the English reader. The problem is a difficult one. I have chosen "nobility" to translate "*szlachta-shliakhta*" on the grounds that it coincides with general usage for the continental elite groups discussed.

The existence of a distinct European society of corporate orders is argued by Dietrich Gerhard in "Regionalism and Corporate Order as a Basic Theme of European History," in *Studies in Diplomatic History: Essays in Memory of David Bayne Horn*, ed. Ragnhild Hatton and M. S. Anderson (London, 1970), 155–82. (For the original text and complete footnotes, see "Regionalismus und Ständisches Wesen als ein Grundthema Europäischer Geschichte," *Historische Zeitschrift* 174 [1952]: 307–37.) He argues that Western institutions and Western society had become "crystallized" in the eleventh and twelfth centuries, and that by the thirteenth century, under the influence of law and philosophy, the legal forms basic to the structure of social orders and estates had been defined. He sees a merging of Roman, Germanic and Slavonic traditions that created a pan-European social system, albeit one that differed greatly from region to region (see 161–3). Gerhard's view of the distinctiveness of European societies and political institutions is by no means original, but the comparative framework and the discussion of regionalism make this essay essential for studies on the Ukrainian nobility. Gerhard sees the common features of the European social order as encompassing Eastern Europe, but not Russia, in the early modern period. Although he questions Oscar Halecki's definition of Western civilization, he accepts the geographical boundaries Halecki proposes. Oscar Halecki, *The Limits and Divisions of European History* (London, 1950). Halecki devotes considerable attention to the Ukrainian lands, which he sees as a borderland drawn into the sphere of Western civilization in the fourteenth through seventeenth centuries. He, like Gerhard, sees Muscovy as outside this European society. (See note 8 for discussions of the Russian social structure.) Gerhard's discussion of the relationship of regionalism to corporate social orders contributes to the analysis of the Ukrainian nobiity's regional particularism in the Polish-Lithuanian Commonwealth.

8. The great differences between the Russian nobility and the other European nobilities are noted in all works on Russian elites. Because of the adaptation of West European models and the changes in the nobles' positions throughout Europe in modern times, these differences diminished. For discussions of the imperial Russian nobility, see Max Beloff, "Russia," in A. Goodwin, *The European Nobility in the Eighteenth Century*, 172–89; Robert E. Jones, *The Emancipation of the Russian Nobility, 1762–1785* (Princeton, 1973); Marc Raeff, *Origins of the Russian Intelligentsia: The Eighteenth Century Nobility* (New York, 1966) and Aleksandr Romanovich-Slavatinsky, *Dvorianstvo v Rossii ot nachala XVII veka do*

otmeny krepostnogo prava, 2d ed. (Kiev, 1912). Beloff begins his article (173) with a discussion of the Charter of Nobility of 1785, "for it serves as a reminder of how different was the position enjoyed by the Russian nobility from that which characterized the aristocracies of other European countries with their emphasis on blood and landed-property rather than on service to the state."

For the period of this essay, the nature of Muscovite-Russian elite groups has been less studied and is more controversial. Recent research by Western scholars has emphasized the existence of distinct social groupings and certain similarities between the Muscovite elite and European nobilities. See Gunther Stökl, "Gab es in Moskauer Staat 'Stände'?," *Jahrbücher für osteuropäische Geschichte*, new series 11 (1963): 321–42; Shigeto Toriyana, "On Muscovite Autocracy—A Comparative View," *Forschungen zur osteuropäischen Geschichte* 18 (1973): 109–23; John Keep, "The Muscovite Élite and the Approach to Pluralism," *Slavonic and East European Review* 48 (1979): 201–31; A. M. Kleimola, "Up through Servitude: The Changing Condition of the Muscovite Elite in the Sixteenth and Seventeenth Centuries," *Russian History* 6, part 2 (1979): 210–29; Robert O. Crummey, "The Reconstitution of the Boiar Aristocracy 1613–1645," *Forschungen zur osteuropäischen Geschichte* 18 (1973): 187–220; and Harmut Ruess, *Adel und Adeloppositionen im Moskauer Staat* (Wiesbaden, 1975) (Quellen und Studien zur Geschichte des östlichen Europa 7). This new research may finally allow the kind of comparative study that Bloch and Febvre called for and may show that some of the sharp dichotomies traditionally perceived between Muscovy and the West must be modified. Yet scholars are in agreement that there were substantial differences between the Muscovite elite and the European nobilities. These differences are of great importance for studying Ukraine, which so often constituted a transitional border zone.

9. Predictably, scholars from the eastern regions of Europe have been most interested in defining "European" and "European civilization" and in establishing criteria for regional (western, eastern, east central, etc.) designations. The first chapter of Josef Macůrek, *Dějepisectví evropského východu* (Prague, 1946), contains a discussion of various scholars' views. In addition to Halecki's *Limits and Divisions*, J. Perenyi's "L'Est Européen dans une synthèse d'histoire universelle," *Nouvelles études historiques publiées à l'occasion du XIIe Congrès international des sciences historiques par la Commission nationale des historiens hongrois* 2 (Budapest, 1965), 379–405, should be consulted. On contacts within Europe in the Middle Ages, see K. Bösl *et al.*, *Eastern and Western Europe in the Middle Ages*, ed. G. Barraclough (London, 1970).

10. See Otto Hintze's essays, "Staatenbildung und Kommunalverwaltung" and "Weltgeschichtliche Bedingungen der Repräsentativverfassung," *Gesammelte Abhandlungen*, ed. Fritz Hartung, 3 vols. (Leipzig, [1941–3]), 1: *Staat und Verfassung*, 206–31, 130–75 (especially 160–1).

11. For general studies on the Polish nobility, see Jarema Maciszewski, *Szlachta polska i jej państwo* (Warsaw, 1969); Henryk Wisner, *Najjaśniejsza Rzeczpospolita. Szkice z dziejów Polski szlacheckiej XVI–XVII wieku* (Warsaw, 1978); Hans Roos, "Ständewesen und parlamentarische Verfassung" and "Der Adel der Polnischen Republik im vorrevolutionären Europa," in Rudolf Vierhaus, ed., *Der Adel vor der Revolution. Zur sozialen und politischen Funktion des Adels in vorrevolutionären Europa* (Göttingen, 1971), 41–76; Janusz Tazbir, *Kultura szlachecka w Polsce. Rozkwit-upadek-relikty* (Warsaw, 1978), and the essays on the Polish nobility in the special issue "Études sur la noblesse," of *Acta Poloniae Historica* 36 (1977). The best general histories discussing social groups are Andrzej Wyczański, *Polska—Rzecza Pospolita szlachecka* (Warsaw, 1965) and Józef Andrzej Gierowski, *Historia Polski 1505–1764* (Warsaw, 1979) (with excellent bibliographical notes). The role of the nobility in Polish social relations is examined in an excellent, modern synthesis by Antoni Maczak in Ireneusz Ihnatowicz, Antoni Maczak and Benedykt Zientara, *Społeczeństwo polskie od X do XX wieku* (Warsaw, 1979), 227–455. On the nobility's political rights and ideology, see Stanisław Grodziski, *Obywatelstwo w szlacheckiej Rzeczypospolitej* (Cracow, 1963) and Andrzej Zajaczkowski, *Główne elementy kultury szlacheckiej w Polsce. Ideologia a struktury społeczne* (Wrocław, 1961). See the critical reviews of the latter work by Juliusz Bardach, "O ujeciu socjologicznym struktury społecznej i ideologii szlachty polskiej (w zwiazku z pracami Andrzeja Zajaczkowskiego)," *Czasopismo Prawno-Historyczne* 15 (1963): 159–78, and Jarema Maciszewski, "W sprawie kultury szlacheckiej," *Przegląd Historyczny* 54 (1962): 539–46. A recent useful addition to the voluminous literature on Polish Sarmatism is the special volume of the Warsaw journal *Teksty* 1974, no. 4 (especially Janusz Maciejowski, "Sarmatyzm jako formacja kulturowa. Geneza i główne cechy wyodrebniajace," 13–42). On political institutions and political culture, see the articles by Władysław Czapliński, Józef Andrzej Gierowski, Józef Leszczyński and Jerzy Włodarczyk in Józef Andrzej Gierowski, ed., *Dzieje kultury politycznej w Polsce* (Warsaw, 1977). Invaluable for discussions of all aspects of the period are the collections of essays *Polska w epoce Odrodzenia. Państwo, społeczeństwo, kultura*, ed. Andrzej Wyczański (Warsaw, 1970) and *Polska XVII wieku: Państwo, społeczeństwo, kultura*, ed. Janusz Tazbir (Warsaw, 1969). These volumes and their bibliographies should be consulted for the specific topics (social groupings, economic developments, military and foreign affairs, etc.) discussed later in this article. Another indispensable work is the handbook with bibliographies by Zdzisław Kaczmarczyk and Bogusław Leśnodorski that constitutes volume 2 (*Od połowy XV wieku do roku 1795*) of Juliusz Bardach, ed., *Historia państwa i prawa Polski*, 4th ed. (Warsaw, 1972).
12. The elite orders of the Grand Duchy of Lithuania have been quite extensively studied. This literature is best approached through *Bibliiahrafiia*

pa historyi Belarusi, 103–5; Leo Okinshevych, *The Law of the Grand Duchy of Lithuania: Background and Bibliography*, Research Program of the USSR, Mimeo Series 32 (New York, 1953); Juliusz Bardach and Jerzy Ochmański with the co-operation of Oswald Backus, *Lituanie* (Brussels, 1969) (Introduction bibliographique à l'histoire du droît et à l'ethnologie juridique D 14); and Oswald Backus, *Motives of West Russian Nobles in Deserting Lithuania for Moscow, 1377–1514* (Lawrence, Kansas, 1957). Also see Backus' "Die Rechtsstellung der litauischen Bojaren," *Jahrbücher für Geschichte Osteuropas* 6 (1958): 1–32, and "The Problem of Feudalism in Lithuania, 1506–1546," *Slavic Review* 21 (1962): 639–59. For a discussion of social groupings in the Ukrainian lands, see D. I. Myshko, *Sotsialno-ekonomichni umovy formuvannia ukrainskoi narodnosti (Stanovyshche selian i antyfeodalni rukhy na Ukraini v XV-pershii polovyni XVI st.)* (Kiev, 1963).

13. The question of "Russia, Ukraine and Europe" has been fraught with passionate controversies. "Russia and Europe" has troubled generations of Russian historians. At its base has been a perception of substantive differences between Russian society, culture and institutions, and their counterparts to the west. The passion this issue has aroused can largely be explained by nineteenth- and twentieth-century Russians' perception of some sort of inferiority of their own traditions. The reactions have ranged from the self-castigation of ardent Westernizers to bravado manifestos about Russian uniqueness by Slavophiles and Soviet Russian patriots. This well-known problem of Russian intellectual history has a little-studied Ukrainian dimension. Those who have asserted Ukrainian distinctiveness have often dwelt on Ukrainian ties to "Europe" and indeed there has been no "Ukraine and Europe" dichotomy in modern Ukrainian intellectual history. Both Ukrainian political thought and historical writing have been suffused with an admiration for all "European" characteristics in the national past that has negated any need to study and evaluate the actual influence of the West on Ukrainians. For a discussion of the "Europeanness" of Ukrainians, see B. Krupnytsky, "Istorychni osnovy evropeizmu Ukrainy," *Literaturno-naukovyi visnyk* (Regensburg) 32, no. 1 (May 1948); 120–30. Many Russian scholars and publicists have been irritated by the Ukrainians' insistence on their "Europeanness" and have seen German and Polish influences as responsible for bringing impurities to the "South Russians." In addition they have emphasized the "regressive" or "reactionary" nature of the Ukrainians' Western ties (the Polish type of nobility, the union with Rome, the culture of the Counter Reformation). This essential problem in East European history penetrates much of the writing on Ukrainian history of the period from 1569 to 1648. Current Soviet scholarship is particularly adamant about the baneful influences of the West on Ukrainians. For a Soviet attack on scholars who study the problem, see M. M. Varvartsev, "Heopolitychni skhemy v burzhuaznykh falsyfikatsiiakh istorii Ukrainy," *Ukrainskyi istorychnyi zhurnal*, no. 2

(1980): 81–91. For discussions of socio-political systems in Eastern Europe at this time, see Józef Andrzej Gierowski, "L'Europe centrale au XVIIe siècle et ses principales tendances politiques," in Mezhdunarodnyi komitet istoricheskikh nauk, *XIII Mezhdunarodnyi kongress istoricheskikh nauk, Moskva, 16–23 avgusta 1970 goda. Doklady Kongressa* 1, part 5 (Moscow, 1973), 106–23, and Zbigniew Wójcik, "Poland and Russia in the 17th Century: Problems of Internal Development," *Poland at the 14th International Congress of Historical Sciences in San Francisco: Studies in Comparative History* (Wrocław-Warsaw-Cracow, 1975), 114–33.

14. Historically, Podlachia has been an ethnographic border zone of Belorussians, Ukrainians and Poles. The linguistic-ethnic border of Belorussians and Ukrainians has always been vague, and current national and administrative borders cut through the amorphous Polissian region. To a considerable degree, the division of this borderland population between the two cultural-national groups has been dictated by political acts, of which the Union of Lublin was the most important. I include Podlachia in my discussion of the Ukrainian territories because it was annexed to the Kingdom of Poland and I exclude the Brest palatinate because it was retained by the Grand Duchy of Lithuania. The question of Ukrainian-Belorussian relations in the early modern period is extremely complex, particularly because of the two peoples' shared religious-literary culture and, to a considerable degree, common collective consciousness as "Ruthenians." Although the differentiation of the two national communities begins far earlier than the sixteenth century, the period from 1569 to 1648 served to increase their distinctiveness. But this increasing differentiation should not be exaggerated and any study of the nobles of the Ukrainian lands should deal with the question of links among the "Ruthenian" nobility that inhabited both Ukraine and Belorussia. For questions of Ukrainian-Belorussian relations and the impact of the Union of Lublin, see the bibliography to a discussion in a number of East European periodicals in the 1940s. "Discussions on the Origins of the Ukrainian Nation," in Myron Korduba, *La littérature historique soviétique-ukrainienne compte-rendu 1917 1931*, reprint of the Warsaw 1930 edition (Munich, 1972), xxxiv–xxxvi (Harvard Series in Ukrainian Studies 10).

15. The formation of the nobility in the Galician principality and the Ruthenian palatinate constitutes a difficult and controversial topic. Two questions are outstanding. First, it has not been established to what degree the boyars of the Galician-Volhynian principality had taken on the characteristics of a corporate noble order. Second, the origins of the nobles of the Ruthenian palatinate must be examined to determine how many descended from the boyars of the Galician principality and how many descended from later immigrants to the Ukrainian lands. On the social structure of Galicia, see I. A. Linnichenko, *Cherty iz istorii soslovii v Iugo-Zapadnoi (Galitskoi) Rusi XIV–XV vv.* (Moscow, 1894); K. A. Sofronenko, *Obshchestvenno-politicheskii stroi Galitsko-Volynskoi Rusi XI–XIII vv.*

(Moscow, 1955); V. T. Pashuto, *Ocherki po istorii Galitsko-Volynskoi Rusi* (Moscow, 1950); Przemysław Dabkowski, *Stosunki gospodarcze ziemi halickiej w XV wieku* (Lviv, 1927) (Pamietnik Historyczno-Prawny 3, no. 4); and Isydor Sharanevych [Izydor Szaraniewicz], *Rys wewnetrznych stosunków Galicyi Wschodniej w drugiej połowie pietnastego wieku* (Lviv, 1869). The question of the origins of the nobles has recently been examined for the Lviv land by Andrzej Janeczek in his "Polska ekspansja osadnicza w ziemi lwowskiej w XIV–XVI w.," *Przegląd Historyczny* 69 (1978): 597–622. He concludes that by 1578 52.6 per cent of landowning noble families were of Polish descent, 27.3 per cent were of Ruthenian descent and 12.6 per cent were of Moldavian descent (a group that had long been assimilated to the Ruthenians). His figures show a dramatic increase of families of Polish descent between the fourteenth and sixteenth centuries. It is likely that the percentage of nobles of Ruthenian descent was much higher in the Przemyśl and Halych lands, which were less attractive for immigrants from Polish territories. A useful bibliography on the area under Jagiellonian rule is Ewa Maleczyńska's section, "Epoka Jagiellońska (1385–1572)," of "Przegląd literatury do dziejów politycznych ziemi czerwieńskiej," *Ziemia Czerwieńska* 1, no. 1 (1935): 111–15. Also, see Roos "Ständewesen und parlamentarische Verfassung," 360, note 67, and the bibliography in Biernacka, *Wsie drobnoszlacheckie na Mazowszu i Podlasiu* (rich in material on the petty nobles of the Ruthenian palatinate, as well as those of the book's subject, Podlachia and Mazowsze). For family histories, see the works by Dzieduszycki and Drohojowski (mentioned in note 4 above) and Ludwik Wyrostek, *Ród Dragów Sasów na Węgrzech i Rusi Halickiej* (Cracow, 1932) (Rocznik Towarzystwa Heraldycznego we Lwowie 11). For a summary of the controversy over the petty nobles' origins, see Iu. H. Hoshko, *Naselennia ukrainskykh Karpat XV–XVIII st. Zaselennia. Mihratsii. Pobut* (Kiev, 1976), 3–23. On Podillia and its nobility, see Leon Białkowski, *Podole w XVI wieku. Rysy społeczne i gospodarcze* (Warsaw, 1920) and the review of this work by Z. L. Radzimiński in *Rocznik Towarzystwa Heraldycznego we Lwowie* 5 (1920) [publ. 1921]: 111–24.

16. In addition to the literature in note 12, one should consult Oskar Halecki, *Przyłaczenie Podlasia, Wołynia i Kijowszczyzny do Korony w roku 1569* (Cracow, 1915) and Jaroslaw Pelenski, "The Incorporation of the Ukrainian Lands of Old Rus' into Crown Poland (1569): Socio-material Interest and Ideology—A Re-examination," *American Contributions to the Seventh International Congress of Slavicists (Warsaw, August 21–27, 1973)* 3 (The Hague and Paris, 1973), 19–52.

17. On the Chernihiv lands, see Mykola Vasylenko, "Pravne polozhennia Chernihivshchyny za polskoi doby (1618–1648)," in *Chernihiv i pivnichne Livoberezhzhia*, ed. Mykhailo Hrushevsky (Kiev, 1928), 290–300 (VUAN, Zbirnyk Istorychno-filolohichnoho viddilu 95 and Zapysky Ukrainskoho naukovoho tovarystva 23).

18. Wacław Lipiński, "Stanisław Michał Krzyczewski. Z dziejów walki szlachty ukraińskiej w szeregach powstańczych pod wodza Bohdana Chmielnickiego (r. 1648–1649)," in Wacław Lipiński, ed., *Z dziejôw Ukrainy*, 145–513. This work has been reprinted with a Ukrainian translation as *Uchast shliakhty u velykomu ukrainskomu povstanni pid provodom Hetmana Bohdana Khmelnytskoho*, ed. Lev R. Bilas (Philadelphia, 1980) in Viacheslav Lypynsky, *Tvory* 2 in the series Viacheslav Lypynsky, *Tvory, arkhiv i studii*, ed. Roman Zalutsky and Ievhen Zyblykevych of the Skhidno-ievropeiskyi doslidnyi instytut im. V. K. Lypynskoho.
19. For estimates of the commonwealth's population and the percentage of nobles, see Wyczański, *Polska*, 26, and Maciszewski, *Szlachta*, 35. Problems of Polish historical demography are discussed in Irena Gieysztorowa, *Wstęp do demografii staropolskiej* (Warsaw, 1976). For a discussion of difficulties in estimating the number of nobles, see Egon Vielrose, "Przyczynek do demografii szlachty polskiej," *Przegląd Statystyczny* 1 (1938): 328–42; T. Furtak, "Kilka zagadnień z demografii historycznej szlachty polskiej," *Roczniki Dziejów Społecznych i Gospodarczych* 7 (1937): 31–58; and the literature in Roos, "Ständewesen und parlamentarische Verfassung," 313, note 8. Roos directs readers to Julian Bartoszewicz's article "Szlachta polska," in *Encyklopedya powszechna* [Orgelbranda] 24 (Warsaw, 1867), 677–99, for statistics on the sixteenth- and seventeenth-century nobility, but Bartoszewicz did not work out reliable estimates on the basis of a comprehensive study of demographic material.
20. I have computed Jabłonowski's estimate from his introductory essays in *Źrôdła dziejowe*. The figure is rough because his estimate for the Kiev and Bratslav palatinates is for the 1620s. The figure also varies in accordance with the inclusion or exclusion of Podlachia. (Jabłonowski's estimates: Ruthenian and Belz palatinates, 572,648; Volhynian palatinate 293,780; Podillian palatinate 97,736; Podlachia palatinate 233,200; Kiev palatinate 234,040; and Bratslav palatinate 311,340.) A number of Polish scholars assert that the estimates of land taxes and the estimates of population per unit of land by Jabłonowski and his colleague Adolf Pawiński were too low. See Witold Kula, "Stan i potrzeby badań nad demografia historyczna," *Roczniki Dziejôw Społecznych i Gospodarczych* 13 (1951): 24–136; Egon Vielrose, "Ludność Polski od X do XVIII wieku," *Kwartalnik Historii Kultury Materialnej* 5 (1957): 3–49. For a discussion of problems in using hearth taxes for Ukraine, see Zenon Guldon, "Badania nad zaludnieniem Ukrainy w XVII wieku," *Kwartalnik Historii Kultury Materialnej* 13 (1965): 561–6. The Soviet Ukrainian historian Oleksander Baranovych was particularly critical of Jabłonowski's methods and insisted that the population of the Dnieper basin was much greater than the estimates made by Polish historical demographers. See his "Naselenie predstepnoi Ukrainy v XVI v.," *Istoricheskie zapiski AN SSSR* 32 (1950): 198–232, and *Zaliudnennia Volynskoho voievodstva v pershii polovyni XVII st.*,

published by VUAN, Sotsiolohichnyi-ekonomichnyi viddil, Komisiia istorychno-heohrafichna (Kiev, 1930). Soviet Ukrainian historians have frequently sought to portray Polish rule as detrimental to Ukraine and to deny economic and demographic growth. Baranovych goes so far as to speculate that the population may have declined. Baranovych, *Ukraina nakanune osvoboditelnoi voiny*, 128; for his population estimates, see 132. Baranovych's estimates appear to be greatly inflated. The Soviet Ukrainian historian Olena Kompan estimates the population of the Ukrainian lands in the second half of the seventeenth century as 3,230,000. *Mista Ukrainy v druhii polovyni XVII st.* (Kiev, 1963). Also see O. S. Kompan, "Do pytannia pro zaselenist Ukrainy v XVII st.," *Ukrainskyi istorychnyi zhurnal*, no. 1 (1960): 65–77.

21. Jabłonowski's essays in *Źródła dziejowe* include some statistics on noble landholders, but not for all the Ukrainian territories. These should be studied in conjunction with the hearth tax sources used by Baranovych and discussed by Guldon (see note 20 above). Additional materials that must be studied include political documents (oaths to the Union of Lublin, dietine instructions), military registers (particularly for the levy of 1621), ecclesiastical records (episcopal elections and synodal records) and, above all, the juridical records of the noble courts. Non-landowners will always remain an elusive group. One of the few attempts to count the number of noble families was undertaken by Antoni J. Rolle. In order to determine the number of noble families in the Kiev palatinate, he examined the inventories published for the extant court registry books for the period 1584 to 1696 (sixteen volumes of the series *Opis aktovnoi knigi Kievskogo gosudarstvennogo arkhiva*, 60 vols. [Kiev, 1869–1913]). He found 1,579 family names (367). Dr. Antoni J. [Rolle], "Dzieje szlachty okolicznej w owruckim powiecie," *Biblioteka Warszawska*, no. 2 (1881): 19–39, 183–200, 352–67.

22. For Podlachia, Jabłonowski puts the number of sizable landholdings at 950 without estimating the number of nobles inhabiting them and the number of petty nobles at 75,710 (total population 233,200). *Źródła dziejowe* 17, part 3, 34, 77. His discussion of the Ruthenian and Belz palatinates is much less satisfactory. He estimates that there were 530 sizable manors and a mere 1,830 petty noble holders. *Źródła dziejowe* 18, part 2, 143–5. These findings seem suspect. He lists no petty noble holders in the Przemyśl and Sanok lands; but in his description of the Przemyśl region, he mentions numerous villages inhabited by petty nobles, 330–3. Hence his statistics must be viewed as unreliable. For the other Ukrainian lands, Jabłonowski provides no statistics, although his essays contain lists of noble landholders. For landowners in Volhynia, see Baranovych, *Zaliudnennia*. The lesser percentage of nobles and the greater concentration of landholdings in the eastern Ukrainian territories is discussed in Ivan Krypiakevych, *Bohdan Khmelnytsky* (Kiev, 1954), 16.

23. For economic trends in Eastern Europe prior to the sixteenth century, see

Marian Małowist, *Wschôd a Zachôd Europy w XIII–XVI wieku. Konfrontacja struktur społeczno-gospodarczych* (Warsaw, 1973). Since the Second World War, economic history, including studies on the estate management of the nobility, has flourished in Poland. Małowist, Jerzy Topolski, Andrzej Wyczański, Antoni Maczak and many others have produced first rate research, but they have confined their studies to the territories of contemporary Poland. Much of this literature is cited in Andrzej Kamiński, "Neo-Serfdom in Poland-Lithuania," *Slavic Review* 34 (1975): 253–68. Also see Jerzy Topolski, *Gospodarka polska a europejska w XVI–XVII wieku* (Poznań, 1977). The once flourishing Lviv school of Polish socio-economic history, which pursued fundamental research on the western Ukrainian territories under the leadership of Franciszek Bujak between the wars, has not continued in that city and since the Second World War the contributions of Polish historians to the study of the area have been limited (except for Maurycy Horn).

Soviet Ukrainian and Russian historians have lacked the originality of their Polish colleagues and have ignored the economic activities of the nobility as a field of study, but they have made major contributions by their studies of the peasantry and the spread of manorial estates. The state of research in Ukrainian economic history is discussed in glowing terms not justified by the modest accomplishments in S. I. Krandievskij, "Badania z historii gospodarczej w Ukraińskiej SSR w okresie powojennym (1946–1971)," *Roczniki Dziejôw Społecznych i Gospodarczych* 37 (1976): 121–38. Soviet research has not been reflected in new syntheses, and V. O. Holobutsky, *Ekonomichna istoriia Ukrainskoi RSR. Dozhovtnevyi period* (Kiev, 1970) remains the only general work on the economic history of the period. Numerous useful studies have appeared in the annual *Ezhegodnik po agrarnoi istorii Vostochnoi Evropy.* Disputes on colonization patterns are discussed in Baranovich, "Naselenie." To understand the emotion of Ukrainian responses to the Polish role in the colonization and economic revival in Ukraine, see Karol Szajnocha, "Zdobycze pługa polskiego," *Szkice historyczne*, 2d ed., 4 vols. (Lviv, 1857–69), 3: 61–80.

24. Regional differences in the commonwealth are discussed in Kamiński, "Neo-Serfdom." The influence of the Vistula trade route, though with insufficient attention to the Ukrainian territories, is discussed in Honorata Obuchowska-Pysiowa, *Handel wiślański w 1 połowie XVII wieku* (Wrocław, 1964) and Stanisław Mielczarski, *Rynek zbożowy na ziemach polskich w drugiej połowie XVI i w pierwszej połowie XVII wieku. Prôba rejonizacji* (Gdańsk, 1962). Better records for the western Ukrainian territories have permitted more extensive study of estate economies in these lands, but with more attention to royal lands than to private ones. Kazimierz Arłamowski, *Zapatrywania i dążenia gospodarcze szlachty czerwonoruskiej XVII wieku* (Lviv, 1927); V. F. Inkin, "K voprosu ob evoliutsii feodalnoi renty v Galichine v XVI–XVIII vv.," *Ezhegodnik po agrarnoi istorii Vostochnoi Evropy. 1963* (Vilnius, 1964), 224–45;

Iu. M. Grossman, "Folvarki gosudarstvennykh imenii Russkogo i Belzkogo voevodstva vo vtoroi polovine XVI v.," *Ezhegodnik po agrarnoi istorii Vostochnoi Evropy 1961* (Riga, 1963), 135–46; Iu. M. Hrossman, "Orendy maietkiv ta ikh vplyv na stanovyshche zakhidno-ukrainskykh selian v pershii polovyni XVII st.," *Pytannia z istorii SRSR* (1958), 107–19. For a discussion of all the Ukrainian territories, see Baranovich, *Ukraina nakanune*, 67–92. The question of estate records is discussed in V. I. Samoilenko, "Maietkovi akty XIV–XVII st.," *Istorychni dzherela ta ikh vykorystannia* 2 (1966): 5–12.

25. For changes in landholding patterns in the commonwealth, see Wyczański, *Polska*, 207–9. Jabłonowski, *Źródła dziejowe* contains useful materials on the pattern of landholding (noble, royal and ecclesiastical) at the end of the sixteenth century. Also see Baranovich, *Ukraina nakanune*, and Baranovych, *Zaliudnennia*. On the formation of great magnates' estates, see Alina Wawrzyńczykowa, *Rozwój wielkiej własności na Podlasiu w XV i XVI wieku* (Wrocław, 1951) (Prace Wrocławskiego Towarzystwa Naukowego, Series A, no. 48); Władysław Tomkiewicz, *Jeremi Wiśniowiecki (1612–1651)* (Warsaw, 1933) (Rozprawy Historyczne Towarzystwa Naukowego Warszawskiego 12); Aleksander Tarnawski, *Działalność gospodarcza Jana Zamoyskiego, Kanclerza i Hetmana Wielkiego Koronnego 1572–1605* (Lviv, 1935) (Badania z Dziejów Społecznych i Gospodarczych 18); and Franciszek Rawita-Gawroński, "Losy wielkiej fortuny na kresach ukrainnych," in *Studya i szkice historyczne*, series 2 (Lviv, 1903), 1–28 (on the Ruzhynsky family).

26. For the deforming influence of the eastern magnates, see Jarema Maciszewski, "Społeczeństwo," in *Polska XVII wieku*, ed. Janusz Tazbir, 146. For problems of classification of groups of the nobility, see Maciszewski, *Szlachta polska*, 7–23, 54–71. On the relative openness of the magnate elite in the kingdom, see Maciszewski, *Szlachta polska*, 55–6. For a discussion of the magnate stratum, including problems of definition, see Władysław Czapliński and Adam Kersten, ed., *Magnateria polska jako warstwa społeczna* (Toruń, 1974). The magnate stratum in the first half of the seventeenth century has been described in an excellent, albeit popular, book by Władysław Czapliński and Józef Długosz, *Życie codzienne magnaterii polskiej w XVII wieku* (Warsaw, 1976). The authors characterize the life of magnates, but have not carried out systematic research on the stratum. They devote little attention to regional factors or to the role of the magnates in the Ukrainian lands. Although it deals with a later period, the work of Teresa Zielińska, *Magnateria polska epoki saskiej* (Wrocław-Warsaw-Cracow-Gdańsk, 1977) is extremely useful for its examination (on the basis of a comprehensive study of the social group) of what constituted the magnate stratum and how magnate families rose and fell. For an interpretation of Ukrainian society as totally magnate-dominated and sub-infeuded, see Baranovich, *Ukraina nakanune*, 49–53. On the question of "feudalism" in the commonwealth in the early modern period, see

Tadeusz Manteuffel, "On Polish Feudalism," *Mediaevalia et Humanistica* 16 (1964): 94–104. The question of noble-servitors in Volhynia is being researched by Władysław Pleszczyński as a Ph. D. thesis at the University of Indiana. The functioning of magnates' clienteles in Volhynia is treated in Inge Auerbach, "Andrej Michajlovič Kurbskij. Sein Leben und sein Werk" (Habil.-schrift: Marburg University, 1980). On magnates of Ruthenian extraction in the Ukrainian lands, see Wanda Dobrowolska, *Młodość Jerzego i Krzysztofa Zbaraskich (z wstępem o rodzie Zbaraskich i życiorysem Janusza Zbaraskiego wojewody bracławskiego)* (Przemyśl, 1926). Also see the biographies cited in note 71 below. For a description of an indigenous noble's rise to magnate status, see Frank E. Sysyn, "Adam Kysil, Statesman of Poland-Lithuania: A Case Study in the Commonwealth's Rule of the Ukraine" (Ph. D. thesis: Harvard University, 1976). For disputes on the significance of the title "kniaź," see Julian Bartoszewicz, *Kniaź i Xiążę* (Cracow, 1876) and Z. L. Radzimiński, *O tożsamości tytułów kniaź i książę w dawnej Rzeczypospolitej* (Lviv, 1908).

27. The rise of the middle nobility as a political and cultural power in Volhynia is discussed in Dembińska, *Wpływy*, 42–62. For discussions of such families, see Franciszek Rawita-Gawroński, "Kisielowie, ich ród-pochodzenie-posiadłości," *Przewodnik Naukowy i Literacki* 40 (1912): 1,008–23, and Kazimierz Pułaski, "Ród Kierdejów podolskich. Monografia historyczno-genealogiczna," *Szkice i poszukiwania historyczne*, series 3 (Cracow, 1906), 169–94. Also see T. Faraniuk, "Vinnytska shliakhta v XVI v.," *Istorychno-heohrafichnyi zbirnyk* 1 (1927) (UVAN Zbirnyk Istorychno-filolohichnoho viddilu 46).

28. The best bibliography on the petty nobility is in Biernacka, *Wsie drobnoszlacheckie*. Also see Volodymyr Antonovych [Vladimir Antonovich], "Soderzhanie aktov ob okolichnoi shliakhte," in *Arkhiv Iugo-Zapadnoi Rossii* 1, part 4 (Kiev, 1867), 1–62; the introduction by Mykhailo Hrushevsky [Mikhail Grushevsky] to the volume *Materialy dlia istorii mestnogo upravleniia v sviazi s istorieiu soslovnoi organizatsii. Akty Barskogo starostva XVI–XVII v.*, which is volume 1, part 8 of *Arkhiv Iugo-Zapadnoi Rossii* (Kiev, 1893), 1–126; and Hoshko, *Naselennia ukrainskykh Karpat*. On the affair of the bishopric of Przemyśl and the local petty nobility, see Antoni Prochaska, "Władyka Krupecki w walce z Dyzunią," *Przewodnik Powszechny* 139–40 (1918): 731–52; 141–2 (1919): 38–47, 283–94, 359–65; and Władysław Łoziński, *Prawem i lewem. Obyczaje na Czerwonej Rusi w pierwszej połowie XVII wieku*, 5th ed., 2 vols. (Cracow, 1957), 2: 238–49. On the service nobility, see Pleszczyński's work on Volhynia (see note 26). For a discussion of boyars after 1569, see Baranovich, *Ukraina nakanune*, 52–3.

29. On proofs of noble status, see Władysław Semkowicz, *Wywody szlachectwa w Polsce XIV–XVII w.* (Lviv, 1913) (Rocznik Towarzystwa Heraldycznego we Lwowie 3 [1911–12]). There is no contemporary discussion of falsification of noble origins in the Ukrainian lands comparable to Walerian

Nekanda-Trepka, *Liber Generationis Plebeanorum ("Liber Chamorum")*, ed. Włodzimierz Dworzaczek, 2 vols. (Wrocław-Warsaw-Cracow, 1963) for the Cracow area.

30. On the Ukrainian peasantry, see the literature on agricultural production in notes 23 and 24, and I. D. Boiko, *Selianstvo Ukrainy v druhii polovyni XVI–pershii polovyni XVII st.* (Kiev, 1963) and volume 1, ed. V. O. Diadychenko *et al.*, of *Istoriia selianstva Ukrainskoi RSR u 2-kh tt.* (Kiev, 1967). For disorders in the Carpathian region, see V. V. Hrabovetsky, *Antyfeodalna borotba karpatskoho opryshkivstva XVI–XIX st.* (Lviv, 1966) and Maurycy Horn, *Walka chłopów czerwonoruskich z wyzyskiem feudalnym w latach 1600–1648*, part 1: *Zbiegostwo i zbójnictwo karpackie* (Opole, 1974), and part 2: *Chłopi dóbr koronnych w walce przeciw zwiększaniu robocizny i danin* (Opole, 1974) (Zeszyty Naukowej WSP w Opolu, series B, Studia i Monografie 40).

31. On cities and towns in the commonwealth, see Jan Ptaśnik, *Miasta i mieszczaństwo w dawnej Polsce*, 2d ed. (Warsaw, 1949). On the Ukrainian lands, see P. V. Mykhailyna, *Vyzvolna borotba trudovoho naselennia mist Ukrainy (1569–1654)* (Kiev, 1975); P. V. Mykhailyna, *Mista Ukrainy v period feodalizmu. (Do pytannia pro stanovyshche mist v umovakh inozemnoho ponevolennia v kintsi XVI–pershii polovyni XVII st.)* (Chernivtsi, 1971); O. S. Kompan, *Mista Ukrainy v druhii polovyni XVII st.* (Kiev, 1963); *Istoriia Kieva. V 2-kh tt.*, ed. O. K. Kasymenko (Kiev, 1959–60); Maurycy Horn, *Walka klasowa i konflikty społeczne w miastach Rusi Czerwonej w latach 1600–1647 na tle stosunków gospodarczych* (Wrocław-Cracow-Warsaw, 1972), and Elżbieta Hornowa, *Stosunki ekonomiczno-społeczne w miastach ziemi halickiej w latach 1590–1648* (Opole, 1963) (Zeszyty Naukowe WSP w Opolu, series B, Studia i Monografie 40). On Kiev's cultural role, see F. P. Shevchenko, *Rol Kyieva v mizhslovianskykh zviazkakh u XVII–XVIII st.. Dopovidi Radianskoi delehatsii. V mizhnarodnyi zizd slavistiv (Sofiia, veresen 1963 r.)* (Kiev, 1963) and F. Ernst, "Kyivska arkhitektura XVII v.," *Kyiv ta ioho okolytsia v istorii i pamiatkakh*, ed. Mykhailo Hrushevsky (Kiev, 1926), 125–66 (Zapysky Ukrainskoho naukovoho tovarystva 22 and VUAN, Zbirnyk Istorychno-filolohichnoho viddilu, Istorychna sektsiia 45). For noble-burgher relations, see Antoni Prochaska, *Lwów i szlachta* (Lviv, 1919) (Biblioteka Lwowska 24, no. 5) and S. T. Biletsky, "Borotba mishchan Lvova proty zasyllia shliakhty v pershii polovyni XVII st.," *Z istorii zakhidnoukrainskykh zemel* 1 (1957): 15–24.

32. The most recent comprehensive work on the brotherhoods is Ia. D. Isaievych, *Bratstva ta ikh rol v rozvytku ukrainskoi kultury XVI–XVIII st.* (Kiev, 1966).

33. The two best general works on the Cossacks are Zbigniew Wójcik, *Dzikie Pola w ogniu. O kozaczyźnie w dawnej Rzeczypospolitej*, 3d ed. revised (Warsaw, 1968) and V. O. Holobutsky [V. A. Golobutsky], *Zaporozhskoe kazachestvo* (Kiev, 1957). On the social and ethnic composition of the

Cossacks, see Władysław Tomkiewicz, "O składzie społecznym i etnicznym Kozaczyzny Ukrainnej na przełomie XVI i XVII wieku," *Przeglad Historyczny* 37 (1948): 248–60. The noble descent of Hetman Petro Konashevych-Sahaidachny has been disputed. For a thorough discussion of his presumed forebears that constitutes a monograph on the petty nobility of the Przemyśl area, see Bohdan Barvinsky, "Konashevychi v peremyskii zemli v XV i XVI st. Henealohichno-istorychna monohrafiia," *Zapysky Naukovoho tovarystva im. Shevchenka* 100 (1930): 9–175 (Iuvileinyi zbirnyk na poshanu akad. Kyryla Studynskoho, pt. 2).

34. On this element of the population, see Stanisław Grodziski, *Ludzie luźni. Studium z historii państwa i prawa polskiego* (Cracow, 1961).

35. On the position of the Catholic church in this period, see *Kościół w Polsce*, ed. Jerzy Kłoczowski, 2 vols. to date (Cracow, 1966–9), 2: *Wieki XVI–XVIII*; and Janusz Tazbir, *Historia Kościoła Katolickiego w Polsce 1460–1795* (Warsaw, 1966).

36. For an excellent synthesis of scholarship on the Orthodox church, see Kazimierz Chodynicki, *Kościół Prawosławny a Rzeczpospolita Polska 1370–1632* (Warsaw, 1934). For the 1632–48 period, one should turn to the monumental work of S. T. Golubev, *Kievskii Mitropolit Petr Mogila i ego spodvizhniki (Opyt tserkovno-istoricheskogo issledovaniia)*, 2 vols. (Kiev, 1883–98). Of more recent works, see Ludomir Bieńkowski, "Organizacja Kościóła Wschodniego w Polsce," in *Kościół w Polsce* 2: 733–1050 (on the Orthodox and Uniate churches), and Ivan Vlasovsky, *Narys istorii Ukrainskoi pravoslavnoi tserkvy*, 4 vols. in 5 books (New York, 1955–66). There is no work on the Uniate church that equals Chodynicki's work on the Orthodox church. One must still turn to the standard nineteenth-century histories of Mykhailo Harasevych (Harasiewicz), *Annales Ecclesiae Ruthenae* (Lviv, 1862); J. Pelesz, *Geschichte der Union der Ruthenischen Kirche mit Rom von den ältesten Zeiten bis auf die Gegenwart*, 2 vols. (Vienna, 1878–80); and Edward Likowski, *Unia Brzeska (1596)* (Poznań, 1896). This situation is particularly unsatisfactory because, while research on the Orthodox church has stagnated in the last thirty years, numerous sources and specialized monographs have appeared on the Uniates, especially in the *Analecta OSBM*. The only general synthesis is the series of valuable but popular lectures of A. H. Velyky, *Z litopysu khrystyianskoi Ukrainy*, 9 vols. (Rome, 1968–77).

37. For religious affairs in the commonwealth during this period, see Ambroise Jobert, *De Luther à Mohila: La Pologne dans la crise de la Chrêtienté 1517–1648* (Paris, 1974) (Collection historique de l'Institut d'études slaves 21). For literature on the various churches in Ukraine in this period, see Isydor I. Patrylo, *Dzherela i bibliohrafiia istorii ukrainskoi tserkvy* (Rome, 1975) (*Analecta OSBM* 33, series 2, section 1) and his addendum "Dzherela i bibliohrafiia istorii Ukrainskoi tserkvy," *Analecta OSBM* 10, series 2, section 2 (1979): 405–87. Not included in the bibliography is the recent study on Protestants in Ukraine by George H. Williams, "Protestants

in the Ukraine during the Period of the Polish-Lithuanian Commonwealth," *Harvard Ukrainian Studies* 2 (1978): 41–72, 184–210.

38. See P. G. Viktorovsky, "Zapadnorusskie dvorianskie familii, otpavshie ot pravoslaviia v kontse XVI i XVII v.," *Trudy Kievskoi dukhovnoi akademii*, 1908, no. 9, 17–60; no. 10, 189–206; no. 11, 344–60; no. 12, 502–24; 1909, no. 6, 178–214; 1910, no. 3, 339–92; no. 11, 409–20; 1911, no. 2, 259–73; no. 6: 257–72; nos. 7–8: 396–424; K. Gorovsky, "Russkie dvorianskie familii," *Vremmenik Instituta stavropigiiskogo za 1910 god* (Lviv), 8–44, and M. Iuzefovich, "Prilozhenie k predisloviiu. Tablitsa shliakhetskikh rodov iugozapadnogo kraia . . . ," *Arkhiv Iugo-Zapadnoi Rossii* 1, part 4 (Kiev, 1867): i–xiii.

39. For the occupants of sees in the Ukrainian territories, see volume 2 of *Kościół w Polsce*. Piasecki, bishop of Przemyśl, was noted for his chronicle, *Chronica Gestorum in Europa Singularium* (Cracow, 1645). Wereszczyński, bishop of Kiev, was a noble of Ruthenian descent who proposed major reforms in the Ukrainian territories. For a description of how he passed over to the Catholic church, see Szajnocha, "Jak Ruś polszczała," *Szkice historyczne* 4: 173–90. On Wereszczyński's career and thought, see Edward Winkler, "Józef Wereszczyński, biskup kijowski," *Przegląd Powszechny* 147–8 (1920): 243–52; 149–50 (1921): 383–90; 151–2 (1921): 414–21; 153–4 (1922): 120–5.

40. In addition to Williams' "Protestants in the Ukraine," see Gottfried Schramm, *Der polnische Adel und die Reformation* (Wiesbaden, 1965) (Veröffentlichungen des Instituts für europäische Geschichte Mainz 36) and Janusz Tazbir, "Antytrynitaryzm na ziemiach ukraińskich w XVII wieku," *Z polskich studiów slawistycznych*, series 4, Historia (Seventh International Congress of Slavists) (Warsaw, 1973), 91–120.

41. For the social origins of the Orthodox and Uniate clergy, in addition to the literature in note 36, see [Ignacy Stebelski], "Ostatnie prace Stebelskiego," ed. W. Serdyński in *Scriptores Rerum Polonicarum* 6 (1878): 263–396 (Wydawnictwa Komisyi Hist. Akad. Umiejetności w Krakowie 10 and Archiwum Komisyi Historycznej 1); Leonid Sonevytsky, *Ukrainskyi epyskopat Peremyskoi i Kholmskoi eparkhii v XV–XVI st.* (Rome, 1955) (*Analecta OSBM*, series 2, section 1, vol. 6); Sophia Senyk, "Women's Monasteries in Ukraine and Belorussia to the Period of the Suppressions" (Ph. D. thesis: Pontifical Oriental Institute, 1979); Mykhailo Hrushevsky, "Storinka do istorii silskoho dukhovenstva (po sambirskym aktam XVI v.)," *Zapysky Naukovoho tovarystva im. Shevchenka* 34 (1900): 1–82; Orest Levytsky [Levitsky], "Iuzhno-russkie arkhierei XVI i XVII st.," *Kievskaia starina*, no. 1 (1882): 49–100 and Isydor Sharanevych [Izydor Szaraniewicz], *Kościelna unia na Rusi i wpływ jej na zmianę społecznego stanowiska świeckiego duchowieństwa ruskiego* (Lviv, 1899). On the church wealth that endowed ecclesiastical positions and the problem of patronage, see Isydor Sharanevych [Szaraniewicz], *Rzut oka na beneficya Kościoła Ruskiego za czasów Rzeczypospolitej Polskiej pod wzgledem*

historyi, przedewszystkiem o stosunku świeckiego duchowieństwa ruskiego w Galicyi do ziemi w tym okresie (Lviv, 1875) and M. Vladimirsky-Budanov, "Tserkovnye imushchestva v Iugo-Zapadnoi Rossii v XVI veku," *Arkhiv Iugo-Zapadnoi Rossii* 4, part 8 (1907): 3–224. On the greater success of the Union in Belorussia, see Władysław Tomkiewicz, "Dzieje unji kościelnej w Wielkiem Ksiestwie Litewskim (1596–1795)," *Pamiętnik VI Zjazdu Historyków Polskich w Wilnie 17–20 września 1935*, 1 (Lviv, 1935), 325–6.

42. The most recent work on Skarga is Janusz Tazbir, *Piotr Skarga szermierz kontrreformacji* (Warsaw, 1978). For materials on Orthodox clerics' glorification of the nobility, see Kh. Titov, *Materiialy dlia istorii knyzhnoi spravy na Ukraini v XVI–XVIII vv.. Vsezbirka peredmov do ukrainskykh starodrukiv* (Kiev, 1924) (VUAN, Zbirnyk Istorychno-filolohichnoho viddilu 17).

43. On developments in Polish Catholicism in this period, see Janusz Tazbir, "Sarmatyzacja katolicyzmu w XVII wieku," in Janusz Pelc, ed., *Wiek XVII—kontrreformacja-barok. Prace z historii kultury* (Wrocław-Warsaw-Cracow, 1970), 7–38.

44. On the nobility's role in the governance of Reformed churches, see Viacheslav Lypynsky, "Ariianskyi soimyk v Kyselyni na Volyni v maiu 1638 r. (Prychynok do istorii ariianstva na Ukraini)," *Zapysky Naukovoho tovarystva im. Shevchenka* 96 (1910): 41–57, and the literature in note 40 above.

45. On lay influence in the Orthodox church, see Viacheslav Zaikyn [Zaikin], *Uchastie svetskogo elementa v tserkovnom upravlenii. Vybornoe nachalo i sobornost v Kievskoi mitropolii v XVI i XVII v.* (Warsaw, 1930); Orest Levytsky [Levitsky], "Cherty vnutrennogo stroia Zapadno-Russkoi tserkvi," *Kievskaia starina*, no. 8 (1884): 627–54; and Kazimierz Chodynicki, "Z dziejów prawosławia na Wołyniu (922–1596)," *Rocznik Wołyński* 5–6 (1937): 52–60. On the role of Ostrozky, see Kazimierz Lewicki, *Książę Konstanty Ostrogski a Unja brzeska 1596 r.* (Lviv, 1933) (Archiwum Towarzystwa Naukowego we Lwowie 11, section 2), 1–224. For a seventeenth-century discussion of the role of the nobility in the Orthodox church, see A. H. Velyky, "Anonimnyi proiekt P. Mohyly po ziedynenniu Ukrainskoi tserkvy 1645 r.," *Analecta OSBM* 4 (10), series 2, section 2 (1963): 484–97.

46. The letters of Metropolitan Iosyf Rutsky illustrate the clerical control of the Uniate church. Athanasius G. Welykyj, ed. *Epistolae Josephi Velamin Rutskyj Metropolitae Kioviensis Catholici (1613–1637)* (Rome, 1956) (*Analecta OSBM*, series 2, section 3, Epistolae Metropolitarum, Archiepiscoporum et Episcoporum, 1).

47. Vyshensky has consequently enjoyed popularity among Soviet scholars as a democrat. See the selection from his works in Biletsky, *Khrestomatiia*, 123–55.

48. For the commonwealth as a whole, see Karol Górski's studies, "Religijność

sarmatyzmu a kwietyzm," *Teksty*, no. 4 (1974): 58–75 and *Od religijności do mitsyki. Zarys dziejów życia wewnetrznego w Polsce*, (Lublin, 1962), part 1: 966–1,795.

49. On Nemyrych, see Stanisław Kot, *Georges Niemirycz et la lutte contre l'intolérance au 17-e siècle* (The Hague, 1960). Nemyrych did not remain dedicated to Anti-Trinitarianism. His conversion to Orthodoxy and call for Protestants to accept Orthodoxy in order to fulfil their desire to return to the early Christian faith represent an interesting chapter of inter-religious relations in Ukraine.

50. *Memoriale Rerum Gestarum in Polonia 1632–1656*, 5 vols. (Wrocław-Warsaw-Cracow, 1968–75) (Polska Akademia Nauk, Oddział w Krakowie, Materiały Komisji Nauk Historycznych, 15, 18, 22, 25, 26).

51. For wills by major Orthodox leaders, see those of Adam Kysil in "Try testamenty Adama Kysilia," *Ukraina*, no. 1–2 (1918): 49–67, and of Halshka Hulevychivna in S. Golubev, *Istoriia Kievskoi dukhovnoi akademii*, 1: *Period do-Mogilianskii* (Kiev, 1886), "Prilozheniia," 113–17. The proliferation of monasteries in Volhynia is documented in Max Boyko, *Bibliography of Church Life in Volhynia* (Bloomington, Indiana, 1974), 51–73 (Publications of the Volhynian Bibliographic Center 9).

52. On Rutsky's activities, see Mirosław Szegda, *Działalność organizacyjna Metropolity Józefa IV Welamina Rutskiego (1613–1637)* (Warsaw, 1967).

53. For the problem of religious tolerance and the growth of intolerance, see Janusz Tazbir, *Państwo bez stosów. Szkice z dziejów tolerancji w Polsce XVII wieku* (Warsaw, 1958); Myrosław Korolko, *Klejnot swobodnego sumienia. Polemika wokół konfederacji warszawskiej w latach 1573–1658* (Warsaw, 1974); and Henryk Wisner, "Walka o realizacje konfederacji warszawskiej za panowania Zygmunta III w latach 1587–1632," *Odrodzenie i Reformacja w Polsce* 19 (1974): 129–49. For the influence of the Counter Reformation and the cultural trends of the seventeenth century, see Janusz Tazbir, *Rzeczpospolita i świat. Studia z dziejów kultury XVII wieku* (Wrocław-Warsaw-Cracow, 1971); Pelc, ed., *Wiek XVII* (in particular Jarema Maciszewski's essay "Mechanizmy kształtowania sie opinii publicznej w Polsce doby Kontrreformacji," 55–70); and the discussion "Umysłowość i ideologia polska XVII w.," *VIII Powszechny Zjazd Historyków Polskich we Krakowie 14–17 września 1958*, 3, ed. Kazimierz Lepszy (Warsaw, 1960), 121–54.

54. The most recent significant Soviet contribution to the history of the Jews in Ukraine is S. Ia. Borovoi, "Natsionalno-osvoboditelnaia voina ukrainskogo naroda protiv polskogo vladychestva i evreiskoe naselenie Ukrainy," *Istoricheskie zapiski AN SSSR* 9 (1940): 81–124.

55. Salo Wittmayer Baron, *A Social and Religious History of the Jews*, 2d ed., 16: *Poland-Lithuania 1500–1650* (New York-London, 1976). Baron uses Samuel Ettinger's doctoral thesis and articles on Jewish colonization of Ukraine, 192–213, 401–2, note 20. Also see Bernard Weinryb, *The Jews of Poland: A Social and Economic History of the Jewish Community in*

Poland from 1100 to 1800 (Philadelphia, 1972).

56. Maurycy Horn, *Żydzi na Rusi Czerwonej w XVI i pierwszej połowie XVII w. Działalność gospodarcza na tle rozwoju demograficznego* (Warsaw, 1975).

57. Baron, *A Social and Religious History*, 16:192. For a discussion of Jewish military taxes and duties, see Maurycy Horn, *Powinności wojenne Żydów w Rzeczypospolitej w XVI i XVII wieku* (Warsaw, 1978). On anti-Semitism in literature, see Kazimierz Bartoszewicz, *Antysemityzm w literaturze polskiej XV-XVII w.* (Cracow, 1914). On converts from Judaism who became nobles (few are listed before the eighteenth century), see the two volumes of Ludwik Piotrkowski [Korwin], *Szlachta mojżeszowa* (Cracow, 1938) and *Szlachta neoficka* (Cracow, 1939).

58. In particular, see his *Armianskie kolonii na Ukraine v istochnikakh i literature XV–XIX vekov (Istoriograficheskii ocherk)* (Erevan, 1962); his contributions to the volumes *Istoricheskie sviazi i druzhba ukrainskogo i armianskogo narodov: Sbornik materialov Nauchnoi sessii* (Erevan, 1961), *Sbornik materialov Vtoroi ukrainsko-armianskoi nauchnoi sessii* (Kiev, 1965) and *Sbornik dokladov* (Erevan, 1971); and his article "The Armenians in the Time of Hetman Bohdan Xmel'nyc'kyj," *Harvard Ukrainian Studies* 3–4 (1979–80): 166–88. On Armenian noble families, see [Ludwik Piotrkowski], *Ormiańskie rody szlacheckie* (Cracow, 1934).

59. For the nobility's pacifism in foreign policy, see the discussions in *VIII Powszechny Zjazd* 3: 70–119; Jarema Maciszewski, *Polska a Moskwa 1603–1618. Opinie i stanowiska szlachty polskiej* (Warsaw, 1968); and Henryk Wisner, "Opinia szlachecka Rzeczypospolitej wobec polityki szwedzkiej Zygmunta III w latach 1587–1632," *Zapiski Historyczne. Kwartalnik Poświęcony Historii Pomorza i Krajów Bałtyckich* 38, no. 2 (1973): 9–50. On the commonwealth's international situation, also see the essay by Wójcik in *Polska XVII wieku*, 13–51. On the military, see Jan Wimmer, *Zarys dziejów wojskowości polskiej do roku 1864*, 2 vols. (Warsaw, 1965–6) and Bohdan Baranowski, *Organizacja wojska polskiego w latach trzydziestych i czterdziestych XVII wieku* (Warsaw, 1957) (Prace Komisji Wojskowo-Historycznej Ministerstwa Obrony Narodowej, series A, 10).

60. On the size and cost of the army, see Jan Wimmer, "Wojsko i skarb Rzeczypospolitej u schyłku XVI i w pierwszej połowie XVII wieku," *Studia i Materiały do Historii Wojskowości* 14, no. 1 (1968): 3–91. For an example of a career made in the military, see Adam Kersten, *Stefan Czarniecki, 1599–1665* (Warsaw, 1963). On the place of the army in the society of the Grand Duchy of Lithuania, see Henryk Wisner, "Wojsko w społeczeństwie litewskim pierwszej połowy XVII wieku," *Przeglad Historyczny* 66 (1975): 41–60.

61. On Tatar attacks, see Marycy Horn, "Chronologia i zasieg najazdów tatarskich w latach 1600–1647," *Studia i Materiały do Historii Wojskowości* 7 (1962): 3–71 and his *Skutki ekonomiczne najazdów*

tatarskich z lat 1605–1633 na Ruś Czerwoną (Wrocław-Warsaw-Cracow, 1964). In the middle of the sixteenth century, the Volhynian nobility had registered its complaints about its exceptionally heavy military service because it was constantly engaged against the Tatars, while the nobilities of other lands of the grand duchy fought only occasionally, and then against the Muscovites. Jabłonowski, *Źródła dziejowe* 6, xiv.

62. For discussion of the recognition of the delegates from the Ukrainian lands that military expenditures were essential to their lands' defence, see Frank Sysyn, "Adam Kysil," 156–8. On a hetman's career, see Antoni Prochaska, *Hetman Stanisław Żółkiewski* (Warsaw, 1927). On the role of confederations, see Kaczmarczyk, *Historia*, 128, 243–5, and Jarema Maciszewski, *Wojna domowa w Polsce (1606–1609)*, 1 (Wrocław-Warsaw-Cracow, 1960). For nobles' attitudes toward levies in the western Ukrainian lands, see Kazimierz Hahn, *Pospolite ruszenie wedle uchwał sejmikowych ruskich od XVI do XVIII wieku* (Lviv, 1928) (Pamietnik Historyczno-Prawny 9, no. 4).

63. Łoziński, *Prawem i lewem*. On magnates' armies, see Krzysztof Dembski, "Wojska nadworne magnatów polskich w XVI i XVII wieku," *Zeszyty Naukowe Uniwersytetu im. A. Mickiewicza w Poznaniu. Historia* 1 (1956): 49–96.

64. On magnates' initiation of foreign adventures, see Kaczmarczyk, *Historia*, 179–80, and Maciszewski, *Polska a Moskwa*.

65. On the conduct of foreign affairs, see Zbigniew Wójcik, ed., *Polska służba dyplomatyczna XVI–XVIII wieku* (Warsaw, 1966). On relations with the Tatars, see Bohdan Baranowski, *Stosunki polsko-tatarskie w latach 1632–1648* (Łódź, 1949) (Prace Instytutu Historycznego Uniwersytetu Łódzkiego 1). On the role of the hetmans in foreign policy, see Wacław Zarzycki, *Dyplomacja hetmanów w dawnej Polsce* (Warsaw-Poznań, 1976) (Bydgoskie Towarzystwo Naukowe, Prace Wydziału Nauk Humanistycznych, Series E, 8). On the selection of hetmans, see Włodzimierz Dworzaczek, "Kto w Polsce dzierżył buławy?" *Przegląd Historyczny* 39 (1949): 163–70.

66. Orest Levytsky wrote a number of excellent studies on the Ukrainian nobility of the sixteenth and seventeenth centuries. See his "Ganna Montovt," *Kievskaia starina*, no. 1–3 (1888): 94–161; "Ocherki starinnogo byta Volyni i Ukrainy," *Kievskaia starina*, no. 4 (1889) 99–123; no. 11 (1889): 350–68; no. 1 (1891): 19–39; no. 2 (1891): 269–80; "Anna-Aloiza kniazhna Ostrozhskaia," *Kievskaia starina*, no. 11 (1883): 329–73; and his introduction, "Akty o brachnom prave i semeinom byte v Iugo-Zapadnoi Rusi v XVI–XVII vv.," to *Arkhiv Iugo-Zapadnoi Rossii* 3, part 8 (Kiev, 1909). For bibliographies of the major Polish scholars who wrote on Ukrainian history in this period, see Leonyd Dobrovolsky, "Edvard-Leopold Rulikovsky, znavets Kyivshchyny (1825–1900)," *VUAN. Zapysky Istorychno-filolohichnoho viddilu* 18 (1928): 75–112. Also see Zygmunt Luba Radzimiński *Ś. Kazimierz Pułaski (1845–1926). Wspomnienie*

pośmiertne (Cracow, 1928); Antoni J. [Rolle], *Wybór pism*, ed. Wacław Zawadzki, 3 vols. (Cracow, [1966]) (there is a list of his publications in volume 1, page 18); K. Sochaniewicz, "Ś. Zygmunt Luba Radzimiński. Prezes honorowy Polskiego Towarzystwa Heraldycznego," *Rocznik Towarzystwa Heraldycznego we Lwowie* 9 (1928–29) [publ. 1930]: 301–18; and Z. L. Radzimiński, "Jaren Marek Gozdawa Giżycki. Wspomnienie pośmiertne," *Rocznik Towarzystwa Heraldycznego we Lwowie* 6 (1924–25) [publ. 1926]: 233–43.

67. Art historians have perforce dealt with "elitist" culture. See Platon Biletsky, *Ukrainskyi portretnyi zhyvopys XVII–XVIII st.. Problemy stanovlennia i rozvytku* (Kiev, 1969); the Lviv art historian Mieczysław Gebarowicz, *Portret XVI–XVIII wieku we Lwowie* (Wrocław-Warsaw-Cracow, 1969); and P. M. Zholtovsky, *Ukrainskyi zhyvopys XVII–XVIII st.* (Kiev, 1978). The best ethnographic work dealing with the petty nobility in this period is Hoshko, *Naselennia ukrainskykh Karpat.* Soviet research currently being conducted on "Boikivshchyna" should result in materials on the life expectancy, diet, fertility and farming techniques of the petty nobles of the Carpathians.

68. Particularly useful are Jan Stanisław Bystroń, *Dzieje obyczajów w dawnej Polsce. Wiek XVI–XVIII*, 2 vols. (Warsaw, 1960); Władysław Czapliński, *Dawne czasy. Opowiadania i szkice historyczne z XVII wieku* (Wrocław 1957); Zygmunt Gloger, *Encyklopedja staropolska*, 4 vols. (Warsaw, 1900–3); Władysław Łoziński, *Życie polskie w dawnych wiekach*, 6th ed. (Warsaw, 1937); Maria Koczerska, *Rodzina szlachecka w Polsce późnego średniowiecza* (Warsaw, 1975); and Aleksander Brückner, *Dzieje kultury polskiej*, 2d. ed., 3 vols. (Warsaw, 1957–69).

69. The most penetrating analysis of the elements and changes in Ukrainian culture in the sixteenth century is Orest Zilynsky, "Dukhova heneza pershoho ukrainskoho vidrodzhennia," *Stezhi. Zhurnal ukrainskoho studentskoho seredovyshcha Nimechchyny ta Avstrii* 1, nos. 7–10 (1946–7): 6–20. For a critical view of Ukrainian spiritual culture, see Georgii Florovsky, *Puti russkogo bogosloviia* (Paris, 1937). Florovsky particularly condemned the decline of Byzantine spirituality and the Latinizing tendencies of Mohyla. On Byzantine influences, see Ihor Ševčenko, "Byzantium and the Eastern Slavs after 1453," *Harvard Ukrainian Studies* 2 (1978): 5–25.

70. Although Polish scholars have frequently lauded the spread of "Polish culture" and "Western civilization" to the Ukrainian lands, they have seldom examined the process, defined its components and analysed the changes. Frequently, "Poland-West-Europe" is assumed to be a monolithic concept associated with a "higher civilization." No attempt has been made to study the possible regeneration of Byzantine or pan-Christian elements in Ukrainian culture or to establish which new influences were specifically Polish as opposed to pan-European, German or Italian. Thus an important problem has been obscured by lofty eulogies to the Polish civilizing mission

and virulent reactions by fervent Orthodox and by patriotic Ukrainians. For examples of the mission mentality in the works of reputable scholars, see Aleksander Jabłonowski, *Historya Rusi Południowej do upadku Rzeczypospolitej* (Cracow, 1912) and Szajnocha, "Zdobycze pługa polskiego." On "Occidentalism" in Polish historiography, see Andrzej Wierzbicki, "Okcydentalizm w historiografii polskiej. Próba konstrukcji modelu," *Przeglad Humanistyczny* 19, no. 8 (1975): 35–43. The best discussion of Polish cultural influence on eastern peoples of the commonwealth is Aleksander Brückner, "Wpływy polskie na Litwie i słowiańszczyźnie wschodniej," in *Polska w kulturze powszechnej*, ed. Feliks Konieczny, pt. 1 (Cracow, 1918), 153–66. On German influences in Ukraine, see Josef Matl, "Der Anteil des deutschen Geisteslebens an der Verwestlichung der ukrainischen und grossrussichen Kultur (15–17 jh.)," *Südostdeutsche Forschungen* 4 (1939): 14–55. For a discussion of Polish influences on the life of the Ukrainian nobility, see Anna Dembińska, *Wpływy kultury polskiej na Wołyń w XVI wieku (na łonie warstwy szlacheckiej)* (Poznań, 1930) (Prace Komisji Historycznej Poznańskiego Towarzystwa Przyjaciół Nauk 16).

71. For memoir literature of this period, see I. Krypiakevych, "Memuary ukraintsiv XVI–XVIII st.," *Stara Ukraina* 9–10 (1924): 126–32. In addition to the biographical works already cited (Tomkiewicz, *Jeremi Wiśniowiecki*; Sysyn, "Adam Kysil"; Golubev, *Mitropolit Petr Mogila*; Lewicki, *Książę Konstanty Ostrogski*; Levytsky (Levitsky), "Ganna Montovt" and "Anna-Aloiza kniazhna Ostrozhskaia"; Prochaska, *Hetman Stanisław Żółkiewski*; Kot, *Georges Niemirycz*; Krypiakevych, *Bohdan Khmelnytsky*; and Dobrowolska, *Młodość Jerzego i Krzysztofa Zbaraskich*); see Antoni J. [Rolle], "Samuel Łaszcz (Kartka z dziejów swawoli kresowej XVI–XVII w.)," *Szkice i opowiadania*, series 5 (Cracow-Warsaw, 1887), 37–141; Klemens Dzieduszycki, *Jan Herburt. Kasztelan Sanocki. Rys biograficzny* (Lviv, 1879); Arkadii Zhukovsky, *Petro Mohyla i pytannia iednosty tserkov* (Paris, 1962) (with a bibliography of earlier biographies); Meletii Solovii, *Meletii Smotrytsky iak pysmennyk*, 2 parts (Rome-Toronto, 1977–8) (Analecta OSBM 36–7, series 2, section 1, 36–7): Antoni Prochaska, "Wyhowski, twórca Unji hadziackiej i jego rodzina," *Przewodnik Naukowy i Literacki* (1920): 18–33, 113–25, 209–21, 305–23, 399–411; Adam Witusik, *Młodość Tomasza Zamoyskiego* (Lublin, 1977); Mieczysław Lepecki, *Pan Jakobus Sobieski* (Warsaw, 1970); and Leszek Podhorodecki, *Stanislaw Koniecpolski ok. 1592–1646* [Warsaw, 1969]. The compilation of a complete list of biographic studies of nobles of the period is necessary for further research on the nobility. The *Polski Słownik Biograficzny* published in Cracow since 1935 will be of great assistance in this task.

72. Much of the commentary on Islamic, Tatar and Turkish influences in Ukraine was culturally biased and based on various racial theories, in particular Turanianism. Such comments were common in the works of

Polish nationalist historians such as Franciszek Rawita-Gawroński, *Kozaczyzna Ukrainna w Rzeczypospolitej Polskiej do końca XVIII-go wieku. Zarys polityczno-historyczny* (Warsaw, [1923]), but he sought to exclude the nobility, as opposed to the Cossacks and peasants, from racial taints. Art historians and folklorists have been in the forefront of study of Eastern influences. See for example, Biletsky, *Ukrainskyi portretnyi zhyvopys* and Tadeusz Mańkowski, *Orient w polskiej kulturze artystycznej* (Wrocław, 1979). Also see Bohdan Baranowski, *Znajomość Wschodu w dawnej Polsce do XVII w.* (Łódź, 1950) and Janusz Tazbir, "Les influences orientales en Pologne aux XVI-XVIII siècles," *La Pologne au XV Congrès international des sciences historiques* (Wrocław-Cracow-Gdańsk, 1980), 214–39.

73. For sources on Ukrainian culture, see Ia. D. Isaievych, *Dzherela z istorii ukrainskoi kultury doby feodalizmu XV–XVIII st.* (Kiev, 1972). The best general outline on cultural developments is Mykhailo Hrushevsky, *Kulturno-natsionalnyi rukh na Ukraini XVI–XVII st.*, 2d ed. (n.p., 1919). On language usage, including among the nobility, see Antoine Martel, *La langue polonaise dans les pays Ruthènes: Ukraine et Russie Blanche, 1569–1667* (Lille, 1933) (Travaux et mémoires de l'université de Lille, Nouvelle série: Droît et lettres 20). On schools, see E. N. Medynsky, *Bratskie shkoly Ukrainy i Belorusi XVI–XVII vv.* (Kiev, 1954); K. V. Kharlampovich, *Zapadno-russkie pravoslavnye shkoly XVI i nachala XVII veka, otnoshenie ikh k inoslavnym, religioznoe obuchenie v nikh i zaslugi ikh v dele zashchity pravoslavnoi very i tserkvi* (Kazan, 1898); J. K. Kochanowski, *Dzieje Akademii Zamojskiej (1594–1784)* (Cracow, 1899–1900) (Fontes et Commentation Historiam Scholarum Superiorum in Polonia Illustrantes 7) (the unpublished matriculation book of the Academy is in Biblioteka Narodowa [Warsaw], Biblioteka Ordynacyi Zamoyskich MS 1598); Alexander Sydorenko, *The Kievan Academy in the Seventeenth Century* (Ottawa, 1977) (University of Ottawa Ukrainian Series 1) (with a complete bibliography of earlier works); and Bronisław Natoński, "Szkolnictwo jezuickie w dobie kontrreformacji," in Pelc, ed., *Wiek XVII*, 309–38. On Ukrainian students abroad, see Domet Olijančyn, "Aus dem Kultur- und Geistesleben der Ukraine. II. Schule und Bildung," *Kyrios* 2 (1937): 38–69, 143–57, 265–78, 351–66; D. Blazejowskyj, "Ukrainian and Bielorussian Students in the Pontificio Collegio Urbano de Propaganda Fide (1627–1846)," *Analecta OSBM* 9 (14), series 2, section 2 (1974): 202–22; and Ihor Losky, "Ukraintsi na studiiakh v Nimechchyni v XVI–XVIII st.," *Zapysky Naukovho tovarystva im. Shevchenka* 151 (1931): 99–110. For a discussion of the education of nobles in the commonwealth, see J[udyta] Freylichówna, *Ideał wychowawczy szlachty polskiej w XVI i początku XVII wieku* (Warsaw, 1938) and Stanisław Łempicki, *Działalność Jana Zamoyskiego na polu szkolnictwa, 1573–1605* (Cracow, 1921) (Prace Monograficzne z Dziejów Wychowania i Szkolnictwa w Polsce 2).

74. St. Śreniowski, *Organizacja sejmiku halickiego* (Lviv, 1938) (Studja nad

Historja Prawa Polskiego imienia Oswalda Balzera 16, no. 3); Stanisław Piotrkowski, *Uchwały podatkowe sejmiku generalnego wiszeńskiego 1572–1772* (Lviv, 1932) (Studja nad Historja Prawa Polskiego imienia Oswalda Balzera 13, no. 4); Antoni Prochaska, "Sejmiki wiszeńskie w czasach trzech elekcyi pojagiellońskich," *Kwartalnik Historyczny* 17 (1903): 363–404, 544–95; Tadeusz Kostkiewicz, *Działalność kulturalna sejmiku ruskiego* (Lviv, 1939) (Pamietnik Historyczno-Prawny 13, no. 2) and Antoni Prochaska, "Z dziejów samorzadu ziemi chełmskiej," *Przegląd Historyczny* 6 (1908): 33–49, 155–72, 306–21. On the eastern Ukrainian lands, there is only the introduction to a volume of instructions of the dietines by N. Ivanishev in *Arkhiv Iugo-Zapadnoi Rossii* 1, part 2 (Kiev, 1861), xv–lxiv and N. V. Storozhenko, *Zapadno-russkie provintsialnye seimiki vo vtoroi polovine XVII veka (Issledovanie po arkhivnomu materialu)* (Kiev, 1888). For the function of the dietines in shaping the political culture of the nobility, see the essays by Jerzy Włodarczyk, "Sejmiki jako szkoła wychowania obywatelskiego (na przykładzie sejmików sieradzkiego i łeczyckiego)," 69–86, and Leszczyński, "Siedemnastowieczne sejmiki a kultura polityczna szlachty," 51–68, and in Gierowski, ed. *Dzieje kultury politycznej w Polsce.*

75. For the dietines of the Ruthenian palatinate, see *Akta grodzkie i ziemskie z czasów Rzeczypospolitej Polskiej z Archiwum tak zwanego Bernardyńskiego [Archiwum Ziemskiego] we Lwowie*, 25 vols. (Lviv, 1868–1935), 20, 24. For the eastern lands see *Arkhiv Iugo-Zapadnoi Rossii* 1, part 2 (Kiev, 1861).

76. On the role of the Diet in forming the political culture of the nobility, see Władysław Czapliński, "Rola sejmów XVII wieku w kształtowaniu sie kultury politycznej w Polsce," in Gierowski, ed. *Dzieje kultury politycznej w Polsce*, 42–50. For information on published and manuscript "diaries," see Władysław Konopczyński, *Chronologia sejmów polskich 1493–1793* (Cracow, 1948) (Archiwum Komisji Historycznej, Polska Akademia Umiejetności 4, series 2, no. 3); Henryk Olszewski, "Nowe materiały do chronologii sejmów polskich," *Czasopismo Prawno-Historyczne* 9 (1957): 229–58; and Zbigniew Radwański, "Uzupełnienie do chronologii sejmów polskich," *Czasopismo Prawno-Historyczne* 2 (1949): 449–51. Professor Andrew Pernal of Brandon University is planning to publish the little-utilized, but extremely valuable German language "diaries" of Gdańsk.

77. P. N. Zhukovich, *Seimovaia borba pravoslavnogo zapadno-russkogo dvorianstva s tserkovnoi uniei (do 1608)* (St. Petersburg, 1901) and *Seimovaia borba zapadno-russkogo dvorianstva s tserkovnoi uniei (s 1609)*, 6 parts (St. Peterburg, 1902–12).

78. [Volumina legum] *Prawa, konstytucye y przywileie Królewstwa Polskiego, y Wielkiego Xiestwa Litewskiego.* ed. Stanisław Konarski, 8 vols. (Warsaw, 1732–82) and Vasyl Bidnov [Vasilii Bednov], *Pravoslavnaia tserkov v Polshe i Litve po "Volumina Legum"* (Katerynoslav, 1908).

79. A listing of the major laws is in Kovalsky, *Istochnikovedenie*, part 3, 14–19.

80. On office holders in the Ukrainian lands, see Karol Maleczyński, *Urzednicy grodzcy i ziemscy lwowscy w latach 1352–1783* (Lviv, 1938) (Zabytki Dziejowe, Towarzystwo Naukowe we Lwowie, 6, no. 1); Leon Białkowski, "Urzędnicy ziemscy podolscy wieku XVI i pocz. XVII," *Rocznik Towarzystwa Heraldycznego we Lwowie* 8 (1926–27) [publ. 1928]: 174–80; Maurycy Dzieduszycki, "Starostowie ruscy i lwowscy," *Przewodnik Naukowy i Literacki* 3 (1875): 428–45; K[azimierz] P[ułaski], "Wojewodowie kijowscy w XV i XVI wieku," *Przewodnik Naukowy i Literacki* 4 (1876): 621–40. Considerable material exists in MSS 493 and 494 collected by J. W. Smoniewski in Biblioteka PAN in Cracow.
81. See Archiwum Główne Akt Dawnych (Warsaw), Tak zwana Metryka Litewska VII–I, "Index actorum publicorum albo regestr xiag y w nich spraw, przywileiów, dekretów królewskich do woiewództw czterech, Kiiowskiego, Wołyńskiego, Bracławskiego y Czerniechowskiego ferowanych y wydanych z Kancellariey Koronney, poczawszy od roku Pańskiego 1569 aż do roku 1673 inclusive za staraniem, praca y kosztem własnym urodzonego Stefana Kazimierza Hankiewicza IKM 1673."
82. For works on the Lithuanian statutes, see Okinshevich, *The Law*. A recent work that examines the relationship of law and practice in the Ukrainian territories is Oswald P. Backus, "Mortgages, Alienations, and Redemptions. The Rights in Land of the Nobility in Sixteenth Century Lithuanian and Muscovite Law and Practice Compared," *Forschungen zur osteuropäischen Geschichte* 18 (1973): 139–67. For the Grand Duchy of Lithuania, Backus concentrates on Volhynia and observes many similarities in the privileges gained by the nobilities of Lithuania and Muscovy.
83. On the Lutske Tribunal, see the articles by M. N. Iasinsky in *Chteniia v Istoricheskom obshchestve Nestora Letopistsa*: "Lutskii tribunal, kak vysshaia sudebnaia instantsiia dlia Volynskogo, Bratslavskogo i Kievskogo voevodstva v poslednei chetverti XVI v.," 14 (1900), pt. 2: 3–72 and "Materialy dlia istorii Lutskogo tribunala (1578–1589)," 13 (1899), pt. 3: 3–34. The lapsing of the separate tribunal at Lutske was long a matter of particular discontent. See Jabłonowski, *Źródła dziejowe* 6, cvii.
84. *Źródła dziejowe* 21 (1894): *Wyciągi z summaryusza aktów trybunalskich* (for the Kiev and Bratslav palatinates).
85. In particular, *Arkhiv Iugo-Zapadnoi Rossii* and *Akta grodzkie i ziemskie.*
86. *Opis aktovnoi knigi Kievskogo tsentralnogo arkhiva oznachennoi po spisku onogo* ..., publ. Kievskii tsentralnyi arkhiv, 60 vols. (Kiev, 1869–1913). See L. A. Protsenko, "Aktovi knyhy iak dzherelo do vyvchennia spetsialnykh istorychnykh dystsyplin," *Istorychni dzherela ta ikh vykorystannia* 1 (1964): 52–62.
87. See the articles by Zdzisław Kaczmarczyk, "Typ i forma państwa polskiego w okresie demokracji szlacheckiej," *Odrodzenie w Polsce*, 5 vols. (Warsaw, 1955–8) 1: *Historia*, ed. Stanisław Arnold, 479–528, and "Oligarchia magnacka w Polsce jako forma państwa," *VIII Powszechny Zjazd Historyków Polskich w Krakowie 14–17 września 1958*, 7 (Warsaw, 1959),

61–76. Also, see Władysław Czapliński, "Rzady oligarchii w Polsce nowożytnej," *Przegląd Historyczny* 52 (1961): 445–65.

88. Frank E. Sysyn, "Ukrainian-Polish Relations in the Seventeenth Century: The Role of National Consciousness and National Conflict in the Khmelnytsky Movement," in Peter J. Potichnyj, ed., *Poland and Ukraine: Past and Present* (Edmonton-Toronto, 1980), 58–82. In addition to the literature cited in the article, see Władysław Czapliński, "Myśl polityczna w dobie kontrreformacji (1573–1655)," *Wiek XVII. Kontrreformacja. Barok*, ed. Janusz Pelc (Wrocław, 1970), 39–54; *Swojskość i cudoziemszczyzna w dziejach kultury polskiej*, ed. Zofia Stefanowska (Warsaw, 1973); the sections on Lithuania in Wisner, *Najjaśniejsza Rzeczpospolita*; and Tomasz Venclova, "Mit o poczatku," *Teksty*, no. 4 (1974): 104–16.

89. For short-term influences, see Andrzej Kamiński, "The Cossack Experiment in *Szlachta* Democracy in the Polish-Lithuanian Commonwealth—The Hadiach (*Hadziacz*) Union," *Harvard Ukrainian Studies* 1, no. 2 (1977): 178–97. For long-term influences, see Zenon Kohut, "A Gentry Democracy within an Autocracy: The Politics of Hryhorii Poletyka (1723/25–1784)," in *Harvard Ukrainian Studies* 3–4 (1979–80): 507–19.

Zenon E. Kohut

Problems in Studying the Post-Khmelnytsky Ukrainian Elite (1650s to 1830s)

The study of elites has become a major task of modern sociology and political science. Its popularity is due to the social scientist's growing realization of an intrinsic link between modernization and social change. In attempting to assess the direction and intensity of social change, the social scientist frequently looks for clues in the nature of the elite. The role of the elite, its structure, the extent to which it is opened or closed to new members, the way it exercises power, the degree to which it is accountable to the rest of society and its ideological presuppositions—all these factors are considered crucial in answering such basic questions about society as whether it is democratic or authoritarian, whether it has a potential for social order or disorder and whether it is politically stable or unstable.

While the social scientist focuses primarily on modern or modernizing societies, the historian must also deal with traditional societies. Historians have long recognized that from early modern times to the twentieth century, the social structure of Europe underwent a profound transformation. Most, whether Marxist or non-Marxist, have agreed that during the period social classes replaced a society defined by orders (legally recognized estates). However, with its emphasis on capitalism, industrialization, market economy and class struggle, the Marxist interpretation offered little for the understanding of a traditional pre-industrial elite. Thus, for a long period, social historians wrote descriptive studies of recognized nobilities rather than applying the concept of elites. Recently, the social historian has turned again to the social sciences for aid in studying pre-industrial traditional elites. What differentiates the new social historian of elites from the conventional student of European nobilities is his manner of approach. He views the social structure as a system, the criteria for determining an elite being not merely legal, but dependent upon the function or roles of various groups within the social system. Such an approach permits a closer scrutiny of existing elites, a greater level of generalization, and provides the methodology for comparative analysis. For example, in a recent study, Peter Burke was able to compare the nobility of Venice with the non-noble elite of Amsterdam on the basis of function within the society.[1]

Most social historians accept Max Weber's three criteria of class (wealth), status (estate) and party (power) in ranking people within a society. Class refers to an individual's economic position, status denotes his prestige in society, and party defines his place in the political order.[2] The subsequent theoretical literature on elites has, to date, made little impact on the social historian. Vilfredo Pareto made the historian more aware of the multiplicity of elites (military elite, political elite, economic—rentiers and speculators) and their "circulation" (ascendancy or descendancy) as a mechanism of social equilibrium.[3] Gaetano Mosco and C. Wright Mills focused on the problem of power and came to the conclusion that a "ruling class" or "governing elite" rules society.[4] Brilliant as these analyses may be, they operate at such an abstract level that they offer little practical guidance for the social historian. On the whole, the social historian of traditional elites is primarily concerned with the overlap of status, wealth and power. In addition, he is interested in how access to the elite is regulated, in whether a specific life-style emerges and in the development of certain attitudes, including a political outlook.

In European society under the old regime, the greatest congruence of wealth, status and power was enjoyed by the nobility or a group functionally similar to a legally recognized nobility. Even a cursory glance at the nobility in Ukraine reveals two basic problems. First, for long periods of history non-Ukrainian nobilities predominated in Ukraine. Second, when a Ukrainian nobility or functionally similar group did exist, it was soon incorporated into the Polish or Russian aristocracies and at least partially assimilated into a non-Ukrainian culture. In a traditional society, in which political leadership was dominated by the aristocracy, the absence of a native nobility or the assimilation of the native elite to another culture meant the lack or loss of national political representation. In the Ukrainian case, as Ivan L. Rudnytsky has pointed out, this led to a rupture in historical continuity and the reduction of the Ukrainian people to what some historians call a "non-historical" nationality.[5]

A Ukrainian elite which functioned as a nobility developed in the Hetmanate. It evolved after the Khmelnytsky revolution and was incorporated at the end of the eighteenth century into the Russian nobility. As a result, the Poltava and Chernihiv provinces—the territory of the former Hetmanate—contained a native Ukrainian nobility. According to the first all-Russian census, taken in 1897, 68 per cent of the hereditary nobles of Poltava province and 41 per cent of the hereditary nobles of Chernihiv province listed Ukrainian as their native language. This percentage far exceeded the number of Ukrainian-speaking nobles for any other Ukrainian territory in the Russian empire.[6] As bearers of a certain historical tradition, the nobles of the Hetmanate provide a modicum of continuity from the post-Khmelnytsky period well into modern times.

Having indicated the importance of the Hetmanate's elite, let us turn to the state of research. Although numerous studies have dealt with various aspects of the elite, there is no single comprehensive work of synthesis covering the entire period. Nor is it possible to write such a monograph without substantial additional research. But before examining what has been studied and what could and should be studied, let us first consider the general attitudes of the historians who have treated the topic.

The earliest writings about the elite were produced by members of that elite and their descendants. These works were to honour ancestors and to establish an indisputable case for considering the Ukrainian elite a genuine hereditary nobility. As such, they cannot be considered scholarly. Yet, the works of the aristocrats do provide valuable information about the composition and outlook of the elite.[7]

The first professional historians to study the elite were the populists. On the whole, they were not as interested in the elite as in its antithesis, the peasantry. The populists viewed the whole post-Khmelnytsky era as a struggle of the masses (peasantry and rank-and-file Cossacks) for freedom and social justice against an exploitative and parasitical elite. Oleksandra Iefymenko, who wrote the only overall synthesis on the subject (*Malorusskoe dvorianstvo i ego sudba*), asserted that after the Khmelnytsky revolution the old order was swept away and Ukrainian society was equalized, but that after several generations the new Cossack elite was able to usurp for itself the socio-economic position once enjoyed by the Polish *szlachta*.[8] Iefymenko condemned the Ukrainian elite for having betrayed all political ideals—i.e., maintaining Ukrainian autonomy—in order to enserf the populace. Iefymenko's study was followed by the much more detached work of Dmytro Miller. As a legal historian, Miller was primarily concerned with the juridical steps by which the Ukrainian elite was incorporated into the Russian nobility and the struggle of the Ukrainian aristocrats for imperial recognition of their titles.[9] But writing when populism was at its peak, Miller, in the end, came to conclusions similar to Iefymenko's. This attitude was shared by Oleksander Lazarevsky—the most respected and prolific historian of Cossack Ukraine. Lazarevsky was the first scholar to offer proof that the Ukrainian peasants were gradually enserfed by the elite, well before Catherine II's *ukaz* of 1783. Although he did not study the Ukrainian elite specifically as a social group, in over four hundred works Lazarevsky touched upon every aspect of its life; of particular value is his description of the elite's offices and biographical information about the elite's leading personalities and major families.[10] In general, the populists produced relatively few works of synthesis. However, they did publish archival materials and contributed a number of monographs on the Hetmanate's social structure, which still remain the basic sources for any student of the Ukrainian elite.

At the beginning of the twentieth century, a new generation of Ukrainian historians revolted against populism and followed a new "statist" orientation. They viewed the Hetmanate as a virtually independent state and concentrated their research on such indicators of this status as foreign relations, internal administration and law. Study of the elite per se was revolutionized by Viacheslav Lypynsky, who was the first to discover that considerable numbers of the *szlachta* had joined Khmelnytsky and that the Khmelnytsky revolution did not totally sweep away the old order.[11] Subsequently, interest in the elite primarily centred on how this elite either defended or failed to defend the state interests of the Hetmanate. Relatively little attention was paid to the elite as a social group. Most works concentrated on political history, particularly of the earlier period when the Hetmanate still played a political role. In dealing with the later period, the state-school historians studied various instances of opposition to imperial integration. Special mention must be made of Oleksander Ohloblyn, who did much to identify various oppositionist circles and contributed to the biographies of many members of the elite.[12] Because of its outlook, the state school could flourish only in interwar Galicia and in emigration.

In Soviet Ukraine, several schools coincided and overlapped during the 1920s. When writing about manufacturing in the Hetmanate, Ohloblyn represented a school of economic history, but his work on political thought in the Mazepa era shows the clear imprint of the state school.[13] Economic history was stimulated by Marxism but was not necessarily Marxist in approach. Mykhailo Slabchenko and his students contributed most to research on the economic history of the Hetmanate.[14] A Marxist interpretation was offered by Matvii Iavorsky, but he did not dwell much on either the Hetmanate or its elite. The topic was much more fruitfully pursued by a juridical school of historians interested in the institutions of the Hetmanate. In this respect, Lev Okinshevych's studies of the Council of Officers and Notable Military Fellows are of particular importance.[15]

All these trends were cut short by the liquidation of Ukrainian scholarship in the 1930s and the adoption of an official Soviet interpretation. Although on some topics this interpretation occasionally changes, it has been consistent and uniform in reference to the elite. Following the populist tradition, Soviet historians have emphasized the development of serfdom, Ukrainian class antagonism and the Ukrainian elite's alliance with the Russian autocracy in order to exploit the masses (although any sign of opposition to the autocracy is also considered treason). The Soviets have not only condemned the Ukrainian elite, but also have stopped studying it. Their contribution has been limited to a few new details about Cossack and peasant uprisings.[16]

If one accepts the sociological model that status, power and wealth are the basic dimensions in studying any elite, one must conclude that, at various times, Ukrainian historiography has been remarkably one-dimensional. The aristocrats were interested in status, the populist and Soviet scholars were concerned with wealth and the state-school historians dealt solely with politics. Only in the 1920s and early 1930s was there a genuine multiplicity of approaches and even some overlap between them. Since no work can present a problem in all its dimensions, it is perfectly legitimate to concentrate on one aspect of a topic. However, it can hardly be conducive to scholarship for all historians to focus on one aspect to the exclusion of all others. A meaningful synthesis about the Ukrainian elite could only be achieved by undertaking serious research covering all three dimensions of the model accepted here.

All three factors were regulated by two centres: one in the Hetmanate, the other first in Moscow and then in St. Petersburg. The structure of the elite and the hierarchy of ranks were, in the end, determined by the Hetmanate's central authorities. Moreover, the Hetmanate distributed land to the elite or, in rare instances, confiscated land from them. Those in power attempted to exclude their political enemies. Thus, the Hetmanate's elite, particularly the upper echelons, struggled to control its institutions, which, in turn, arbitrated questions of power, status and wealth for at least another part of the elite. While several factions of the elite struggled to control the local centre, they had little influence over the second more powerful centre in St. Petersburg. The imperial government was free to recognize or deny the status of the Ukrainian elite. It could question the rights of ownership of estates. The tsar could and did demote members of the elite, confiscate their estates and exile or imprison them.[17] Therefore, the social, economic and political position of the elite was part of a dynamic system, arbitrated by two unequal power centres.

With these important qualifications in mind, let us now turn to the first dimension of social rank, namely, status. By status we mean the amount of prestige or honour one enjoys by virtue of occupying a certain position in society. The position may be defined by custom or law. In the Hetmanate, one's position was recognized largely by custom, but customary practices were beginning to enter into the law codes, particularly the *Laws by Which the Little Russian People Are Judged*.[18]

The social group in the Hetmanate which enjoyed the greatest honour and prestige was the elite that we are considering. By the eighteenth century it was called "Little Russian *szlachta*" and was composed of several subgroups. First was the genuine *szlachta* stemming from the pre-Khmelnytsky era. As Lypynsky pointed out, significant numbers of the *szlachta* had joined the Khmelnytsky uprising. However, it had been assumed that these *szlachta* elements did not survive the period of the Ruin and the transfer to Left-Bank Ukraine. Subsequent studies by Serhii Ivanytsky-Vasylenko and Lev Okinshevych indicated that a considerable number of *szlachta* had survived and prospered in the Hetmanate, particularly in the most northern part, which was touched least by the Khmelnytsky upheavals. Moreover, there are indications that the *szlachta* continued to immigrate into the Hetmanate, especially from Belorussia.[19] The question of a genuine *szlachta* presence in the Hetmanate is important, for it could help explain the adoption of *szlachta* political values by the entire elite.

The rest of the Little Russian *szlachta* was composed of Cossack officers and notables, but the clergy and urban patriciate was also represented. In Poland-Lithuania, many Roman Catholic priests had been considered noblemen and this tradition had been copied by the Orthodox clergy of the Hetmanate. On the whole, the clergy was recognized as having *szlachta* status and certain *szlachta* economic privileges but, except for some members of the higher clergy, it neither participated in the Hetmanate's politics nor was it included in the fairly elaborate ranking of the Ukrainian elite.[20] In 1757 Hetman Kyrylo Rozumovsky ordered that the sons of archpriests who did not enter the priesthood could join the lowest rank of the Notable Military Fellows—the secular system of ranks—but that sons of ordinary priests should be registered as free Cossacks.[21] This indicates that the clergy did not enjoy social rank or status equal to that of office-holders but were a subgroup only marginally connected to the *szlachta*.

While some *szlachta* rights for priests were recognized, the urban patriciate had no claim to *szlachta* status. It could enter the "Little Russian *szlachta*" only by assuming an office in the Hetmanate's administration. There are indications that at the end of the seventeenth and the beginning of the eighteenth centuries, a number of merchants and craftsmen were able to enter the elite or, at least, had familial ties with the elite.[22] Unfortunately, the social roles of the urban patriciate and clergy have not as yet been studied. My very preliminary observations are based on an impressionistic reading of the sources.

Honour and prestige were not meted out equally to all who claimed to belong to the Little Russian *szlachta*, but depended on either government office or rank in the Society of Notable Military Fellows. A person with a *szlachta* title stemming from Polish times could quite easily be ranked below someone who had risen through the Cossack military hierarchy. The institution for determining social rank, rather than political office, was the Society of Notable Military Fellows, consisting of landowners who could require peasants to perform labour obligations (peasants were not as yet serfs because they could seek better conditions by moving to another landlord). In return for this basic *szlachta* right, notables were required to perform certain duties and were listed in an official register. When a notable assumed a military or administrative position, he was dropped from the register, since he was no longer capable of performing the required duties. With the exception of the infirm or aged, all Notable Military Fellows were liable for the military levy in times of war and for various incidental duties during times of peace, such as service as couriers, judges or criminal investigators.

Since virtually all administrative and military officers were filled by Notable Military Fellows, social status was closely connected with power. By the 1720s the structure of the Notable Military Fellows had evolved into an elaborate hereditary hierarchy of three levels. The highest ranking notables were called the Fellows of the Standard (*bunchukovi tovaryshi*). They were under the direct authority of the hetman and thus immune from the Hetmanate's local administration. The highest officials of the land—the general staff, the colonels and regimental staffs—were drawn almost exclusively from the ranks of the Fellows of the Standard. Below the Fellows of the Standard came a large middle layer called the Military Fellows (*viiskovi tovaryshi*), who were under the jurisdiction of the Hetmanate's central administration. The company captains and senior chancellery clerks usually came from the Military Fellows. At the base of the Society of Military Fellows were an even larger number of mere Fellows of the Banner (*znachkovi tovaryshi*). They provided the administration with lower company officers and clerks.

Lev Okinshevych was the first to study the Society of Notable Military Fellows and to show that it was primarily a hierarchy of social rank—or status—rather than a peculiar Cossack military office.[23] Because the notables performed state service, many historians have treated them as state officials, although they were unsure whether to place them in the military or administrative hierarchy. The correlations between the ranks of notables and certain offices are mine. If they stand, then I believe that the basic relationship between the status hierarchy and the power hierarchy has been resolved. We can then proceed to tackle questions regarding the openness or impenetrability of the elite and social mobility into and within the elite.

Considering the present state of research on status and power, the next step, in my opinion, should be to establish or reconstruct memberships in the elite. There exists a good base of published sources for such a project, including works by Modzalevsky, Myloradovych, Pavlovsky and Lazarevsky.[24] That it can be done has been demonstrated by George Gajecky, who was able to reconstruct the central and regimental staffs.[25] As a result of Gajecky's project we now possess lists of the most important office-holders throughout the existence of the Hetmanate. If these could be correlated with lists of Notable Military Fellows, we would know the membership of the entire elite. Unfortunately, lists of Notable Military Fellows have not been published and we are not quite sure how many are available in Soviet archives. But even without the Soviet archives, it is possible to establish a fairly comprehensive list of the elite, at least for a certain period. If such lists were available for several periods, then a simple comparison could tell us what new families had entered the elite, the length of time it took for a family to move from one level of the Notable Military Fellows to the next, whether certain families controlled a particular office, whether certain families fell in the status and power hierarchies and many related questions. Ideally, the status and power hierarchies should also be correlated with wealth. However, as will be shown subsequently, the current state of research does not permit the utilization of this category. Consequently, let us first determine the membership of the elite and their rates of mobility. Only then can one concentrate on explaining the reasons for such mobility.

The elite's power was exercised not only through the possession of offices, but also through control of institutions. In the Hetmanate, views of the elite found expression through a quasi-parliamentary body called the Council of Officers. It evolved from a council of military officers of the Cossack Army into a representative body of the "Little Russian *szlachta*." Meeting between Christmas and Epiphany and during the Easter holidays, the council discussed all important pending matters, especially foreign affairs, finance, taxation and judicial reforms. By the mid-eighteenth century such councils met for longer sessions with elaborate agendas, and the hetman did not initiate important judicial or civil reforms without the approval of a council. Finally, the council meeting in 1763 petitioned Catherine II to approve a regular Diet of the Nobility for the Hetmanate.

The Council of Officers is only the most outstanding example of an institution through which the elite could exercise power. Others included the general staff, the various judicial bodies, the central treasury and the regimental staffs. Fortunately, thanks to the juridical school of the 1920s, many of these institutions have been studied. Undoubtedly, the most important scholar of institutional history is Lev Okinshevych, who was the first to trace the evolution of the Council of Officers into a quasi-parliamentary body of the aristocracy and to give a comprehensive analysis of the general staff.[26] Yet, many questions about the nature and limits of power as expressed through institutions remain unresolved. For example, the exact constitutional relationship between the hetman and the Council of Officers remains unclear. Was the hetman obliged to call a council on a regular basis? How, exactly, was representation determined? How were decisions made? Did the Russian authorities influence the relationship between the hetman and the council? Similar questions could be asked about other institutions. Thus, while we are informed about the basic functions of institutions and governmental offices, knowledge about the way power was distributed among various institutions controlled by the elite awaits further research and elaboration.

The local power enjoyed by the Ukrainian elite was also limited by an outside force, the Russian central administration. The relationship between the two power centres is regularly the subject of political history. Although many more details about this relationship are yet to be discovered, the general contours are well known, and I shall not dwell upon them here. Instead, I would like to mention a few words about the political outlook of the elite which, to a large extent, motivated its political behaviour.

From the time of Khmelnytsky to the end of the eighteenth century, the political outlook of the elite changed according to political circumstance and alterations within its structure. In the early stages, the elite's orientation was mainly that of the Cossacks, who in a patrimonial relationship served their king or tsar in return for cash payments and economic prerogatives. The Cossacks did not claim that they represented a specific land or manifest any particular territorial patriotism. The successful Khmelnytsky revolution, the influx of *szlachta* members into the Cossack elite and the reality of an existing state forced a revaluation of the basic political presuppositions. The Cossack view was challenged by a territorial concept, the Great Principality of Rus', as expressed in the Treaty of Hadiach (1658). According to the treaty, the Rus' principality was to have been a separate state, with its own administration, finances and currency, and it was to have joined Poland and Lithuania in a tripartite commonwealth. The three equal partners would have had a common king and Diet. In the Diet, the *szlachta* of Rus' (expanded by the ennoblement of Cossack officers) was to have been the representative of the territorial interests of Rus'—thus functioning as a representative nobility of the European type. With conditions unacceptable to both Muscovy and the rank-and-file Cossacks, the Union of Hadiach failed.

During the Mazepa era, when the Cossack officers began to assume the role of a *szlachta*, the idea of a contractual relationship between a monarch and a nobility representing a specific territory re-emerged, but it was challenged by the old Cossack notion of a contractual relationship between a monarch and the Cossack army. Only in the mid-eighteenth century, with the development of a quasi-parliament, did the Little Russian *szlachta* begin to express the concept that it was responsible for the territorial integrity and constitutional arrangement of its *patria*, the Hetmanate. But this breakthrough in political thought occurred when the Russian empire was being transformed from a patrimonial into a centralistic, absolutist state—a state that could not tolerate an autonomous territorial elite.

On the whole, the study of political thought is fairly well developed. For the Khmelnytsky period, too much attention has been focused on the nature of the Pereiaslav treaty, and not enough on the political outlook and expectations of the Cossack officer class. The Hadiach Union has been thoroughly analysed by Mykhailo Hrushevsky and more recently by Andrzej Kamiński.[27] Political thought in the Mazepa era has been elucidated by Oleksander Ohloblyn and Orest Subtelny.[28] I have analysed mid-eighteenth century constitutional thought, particularly the territorial *szlachta* concept.[29] Early nineteenth-century political thought, represented by such works as *Istoriia Rusov*, has been covered by Ohloblyn, Andrii Iakovliv and many other scholars.[30] Therefore, while many details and undercurrents still need further study, the major steps in the evolution of political thought are now known. The next step should be a synthesis of political ideas from the time of Khmelnytsky to the early nineteenth century.

Let us now turn to the third criterion for ranking elites, namely wealth. Paradoxically, after a century of research by populist and Soviet historians, this criterion remains the least known. The populists had carefully established the legal steps by which the peasants had become enserfed. The second discovery of the populist historians was that the Ukrainian elite had gradually accumulated more and more land. The figures which are given vary and are often contradictory, depending on the sources used. But the trend is unmistakable: by the 1780s crown lands (rank lands) given temporarily for service had been greatly reduced; the plots of the free peasantry had virtually disappeared; and the Cossack homesteads had become much smaller and more impoverished.[31] Although no exact figures exist, it seems that through purchase, outright seizure and court actions, the seigniors (the elite and monasteries) were able to obtain the greater part of the Hetmanate's cultivated land area.

Having made these important discoveries, the populist historians smugly condemned the elite and saw no need for further study of its landholdings. Soviet scholars have followed suit by focusing exclusively on peasant and Cossack resistance to socio-economic exploitation. Peasant revolts, landlords' seizure of peasant lands and court cases over land and status (whether one is Cossack or peasant, free or dependent) have become the mainstay of Soviet historiography.[32] But these studies tell us virtually nothing about the wealth of the elite or seigniorial economics. What was the size of a typical estate? How many peasants worked on it? What were its products? Were the products consumed on the estate or was there a surplus for a market? These important questions—basic for any Marxist approach to history—seem of no concern to the Soviet historian of the Hetmanate.

In researching any aspect of the Hetmanate, one inevitably comes across documentation that some families were exceedingly wealthy. For instance, the Kochubei, Galagan, Lyzohub, Myklashevsky, Markovych, Mazepa, Skoropadsky, Apostol and Rozumovsky families owned hundreds of estates and had up to thirty thousand peasants attached to the family manor. But these were the wealthiest and among the most powerful families in the Hetmanate. My impression is that the vast majority of the elite owned middle-sized estates, probably smaller with fewer dependent peasants than the typical central Russian or Right-Bank Ukrainian estate. This impressionistic view has been partially confirmed in a recent pioneering work by E. M. Kabuzan and S. M. Toritsky, who calculated the number of serfs per nobleman for all regions of the Russian empire. From this work it is clear that between 1782 and 1795 there were more nobles and fewer serfs in the Hetmanate than in any other region of the empire. In fact, per nobleman, the Ukrainian elite averaged only one-third the number of serfs owned by the nobles in the central Russian regions.[33]

The number of serfs per nobleman is a rather crude estimate of wealth.

More refined studies are necessary. As is well known, the Hetmanate underwent numerous censuses and revisions throughout its existence. Most of them contained material concerning landholdings. Some parts of these censuses have been published and various works based on these statistical materials have appeared. I once attempted to collect all these published sources to see what could be learned about the landholdings of the elite. I soon discovered that the sources rarely used the same categories (homesteads, estates, houses) and never seemed to cover the same geographical region over any significant period of time. But such a study is feasible if one has access to archival materials, particularly the 1764 Rumiantsev census. This is proved by M. Tkachenko's brilliant analysis of economic relations in the Kaniv company of the Pereiaslav regiment, published in 1926.[34] Unfortunately, it covers only a tiny part of the Hetmanate, and it is essential to investigate the landholdings for at least one or two full regiments before coming to any general conclusions.

In addition to the major concerns of status, power and wealth, the social historian is also interested in the education, culture and life-style of an elite. Sources that provide invaluable materials for this topic are family papers, memoirs and diaries; works describing the educational system in eighteenth-century Ukraine, St. Petersburg and Moscow; lists of students in West European universities; and analyses of private libraries. Space, however, does not permit me to discuss the culture or life-style of the Ukrainian elite. Instead, I would like to pose one concluding question which should be of particular concern to the historian of Ukraine—the relationship between the traditional elite and modern Ukraine.

If the elite of the Hetmanate provides one of the few instances of a traditional Ukrainian aristocracy surviving into modern times, then its impact on modern Ukrainian history becomes a crucial question in determining the degree of continuity or discontinuity in the Ukrainian historical process. As with many questions of Ukrainian history, it has not been thoroughly studied, but only touched upon by scholars.[35] In dealing with this problem, it must be remembered that the Hetmanate was only a small part of Ukraine and its elite represented an even smaller part of the Ukrainian population. Other social groups and other regions played a crucial role in the formation of a modern Ukraine.

In my opinion, three questions about the role of the Hetmanate's elite merit particular attention: (1) What was the impact of its political and historical traditions on Ukrainian political thought and historical consciousness? (2) What was its role in the formation of a Ukrainian intelligentsia? (3) What was its impact on the Ukrainian cultural and literary revival?

My own rather limited research has convinced me that the elite's political and historical traditions had considerable influence on subsequent political thought—particularly on the Cyril and Methodius Brotherhood—as well as on the preservation of a historical consciousness and on the formation of modern Ukrainian historiography.[36] As far as an intelligentsia is concerned, Omeljan Pritsak's statistics on the social and national origins of the students of Kharkiv University in the first decades of its existence indicate that virtually all its Ukrainian students were either nobles from the Hetmanate (strangely enough, very few were from Sloboda Ukraine) or sons of priests primarily from Right-Bank Ukraine.[37] Moreover, as is well-known, some of the first writers in Ukrainian, including Ivan Kotliarevsky and Ievhen Hrebinka, were nobles from the former Hetmanate. If one adds scholars, particularly historians, to their number, then it seems that the Hetmanate's elite did play a significant role in the creation of a Ukrainian intelligentsia. But the elite's role does not stop here. Has anyone ever considered who purchased the publications of the early intelligentsia? It is becoming more and more apparent that many were bought by the nobles of Little Russia; certainly the nobles subsidized them.[38] In fact, Taras Shevchenko's emancipation, education and the publication of the *Kobzar* would not have been possible without political influence and subsidies provided by "Little Russian" nobles.[39] These are only a few instances of what can and must be thoroughly explored.

In conclusion, our knowledge of the post-Khmelnytsky elite is fragmentary. Bits and pieces of the mosaic have been uncovered but a great deal of the picture is still missing. Some of the missing pieces—particularly those regarding status and power—can be supplied by a judicious interrogation of published sources. Others—mainly dealing with wealth and economics—can be discovered only with extensive archival research. So far, Western scholars have not been given access to this rich archival fund while our Soviet colleagues seem unable or unwilling to tap this resource. Therefore, we must do the best we can on the basis of whatever resources we can muster. The Ukrainian elite, kin to a European nobility, is too rare and important a phenomenon for us to ignore.

Notes

1. P. Burke, *Venice and Amsterdam: A Study of Seventeenth-Century Elites* (London, 1974).
2. M. Weber, *Essays in Sociology* (New York, 1958).
3. V. Pareto, *The Mind and Society*, ed. Arthur Livingston, 4 vols. (New York, 1956).

4. G. Mosca, *The Ruling Class* (New York, 1935); C. Wright Mills, *The Power Elite* (New York, 1956).
5. I. L. Rudnytsky, "The Role of the Ukraine in Modern History," *The Development of the USSR*, ed. D. W. Treadgold (Seattle, 1964), 211–28.
6. Tsentralnyi statisticheskii komitet, *Pervaia Vseobshchaia perepis naseleniia Rossiiskoi Imperii*, 89 vols. (St. Petersburg, 1899–1905). According to the census, the following percentages (computed by the author) of hereditary nobles claimed Ukrainian as their native language: (1) Chernihiv province—41 per cent, 48 "Chernigovskaia guberniia" (St. Petersburg, 1905), 308; (2) Poltava province—68 per cent, 33 "Poltavskaia guberniia" (St. Petersburg, 1904), 286; (3) Volhynia province—26 per cent, 8 "Volynskaia guberniia" (St. Petersburg, 1904), 248; (4) Podillia province—30 per cent, 32 "Podolskaia guberniia" (St. Petersburg, 1904), 256; (5) Kherson province—13 per cent, 47 "Khersonskaia guberniia" (St. Petersburg, 1904), 258; (7) Kharkiv province—14 per cent, 46 "Kharkovskaia guberniia" (St. Petersburg, 1903), 270; (8) Tavrida province—4 per cent, 41 "Tavricheskaia guberniia" (St. Petersburg, 1904), 274; (9) Katerynoslav province—18 per cent, 13 "Ekaterinoslavskaia guberniia" (St. Petersburg, 1904), 206.
7. The historiography of the aristocrats has been discussed in Z. E. Kohut, "The Abolition of Ukrainian Autonomy (1763–1786): A Case Study in the Integration of a Non-Russian Area into the Empire" (Ph. D. thesis, University of Pennsylvania, 1975), 323–33, and in A. Lazarevsky, "Prezhnie izyskateli Malorusskoi stariny," *Kievskaia starina* (hereafter *KS*), no. 2 (1895): 170–94.
8. A. Efimenko, "Malorusskoe dvorianstvo i ego sudba," *Iuzhnaia Rus'. Ocherki, issledovaniia i zametki* 1 (St. Petersburg, 1905), 145–200.
9. D. Miller, "Ocherki iz istorii i iuridicheskogo byta staroi Malorossii. Prevrashchenie malorusskoi starshiny v dvorianstvo," *KS* 1897, no. 1, 1–31; no. 2, 188–220; no. 3, 351–74; no. 4, 1–47.
10. A comprehensive list of Lazarevsky's works has been published by M. Tkachenko, "Spysok prats O. M. Lazarevskoho i prats pro nioho," *Ukrainskyi arkheohrafichnyi zbirnyk* 2 (1927): li–lxxx.
11. W. Lipiński, ed., *Z dziejôw Ukrainy* (Cracow, 1912); V. Lypynsky, *Ukraina na perelomi, 1657–1659* (Vienna, 1920).
12. The most important works of O. Ohloblyn dealing with the elite are the following: *Liudy staroi Ukrainy* (Munich, 1959); *Hetman Mazepa ta ioho doba* (New York, 1960); *Opanas Lobysevych (1732–1805)* (Munich, 1966); "Ukrainian Autonomists of the 1780's and 1790's and Count P. A. Rumyantsev-Zadunaysky," *Annals of the Ukrainian Academy of Arts and Sciences in the United States* 6, no. 3–4 (1958): 1313–26. For a comprehensive listing of Ohloblyn's works, see L. Vynar, "Bibliohrafiia prats prof. d-ra Oleksandra Ohloblyna," *Zbirnyk na poshanu prof. d-ra Oleksandra Ohloblyna* (New York, 1977), 93–126.
13. A. P. Ogloblin, *Ocherkii istorii ukrainskoi fabriki; Manufaktura v*

Getmanshchine (Kiev, 1925); O. Ohloblyn, "Do istorii ukrainskoi politychnoi dumky na pochatku XVIII viku," *Zapysky istorychno-filolohichnoho viddilu Vseukrainskoi Akademii nauk* (henceforth *ZIFV VAN*) 19 (1929): 231–41.

14. M. Slabchenko, *Khoziaistvo Getmanshchiny v XVII–XVIII st.*, 4 vols. (Odessa, 1925).
15. L. Okinshevych, *Tsentralni ustanovy Ukrainy-Hetmanshchyny XVII–XVIII vv.*, part 2: *Rada starshyn,* Pratsi Komisii dlia vyuchuvannia istorii zakhidno-ruskoho ta ukrainskoho prava 8 (Kiev, 1930); L. Okinshevych, *Znachne viiskove tovarystvo v Ukraini-Hetmanshchyni XVII–XVIII st.*, Zapysky Naukovoho tovarystva im. Shevchenka 157 (Munich, 1948).
16. The best general Soviet work is by V. A. Diadychenko, *Narysy suspilno-politychnoho ustroiu Livoberezhnoi Ukrainy kintsia XVII-pochatku XVIII st.* (Kiev, 1959). Other studies include: I. O. Hurzhii, *Borotba selian i robitnykiv Ukrainy proty feodalno-kriposnytskoho hnitu (Z 80-kh rokiv XVIII st. do 1861 r.)* (Kiev, 1958). *Istoriia selianstva Ukrainskoi RSR*, 2 vols. (Kiev, 1967); K. Huslysty, *Turbaivske povstannia* (Kiev, 1947); I. Hurzhii, *Povstannia selian v Turbaiakh (1784–1793)* (Kiev, 1950).
17. For example, the families who had supported Hetman Mazepa's break with Muscovy suffered such consequences. See O. Ohloblyn, *Hetman Ivan Mazepa*, 369, note 49. Moreover, tsarist agents pursued even those members of the elite who had escaped to Western Europe, particularly Mazepa's relative Andrii Voinarovsky. See L. Vynar, *Andrii Voinarovsky* (Munich, 1962).
18. This codification of laws was completed in 1743. A brief appended to the code suggests that penalties be adjusted to take into account the rank of both the victim and offender and lists of the hierarchy of ranks in the Hetmanate. The code has been published in A. Kistiakovsky, ed., *Prava po kotorym suditsia Malorossiiskii narod* (Kiev, 1879). The relevant appendix is to be found on pages 833–8.
19. For the survival of the old *szlachta* and immigration of the *szlachta* from Belorussia, see Okinshevych, *Znachne viiskove tovarystvo*, 5–18, 33–9 and S. Ivanytsky-Vasylenko, "Derzhavske zemlevolodinnia polskoi shliakhty na Hetmanshchyni," *Pratsi Komisii dlia vyuchuvannia istorii zakhidno-ruskoho ta ukrainskoho prava* 1 (Kiev, 1925): 122–80.
20. For example, the brief appended to *The Laws by Which the Little Russian People Are Judged* merely states that clergymen are to be considered as having *szlachta* status, but does not include them in the ranking system. See Kistiakovsky, ed., *Prava po kotorym suditsia*, 833–8.
21. L. Okinshevych, *Lektsii z istorii ukrainskoho prava* (Munich, 1947), 75.
22. Apparently, in the seventeenth century, burghers were connected with the elite and even participated in the Council of Officers. See Okinshevych, *Rada starshyn*, 253.
23. Okinshevych, *Znachne viiskove tovarystvo.*

24. V. L. Modzalevsky, *Malorossiiskii rodoslovnik*, 4 vols. (St. Petersburg, 1904–15); G. A. Miloradovich, *Rodoslovnaia kniga chernigovskogo dvorianstva*, 2 vols. (St. Petersburg, 1901); I. F. Pavlovsky, *Po arkhivnym dannym. K istorii poltavskogo dvorianstva*, 2 vols. (Poltava, 1906). A great many of the over four hundred works of O. Lazarevsky touch upon the life of Ukrainian nobles and cannot be listed here. The following works are in my opinion the most important for studying the elite: "Ocherk stareishikh dvorianskikh rodov v Chernigovskoi gubernii," *Zapiski Chernigovskogo gubernskogo statisticheskogo komiteta* 2 (1868): 35–148; *Sulimovskii arkhiv* (Kiev, 1884); "Ocherki malorossiiskikh familii," *Russkii arkhiv* 1–3 (1875); "Liudy staroi Malorossii," *KS*, 1885: "Lizoguby," no. 1, 101–25; "Miloradovichi," no. 3, 479–98; "Miklashevskie," no. 8, 245–53; "Svechki," no. 8, 253–8.
25. G. Gajecky, *The Cossack Administration of the Hetmanate*, 2 vols. (Cambridge, Mass., 1978).
26. Okinshevych, *Rada starshyn*; L. Okinshevych, "Heneralna starshyna na Livoberezhnii Ukraini XVI–XVII–XVIII st.," *Pratsi Komisii dlia vyuchuvannia istorii zakhidno-ruskoho ta ukrainskoho prava* 2 (1926): 84–171.
27. M. Hrushevsky, *Istoriia Ukrainy–Rusy* 9, part 2 (Kiev, 1931), 292–359; A. Kamiński, "The Cossack Experiment in *Szlachta* Democracy in the Polish-Lithuanian Commonwealth: The Hadiach (Hadziacz) Union," *Harvard Ukrainian Studies* 1, no. 2, (1977): 178–97.
28. O. Ohloblyn, *Hetman Mazepa ta ioho doba*; O. Ohloblyn, "Do istorii ukrainskoi politychnoi dumky"; O. Subtelny, "Mazepa, Peter I, and the Question of Treason," *Harvard Ukrainian Studies* 2, no. 2, (1978): 158–83.
29. Kohut, "The Abolition of Ukrainian Autonomy," 47–58; a fuller treatment is Z. Kohut, "The Ukrainian Elite of the Eighteenth Century and Its Integration into the Russian Nobility," *The Role of the Nobility in Russia and Eastern Europe* (Yale Russian and East European Publications, No. 4), forthcoming.
30. For a thorough review of the varied interpretations as to the authorship and philosophy of *Istoriia Rusov*, see O. Ohloblyn's introduction to a modern Ukrainian translation of the work, *Istoriia Rusiv* (New York, 1956), v–xxix.
31. A. Lazarevsky, *Malorossiiskie pospolitye krestiane (1648–1783 gg.)* (Kiev, 1908); A. Lazarevsky, *Opisanie Staroi Malorossii*, 3 vols. (Kiev, 1888–1902); V. Barvinsky, *Krestiane v Levoberezhnoi Ukraine v XVII–XVIII vv.* (Kharkiv, 1909); V. A. Miakotin, *Ocherki sotsialnoi istorii Ukrainy v XVII–XVIII vv.*, 3 vols. (Prague, 1926).
32. The major Soviet works are listed in note 16.
33. V. M. Kabuzan and S. M. Troitsky, "Izmeneniia v chislennosti, udelnom vese i razmeshchenii dvorianstva v Rossii v 1782–1855 gg.," *Istoriia SSSR*, no. 4, (1971): 153–69. These statistics are corroborated by impressionistic accounts. Iosyp Hermaize provides a good description of the impoverished

petty nobility in his foreword to O. Doroshkevych, ed., *20–40 roky v ukrainskii literaturi* 2 (Kiev, 1924), xi–xii. Recently V. Holobutsky described the estates of the Left-Bank Ukrainian nobles as primarily small to middle size. See V. O. Holobutsky, *Ekonomichna istoriia Ukrainskoi RSR* (Kiev, 1970), 170.

34. M. Tkachenko, "Kanivska sotnia Pereiaslavskoho polku z Rumiantsevskoiu revizieiiu," *ZIFV VAN* 7–8 (1926): 242–308.
35. G. S. N. Luckyj, *Between Gogol and Ševčenko*, Harvard Series in Ukrainian Studies, 8 (Munich, 1971); Kohut, "The Abolition of Ukrainian Autonomy," 281–348; O. Pritsak, "U stolittia narodyn M. Hrushevskoho," *Lysty do pryiateliv*, no. 5–7 (1966): 1–18; I. L. Rudnytsky, "Intellectual Origins of Modern Ukraine," *Annals of the Ukrainian Academy of Arts and Sciences in the United States* 6, no. 3–4 (1958): 1381–1405.
36. Kohut, "The Abolition of Ukrainian Autonomy," 343–7.
37. Professor Omeljan Pritsak of Harvard University compiled these statistics in connection with a course on modern Ukrainian intellectual history. Unfortunately, they have not as yet been published.
38. For a fascinating study of the social profile of Ukrainian book readership, see P. Fylypovych, "Sotsiialne oblychchia ukrainskoho chytacha 30–40 rr. XIX viku," *Pavlo Fylypovych, Literatura, statti, rozvidky, ohliady* (New York, 1971).
39. For a stimulating article about the relationship between Shevchenko and the Ukrainian nobility, see O. Ohloblyn, "Problema ukrainskykh zviazkiv Shevchenka," *Ukrainskyi istoryk*, no. 3–4 (1973): 38–53.

Orest Subtelny

Cossack Ukraine and the Turco-Islamic World

To say that the attitude of the inhabitants of Cossack Ukraine toward the Turco-Islamic world was generally negative is to state the obvious. Every Ukrainian has heard at one time or another, in proverbs, songs or folktales, about the ancient antagonism between the Cossacks and the Turks and Tatars. Even those who have not been exposed to these folk memories can easily deduce that the two societies did not co-exist harmoniously. Common knowledge poses a problem: if at the outset a basic point such as this is taken for granted, what else can one say about Ukrainian attitudes toward the Muslims? We have no startling revisionist argument up our sleeve that might challenge this widespread view. Nor do we have new sources to bring to bear on this topic. But we do hope to contribute to the topic by pointing out nuances in generally held views and elaborating on what has been only vaguely surmised. How precise was the knowledge of the Ukrainians about the Turks? Did different segments of Ukrainian society view this subject differently? How were their attitudes formulated? This paper will address these and similar questions in the hope that by discussing them we can move beyond the bounds of common knowledge.

It is worthwhile to recall the importance of the Turkic element in Ukrainian history. Would Cossackdom have existed without it? If it were not for the Tatars, could Khmelnytsky have succeeded in 1648? Simply in demographic terms, the Tatar impact was staggering. Between the fifteenth and eighteenth centuries Ukraine lost many thousands of people because of their raids. The land would not be called Ukraine ("border territory") if it had not been on the frontier of the Turkic steppe. Indeed, Cossack Ukraine emerged because of the Turkic presence, and as this presence faded in Europe, so too did Ukrainian Cossackdom. In view of the close relationship between the two societies, it is, therefore, necessary to consider how one viewed the other.

From the fifteenth to the seventeenth centuries the Turkish threat was probably the single greatest cause of concern in Europe.[1] In many ways, the confrontation of the Christian and Muslim worlds—Europe's first global conflict—was analogous to the present confrontation of democratic and Communist societies. In Western Europe the conflict was perceived not only as a religious war, but also as one of two competing political and socio-economic systems. Western writers were quick to draw comparisons between the two societies. And the fact that they often found Ottoman ways to be more praiseworthy than their own is convincing proof of how far objective, critical thinking had advanced in the West.[2] One can argue that the extent to which the Turk was perceived accurately in the various lands of Europe was a revealing indication of the given country's political and intellectual sophistication. With this in mind, we may begin to observe how Europe's growing curiosity and knowledge about Turks and Tatars was reflected in Ukraine.[3]

To deal with the Ukrainian perceptions of the Turco-Islamic world one must first distinguish the various types of viewers. There was, first of all, "public opinion" on this subject, that is to say, the views held basically by the Ukrainian peasantry. A second, distinct perspective was that of the Kievan *knyzhnyky* or scholastics. Finally, there were the attitudes of the Ukrainian political elite toward the Ottomans and Tatars.

"Public Opinion"

The primary source for gauging the popular views and attitudes toward the *bisurmeny* (Muslims) are the *dumy*, but to rely on these historical songs is to expose oneself to problems of exaggeration, fabrication and stylization. There is, however, little choice in the matter, especially as the *dumy* are also our only source of public opinion on the topic and despite the various problems associated with their use, are a bountiful source of information. They are, after all, a direct by-product of the confrontation between Turkic and Ukrainian societies and various aspects of this confrontation constitute their most important theme. It would appear, then, that the *dumy* have much to tell us about the *bisurmeny*.

There are three basic contexts in which the Turks and Tatars appear in the historical songs. First, the Tatar raid—this event is always pictured as something unexpected, furious and cruel. For example, a well-known verse reads:

Sei nochi v opivnochi
Shche kury ne pily,

Iak Tatary v nashi hory
Z vitrom naletily.

Sei nochi v opivnochi
Zla hodyna stala,

Oi turetska dyka banda
Krai nash zvoiuvala.[4]

Those villagers who are not killed are herded off to Kaffa, the emporium of the slave trade, which a contemporary described as "the vampire that drinks the blood of Rus'."[5]. The Tatars themselves are seen as a natural disaster similar to lightning, flood or famine. Yet they receive little attention in the *dumy*. The songs' purpose is to describe the moment of shock that a prey feels when struck by a predator, without dwelling on the predator himself.

Second, the songs which deal with the Cossack-Tatar duel in the steppe (example: "Kozak Holota") have a more confident, sometimes even humorous tone, probably because the Cossack often emerges as the victor in the struggle. But although the duel involves two opponents, the Cossack receives most of the attention. The Tatar's role is primarily that of a foil for the Cossack's heroics. The main message of the *duma* is to praise the Cossack because he acts as a defender of the land.

Third, a prevalent theme in the *dumy* is Turkish slavery, which is always represented as a condition of slow, prolonged anguish. We usually have a picture of the physical conditions of slavery, invariably followed by a lament about the emotional anguish of separation from home and one's loved ones. What is striking here, especially in situations where the captive spends ten, twenty or thirty years in captivity, is how little is said about the Turks and their land. The "*turetskaia zemlia*" is seen as a barrier which separates the captive from his homeland. It receives little attention in itself. The focus is on the condition and feelings of the captive and there is a total lack of interest in his surroundings.

Turkish slavery is never indefinitely prolonged. It is resolved in one of several ways. Often it ends with the death of the captive far from home. Another resolution is escape. Two well-known *dumy* which deal with such an event are "Ivan Bohuslavets" and "Samuil Kishka." The latter is based on an actual escape of a large number of Ukrainian and Russian captives in the 1640s.[6]

Finally, another way out of slavery is to become a renegade. In general, the *dumy* condemn renegades, but there is a good deal of ambiguity on this score, since escape from Turkish slavery is almost always accomplished with their aid. The most famous *duma* which describes an episode of this type is that of "Marusia Bohuslavka," the heroine of which is modelled on the famous Roxolana.[7] Because she has accepted Islam, she has the trust of her master and she takes advantage of it to free seven hundred Cossack captives. But she does not join them in returning home because "... *vzhe ia poturchylasia, pobisurmenylasia, dlia rozkoshi turetskoi, dlia lakomstva neshchasnoho.*"[8] We might note in this connection an episode from Velychko's chronicle. In 1675 the famous Zaporozhian *koshovyi*, Ivan Sirko, made an especially daring raid on the Crimea, during which he freed over seven thousand captives. To his astonishment, he learned that about three thousand of them did not want to return to their homes, but preferred to stay among the Muslims. His reaction was an example of Christian commitment; he ordered all three thousand to be slaughtered to a man, and, as he looked at the piles of corpses, he sorrowfully proclaimed: "Brothers, forgive me, but it is better that you should lie here awaiting the terrible judgment of God than go back to Crimea to help them increase in numbers and risk the eternal damnation of your souls."[9] Episodes such as these indicate that apostasy, while condemned, was more widespread than commonly thought. In fact, there is some evidence that nineteenth-century versions of the *dumy* condemn apostasy much more strongly than did the original sixteenth-century versions.

To summarize, although the major themes of the *dumy* deal with Muslims, there is surprisingly little information about or attention given to the Turks and Tatars themselves. This contrasts sharply with German historical songs of this period which are replete with historical details about the infidel.[10] How then can this myopic vision of the *dumy* be explained? It seems that a large part of the explanation lies in what an older generation of anthropologists called the primitive or peasant mind. According to his theory, a peasant always thinks in personal and concrete terms. His vision is limited to his own immediate environment. It is this mentality that prevents the formulators and audience of the *dumy* from looking beyond the effects of raids and slavery to the people who were the cause of these calamities.

The Galician and Kievan Scholastics

One might expect an absence of curiosity and broader knowledge about the Turks and Tatars among the general Ukrainian populace. But what was the attitude toward and knowledge about the Turks among the scholastics of early seventeenth-century Galicia and of Kiev, which in the latter part of the seventeenth century became the centre of Orthodox scholarship? In general, as might be expected, the attitude was negative. More surprisingly, the knowledge was not very deep. However, in the case of Galicia, there was a rare and brief moment when some Orthodox polemicists took a positive view of the Ottoman empire.

It is not difficult to find the reason for this passing Turcophile interlude. As a result of the Union of Brest of 1596 the Orthodox Ukrainians were exposed to the increasingly militant and oppressive Catholicism of the dominant Poles. Reacting to this oppression, Orthodox polemicists loved to point out that even the "heathen" Ottomans treated their Orthodox subjects more fairly than did the Poles. Indeed, compared to the intense religious conflicts that wracked Europe during this period, the Ottoman empire was a model of religious tolerance (partly because Islam forbade the taxation of Muslims and so proselytizing efforts were discouraged by the porte). Thus, in 1605 the widely distributed anti-Uniate polemic *Perestoroha* (A Warning), ascribed to Ivan Boretsky, praised the Ottomans for their treatment of the Orthodox.[11] The same theme was repeated in another anti-Uniate polemic, Zakhariia Kopystensky's *Palinodiia* (A Retraction), which appeared in 1621–2.[12] However, as Ottoman aggressiveness revived in the latter part of the century, this wave of Turcophilia, which, it may be added, was also evident (but for different reasons) in Poland and Muscovy, quickly passed.

As the seventeenth century came to an end, the Turkish threat again became a predominant theme in Europe. One would expect that Ukrainians, who had experienced a great Ottoman invasion in 1672, would have taken a deep interest in their invaders. But while in the West a veritable flood of books, pamphlets and accounts about the Ottomans continued to appear, relatively little was written on the topic in Ukraine. In fact, only three churchmen—all products of the Kiev Collegium—were known for their works on Islam: Simeon Polotsky, who moved to Moscow where he wrote several attacks against Islam; Lazar Baranovych, who preached fiery sermons against the Muslims and wrote anti-Turkish and anti-Tatar poems, which urged Poles and Ukrainians to forget their differences and unite against the common Ottoman threat;[13] and his pupil, Ioannikii Galiatovsky, who was a rector of the Collegium and who, of the three, was the best known "specialist" on Islam. It is to the works of the last-mentioned that we must turn to find the most extensive commentaries by the Kievan scholastics on Islamic religion and society.

Galiatovsky's first book on this topic, entitled *Łabedź* (The Swan) and written in Polish, appeared in 1679, soon after the Ottoman invasion of Podillia.[14] The purpose of the book, which, incidentally, was dedicated to Hetman Ivan Samoilovych, was to "rouse Christians to war against the Muslims and to show the devices and means whereby they might defeat Muslims in war and erase the foul Muslim name from the earth." Islam, rather than the Ottomans or Tatars, was the focus of the author's attack. Galiatovsky presented what he considered to be the key issues of Islam and then proceeded to respond to them.

The first question the author poses is why Islam has lasted longer than any other heresy. Among the explanations which he proposes are the following: it is God's way of testing the Christians; it is a punishment for their sins; it is the result of Christian disunity. As for the question of why people accepted Islam in the first place, he suggests: because of the threat of death; due to the temptations of carnal pleasure; as a result of the *devşirme* system (the so-called "blood tribute": forcible recruitment of Christian boys into the Ottoman establishment); because hell must be filled up in some way and Muslims can best be used for this purpose. Galiatovsky maintains that the Turks managed to rouse their faithful to war against the Christians by means of threats and by the promise of carnal rewards. He ends his polemic on a practical note. In an effort to encourage Christians, he enumerates a series of ruses that may be used to defeat the *bisurmeny*. Among the more effective tactics, he suggests the use of the Trojan horse and Princess Olha's trick with the burning pigeons.

Galiatovsky's other book on an Islamic topic was *Alkoran* (The Koran, 1683), which he dedicated to Tsars Ivan and Peter. The purpose of this book, which was written in the form of a debate between a Muslim and a Christian, was "that Christians reading my arguments against the Koran might know how to reply to inquiring Muslims and teach them the truth."[15] Although *Alkoran* is hardly a model of objectivity, it probably contains more factual data about Islam and Islamic society than any other work written in Ukraine during the sixteenth-seventeenth centuries. In attacking the basic tenets of Islam—the genuineness of Mohammed as a prophet, the divine origin of the Koran, the need to fast during Ramadan, the duty to pray five times daily, the abstinence from wine, the dervish orders—Galiatovsky inadvertently informed his readers about the actual content of Islam.

Most revealing is the question of Galiatovsky's sources. There is no attempt on his part to obtain first-hand information from returning captives, travellers or Greek ecclesiastics who were constantly on the move between Constantinople, Kiev and Moscow. Paradoxically, this scholastic living on the borders of the Islamic world learned about Islam primarily from Polish written sources (the chronicles of Stryjkowski, Bielski) which, in turn, depended on Italian sources. His most reliable and informative source is the work of the English traveller, Paul Rycaut, entitled *The Present State of the Ottoman Empire*, of which a Polish translation was made in 1678.[16] Thus, Ukrainians, who were constantly exposed to Muslims, depended on Western works to learn about various aspects of Islamic society. The fact is that Galiatovsky and his milieu had no objective interest in information about Islam or Muslims; their primary objective was to use this information for polemical purposes. Galiatovsky clearly states that his interest in Islam goes only so far as it can be related to Christianity, for "like grain among chaff, one can find truth about Christianity among the falsehoods of Islam." Little beyond their own immediate religio-cultural environment—and certainly not Islam—could have relevance for the Kievan scholastics. In this sense, although more sophisticated in the sense of book learning, their vision was not much broader than that of the creators of the *dumy*.

There is a tendency for Ukrainians to be self-congratulatory when they compare the cultural level of Ukraine with that of Muscovy in the seventeenth century. Undoubtedly, the cultural level in Ukraine was higher; Galiatovsky's works, for example, were quickly and enthusiastically translated into Russian as the last word on the subject of Islam. However, if we compare his works with those which appeared in the West on the same topic, then Galiatovsky's inability to break out of the theological framework, to take an interest in a different culture and to value knowledge for its own sake contrasts sharply with the well-informed, first-hand and often objective and probing accounts about Islam and Islamic society which had been appearing in the West since the fifteenth century. Closer to home—in Poland—two decades before the appearance of Galiatovsky's works, the periodical journal, *Merkuriusz Polski*, carried accurate, up-to-date information about developments in the Ottoman empire and the Crimea.[17] In Moldavia, a few decades after Galiatovsky wrote, Cantemir began writing his history of the Ottoman empire which would not be superseded until the nineteenth century.[18] The narrowness of the Kievan scholastics' world-view stemmed from the fact that the culture of seventeenth-century Ukraine was non-secular, its orientation —theological, and its learning—purely scholastic. The intellectual curiosity which had been the hallmark of the Renaissance in Europe was still missing in Kiev.

There were, finally, important political implications to these views on the Muslims. Because the Kievan scholastics saw the conflict with the Muslim strictly in religious terms (Europe had long since abandoned this view), they turned to the leading Orthodox ruler, the Muscovite Tsar, for political and military leadership. Thus, their view of the Muslims encouraged Ukrainian ecclesiastical circles to focus their political loyalties on the tsars rather than on the hetmans.

The Political Elite

It should come as no surprise that the primary characteristic of the approach of the Ukrainian political elite to the Turco-Islamic world was pragmatism. By the political elite we mean here the political decision-makers in Cossack Ukraine: the hetmans, *polkovnyky* (colonels) and *heneralna starshyna* (general staff officers). Indeed, there existed an interesting correlation between pragmatism in dealings with the Muslims and the level of political sophistication and individualism on the part of the elite. The more conscious the Cossack leadership became of its political role, the closer and more intimate became its ties with the Ottoman porte and the Crimean khanate. Conversely, when Ukrainian Cossackdom did not play a prominent political role, as was the case in the sixteenth or eighteenth centuries, relations with the Muslims were, of necessity, strictly antagonistic.[19]

In 1624, at the time when the Zaporozhian Host assumed patronage over the Orthodox church and the *bratstva* (fraternities) and became in effect the defender of Ukrainian rights against Polish-Catholic pressure, Hetman Mykhailo Doroshenko intervened for the first time in an internecine struggle in the Crimean khanate at the request of one of the claimants to the throne.[20] What this event signified was that, simultaneously with the expansion of the Zaporozhians' political role at home, there was a corresponding growth of their political sophistication abroad. Henceforth, the Tatar was no longer seen as an implacable, uncompromising enemy, but rather as an entity with which it was possible to come to a political understanding. For the history of Cossack Ukraine, this was a crucial psychological breakthrough.

Without this realization, it is unlikely that Khmelnytsky's uprising would have succeeded. Khmelnytsky, however, carried this idea even further. Rather than viewing the relationship of Cossacks to Tatars and

Turks as a prolonged conflict punctuated by occasional moments of co-operation, Khmelnytsky began to negotiate Ukraine's acceptance of Ottoman suzerainty.[21] This was a daring and innovative step. For a Christian society which was formed to a large extent out of the conflict with the Muslim infidels, to accept voluntarily the suzerainty of the latter was unprecedented. What prompted Khmelnytsky to take such a step? No doubt, at the time he negotiated with the porte, his options were limited and this was a way of bringing pressure to bear on the tsar. Nevertheless, the hetman was quite serious about his talks with the Ottomans. He saw the relative freedom of action which Moldavia, Wallachia and Transylvania enjoyed under Ottoman tutelage, and concluded, despite the traditional prejudice, that a similar arrangement would best serve Ukraine's interests. Thus, it was *Realpolitik* that dictated his policy toward the Muslims. However, because of the inability of the rest of Ukrainian society to think in these terms, the hetman's plans could not be pursued any further.

Petro Doroshenko was probably the most altruistic of the Cossack hetmans. He had a well-earned reputation for placing the general welfare of Ukraine above narrow, personal interests, and it was the conviction of this experienced leader that his land's political interests could best be served as an Ottoman protectorate.[22] Like Khmelnytsky, he found the arrangement that Moldavia had with the porte to be the most attractive option open to the Ukrainians. In general outline, the terms of such an agreement which Doroshenko and later Orlyk concluded were as follows: the hetman was to have supreme and exclusive authority over the Cossacks; the Cossacks and the entire Ukrainian population were to be guaranteed their freedom; the hetman was to be freely elected; the porte was to be obligated not to interfere in Cossack affairs; Ukraine was to pay no taxes or tribute to the porte.

On the other hand, the duties and obligations of the Cossacks to the porte were the following: the porte was to have the hetman's and the Cossacks' constant loyalty; the Cossacks were to partake in the defence and military campaigns of the Ottoman empire; the hetman, Cossacks and all inhabitants of Ukraine were to acknowledge the protectorate of the sultan.[23]

The desire of pro-Ottoman hetmans for an accommodation with the porte was not one-sided. The Ottomans and Tatars were very much interested in the establishment of a Cossack principality which they hoped would act as a barrier to Muscovite expansion. In fact, in the latter part of the seventeenth century, the establishment of such a Ukrainian principality became one of the major goals of their foreign policy and provided the impetus in 1672 for their great campaign to the north. Thus, consciousness of common interests was very strong on both sides. One could argue that, in terms of political goals, most Ukrainian hetmans could come to an understanding with the Muslim Tatars or Turks much more easily than with the Polish *szlachta* or the Muscovite tsars.

In view of these pro-Ottoman tendencies, we might wonder how much the hetmans actually knew about their Muslim allies. In general, the political elite was better acquainted with the Ottomans and Tatars than with any other segment of the population. Several of the hetmans—Bohdan and Iurii Khmelnytsky and Pylyp Orlyk—were Ottoman captives for extended periods of time. At this point, we might note that the members of the *starshyna* who were taken into captivity were often ransomed and could later make use of their knowledge of the Muslims. This was seldom the case with peasants. Kievan scholastics, on the other hand, rarely fell into captivity. Bohdan Khmelnytsky was supposed to have known Turkish and studied Islam. His son knew the language and culture of the Ottomans well. Orlyk was personally acquainted with many of the leading Crimean and Ottoman statesmen. Doroshenko had about twenty years of experience in dealing with the Ottomans and Tatars. Moreover, there were a number of leading *starshyna* families of Tatar origin—for example, the Kochubei and Dzhalalii families. Many of the *starshyna* spent much time in Istanbul or the Crimea as members of embassies and delegations. Finally, a hetman like Ivan Mazepa had an elaborate system of spies in Crimea and in the principalities (Moldavia and Wallachia) and these regularly informed him in great detail of what was taking place in the khanate and the empire. Thus, we see that the political elite had vast personal experience and a steady flow of information about the Muslims at its disposal.

This is not to say, of course, that hetmans who wanted to establish Ukrainian independence or autonomy were ipso facto Turcophiles. Indeed, even those who were most familiar with the Ottomans and Tatars and co-operated most closely with them often harboured feelings of deep personal antagonism toward them. A revealing example of this tension between political interests and personal convictions was the case of Pylyp Orlyk.[24]

Orlyk's view of the Turks and Tatars was influenced by two assumptions: that the khans and the porte were the only powers capable of supporting the cause of an independent or autonomous Ukraine, and that the Ukrainians and the Ottomans and Tatars faced a common enemy. This theme of co-operation was strongly emphasized in the hetman-in-exile's first political statement, the so-called Bender Constitution. Article three of that document reads:

> Whereas we always need the neighbourly friendship of the Crimean realm, whose aid the Zaporozhian Host requested more than once for its defence, it should be possible now as formerly, for His Excellency the Illustrious Crimean Khan, through his envoys to renew the ancient bond of fraternity, military alliance and to confirm eternal friendship with the Crimean realm.[25]

Thus, the very constitution of the Mazepist émigrés acknowledged and encouraged the need for a positive approach to the Tatars and Ottomans.

To dramatize to the porte and to the khans the danger which they shared with the Ukrainians, Orlyk participated in the fabrication of the so-called "Project of Peter I" which, as we have shown elsewhere, was the forerunner of the famous "Testament of Peter the Great."[26] Essentially, this fabricated document, which Orlyk submitted to the porte on several occasions, argued that Moscow had a systematic plan for absorbing Ukraine, the Crimea and, finally, the Ottoman empire itself. Orlyk proposed a measure to counter these aggressive ambitions of the Muscovites that has a surprisingly modern ring to it. He pointed out that the tsar's Turkic subjects, primarily the Kazan Tatars, presented a serious problem for Moscow. Because there existed a consciousness of community among all Turkic Muslims both within the tsarist realm and beyond it, Orlyk urged the porte to consider forming a grand coalition of Turco-Islamic peoples stretching from the Bucak to the Urals.[27] In emphasizing the problem of the Ukrainians and bringing to the attention of the porte the plight of the tsar's Turco-Islamic subjects, the émigré hetman was one of the first political figures to stress the diverse ethnic composition of the nascent Russian empire and to urge exploitation of this fact.

But this widespread coalition of Turco-Islamic peoples was to be only a part of an even broader coalition of forces including Sweden and Poland, with Ukraine in the pivotal position. This inclusion of other Christian powers into Ukraine's dealings with the Tatars and Ottomans is very characteristic of Orlyk. He was willing to co-operate with the Muslim but only if he had other Christian states for company. Here he differed from Doroshenko and Khmelnytsky who were willing to accept Ukraine's relationship with the Ottoman porte on a one-to-one basis.

Such were the views which Orlyk espoused when he felt that the Ottomans and Tatars might be helpful in achieving his maximum goal—the establishment of a Ukrainian principality. But what were his views on his erstwhile Muslim allies when, as often happened in his career, such maximal goals seemed hopeless? In moments such as these Orlyk retreated into his minimal programme, that is, he attempted to reach an accommodation with the Poles or, less eagerly, with the Russians that would grant him and his Zaporozhians an appropriate socio-economic—but not political—position in Ukraine.

During these times of flagging confidence, Orlyk's attitudes toward the Muslims changed drastically. He continued to perceive the Ottomans and Tatars in a broad context, but now he operated not on a geopolitical level, but on a religious one. (We might recall at this point that Orlyk was a product of the Mohyla Academy and had been exposed to the works of Baranovych and Galiatovsky.) The basic conflict was no longer between an aggressive Russia and a defensive alliance of all her neighbours, but between two irreconcilable religions—Christianity and Islam—and their respective secular representatives. In this context, Orlyk felt that the greatest danger to him and his Zaporozhians was not the liquidation of their rights and privileges, but rather the damnation of their souls for associating with the infidel. In 1713, when the Ottomans no longer seemed to be interested in supporting the Mazepist émigrés, Orlyk wrote to the Zaporozhians of the Turks that "from the very inception of their accursed [Islamic] religion, they have been the primary enemies of Christendom and seek nothing more than to destroy the Christian people."[28] Several months later, after hearing a rumour that his patron, Charles XII of Sweden, might make peace with Peter I, the hetman-in-exile asked:

> What could be more pleasing to God and simultaneously agreeable and desirable to the general expectations of all Christianity than if His Royal Majesty concluded peace with Moscow, combined his armies with hers and together turned against the major enemies of the Christian peoples [i.e., the Ottomans]?[29]

Further, in 1728, while trying to receive a pardon from the Russian court, Orlyk wrote to St. Petersburg:

> I openly proclaim that it is more because of religious zeal and remorse than hope of private gain that I wish to return to the faithful obedience of His Imperial Majesty, with my very numerous army, so that I will not be implicated in the Turkish war and in the spilling of Christian blood.[30]

We see that in cases when Orlyk was free of the political obligations, which had forced him to deal with the Muslims rationally, he quickly reverted to his blind antagonism toward them—an antagonism which characterized so much of Ukrainian society. We may therefore conclude that the Ukrainian elite was forced by political necessity to be innovative in its approach to the Muslims, to view them objectively and to deal with them in a rational manner.

Notes

1. Cf. R. Schwoebel, *The Shadow of the Crescent: The Renaissance Image of the Turk* (Nieuwkoop, 1967).
2. A good example of such attitudes is the work by O .G .de Busbeq (1522–92), *Travels in Turkey, a Translation from the Latin Containing the Most Accurate Account of the Turks and Neighbouring Nations, the Manners, Customs, Religions, etc.* (London, 1744).
3. For an overview of Ukrainian Oriental studies see J. Reychman, "Z dziejów ukraińskiej orientalistyki i stosunków kulturalnych Ukrainy ze Wschodem," *Przeglad Orientalistyczny* 49 (1964): 53–60.
4. *Istorychni pisni*, ed. I. P. Berezovsky, et al. (Kiev, 1961), 63, 100. In literal translation: "This night at midnight/ Before the cocks crew/ The Tatars raided our mountains/ Coming like the wind./ This night at midnight/ An evil hour has struck:/ The savage Turkish band/ Has conquered our land."
5. A first-hand account of the plight of these captives is given by M. Lytvyn (Lituanus), *De moribus Tartarorum, Litvanorum et Moschorum* (Basel, 1615). A discussion of this source and a good treatment of the fate of Ukrainian captives in the Ottoman empire is found in A. Krymsky, *Istoriia Turechchyny* (Kiev, 1924), 167–70, 174–83. The question of the number of captives taken by Tatars and Turks in Ukraine has not been properly elucidated as yet. Traditionally, Ukrainian historians have given figures as high as 20-30,000 taken in a single raid (see Krymsky, *Istoriia Turechchyny*, 174). However, A. A. Novoselskii (*Borba Moskovskogo gosudarstva s tatarami v pervoi polovine XVII veku*, Moscow-Leningrad, 1948, 434–5) states that the average number of captives taken in a single Tatar raid was between 2-3,000 people, of which less than twenty lost their lives in the process. These lower figures are corroborated by A. Fisher (lecture at the Harvard Ukrainian Research Institute, April 1978, entitled "The Ottoman Crimea in the Sixteenth Century") who states that the highest number of captives all the Crimean cities handled in one year was about 2,200.
6. Cf. B. P. Kyrdan, *Ukrainskie narodnye dumy (XV-nachalo XVII v.)* (Moscow, 1962), 122, 129.
7. A detailed discussion of Suleiman the Magnificent's famous wife, Roxolana (d. 1558), a priest's daughter from Rohatyn, may be found in Krymsky, *Istoriia Turechchyny*, 184–96.
8. Kyrdan, *Ukrainskie narodnye dumy*, 101. " . . . I have turned Turkish and infidel, for the sake of Turkish luxury, and because of miserable greed." English translation from *Ukrainian Dumy*, trans. G. Tarnawsky and P. Kilina (Toronto-Cambridge, Mass., 1979), 41.
9. Krymsky, *Istoriia Turechchyny*, 184–96.
10. See R. Wolkan, "Zu den Türkliedern des XVI Jahrhunderts," *Festschrift zum VIII Allgemeinen Deutschen Neuphilologentage* (Vienna-Leipzig, 1898).
11. For a full text of the "Perestoroha," see M. Vozniak, *Pysmennytska*

diialnist Ivana Boretskoho na Volyni i u Lvovi (Lviv, 1954).

12. Cf. "Palinodia" in *Pamiatniki polemicheskoi literatur v Zapadnoi Rusi* 4, part 1 (St. Petersburg, 1878). Excerpts from the work may also be found in O. I. Biletsky, comp., *Khrestomatiia davnoi ukrainskoi literatury (do kintsia XVIII st.)* (Kiev, 1967).
13. For the texts of Baranovych's poems see R. Łużny, *Pisarze kregu Akademii Kijowsko-Mohylańskiej a literatura polska* (Cracow, 1966), 150–6. Some of the poems bear the following titles: "Aby kozacka łódka k Turkom a płyła pobudka," "Nie bedzie, jako świat światem, Rusin Polakowi bratem," and "Na jak masz cere obrócić cholere!".
14. D. Waugh in his dissertation has summarized Galiatovsky's works on Islamic topics: "Seventeenth Century Muscovite Pamphlets with Turkish Themes: Towards a Study of Muscovite Literary Culture in its European Setting" (Ph. D. thesis, Harvard, 1972), 161 ff.
15. *Ibid.*, 162.
16. *Ibid.*, 165.
17. For the deep interest in Islam and other Oriental topics evoked in seventeenth-eighteenth century Poland, see J. Reychman, *Orient w kulturze polskiego Oświecenia* (Wrocław-Warsaw-Cracow, 1964). On the other hand, the Ottomans also had people who evinced an interest in Christian lands and specifically in Ukraine. Cf. Evliia Chelebi, *Kniga Puteshestviia (Moldaviia i Ukraina)*, vyp. 1 (Moscow, 1961).
18. The first printed version of Cantemir's (1673–1723) work, *The History of the Growth and Decay of the Ottoman Empire*, was published in London posthumously in 1734–5. However, manuscript copies of the work were in circulation earlier and on the basis of this work Cantemir was made a member of the Berlin Academy of Sciences.
19. For a study of Cossack-Muslim conflicts in the sixteenth century, see C. Lemercier-Quelquejay, "Un condottieri Lithuanien du XVIe siècle le Prince Dimitrij Višneveckij et l'origine de la Seč zaporogue d'après les archives ottomanes," in *Cahiers du Monde Russe et Sovietique* 10 (1969): 258–79. A study which deals with the Ukrainian Cossack wars with the Tatars and Turks in the eighteenth century is O. M. Apanovych, *Zbroini syly Ukrainy pershoi polovyny XVIII st.* (Kiev, 1969).
20. A detailed study of these events is B. Baranowski, *Polska a Tatarszczyzna w latach 1624–1629* (Łódz, 1948). Also see M. Hrushevsky, *Istoriia Ukrainy-Rusy* 7 (New York, 1956), 513 ff.
21. The general question of Cossack-Muslim relations during the seventeenth century is treated by V. Dubrovsky, "Pro vyvchennia vzaiemyn Ukrainy ta Turechchyny u druhii polovyni XVII st.," *Skhidnyi svit*, no. 5 (1928): 172–82. On the specific topic of Khmelnytsky's relations with the Ottomans and Tatars see N. Kostomarov, "Bogdan Khmelnitsky, dannik Ottomanskoi Porty," *Sobranie sochinenii*, Book 5, vol. 14 (St. Petersburg, 1905); M. Hrushevsky, *Istoriia Ukrainy-Rusy* 9, *passim*; O. Pritsak, "Das erste türkisch-ukrainische Bündnis, 1648," *Oriens* 6 (1953): 266–98;

B. Baranowski, "Geneza sojuszu kozacko-tatarskiego z 1648 r.," *Przegląd Historyczny* 37 (1948): 276–87; J. Rypka, "Z korespondence Vysoké Porty z Bohdanem Chmelnyckim," *Bidliiv Sbornik* (Festschrift Jaroslav Bidlo) (Prague, 1928), 482–98.

22. A thorough analysis of Doroshenko's relations with the Ottoman porte is D. Doroshenko and J. Rypka's "Hejtman P. Dorošenko a jeho turecká polityka," *Časopis Národního Musea*, nos. 1–2 (1933): 1–55. Also see O. M. Apanovych, *Zaporizka Sich u borotbi proty turetsko-tatarskoi ahresii* (Kiev, 1961) and Z. Wójcik's two studies *Traktat andruszowski i jego geneza* (Warsaw, 1959) and *Miedzy traktatem andruszowskim a wojna turecka* (Warsaw, 1968). A Polish translation of Ottoman chronicles dealing with their invasion of Ukraine in 1671–2 is J. S. Sekowski's *Collectanea z dziejopisów tureckich* 2 (Warsaw, 1825).

23. For a summary of Doroshenko's treaty see *Sbornik statei i materialov po istorii Iugo-zapadnoi Rossii* (Kiev, 1916), 75 (hereafter: *Sbornik*).

24. For a more detailed discussion of Orlyk's relations with Ottomans and Tatars, see O. Subtelny, "The Unwilling Allies: The Relations of Hetman Pylyp Orlyk with the Ottoman Porte and the Crimean Khanate, 1710–1742" (Ph. D. thesis, Harvard, 1973). Also see Subtelny, "Political Cooperation and Religious Antagonism: Aspects of Pylyp Orlyk's Relations with Turks and Tatars," in *Zbirnyk na poshanu Oleksandra Ohloblyna* (New York, 1977), 454–65, and "From the Diary of Pylyp Orlyk," *Ukrainskyi istoryk* 8 (1971): 95–105.

25. Cf. A. O. Bodiansky, "Perepiska i drugiia bumagi shvedskogo korolia Karla XII . . . ," in *Chteniia v Imperatorskom Obshchestve istorii i drevnostei rossiiskikh pri Moskovskom universitete*, no. 1 (Moscow, 1847), 6.

26. O. Subtelny, "Peter I's Testament: A Reassessment," *Slavic Review* 33 (1974): 663–78.

27. *Sbornik*, 60. Also see Subtelny, "Unwilling Allies," 133 ff.

28. Orlyk to the Zaporozhians, 30 March 1713, *Biblioteka Czartoryskich* (Cracow), fol. 5907, no. 28530.

29. Orlyk to Müllern, 11 October 1711, in B. Krupnytsky, *Hetman Pylyp Orlyk (1672–1742)* (Warsaw, 1938), 212.

30. Orlyk to Sztenflict, 26 June 1726, in his "Diariusz podróżny . . . ," located in *Archives du Ministère des Affaires étrangères* (Paris), Mémoires et Documents. Pologne, 9, fol. 204.

Patricia Herlihy

Ukrainian Cities in the Nineteenth Century

The most salient characteristic of urbanization in Ukraine in the nineteenth century is that, on the whole, there was so little of it. Or, to be precise, urbanization occurred in Ukraine, but without substantial participation by Ukrainians. As late as 1897, less than 16 per cent of the Ukrainian population could be described as town dwellers.[1] Within the cities themselves, Ukrainians constituted only about one-third of the inhabitants.[2] The reasons for this retarded urbanization of Ukrainians seem to have been principally two. The Ukrainians themselves were predominantly a peasant people with deep attachment to the soil. When they faced overcrowding in their old rural homes, they preferred to seek out new agricultural lands, sometimes in distant places, rather than migrate into cities. Secondly, the Russian imperial government, while anxious to promote the growth of urban centres within Ukraine, favoured, for reasons we shall presently note, Russian rather than Ukrainian settlements within them.

While the process of nineteenth-century urbanization shows certain large uniformities across Ukraine, there are nonetheless substantial differences within this movement too. These are best revealed by considering the development of particular cities, set within varying geographic, economic and political surroundings. Some of the cities grew slowly but steadily; others experienced bursts of expansion (see Table 1). In some urban centres, concomitant industrialization was important, while in others political, agricultural and cultural functions seem to have acted as the principal stimuli. Here, we shall single out for particular scrutiny five Ukrainian towns in the nineteenth century: Kiev, Kharkiv, Lviv, Odessa and Luhanske. In sketching their histories, our strokes must be bold and broad; shadings will be added later.

TABLE 1. POPULATION OF THE CITIES OF KIEV, KHARKIV, LVIV, ODESSA AND LUHANSKE IN THE NINETEENTH CENTURY

Year	Kiev	Kharkiv	Lviv	Odessa	Luhanske
1772			20,000		
1786			25,000		
1787		10,967			
1795			39,000	2,345	3,000
1808			41,500	12,500	
1810			43,522		
1814				25,000	
1815		12,600			
1817				32,700	
1820			46,000	40,000	
1827			55,460		
1840	44,683			68,765	
1842				76,862	
1848			68,000		
1850			70,000		
1856		35,600		101,320	
1857			70,384		
1860	55,000	50,000		112,500	9,000
1861	65,000	50,301			
1862	70,341				6,643
1863		52,000			
1864	70,590				
1869			87,100	118,977	
1871		85,561			
1873				193,513	
1874	127,251				
1880			100,000	219,300	
1881		128,445			
1883				244,609	
1892				340,526	
1897	247,723	155,000		403,815	20,400
1900			159,870	450,000	34,175
1901			198,237		
1903	319,000				
1912	410,000	250,000			
1914			212,030	630,000	68,500
1916	506,000	248,000	220,000		
1917		288,000			
1918			197,431		

SOURCE: The figures are taken from the entries of the towns in the appropriate volumes of *Istoriia mist i sil Ukrainskoi RSR*, 26 vols. (Kiev, 1967–74).

Kiev

Traditionally the "mother" of Ukrainian cities, probably the region's most ancient and surely its most historic urban settlement, is Kiev. Despite its ancient origins, this "Ukrainian Jerusalem" supported in 1840 fewer than 45,000 inhabitants.[3] Its location close to the confluence of the Pripet, upper Dnieper and Desna rivers made it a favourable market site, where forest products, brought largely from the north, could be exchanged for the produce of the southern steppe. From the end of the eighteenth century the great "Contracts" fairs were held in Podil, one of the city's three quarters. Yet this lively commerce did not result in substantial urban growth during the first half of the nineteenth century. On the contrary, between the urban enumerations of 1840 and 1860, the population increased by little more than 10,000 persons.[4] In the decades before the advent of the railroad, this small market town adequately served the needs of its predominantly agricultural region. After 1861 the pace of urban growth dramatically quickened. According to the census of 1874, the number of urban residents was nearly double that of 1861.[5] The rate of growth remained high during the subsequent decades. The all-Russian census of 1897 reveals that the city's population had once more nearly doubled, reaching 247,723 persons. Kiev was by then the second most populous city of Ukraine, surpassed only by Odessa.

What factors or functions supported this rapid expansion? An analysis of the census of 1874 shows that urban industries were still new and small, and that industrialization was not the major factor in this expansion, at least not in its early stages. The large preponderance of males over females within the urban population gives us some hints as to why Kiev was growing. In 1864 males outnumbered females by 41,000 to 29,000 within the city. In 1874 more than 72,000 males shared the city with 55,000 females.[6] The population was composed chiefly of students, soldiers, monks and bureaucrats—nearly all of them males and most of them unmarried.

The government acted as prime mover in bringing males into the city. Kiev had been affected by the Polish uprising of 1831. Responding by increased centralization, the imperial government abolished the favourable regime of the Magdeburg Law, under which the citizens had hitherto lived. By 1840 Kiev had passed fully under the general laws of the empire, and this resulted in a considerable loss of municipal autonomy. In 1834 the government moved the university at Vilnius to Kiev. The act served to punish students who had taken part in the anti-Russian agitation; it also anchored a Russifying institution in a strategic area. With like intent, the government transferred the headquarters of the First Army from Mogilev to Kiev. Tsarist policy sought to attract Russian merchants to the city. An *ukaz* of 1835 extended to merchants who might emigrate from Russian guberniias to Kiev exemption from taxes for three years.[7] The second Polish uprising of 1863 added vigour to the efforts of the Russian government to cultivate a strong Russian presence in this strategic town.

The censuses measure the results of these policies. In 1874 nearly 40 per cent of the population declared Russian to be their mother tongue. Only a little more than 32 per cent of the inhabitants reported Ukrainian as their first language. Jews were comparatively few in Kiev and constituted only 5 per cent of the total population in the late 1860s—but their numbers were growing, attaining 10 per cent by 1874 and 12 per cent in 1897.[8] This delayed growth in the number of Jewish residents probably reflects the lingering effects of the legal obstacles which the government had established against Jewish settlements within the city in 1835. The restrictions on Jewish settlement doubtlessly handicapped the growth of those light industries—chiefly clothing and metalwork—in which Jews were especially prominent. On the other hand, the substantial size of the Russian sector of the population (54.2 per cent in 1897: see Table 2) reflects the city's established importance as a cultural, administrative and military centre.

Important too in supporting the city's early growth were its ancient churches and holy places—notably the famous "Monastery of the Caves," one of the greatest shrines in all Orthodox Christendom. By the end of the century nearly a quarter of a million devotees, by contemporary estimate, descended annually on Kiev to gain spiritual benefit from these sacred places.[9] The annual influx of pilgrims stimulated the growth of hotels, restaurants and shops within the city. Foreigners, too, regularly came to visit this beautiful town on the Dnieper. The census of 1874 even counts among the resident population two Africans, five Americans and one Dutchman.[10] We would like to know what brought these persons to Kiev, and what retained them, but here our sources fail us.

At Kiev, industry made only a belated contribution to urbanization. In 1845 there were in the city only seventy-nine enterprises, which employed 820 workers, chiefly artisans and craftsmen. They produced bells, books and candles, as well as leather, tin, bricks, glass, flour and spirits. The total product from these small manufactures amounted to 737,600 silver rubles annually. Sixteen years later, in 1861, industrial production had tripled, reaching 2.3 million rubles per year.[11] Growth had been impressive, but still Kiev's industries would have to be judged modest in size and output.

However, foundations were being laid for much more substantial advances. The government promoted the construction of good roads leading to this garrison town. In 1853 an engineering marvel, a bridge of unprecedented size, was completed over the Dnieper river. In the words of an admiring Englishman, the bridge was "considered unequalled for length and width of span by any other bridge in Europe."[12]

The centre of a large and fertile agricultural region, Kiev had long engaged in the processing and marketing of farm products. The adoption of steam power, although slow, nevertheless allowed the construction of ever more numerous and ever larger grain mills and especially sugar-beet refineries. By the 1870s 230 sugar refineries were located at or near Kiev, the densest concentration in the entire empire. Kiev also possessed the only sugar exchange in the imperial territories, where all sugar transactions were registered.[13] At this time the manufacture of and trade in sugar was the region's most profitable, and most volatile, business. Fortunes were rapidly accumulated, and some of them rapidly lost. According to an English traveller, numerous sugar barons rose from the ranks of itinerant traders or other modest origins. In spite of, or perhaps because of, their lowly background they were prone to construct huge stone houses, which reminded our traveller of Venetian palaces.[14] By 1897 the value of refined sugar represented one-quarter of the city's entire industrial output,[15] and Kiev also led all Ukrainian cities in the milling of flour and bran. In sum, over a thirty-seven year period (1860–97), the number of factories in Kiev increased four times, the number of workers 7.5 times, and the value of the manufactured products eleven times.[16]

At Kiev the relationship of urbanization and industrialization was complex and subtle. Industrial growth, it appears, did not so much stimulate immigration, as did immigration promote industrial growth. In other words, the presence of an already large population and a sizable labour force, as well as active markets, created favourable conditions for the growth of industries. Critical, then, for the expansion of the city and the establishment of a strong industrial base was the improvement in sanitary conditions, in public health and hygiene.

In the early decades of the nineteenth century, natural disasters had severely limited the growth of population. The great fire of July 1811, for example, raged for several days and destroyed 1,176 houses, 19 churches and 3 monasteries.[17] Smallpox, typhus, scarlatina, scrofula, dysentry and cholera repeatedly flayed the urban population. As late as 1874, only 28.3 per cent of the city's population had been born in Kiev and its environs—a figure which reflects not only substantial immigration but the huge losses, which a persistently high urban death rate continuously claimed. Unable to maintain its own numbers through natural reproduction, the city was forced to recruit rural immigrants in substantial numbers.[18]

In nineteenth-century Kiev it was vital to provide the urban population with adequate quantities of pure water. By 1872 the city daily pumped some 500,000 vedros (about 1.3 million gallons) of sand-filtered water from the Dnieper river. Still, the good water benefited largely the wealthy. Most of the population drank the suspect water from the city's 1,300 wells. Over the next two decades the urban government undertook the construction of a sewage system, and progress was more rapid at Kiev than at Moscow.[19] By 1894 several sections of the city enjoyed both good water and efficient sewage disposal. To be sure, in the impoverished Podil quarter, open sewers still gave off a horrible stench, which the wastes from soap factories rendered even more pungent. Still, the city was by then well on its way toward achieving acceptable conditions of public hygiene. Basking in the government's favour, Kiev confronted and overcame these acute problems of growth sooner and more efficiently than most Ukrainian or Russian towns.

Between 1863 and 1897 the population of Kiev grew more rapidly than that of the empire as a whole. Substantial industries were supporting old residents and attracting new. Already by 1884 the sex ratio had swung into near balance, with 79,000 men and 76,000 women.[20] The city glowed with an unmistakable aura of prosperity. In 1892 it constructed an electric tramway—the first city in the Russian empire to be served by electric streetcars. By 1890 over six thousand factory workers found employment in the railroad repair shops, the refineries, tobacco firms, the arsenal and other enterprises.

This brief glance at Kiev's development can perhaps support the following conclusions. The initial stimuli to urban expansion derived from governmental policies, which aimed at establishing a strong Russian presence in a strategic and long contested area. For this reason, the government brought Russian students and teachers to Kiev's new university, stationed Russian troops in the city's garrison, and invited Russian merchants and artisans to ply their trades in the town. The policy was on the whole a success, and Kiev in the late nineteenth century was an enclave of largely Russian settlement within the Ukrainian countryside.

Kharkiv

Founded about 1650, set within the Donets valley at the border of forest zone and steppe, Kharkiv was in origin a frontier fortress, designed to defend Muscovite tsardom from Tatar incursions and to serve as a staging point for further Russian expansion to the south and east. The tsars actively encouraged Ukrainian, especially Cossack, settlement within the new town and its thinly settled environs. The chief advantage of the new city was perhaps its distance from other cities. Without a rival, it soon became the military, economic, religious and intellectual capital of northeastern Ukraine. The open land was ideally suited for hunting and bee-keeping. Given the abundance of grasses, the raising of horses and cattle took early root, to be followed by cereal cultivation on the fertile soil. By the early nineteenth century Kharkiv possessed a population of about 12,600. It was the see of an archbishop and a university founded in 1805; and it retained its large garrison. Its inhabitants were chiefly small tradesmen and artisans, who tanned leather, made boots, washed wool and baked bricks. When the town was made the capital of the Kharkiv *general-gubernatorstvo* in 1835, the attendant bureaucrats further swelled the city and enriched its economy.

Kharkiv's lonely place on the urban map of the Russian empire lent it great strategic importance. It gathered and knotted the principal routes connecting Moscow and St. Petersburg with the Crimea and Caucasus. Moreover, the produce from vast areas of steppe and forest regions flowed through it, on its way to its ultimate consumers. The city annually hosted four fairs, each lasting approximately one month. According to a resident English engineer named George Hume, the commerce of the city was second only to that of Nizhnii-Novgorod, the liveliest of the fair towns of central Russia. He described the active wool fair held in June, when thousands of bales of wool, of every sort and quality, lined the streets.[21]

The earliest small industries of the town used local agricultural products. In comparable fashion, the discovery and exploitation after the Crimean War of the rich mineral deposits of the Donbas and the Kryvyi Rih regions added vitality to Kharkiv's economy. In 1867 the English engineer George Hume, cited earlier, arrived in Kharkiv to manufacture steam threshing machines. Versatile in his skills and insatiable in his ambitions, he also built a steam flour mill, equipped a sugar refinery with machinery, and provided the Grand Duchess Elena Pavlovna, aunt of the emperor, with vats for her distillery. His industrial empire, built over thirty-five years, had its headquarters in a large building on the principal street of Kharkiv, with branch offices in Kiev (300 miles to the west), Taganrog (427 miles to the south) and Baku (1300 miles to the southeast). He himself described Kharkiv as a city of "the greatest strategic and commercial importance."[22] He and similar entrepreneurs gave Kharkiv stature and renown in the manufacture of light machinery and tools. The city's largest industry was a machine manufacturing plant, constructed in 1879.[23] Again, Kharkiv's isolation as an urban centre buttressed the town's importance.

In 1869 railroads linked the city with Kursk and Azov. By the end of the century it was a major station on the trunk lines joining Moscow and Sevastopil, and Moscow and Mykolaiv. By 1861 it was one of the few cities in the empire with a population of over 50,000. Between 1801 and 1901 its population grew by twenty times, making it one of the most rapidly expanding cities in the empire.[24]

Location, even more than trade and industry, best accounts for this rapid population increase. In 1839 Kharkiv acquired a school of veterinary science, which gave substantial support to animal husbandry in the region. The guberniia and its neighbours furnished the Russian army with large numbers of its mounts. With the growing mineral output from mines in the Donbas and Kryvyi Rih came a demand for engineers. In 1885 there opened in the city a new technological institute. Middle schools, trade schools, technological schools and railroad schools of all kinds were established. Art was not sacrificed for science. Kharkiv, prosperous and booming, was noted also for its painting, music, theatre and for public interest in its short but colourful history.

Rapid growth gave the town a chaotic appearance; no architectural unity could be found in its irregular streets and haphazardly constructed buildings. Like most nineteenth-century cities, Kharkiv suffered from the absence of paving, from the ubiquity of mud in autumn and spring and of dust in summer.[25] Water too remained in short supply until 1879, when the city at last began to pump pure water from distant sources. But not until 1904 were the first dozen water hydrants placed at the service of the citizenry.

Although Ukrainians predominated among the earliest settlers of Kharkiv, the development and diversification of the economy attracted a variegated lot of inhabitants, including foreigners such as Hume. Belgians, employed by the mining and metallurgical firms, gladly chose to reside in Kharkiv, a town of some amenities. Although Russians were numerous, Ukrainians figured prominently in university life; some of them, such as Dmytro Bahalii, achieved distinction both as university rectors and city mayors. Kharkiv's was in fact the first modern secular university in Ukraine (apart from Lviv), and gave major impetus to the development of the Ukrainian national consciousness. Ukrainians predominated in the countryside, and also gathered into the small towns which dotted the guberniia. By the first decade of the twentieth century, within the guberniia as a whole, about 15 per cent of Ukrainians lived in some sort of urban centre. Here the percentage of urbanized Ukrainians roughly corresponds with the percentage of urban dwellers in the population as a whole—14 per cent. Still, Kharkiv claimed few of them. Writing about

1912, Steven Rudnitsky, author of a comprehensive survey of Ukrainian cities, remarked: "But we note for the first time here the remarkable fact that in all the district cities, the Ukrainians are much more numerous than the Russians. Only in the capital city, Kharkiv, are they in the minority, and comprise little more than one-fourth the population."[26]

In summary then, Kharkiv, much like Kiev, drew initial life from local agricultural production, especially the breeding of horses, cattle and sheep, and the raising of wheat. Agricultural surpluses in turn attracted traders and fed the region's vigorous fairs. Commercial traffic also brought about improved communications. The subsequent exploitation of the mineral wealth of the Don basin gave an added stimulus to the town's economy. Metallurgical factories and machine works soon formed an important part of Kharkiv's economic life. Beyond these primary industries, the growth of manufactures such as textiles may have been retarded, as the imperial government deliberately sought to protect the cloth industry in the central Russian provinces. As a military post and an administrative and educational centre, Kharkiv absorbed a large Russian population, despite the fact that Ukrainians in the district favoured urban settlement in uniquely large proportions. At all events, Kharkiv grew because it was a new town, and appropriated from its origins the functions of a military, administrative, commercial and cultural centre with a vast region. It served its region in multiple ways, and this in large part explains its fortunes and its history.

Lviv

Lviv, in contrast, is a much more ancient city. Founded in the thirteenth century on an important trade route, it developed as a major commercial and cultural centre. Unlike Kiev and Kharkiv, Lviv in the nineteenth century was under Austrian rather than Russian rule. It was the capital of the province of Galicia from 1772 to 1918 and thus the principal urban centre in Eastern Galicia, a region largely populated by Ukrainians. (According to the census of 1900, out of 4.8 million inhabitants of Eastern Galicia, 3 million, or 62.5 per cent, were Ukrainians.)[27] Lemberg, as the Austrians called the town, already possessed in 1857 a population of 70,384 inhabitants.[28] It has always ranked among the five largest cities of both Russian and Austrian Ukraine.

Galicia was not a rich province, either in agriculture or in minerals, and the commercial and industrial development of Lviv progressed only slowly. In 1850 the city contained only nine industries, engaged in the manufacture of matches, textiles and beer.[29] Later, the production of construction materials—bricks, tiles, lime and cement—gained some importance. The city concentrated its efforts on light industries: shoemaking, tailoring, and food processing, especially the milling of flour. Metallurgy and machine making, on the other hand, were marked by lethargic growth. The coming of the railroad gave the chief and virtually the only stimulus to such employment, as the city became an important railroad centre with its own repair shop. By 1871 Galicia was linked by rail with the Ukrainian lands under Russian rule. Still, by the end of the century, only about a thousand workers were engaged in machine making or in repair. In the opinion of most Ukrainian economists, the imperial Austrian government did not favour industrial development in Eastern Galicia.[30] Rather, it sought to preserve the region as a supplier of raw materials to, and a purchaser of finished products from, the central Austrian provinces. It did not want to foster competition within the empire to Viennese and Bohemian industries.

Lviv first served the Austrians as an administrative centre, but it also functioned after 1848 as a kind of cultural capital for the subject nationalities (Poles and Ukrainians) of Galicia. In 1900, Poles, who made up only 23 per cent of Eastern Galicia's population, formed a majority (51.6 per cent) of the inhabitants of Lviv. Although the Ukrainians at this time made up only 18.3 per cent of the city's population, they also took advantage of the relative leniency of the Austrian government to launch a highly influential political and cultural movement. From the 1870s Galicia served the Ukrainian people as a kind of Piedmont, where cultural and political activities banned in Russian-ruled Ukraine could find an outlet. The Ukrainians, for example, founded the *Prosvita*, or Enlightenment, Society, in 1868, which provided a focal point for Ukrainian cultural and educational activities until 1939.[31] By 1912 it claimed a membership of 35,000, with branches scattered over some seventy-four towns and cities. It maintained its own library and reading rooms, and sponsored a press, which published both books and periodicals. In 1912 it even founded at Lviv a two-year commercial high school, for both boys and girls. Moreover, at the University of Lviv, Ukrainian was one of three official languages, and, significantly, from 1849 Ukrainian professors held chairs throughout the faculties and not only in languages.

Lviv was, moreover, the headquarters of a Ukrainian retail co-operative—the *Narodna torhivlia* society, founded in 1883—of a federation of credit unions—the *Kraievyi soiuz kredytovyi*, founded in 1898—and of a Ukrainian insurance company, the Dnister Mutual Fire Insurance Company, founded in 1892. Toward the end of the century, a pedagogical institute and two schools for girls opened their doors. On the eve of the First World War there were fourteen private and state Ukrainian schools at Lviv. In the words of one historian, "at the time of the outbreak of World War I, Ukrainian cultural life in Lviv had already attained a high level of development."[32] Apart from schools and credit institutions, Ukrainians in Lviv could take advantage of an agricultural society and the Shevchenko Society (1873), which twenty years later became the Shevchenko Scientific Society and was tantamount to a Ukrainian Academy of Sciences. Nowhere was national consciousness and cultural activity so lively as in Lviv.

Lviv was a stately city adorned by large buildings: hospitals, schools, government structures, palaces, churches and monasteries. Gas lights illuminated its streets as early as 1858 and by 1880 they had been replaced by electric lamps. In 1894 electric trams served the public, replacing the horse-drawn cars installed by the Società Triestina in 1880. Bicycles from 1879, and automobiles from 1890, accelerated urban transport. Telephones first began to ring in 1884; fourteen years later, 659 subscribers had joined the system. A modern sand filtering water system was installed fairly late—in 1901—and a modern sewage system was completed only in 1914. By then, the processes of modernization had run to term.

In summary, Lviv's growth in the nineteenth century was slow but steady. Industry played a restricted role in luring immigrants to the city. Administration, education, finance and culture sustained Lviv's population, but could not generate a true urban boom. And yet, in spite of its small industrial base and limited wealth, the city assumed a major role in the history of its region, and of the Poles and Ukrainians, as well as the numerous Jews, Armenians and Germans settled within it. Although the Ukrainians themselves were a small component of the urban population, their intellectual leaders established a network of national institutions which improved their standards of living and enriched their cultural endowment. Given a certain latitude not allowed within the Russian empire, Ukrainians in Lviv were able openly, even brilliantly, to nurture their national culture and spirit.

Odessa

In 1794 Empress Catherine II ordered the building of a new city on the northwest shore of the Black Sea, on the site of a former Turkish fortress. Odessa, as she called the new foundation, was to serve both as a military outpost and a commercial port. Catherine and her successors encouraged Bulgarians, Greeks and Germans to settle in the new city and its environs, and other foreigners—Italians, French, Armenians, Tatars—soon joined them. New arrivals flocked in from the hinterland; Russians, Ukrainians, Belorussians, Jews and Poles.[33]

The rate of growth of Odessa's population in the nineteenth century was the most dramatic in the Russian empire, and can be matched only in the history of such great western American cities as Chicago. As early as 1856 it surpassed 100,000 persons, and achieved the status of the third city (after Moscow and St. Petersburg) in the empire. By 1878 the city had a radius of about seven miles and contained more than 200,000 people. It entered the twentieth century with 400,000 inhabitants; it had long been the largest city in Ukraine.

From the beginning, foreign trade built Odessa's fortunes. Following the Napoleonic wars, an enormous demand for wheat was developing in Western Europe. Industrialization in the West, the abolition of the corn laws and the triumph of free trade opened up vast new markets. The emancipation of the serfs in the Russian empire (1861) and the liberal reforms of Alexander II stimulated the production of wheat for market, most notably on the Ukrainian steppes. Odessa served the steppes as the most convenient port of export. In 1860 cereal exports through Odessa were about 7 million quintals; they soared to more than 28 million in 1878.[34]

Industry too made a belated but growing contribution to the support of this huge urban population. At Odessa, as at Kharkiv, industries initially exploited the agricultural produce of the surrounding region. The manufacture of tallow, soap, candles and rope were among the first industries to take root in the city. Factories making vodka, macaroni, bricks and tiles—all destined for local consumption—followed soon after.

Several obstacles obstructed and delayed the foundation at Odessa of large-scale manufactures. Perennial shortages of capital, labour, water and fuel handicapped the entrepreneur. Capital, which abounded in foreign commerce, was largely controlled by foreigners and rarely diverted to local, inland enterprises. In the opinion of Soviet historians, the presence of the port even obstructed industrial development.[35] The wealthy residents of the city spent their money on luxury goods available in the free port, or satisfied their expensive tastes with smuggled commodities; at all events their money flowed abroad and gave no stimulus to local enterprises. Only late in the century did foreign capitalists seek out investment opportunities in Odessa and its hinterland. Belgians, for example, financed and constructed the city's first electric tramway in the 1890s.

Moreover, in this nineteenth-century boom town, labour costs remained high, buoyed by the high costs of housing, food, water and fuel. For long the cheapest accessible coal was from Britain. One further hindrance to early industrial development in Odessa was the lack of railroads. The first line opened in 1865, but remained for several years a local service. Not until 1872 was Odessa connected to Moscow by rail, and not until 1876 could one take a train to Kiev. Nonetheless, during the great push for industrialization which marks economic development in the Russian empire from the 1890s Odessa did achieve substantial industrial expansion. By 1899 over five hundred enterprises were functioning within the city. During the fifteen-year period from 1885 to 1899, both the value of industrial output and the number of employees increased by a factor of three. (The size of the total urban population had meanwhile not quite doubled.) To be sure, the ten years before the outbreak of the First World War were difficult for Odessa. Depression, unemployment, industrial unrest, strikes and revolutionary agitation slowed to a halt the hitherto galloping expansion. Even the imperial government, which viewed the town as a nest of conspirators, appeared to promote the port of Mykolaiv at Odessa's expense. But in spite of these setbacks, Odessa held its rank as Ukraine's largest city.

This spectacular growth would not have been possible without the improvement of public hygiene. In the early nineteenth century Odessa faced formidable problems with its unpaved streets, which mud made impassable in winter and dust unbearable in summer; with wells, the water from which soon became insufficient in quantity and unacceptable in quality; and with its open gutters and ditches which were designed to carry away the sewage. Moreover, the growing concentration of human beings in a small area raised the threat of communicable diseases—typhus, typhoid and tuberculosis.[36]

Against all these obstacles to urban growth, the city, especially from the 1870s, made remarkable progress. By 1873, 71 per cent of the houses had running water, and the water itself was piped in in large volumes from the Dniester river, some twenty-seven miles distant. At this time about 45 per cent of the houses were connected to a central sewer network. By 1878 the major sewer system was completed. Gradually the streets were paved and by 1895 all the central area of the city and much of the outlying districts had been successfully covered. The fruit of all these improvements was a dramatically lowered death rate. In this opportune change, Odessa was initially more favoured than either Moscow or St. Petersburg. During the 1880s the death rate fell below the urban birth rate, and the city was no longer dependent upon immigration simply to maintain its size. In achieving demographic self-sufficiency, Odessa had also, in a real sense, become a modern city.

Odessa's society showed certain qualities which rendered it unique among Ukrainian cities. More than any other town, it retained a highly cosmopolitan character, with large numbers of foreign visitors and immigrants. The census of 1897 records that no fewer than fifty languages were spoken in the city, excluding Russian. It was also a major centre of Jewish settlement; Jews by the late nineteenth century constituted about one-third of the urban population. Curiously, this ostensibly Ukrainian city contained very few Ukrainians. To be sure, in reporting their language and origins to the census takers, many true Ukrainians preferred to pass themselves off as Russian in order to procure the economic and political advantages of membership in the empire's dominant national group. Still, in 1897 only 5.7 per cent of Odessa's population identified Ukrainian as their first language. Even Russians formed only 41.2 per cent of the urban residents.

Several factors explain the small numbers of Ukrainians in Odessa. Overseas trade, which established Odessa's early prominence, was a risky business. Those involved in it had to have experience in foreign markets; usually too, they had to rely upon a network of foreign correspondents and have ready access to capital. Both Ukrainians and Russians had little knowledge of overseas commercial affairs. The successful merchants were initially Greeks, Frenchmen and Italians, and, later in the century, Jews. Ukrainians (and Russians too) scarcely participated in this lucrative economic activity.

As seen in the census of 1897, most Ukrainian immigrants to Odessa were male, poor and unmarried. Of the 11,172 Ukrainian males then residing in Odessa, only 224 were independently wealthy, supported by interest on savings or stocks; and only 100 were rentiers, living from land rents. More Ukrainians were in the military than in any other profession. The high echelons of the civil service were, on the other hand, a predominantly Russian domain. About 14 per cent of the Ukrainian males were employed in the local quarries and mines, as unskilled, manual labourers. About 12 per cent engaged in manufacturing on a small scale, and 8 per cent were in transport. The Ukrainian carter, the *chumak*, had long been a familiar sight on the roads leading to Odessa, driving his grain-laden wagons to port. By 1897 the railroad had largely replaced the wagons, but Ukrainians continued to labour on the river barges, which still performed vital services to the local economy.

Few Ukrainian women came to Odessa (the sex ratio among Ukrainians was 159 males for every 100 women), and the census indicates that the birth rate was comparatively low, whereas rates of child mortality were high. Few marriages, few babies and low-skilled employment indicate that most Ukrainians were of humble socio-economic status. Among them, only the destitute and the desperate found their way to Odessa. Perhaps the keen competition among merchants, traders and shopkeepers discouraged them from seeking a new life within the city.

In summary, then, Odessa owed its origins and its early growth to the favour of the imperial government and to the unexpected development of massive cereal export to Western Europe. The city attracted a variegated population, who took advantage of opportunities in government, trade and industry. However, the Ukrainians themselves were ill-equipped to participate intimately in the life of the new and booming city, owing to their rural origins and political disabilities. Perhaps it is indicative of their general relationship to urbanism, that the largest city in Ukraine was also the least Ukrainian.

Luhanske

In 1795, hardly more than a year after the creation of Odessa, the imperial Russian government founded another new town, Luhanske. Located on the Luhan river in the northern Donets basin, the town was destined to become a principal industrial centre in the guberniia of Katerynoslav. Indeed, in origin Luhanske was not so much a town as a factory. The *ukaz* of 1795 which gave birth to Luhanske ordered that iron works be constructed on the site. The government further allocated some 715,733 rubles to an English entrepreneur named Gascoigne, the director of the project. It also ordered that some three thousand serfs be shipped from the central Russian provinces in order to supply the needed labour force. The new works, it was envisioned, could exploit the iron deposits of the region and provide cannon and shot to the fledgling Russian navy on the Black Sea. Given the distance to the sea, the venture at first fared poorly. But the gathering storms of the Napoleonic wars showered the new factory with demands for armaments and allowed it to flourish. So also, during the Crimean War, Luhanske served as an important source of supply to the empire's beleaguered southern army, pinned down at Sevastopil.[37]

Apart from its military-industrial functions, Luhanske served also as a transportation centre and a market town. The highways from the central gubernii to the port cities of Rostov and Taganrog passed through it. Two fairs were held each month at Luhanske, but their importance never extended beyond the immediate region. Still, the inhabitants of the surrounding area—peasants and *pomishchiky*—purchased metals, tiles, bricks, coal, building stones, honey, wax, cattle, grain, meat, wool and leather, and other typical products of the southern economy.

By the middle of the century the factory town attracted its first manufactures of non-military items: tallow, wax, candles, soap, oils, tiles, bricks, lime and flour. Again the exploitation of local, largely agricultural, products, typical of industrial development in Ukrainian cities, should be apparent. Even with this industrial diversification, Luhanske remained for the most part a one-company town. Alongside the factory were the administrative offices, courthouse, police station, two dispensaries, the poorhouse, a pharmacy, two schools, a library and a small museum, a meteorological station and two churches. Most of the iron workers lived in cottages or in barracks holding from twenty-five to thirty men. The nearby village of Kamianyi Brid, where other workers resided, contained some 1,558 stone and 227 wooden houses. The managers of the factory resided in ten comfortable stone houses.[38]

Moreover, the prosperity of the iron industry largely determined the fortunes of the town. After the Crimean War, the iron factory entered upon a period of hard times. The population of Luhanske shrank from 9,000 in 1861 to 6,643 in 1862.[39] Finally, in 1887 the factory closed down altogether[40] and was not reopened until 1895. Meanwhile, the railroad reached Luhanske, rather belatedly in 1874, and by 1897 the town was joined to the Azov line. At this time the town had only 20,404 inhabitants, but Luhanske was slowly reorganizing and rebuilding its economy, and producing iron products for peaceful purposes. A German entrepreneur by the name of Hartmann built there the largest steam-engine factory in Russia, with the capacity of producing as many as twenty engines per month. By 1905 this single factory manufactured 21.1 per cent of all the steam engines made in Russia. From 1900 to 1903 the enterprise reportedly returned to its owner a profit of three million rubles. Other foreign entrepreneurs exploited and enjoyed the period's "shower of gold." In 1896 a Belgian stock company established an enamel works. Now long since nationalized, it still survives. Belgians also set up foundries, bone meal factories, distilleries, leather works and so on. By 1900 some 10,000 workers labouring in 230 factories had settled in Luhanske; they comprised about half the population of the town.

In the fourteen years before the First World War, the town's population tripled, but the available amenities and services did not expand at a comparable rate.[41] In 1912 there were only 7,993 private dwellings—mostly one-storey edifices constructed from local stone; more than a thousand of them had roofs of clay or mud. Only fourteen streets were paved and only 513 kerosene lamps lit the centre of the city. There was no sewage system and no adequate supply of water. The city lacked a telephone system and only the very rich could afford private lines. Medical facilities consisted of a single hospital, constructed as late as 1894, and there was only one doctor for every 1,365 inhabitants. Little wonder that typhus and cholera repeatedly ran through the populace—notably in 1908, 1909 and 1910. Schools were few and cultural centres rare. The latter consisted of a seasonal theatre, two clubs, a city library and three movie theatres. In terms of per capita expenditures on city services, the government of Luhanske was the most parsimonious in the entire guberniia of Katerynoslav.

Luhanske (now Voroshylovhrad) was not a predominantly Ukrainian town. The factory serfs and plant managers who originally settled it were drawn from central Russia. Other workers immigrated over the years into the city, but included few Ukrainians. In 1897 only 19.1 per cent of the urban population was Ukrainian (see Table 2). Perhaps because of its artificial creation and close connection with the imperial army, Luhanske possessed a greater proportion of Russians (68.2 per cent) than any of the Ukrainian cities listed in Table 2.

TABLE 2. NATIONAL COMPOSITION OF THE POPULATION IN FOUR UKRAINIAN CITIES IN 1897

City	Ukrainians	Russians	Jews	Poles
Kiev	22.23	54.20	12.08	6.69
Kharkiv	25.92	53.17	5.66	0.28
Odessa	5.66	40.79	32.50	4.48
Luhanske	19.12	68.16	7.10	0.50

SOURCE: *Pervaia vseobshchaia perepis Rossiiskoi imperii, 1897 g.*, prepared by the Tsentralnyi komitet Ministerstva vnutrennikh del, under the supervision of N. A. Troinitskii, 80 vols. (St. Petersburg, 1899–1905). The data for Kiev appear in vol. 16; for Kharkiv in vol. 46; for Odessa in vol. 47; and for Luhanske in vol. 15.

Of the five Ukrainian cities here considered, Luhanske was unique for the early and continuing importance of its industry. It was, on the other hand, singularly lacking in charm and comfort. If the commercial, administrative and cultural centres previously studied attracted few Ukrainian immigrants, an industrial city such as Luhanske attracted fewer still. Like Odessa, it was an entirely new town, but unlike Odessa, it did not progressively assume functions beyond its original purpose; it never became in our period an important market town or intellectual centre. While large commercial cities, as we have seen, eventually invited industrialization, this purely industrial town did not assume important commercial or cultural functions. Luhanske remained in its development what it had been in its origins: a factory city.

Summary

In this sketch of five Ukrainian cities in the nineteenth century, is it possible to discern common patterns? Clearly, few Ukrainians were attracted to any form of urban life. Their intellectual leaders, we might note, themselves smitten by a kind of romantic attachment to the countryside, frowned upon settlement in the supposedly corrupt cities. Moreover, within the Russian empire land still abounded, and agriculture held the principal interest of the Ukrainians. To be sure, the constraints of serfdom limited their movement in the first half of the century. But many peasants (sometimes entire villages) made their way to underdeveloped and underpopulated southern Ukraine. After emancipation in 1861, as the empty southern lands were largely claimed and settled, Ukrainians moved in large numbers to the region of the Northern Caucasia.[42] To a lesser extent they settled in enclaves, set within the vast spaces of the Ural mountains and the Volga basin. Some pushed even farther to the east through Siberia, into Central Asia, Kazakhstan and finally to the basin of the Amur river. Before the First World War some two million Ukrainians had emigrated to the eastern reaches of the Russian empire. With so much land inviting colonization, the Ukrainians not surprisingly largely avoided the great urban centres, where their skills earned them little reward. In Eastern Galicia, on the other hand, the most densely settled of all Ukrainian regions, open land was not so easily found. Here, the Ukrainians faced a difficult choice: either they would have to move to cities to earn their ways as labourers; or they could seek new farms or jobs in the United States, Canada, Brazil, Argentina and other newly settled territories. Between 1890 and 1913 numerous Ukrainians from the lands of Austria-Hungary came to seek their fortunes in the New World; estimates of their number vary, but range between 300,000 and 800,000.[43]

What contribution did industrialization make to urban growth? Among the five cities, only at Luhanske did industry make an early and substantial contribution to urban expansion. The other towns were all initially administrative, commercial and cultural centres. Most notably at Kiev and Odessa, governmental favour was also a significant factor in promoting the growth of cities. With much reason, therefore, scholars have recently questioned the tight linkages, presumed to have existed between industrialization and urbanization in the nineteenth century.[44]

On the other hand, the importance of industrialization in the growth of these cities cannot be entirely discounted. All five achieved some industrialization, especially after the coming of the railroad (here Odessa was less favoured than the others). The earliest industries typically processed local raw materials, both agricultural and mineral.

Industrialization, in turn, heightened the rate of population expansion within these already established urban communities. Between 1861 and the First World War the population of Kiev increased eight times; Luhanske, ten times; Odessa, six times; Kharkiv, five times; and Lviv, three times. There seems, in other words, to be a rough correlation between the degree of industrialization and the rate of subsequent urban expansion. This observation lends support to Roger Thiede's contention that "industry played a greater role than trade in the urbanization process."[45]

In more specific terms, industrialization appears to have been a significant factor not during the establishment of most Ukrainian cities, but during a subsequent, specific stage in the process of urban growth. Although trade, administration and culture are all important in the formation of urban nuclei and although cities can survive indefinitely as commercial, administrative and cultural centres, nevertheless industrialization alone provides the impetus to sustained and substantial urban growth. In Ukraine, as in the world, it made an essential contribution to the appearance of the first, truly great, truly modern cities.

Notes

1. *Ukraine: A Concise Encyclopaedia*, ed. V. Kubijovyč, 2 vols. (Toronto, 1963–71), 1: 169.
2. J. Borys, *The Sovietization of Ukraine 1917–1923: The Communist Doctrine and Practice of Self-Determination* (Edmonton, 1980), 66.
3. *Istoriia Kieva* 1 (Kiev, 1963), 248.
4. *Ukraine: Encyclopaedia* 1: 199.
5. *Istoriia Kieva* 1: 248, gives the population in 1861 as 65,000. Serhii Shamrai, "Kyivskyi odnodennyi perepys 2-ho bereznia 1874 roku," *Kyiv ta ioho okolytsia v istorii i pamiatkakh*, ed. M. Hrushevsky (Kiev, 1926), gives the population as 127,251 in 1874.
6. For the figures from 1861, see N. Sementovsky, *Kiev, ego sviatyni, drevnosti, dostopamiatnosti i svedeniia neobkhodimyia dlia ego pochitatelei i puteshestvennikov* (Kiev, 1864), 17. The numbers are 41,327 males and 29,263 females. For the figures from 1874, see *Kyiv ta ioho okolytsia*, 367.
7. *Istoriia Kieva* 1: 254.
8. *Kyiv ta ioho okolytsia*, 367. *Trudy etnograficheskο-statisticheskoi ekspeditsii v zapadno-russkii krai*, ed. P. P. Chubinsky, vol. 7 (St. Petersburg, 1872), 179.
9. For a colourful description by a German woman of the pilgrims coming to Kiev in 1900, see R. Binion, *Frau Lou* (Princeton, 1968), 271–3.
10. *Kyiv ta ioho okolytsia*, 372. An Englishwoman noted the influx of pilgrims to Kiev in 1890 and spoke also of English visitors to the city: "There are

very few fixed English residents in Kieff, but our country is always fairly represented by a floating population of travellers, military officers, commercial gentlemen, and governesses, most of whom I met." She then observed that military officers from Indian stations often came to board with native families in order to master the language. See I. Morris, *A Summer in Kieff or Sunny Days in Southern Russia* (London, 1891), 63, 82.

11. *Istoriia Kieva* 1: 253.
12. G. Hume, *Thirty-Five Years in Russia* (London, 1914), 255. The iron for the bridge was partially prepared in Birmingham, England; the construction machinery also came from England. It took sixteen ships to carry the materials from Liverpool to Odessa. Carl Vignoles, the English chief engineer, brought his two sons and two helpers to aid the work. The bridge was built mostly by local labourers at a cost of 2.5 million rubles. See *Kiev, ego sviatynia*, 12.
13. O. Parasunko, *Massovaia politicheskaia zabastovka v Kieve v 1903 g.* (Kiev, 1953), 16.
14. Hume, *Thirty-Five Years*, 257.
15. *Istoriia Kieva* 1: 344.
16. *Istoriia mist i sil Ukrainskoi RSR: Kyiv* (Kiev, 1968), 130.
17. *Istoriia Kieva* 1: 262.
18. *Ibid.*, 339.
19. *Ibid.*, 358–9.
20. *Ibid.*, 340.
21. *Thirty-Five Years*, 115. For more details on Kharkiv's fairs, see I. O. Hurzhii, *Ukraina v systemi vserosiiskoho rynku 60-90kh rokiv XIX st.* (Kiev, 1968), 114–15.
22. *Thirty-Five Years*, 115.
23. *Kharkov. Spravochnaia kniga* (Kharkiv, 1957), 23.
24. *Ibid.*, 24. From the 1860s, heavy industry concentrated in the city.
25. *Ibid.*, 28.
26. *Ukraine: The Land and its People* (New York, 1918), 141.
27. A. Zuk, "Lviv, Center of Ukrainian Economy in Galicia," *Lviv. A Symposium on Its 700th Anniversary* (New York, 1962), 305.
28. *Statistische Übersichten über die Bevölkerung und den Viehstand von Österreich nach der Zählung vom 31 Oktober 1857* (Vienna, 1859), 21. For discussion of the economic importance of the city in the nineteenth century, see *Naryry istorii Lvova*, ed. I. Krypiakevych et al. (Lviv, 1956), 115–16.
29. S. Y. Prociuk, "Economic Development of the City of Lviv," *Lviv. A Symposium*, 377.
30. Zuk, "Lviv," 312.
31. *Ibid.*, 314.
32. V. Radzykevych, "Lviv—A Center of Ukrainian Culture between Two World Wars," *Lviv. A Symposium*, 203.
33. For the ethnic composition, commerce, industry and urban growth, see my

articles, "The Ethnic Composition of the City of Odessa in the Nineteenth Century," *Harvard Ukrainian Studies* 1 (March 1977): 53–78; "Odessa: Staple Trade and Urbanization in New Russia," *Jahrbücher für Geschichte Osteuropas*, 22 (1973): 184–95; "Russian Wheat and the Port of Livorno, 1794–1865," *The Journal of European Economic History* 5 (Spring 1976): 45–68; "Greek Merchants in Odessa in the Nineteenth Century," *Harvard Ukrainian Studies* 3–4 (1979–80): 399–420.

34. M. V. Kaspéroff, "Commerce des céréales," *La Russie à la fin du 19e siècle*, ed. M. W. De Kovalevsky (Paris, 1900), 724–43, for the growth in grain exports.
35. V. A. Zolotov, *Vneshniaia torgovlia Iuzhnoi Rossii v pervoi polovine XIX veka* (Rostov, 1963), 145.
36. P. Herlihy, "Death in Odessa: Population Movements in a Nineteenth Century City," *Journal of Urban History* 4, no. 4 (August 1978): 417–42.
37. *Istoriia mist i sil Ukrainskoi RSR. Luhanska oblast* (Kiev, 1969), 67.
38. *Lugansk. Istoricheskii ocherk* (Donetsk, 1969), 10.
39. *Istoriia mist i sil. Luhanska oblast*, 68, and *Lugansk*, 21.
40. *Istoriia mist i sil. Luhanska oblast*, 69.
41. *Ibid.*
42. *Ukraine: Encyclopaedia* 1: 196–7.
43. See *The Ukrainians in America* ed. V. Westman (New York, 1976), 68–9.
44. See, for example, D. Brower, "L'urbanisation russe à la fin du XIXe siècle," *Annales-Economies-Sociétés-Civilisations*, 32 (1977): 83.
45. R. L. Thiede, "Industry and Urbanization in New Russia from 1860 to 1910," *The City in Russian History*, ed. M. F. Hamm (Lexington, Kentucky, 1976), 136.

Steven L. Guthier

Ukrainian Cities during the Revolution and the Interwar Era

Cities have played a pivotal, though not always propitious, role in the modern history of the Ukrainian nation. The urbanization process before the revolution failed to attract a substantial number of Ukrainians to the cities. Thus well into the Soviet period, one could speak of the cities of Ukraine, but not of Ukrainian cities as communities where the Ukrainian language and culture predominated. With rare exceptions the major cities of Ukraine were Russian and Jewish in ethnic composition and Russian in national sentiment. This circumstance created problems for Ukrainian nationalism in two significant respects. First, in the struggle for Ukrainian self-determination from 1917 to 1920, the Russian urban population played the role of a sizable "fifth column," strategically situated at the centres of the production and distribution of Ukraine's resources. Second, both before and after 1917 ethnically Ukrainian residents in the cities were submitted to intense Russification.

This essay examines the impact of the cities on Ukrainian nationalism during the revolutionary and interwar eras. Part one discusses the weakness of the Ukrainian nationality in the cities as a contributory factor in the defeat of the Ukrainian Revolution. Part two considers the extent to which Ukrainians improved their representation in the urban population during the first two decades of Soviet rule. It also analyses the problem of assimilation as an aspect of the urbanization process in Ukraine.

The Cities in the Ukrainian Revolution

The pre-revolutionary cities in Ukraine were islands of alien language and culture in a Ukrainian peasant sea. At the turn of the century urbanization had as yet made little impact on the demographic structure of Ukraine. According to the imperial Russian census of 1897, 13 per cent of the region's population lived in official towns or *goroda*; a bare 7 per cent lived in cities with 50,000 or more inhabitants.[1] Not only was the level of urbanization low, but Ukrainians were also the least urbanized national group within their ethnic territory. Whereas Ukrainian speakers constituted 80 per cent of the rural population, they comprised only one-third of the urban population. Moreover, as the size of towns increased, the Ukrainian element became progressively weaker. Table 1 groups towns by size and indicates the proportion of Ukrainians, and Table 2 presents a breakdown by native language of the population in the cities of Ukraine with over 50,000 inhabitants in 1897.

TABLE 1. DISTRIBUTION OF UKRAINIANS BY TOWN SIZE IN 1897

Size of Towns	No. of Towns	Total Population	Ukrainian Population	Percentage of Ukrainians
Under 20,000	86	870,981	535,297	61.5
20,000–50,000	16	438,580	158,411	36.1
50,000–100,000	7	448,532	96,507	21.5
Over 100,000	4	938,366	155,868	16.6
All Towns	113	2,696,459	946,083	35.1

SOURCE: *Pervaia vseobshchaia perepis naseleniia Rossiiskoi imperii 1897 goda.* (St. Petersburg, 1897–1905).

These tables show that Ukrainians were considerably underrepresented in those towns that were large enough to have an impact on the upcoming revolutionary struggles in Ukraine. Poltava, a town of very localized social and economic influence, was the only city with over 50,000 inhabitants and the only provincial capital in which Ukrainians constituted a majority. In Kiev, Odessa, Kharkiv and Dnipropetrovske, Russians heavily outnumbered Ukrainians. These four cities represented major concentrations of trade, manufacturing and transportation. Kiev, Odessa and Kharkiv were in addition the pre-eminent centres of administration, media and education in the region. The dominance of Russians in the population meant that opponents of Ukrainian national aspirations controlled the foci of socio-economic power in Ukraine.

In the two decades before the revolution, the pace of urbanization accelerated in Ukraine. On the eve of the First World War, there were

TABLE 2. POPULATION OF MAJOR CITIES BY NATIVE LANGUAGE, 1897

City	Total Population	Ukrainian	Russian	Jewish
		(Percentage of Total)		
Odessa	403,815	9.4	49.0	30.8
Kiev	247,723	22.2	54.2	12.1
Kharkiv	173,989	25.9	63.2	5.7
Dnipropetrovske[a]	112,839	15.8	41.8	35.4
Mykolaiv	92,012	8.5	66.3	19.5
Zhytomyr	65,895	13.9	25.7	46.4
Kremenchuk	63,007	30.1	19.3	46.9
Kirovohrad[b]	61,488	23.6	34.6	37.8
Kherson	59,076	19.6	47.2	29.1
Poltava	53,703	56.0	20.6	19.9
Berdychiv	53,351	8.2	8.6	77.1

SOURCE: *Pervaia vseobshchaia perepis naseleniia Rossiiskoi imperii 1897 goda.*

[a] Katerynoslav in 1897.

[b] Ielysavethrad in 1897.

twenty-two cities of over 50,000 in population with a total of three million residents.[2] The population of Kiev grew two and one-half times in this period; by 1913 it had 600,000 inhabitants and was rivalling Odessa as Ukraine's largest city. Regionally, the factory towns of the Donets basin and Dnieper industrial districts exhibited extraordinary growth. Between 1897 and 1914 the cities of Katerynoslav (Dnipropetrovske), Luhanske (Voroshylovhrad), Iuzivka (Donetske), Oleksandrivske (Zaporizhzhia) and Kamianske (Dniprodzerzhynske) all at least doubled their populations.

The acceleration of urban growth before the revolution was not paralleled by any significant improvement in the position of the Ukrainian nationality in the cities. This circumstance reflected, on the one hand, the relatively weak flow of migrants from the Ukrainian countryside to the cities, and on the other hand, the inroads of Russification among the Ukrainian urban minority. In the last decades of the Russian empire, rural overpopulation forced hundreds of thousands of Ukrainians out of their native villages. Most of them, however, sought to improve their lot as agricultural colonists in the Kuban and Siberia. The overwhelming majority of Ukrainians were peasant farmers, strongly attached to the land and lacking in skills that were readily transferable to urban trades. Migration to the cities meant accepting the most menial jobs. Moreover, the town was perceived as a foreign and intimidating environment. A participant in the Ukrainian Revolution characterized the villagers' attitude toward the pre-revolutionary city as follows:

> The city rules the village and the city is "alien." The city draws to itself all the wealth and gives the village almost nothing in return. The city extracts taxes which never return to the village in Ukraine. In the city one must pay bribes to be freed from scorn and red tape .... The city is aristocratic, it is alien. It is not ours, not Ukrainian. It is Great Russian, Jewish, Polish, but not ours, not Ukrainian.[3]

In Ukraine the social gulf separating town and country was significantly widened by ethnic cleavages. This circumstance, combined with the Ukrainian peasants' attachment to farming, restricted rural migration to the cities.

Those Ukrainians who found themselves in the cities were subjected to powerful assimilatory pressures. Until 1905 Ukrainian language publications were banned in the Russian empire. The removal of this ban stimulated a flurry of Ukrainian-language publishing activity, and in 1906 almost every town had its own Ukrainian newspaper. By 1908, however, official harassment and financial failures had reduced the field of the Ukrainian popular press to one daily, *Rada* in Kiev, and a few weeklies of irregular issue.[4] The Ukrainian communities in the great cities of Odessa, Dnipropetrovske and Mykolaiv were without native-language newspapers in the decade before the revolution; in the same period Kharkiv had two short-lived weeklies.[5] Instruction in the Ukrainian language was not permitted in the schools, even at the primary level, until 1917. The discriminatory policies aimed at Ukrainian language and culture were enforced with particular effectiveness in the larger cities, where the unremitting Russian character served to denationalize many urban Ukrainians.

Direct demographic evidence concerning the position of the Ukrainian nationality in the cities at the time of the revolution is available only for Kiev. In September 1917 a census was conducted which collected data on the nationality and occupational distribution of the civilian population. Since Kiev was the centre of nationalist activity both before and during the revolution, Ukrainians were as well if not better placed here than in other cities of Ukraine. Moreover, as noted above, Kiev was one of the most rapidly growing urban centres in Ukraine; the situation in Kiev was characteristic of the impact which urbanization was having on the ethnic structure of the cities. Table 3 presents a breakdown by nationality of Kiev's population. The deteriorating position of the Ukrainians from 22.2 per cent in 1897 to 16.4 per cent in 1917,[6] reflected the dual effects of relatively small-scale Ukrainian influx to Kiev and the Russification of Ukrainians who did settle there. The rise of Kiev to one of the empire's chief trade and manufacturing centres, combined with the city's extensive

TABLE 3. POPULATION OF KIEV BY NATIONALITY IN 1917

	Total	Ukrainian	Little Russian (Percentage of Total)	Russian	Jewish	Polish
Civilian Population	467,591	12.0	4.4	49.5	18.7	9.2
Those Engaged in:						
Industry and Manufacturing	57,220	11.9	3.8	43.3	20.3	9.4
Transport and Communications	33,281	18.8	4.6	52.1	3.1	8.2
Trade and Credit	33,740	9.1	3.3	39.5	34.3	8.1
Free Professions[a]	16,111	7.1	2.9	46.8	23.3	11.8
Students[b]	3,864	7.7	3.4	49.3	24.1	10.8
Church, Administration, Courts and Police[a]	26,291	12.3	5.5	55.2	10.3	9.4

SOURCE: I. S. Bisk, *K voprosu o sotsialnom sostave naseleniia g. Kieva (po dannym perepisi 1917 g.)* (Kiev, 1920), 3, 12.

NOTE: Nationality was determined by the self-identification of the census respondents.

[a] Does not include *rabochie*.

[b] Those older than fourteen and not living at home.

administrative functions to attract large numbers of Russian and Jewish residents. Thus between 1897 and 1917, whereas the Ukrainian population of Kiev increased by 60 per cent, the Russian population doubled and that of Jews tripled; these growth rates far exceeded the natural population increase.

Assimilation further undermined the strength of Ukrainians in Kiev. The 1917 census collected data on nationality (*natsionalnost*) by self-identification in contrast to the native language criterion applied in 1897. Thus people who had Ukrainian forebears and whose native language was Ukrainian, would often identify themselves and appear in the later census as Russians. In the absence of accompanying data on native language or ethnic origins for 1917, it is impossible to pinpoint the degree of Russification; however, it was undoubtedly considerable. Because of the nearly exclusive availability of schooling, newspapers and skilled employment in the Russian language, the impact of assimilation should have been felt most strongly in the educated strata. As Table 3 indicates, Ukrainians were significantly underrepresented among professionals and students, even though Kiev had long been a mecca for national-conscious Ukrainian intellectuals.

One other aspect of the results of the 1917 Kiev census should be noted: that over a quarter of the Ukrainians identified themselves as "Little Russians." The choice of this designation at a time when the most nationalistic layers of Ukrainian society viewed *malorossy* as a demeaning and even pejorative term, raises serious questions about the political orientation of the "Little Russian" element. One could hypothesize that Little Russians represented poorly educated, unmobilized segments of Ukrainian society with a low level of national consciousness. This appraisal, however, is not supported by any evidence. As Table 4 indicates, there was little difference in the social composition of the *malorossy* and the *ukraintsy*, though "Little Russians" were marginally better represented in the upper classes. The existence of a "Little Russian" element in Kiev's population suggests that decades of official suppression of Ukrainian national consciousness had left some ethnic Ukrainians with no clear attachment to their own political nation.

In the absence of census data for other cities, the results of the election to the Russian Constituent Assembly can help provide a broader picture of the situation of Ukrainians in the cities during the revolution. The democratic election process and the high level of participation make the returns an exceptionally useful gauge of popular sentiment and political identity in 1917. Appendix 1 (pp. 173–4) presents detailed results in thirteen major cities while Table 5 indicates the proportion of votes

TABLE 4. *UKRAINTSY* AND *MALOROSSY* IN KIEV BY SOCIAL STATUS, 1917

Occupation	Ukraintsy	Malorossy
	(Percentages)	
Workers	47.0	39.6
Household Servants	15.1	15.8
Office Workers[a]	11.5	11.9
Church, Administration, Courts and Police	10.7	14.0
Proprietors	9.8	10.9
Professionals[b]	4.7	5.7

SOURCE: Bisk, *K voprosu*, 8.

[a]*Sluzhashchie.*

[b]Includes students over fourteen years old, not living at home.

received by the Ukrainian national parties and their opponents.

One should emphasize that the Ukrainian totals were exaggerated since a substantial part of the vote in urban areas was cast by the military garrisons,[7] which contained a large complement of peasant Ukrainian soldiers. The latter, like their civilian counterparts in the villages, gave a high proportion of votes to Ukrainian socialists.[8] However, the peasant troops represented a transitory force in city politics. War weariness stimulated a high desertion rate and the troops were also anxious to return to the village in order to participate in the spontaneous land reform being carried out by the peasantry. In consequence, large numbers of Ukrainian soldiers returned to the countryside, leaving the national cause in the cities in a more unfavourable position than is suggested by Table 5. Table 6 shows party strength in several cities adjusted to reflect the civilian vote only.

As Tables 5 and 6 indicate, Ukrainian nationalists were outpolled in nearly every city by at least one group which was apathetic or antipathetic toward the Ukrainian cause. In Kiev the Ukrainian bloc was defeated among the civilian electors by the conservative List of Russian Voters headed by the Ukrainophobe Vasilii Shulgin. Only in Poltava did the Ukrainian parties muster a substantial plurality of the vote.

The revolution of 1917 thus found Ukrainian nationalism in a weak position in the cities; the movement had neither the mass support nor the material resources to successfully prosecute the national cause. During 1917 Ukrainian nationalists in Kiev were opposed at every turn by the Russian population in their attempts to Ukrainianize the administrative, cultural and educational institutions of the city.[9] In Poltava a Ukrainian

TABLE 5. CONSTITUENT ASSEMBLY ELECTION RESULTS IN MAJOR CITIES (PERCENTAGES)

City	Ukrainian Parties[a]	Bolsheviks	Kadets	Other Major Lists (over 10%)
Poltava	38	16	18	Zionists-16
Mykolaiv	31	26	14	Zionists-14
Kirovohrad	31	13	16	Zionists-31
Kremenchuk	29	21	7	Zionists-32
Kherson	27	18	14	Zionists-25
Kiev	26	18	10	Russian Voters-20
Vinnytsia	20	21	10	Zionists-23
Chernihiv	19	6	21	Zionists-26
Odessa	22	25	15	Zionists-26
Dnipropetrovske	16	26	12	Zionists-18
Zhytomyr	16	10	15	[b]
Kharkiv	13	28	25	
Voroshylovhrad	9	48	14	

SOURCE: See Appendix 1.

[a] All lists in which Ukrainian parties participated; that includes the UPSR/PSR blocs in Poltava, Kharkiv and Kherson provinces; and the USF/Popular Socialist blocs in Kiev and Chernihiv provinces. See Appendix 1.

[b] The Zionist List and Polish List combined polled 40 per cent.

TABLE 6. CIVILIAN VOTE IN MAJOR CITIES (PERCENTAGES)

City	Ukrainian Parties	Bolsheviks	Kadets	Other Major Lists (over 10%)
Kirovohrad	23	9	19	Zionists-39
Kiev	21	13	12	Russian Voters-29
Chernihiv	19	6	21	Zionists-26
Dnipropetrovske	13	27	13	Zionists-20
Odessa	18	19	17	Zionists-34
Zhytomyr	10	9	14	Poles and Jews-49
Kharkiv	8	23	29	Mensheviks-10

SOURCE: See Table 5 and Appendix 1.

deputy to the City Duma observed that "every kopeck for Ukrainian affairs, every trifle had to be extracted from [the Duma] with a struggle."[10] These unfavourable conditions existed in the two cities with the strongest traditions of Ukrainian nationalism. In other major cities such as Odessa, Kharkiv and Dnipropetrovske, local activists confined their efforts almost exclusively to cultural-educational work. Ukrainian influence in the politics of these cities depended upon the nationalist spirit among the troops in the garrisons.[11] When these soldiers departed, the national cause was left with little urban support. The plight of Ukrainian nationalism in Odessa, as described by the Austrian commander in April 1918, was similar to the situation in major cities and factory towns throughout Ukraine.

> Odessa is a cosmopolitan city and avidly refuses to acknowledge itself as belonging to the newly-created Ukrainian Republic; Ukrainians in Odessa are no more than 10 per cent [of the population]. The Ukrainian tongue enjoys no usage. They completely disespouse the Kiev Rada here and call it the "Impostor Government."[12]

The weakness of the Ukrainian nationality in the cities proved a crucial and perhaps decisive factor in the defeat of the Ukrainian Revolution. Despite demonstrative and overwhelming support for Ukrainian nationalism in the villages, the movement foundered in the cities.[13] Opponents of Ukrainian national aspirations were consistently able to deny Ukrainians access to the industrial resources, communications and transport facilities centred in the towns. This circumstance created insurmountable obstacles to the co-ordination and supply of an all-Ukrainian national effort. Ultimately, the great cities and factory towns provided the Bolsheviks with a decisive foothold in Ukraine from which they were able to reimpose central Russian authority.

The Cities of Soviet Ukraine between the Wars

The revolution and civil war initiated a precipitous population decline in the cities of Ukraine. Hundreds of thousands of people sought relief in the countryside from the food shortages, unemployment and political insecurity which plagued the cities from 1918 to 1921. (See Appendix 2 (p. 175) for the population figures of major cities between 1910 and 1939.) The outflow was particularly heavy among Ukrainian nationals, reflecting the fact that it was a generally inauspicious time for them in the cities. Working-class Ukrainians in the towns often had home villages nearby in which they could seek refuge, while this option was not commonly open to urban Russians and Jews in Ukraine. In consequence, the representation of Ukrainians in the cities reached its nadir during the civil war.

The end of the civil war did not immediately arrest this process of "ruralization." Economic recovery and industrial reconstruction proceeded slowly in the early NEP period, holding down employment opportunities in the cities. This was particularly evident in the metallurgical and mining districts of the Donets basin and Dnieper Bend, where towns continued to suffer population losses after 1920.[14] Odessa was hard hit not only by the dislocation of industry but also by the decline of the Black Sea trade. In 1923 the population of Odessa was barely one-half that of 1914; its subsequent rate of growth was among the lowest of Ukrainian cities between the wars.

By the mid-1920s cities throughout Ukraine were recouping their earlier population losses as evacuees returned and a new wave of migrants arrived. As Table 7 indicates, the revival of the cities was paralleled by an absolute and relative growth in the ethnically Ukrainian urban population.[15]

TABLE 7. UKRAINIANS IN THE URBAN POPULATION, 1920–6

	Ukrainians (in Thousands)			(Percentage)		
	1920	1923	1926	1920	1923	1926
Total Urban	–	2163.3	2536.5	–	44.4	47.3
Major Cities						
Dnipropetrovske	7.7	20.7	83.7	4.7	16.0	36.0
Donetske	4.3	2.2	27.6	11.4	6.9	26.2
Kharkiv	57.4	121.8	160.1	21.3	37.9	38.5
Kiev	52.4	112.0	216.5	14.3	27.1	42.3
Mykolaiv	16.7	14.2	31.4	15.3	17.5	29.9
Odessa	12.5	21.0	73.5	2.9	6.6	17.6

SOURCE: *Statystyka Ukrainy*, no. 28; *Naselenie Ukrainy po dannym perepisi 1920 goda* (Kharkiv, 1923); *Statystyka Ukrainy*, no. 77; *Naselennia v mistakh Ukrainy za dannymy Vsesoiuznoho miskoho perepysu 15 bereznia 1923 roku* (Kharkiv, 1925); *Vsesoiuznaia perepis naseleniia 1926 goda* (Moscow, 1928–33), vols. 11–13, Table 6 (hereafter *1926 Census*).

Nevertheless, in 1926 Ukrainians still remained significantly underrepresented in the cities. Only one out of nine Ukrainians lived in urban settlements where they constituted 47.3 per cent of the population (against 87.5 per cent of the rural population). As in the pre-revolutionary period, most urban Ukrainians congregated in the smaller towns. Of the 2.5 million Ukrainians in urban communities in 1926, two-thirds lived in towns with less than 50,000 inhabitants.[16] Ukrainian nationals continued to form a minority in the major cities while Russian remained the dominant language of city life. Table 8 presents a breakdown of the urban population by nationality and native language in 1926.

The substantial excess of Russian speakers over Russian nationals in Table 8 suggests that the cities remained powerful Russifying environments. The 1926 census correlated *narodnost* with native language.[17] Since the latter determines the national culture to which a person has easiest access, it represents a valuable indicator of assimilation. The

TABLE 8. URBAN POPULATION BY NATIONALITY AND NATIVE LANGUAGE IN 1926 (PERCENTAGES)

	Total Population	Nationality			Native Language	
		Ukrainian	Russian	Jewish	Ukrainian	Russian
Total Urban	5,359,240	47.3	25.1	22.7	36.0	44.5
Over 50,000	2,431,329	35.8	31.9	26.8	22.8	57.9
Under 50,000	2,927,911	56.9	19.4	19.4	47.0	33.4
Major Cities:						
Kiev	512,088	42.3	24.5	27.4	27.9	52.2
Odessa	417,690	17.6	39.0	36.7	10.1	66.1
Kharkiv	415,400	38.5	37.2	19.5	23.8	64.2
Dnipropetrovske	232,336	36.0	31.6	26.7	20.4	63.8
Donetske	105,242	26.2	56.6	10.8	11.1	80.8
Mykolaiv	104,724	29.9	44.6	20.8	10.3	77.8
Subraion:						
Right Bank	1,447,346	49.0	12.2	33.7	43.0	25.3
Left Bank	1,114,474	60.9	19.5	16.9	50.2	37.7
Steppe	1,056,969	33.0	33.2	27.9	21.3	58.2
Donets Basin	848,801	40.6	49.0	4.6	22.2	71.4
Dnieper Industrial	462,926	49.4	25.2	20.0	35.6	51.6
Forest	428,724	52.9	15.4	27.5	39.9	32.7
(Rural)	(23,635,740)	(87.5)	5.6	(1.5)	(85.6)	(8.6)

SOURCE: *1926 Census*, vols. 11–13, Table 6.

tendency of the population to abandon one language for another may signal a long-term reorientation of national identity. The relationship between urbanization and Russification among Ukrainians deserves careful attention, since widespread assimilation in the cities would imply a critical loss of trained and educated cadres for the Ukrainian nationality.

In 1926 a substantial number of Ukrainians in urban centres identified Russian as their native language. Indeed a comparison with the 1897 census data (see p. 158 above) reveals that Ukrainian speakers were scarcely better represented in urban centres in 1926 than three decades earlier. In addition, among Ukrainians in the cities who could read and write, Russian was the most common language. Table 9 groups Ukrainian nationals in the cities according to their native language and language of literacy.

TABLE 9. LANGUAGE USAGE OF UKRAINIAN NATIONALS IN THE CITIES IN 1926 (PERCENTAGES)

	Ukrainians Speaking:		Literate Ukrainians Reading:		
	Ukrainian	Russian	Ukrainian Only	Russian Only	Both Languages
Total Urban	74.5	24.7	18.3	41.1	38.5
Over 50,000	61.9	37.1	12.1	44.6	41.6
Under 50,000	81.0	18.2	22.2	38.9	36.6
Major Cities:					
Kiev	64.4	34.5	13.1	35.2	50.9
Odessa	55.8	43.8	12.2	58.0	29.0
Kharkiv	60.2	38.5	9.1	46.1	42.9
Dnipropetrovske	55.9	43.5	8.2	53.9	33.6
Donetske	41.8	57.4	5.2	69.0	21.6
Mykolaiv	33.6	65.7	6.0	67.3	26.0
Subraion:					
Right Bank	85.1	14.0	27.3	25.2	46.2
Left Bank	81.3	18.0	19.0	35.8	44.0
Steppe	63.1	36.2	12.2	53.1	33.9
Donets Basin	54.1	44.9	6.0	66.6	22.0
Dnieper Industrial	70.7	28.6	17.4	47.6	31.0
Forest	73.1	26.0	18.8	38.9	40.8
(Rural)	(96.5)	(3.2)	(46.9)	(29.8)	(22.2)

SOURCE: *1926 Census*, vols. 11–13, Tables 6 and 6a.

About one out of four Ukrainians in towns gave Russian as their native language in 1926 against one out of thirty in the countryside. Whereas

80 per cent of literate Ukrainians in the cities could read Russian, only 57 per cent were literate in Ukrainian, leaving over 40 per cent with no reading facility in their national language. Within this context of higher assimilation in urban areas there were certain visible patterns. The largest cities predictably proved to be the strongest Russifying environments. As cities grew in size the number of Russians and the ubiquity of Russian-language education and media increased. Regionally, the Ukrainians in the cities of the Right and Left Banks showed the greatest resistance to Russification. Kiev and Kharkiv had the least Russified Ukrainian populations among the great cities. In Poltava and Vinnytsia 90 per cent of Ukrainians spoke their national tongue and three out of four who were literate read Ukrainian. In these cities the absence of large scale commercial and manufacturing activity (except in Kiev and Kharkiv) had retarded the influx of Russians. Moreover, the Ukrainian peasants here had proven particularly receptive to the nationalist message during the revolution.[18] The migrants from the villages of the Right and Left Banks after the civil war were likely to be very conscious of their Ukrainian ethnicity. The relative dearth of Russians and the stronger tradition of Ukrainian nationalism here served to moderate the assimilatory impact of the cities.

At the other extreme were the factory towns of the Donets basin subraion where Russification had made disturbingly deep inroads among the Ukrainian population.[19] In the three large and rapidly growing cities of Donetske, Voroshylovhrad and Makiivka 60 per cent of Ukrainians gave Russian as their native language and 75 per cent of the literate Ukrainians could read only in Russian. The mines and metallurgical plants of the Donets basin had long drawn the bulk of their labour from nearby Great Russian provinces.[20] In 1926 barely one-third of the industrial workers here were Ukrainian nationals.[21] Moreover, during the revolution and civil war the Donets basin was a stronghold of Russian socialist activity rather than Ukrainian nationalism.[22] As a consequence of close association with a Russian proletarian majority and class mobilization under the direction of Russian socialists, the Ukrainian workers of the Donets basin factory towns had experienced extensive assimilation. Similar circumstances had served to Russify a substantial number of Ukrainians in the industrial cities and ports of the steppe region—Odessa, Mykolaiv, Kirovohrad (Ielysavethrad, Zinovevske), Kherson and Zhdanov (Mariupil).

In Ukraine's other major industrial area, the Dnipropetrovske region, urban Ukrainians proved more resistant to assimilation. The heavily Ukrainian rural districts along the Dnieper river provided the bulk of the workers for the local factories and mines. Between 1905 and 1916

TABLE 10. POPULATION GROWTH IN UKRAINIAN CITIES, 1926–39

City	1926	1939	Per Cent Growth 1926–39
Kiev	513,637	846,293	65
Kharkiv	417,342	833,432	100
Odessa	420,862	604,223	44
Dnipropetrovske*	232,925	500,662	115
Donetske*	105,857	462,395	337
Zaporizhzhia*	55,744	289,188	419
Makiivka*	51,471	240,145	367
Zhdanov*	41,341	222,427	438
Voroshylovhrad*	71,765	213,007	197
Kryvyi Rih*	31,285	197,621	532
Mykolaiv	104,909	167,108	59
Dniprodzerzhynske*	34,150	147,829	333
Poltava	91,984	130,305	42
Horlivka*	23,125	108,693	370
Kirovohrad	66,467	100,331	
Kherson	58,801	97,186	65
Zhytomyr	76,678	95,090	24
Konstiantynivka*	25,303	95,087	276
Kramatorske*	12,348	93,350	656
Vinnytsia	57,990	92,868	60
Kremenchuk	58,832	89,553	52
Ienakiieve*	24,329	88,246	263
Melitopol	25,289	75,735	199
Slovianske*	28,771	75,542	163
Kadiivka*	17,224	68,360	297
Chernihiv	35,234	67,356	91
Berdychiv	55,613	66,306	19
Sumy	44,213	66,883	44
Nikopol*	14,214	57,841	307
Artemivske*	37,780	55,165	46
Komunarske*	16,040	54,794	242
Cherkasy	39,511	51,693	31
Berdianske	26,408	51,664	96
Krasnyi Luch*	7,029	50,829	623

SOURCE: *1926 Census*, vols. 11–13, Tables 6 and 10; *Planovoe khoziaistvo*, no. 6 (1939): 14–17.

* City located in Donets basin or Dnieper industrial districts.

Ukrainian nationalists had been active through the *Prosvita* society in the working-class villages surrounding Dnipropetrovske.[23] During the revolution the USDRP and Ukapisty worked extensively in the Dnieper industrial region. These factors held down the Russification of the Ukrainian proletariat. Only in the older and larger industrial city of Dnipropetrovske was there substantial assimilation of Ukrainians. In Zaporizhzhia, Kryvyi Rih and Dniprodzerzhynske 70–90 per cent of Ukrainians habitually spoke their national tongue in 1926.

In the thirties the pace of urbanization accelerated dramatically in Ukraine. Between the all-union censuses of 1926 and 1939 the urban population grew from 5.4 million to 11.2 million.[24] One out of five people in Ukraine lived in a city with over 50,000 inhabitants by 1939, against one in twelve in 1926. Table 10 presents the intercensal growth of the thirty-four cities with 50,000 population on the eve of the Second World War. The introduction of forced draft industrialization via the Five Year Plans was the stimulus behind the breakneck urban growth. Ten new cities, nine of which were centres of industry,[25] achieved the 100,000 population plateau during this twelve-year period.

TABLE 11. NATIONAL COMPOSITION OF KHARKIV, 1926 AND 1939

Year	Ukrainians		Russians		Jews	
	In Thousands	Percentage	In Thousands	Percentage	In Thousands	Percentage
1926	160.1	37.9	154.4	37.2	81.1	19.5
1939	403.6	48.5	274.2	32.9	130.2	15.6

SOURCE: *1926 Census*, vol. 12, Table 6; M. V. Kurman and I. V. Lebedinsky, *Naselenie bolshogo sotsialisticheskogo goroda* (Moscow, 1968), 122.

Because of the emphasis on heavy industry in the planned economy, cities in the eastern mining and metallurgical districts of Ukraine demonstrated extraordinary growth. The population of the eighteen cities located in the Donets basin and Dnieper industrial regions (Table 11) increased by 264 per cent during the intercensal period. Kharkiv doubled its population between 1926 and 1939, and exhibited the largest absolute growth of any Ukrainian city. As a centre of heavy machine construction and the railroad hub of Eastern Ukraine, Kharkiv had strong economic ties to the mining and metallurgical towns of the Donets basin. Kiev, while lagging behind the republic average for urban growth, exhibited an absolute population increase of one-third of a million people. The designation of Kiev as the new capital of the republic in 1934 provided considerable stimulus for growth.

Any characterization of the level of participation of Ukrainians in the accelerated movement to the cities in the 1930s is necessarily sketchy. Detailed results of the 1939 census including nationality profiles of the urban population have not been published. However, the available evidence indicates that the Ukrainian countryside was supplying much of the manpower for the burgeoning industrial cities. The proportion of Ukrainians among metallurgical workers rose from 19.1 per cent in 1925 to 45.9 per cent in 1931, and among miners from 19.4 per cent to 65.0 per cent. The Ukrainian population of Dnipropetrovske rose from 36 per cent in 1926 to 48 per cent in 1933; in Zaporizhzhia the Ukrainian element grew from 48 to 56 per cent in the same period; and in Stalino (Iuzivka, Donetske) from 26 to 31 per cent.[26] Thus the the first Five-Year Plan had a significant impact on the national composition of these major cities. The Ukrainian population of Kharkiv rose by about one-quarter of a million between 1926 and 1939 (see Table 11).

The absence of nationality and native language data for 1939 precludes precise observations concerning assimilation among Ukrainians during this period of intensive urbanization. Yet it must be presumed that the proportion of Russified Ukrainians in the cities declined in the 1930s. The push of collectivization and the pull of industrialization brought a massive influx of Ukrainian peasants to the cities, whose numbers must have strained the assimilatory capacity of the Russian language schools and press.[27] More importantly, the governmental policy of assimilating these urban Ukrainians was temporarily repudiated in the 1930s, and a contrary policy of Ukrainianization in the cities was pursued. Ukrainianization had been decreed as early as 1923, but press developments indicate that urban Ukrainianization was systematically enacted only at the end of the 1920s. In 1929 and 1930 city newspapers were shifted to the Ukrainian language in Kharkiv, Odessa, Dnipropetrovske, Mykolaiv and Zaporizhzhia.[28] Ukrainianization of the press was extended even to the heavily Russified factory towns of the Donets basin, though Donetske itself was excluded. By 1938 official sponsorship of Ukrainianization of the cities had been abandoned. But a complete volte-face to a policy of forced assimilation of the urban population was not attempted. While in the Donets basin there was widespread re-Russification of the press before the Second World War, elsewhere the Ukrainian popular newspapers survived the thirties intact.[29] Thus during Ukraine's most intensive period of urbanization, Ukrainian newcomers to the cities entered an environment in which linguistic and cultural manifestations of Ukrainianism were tolerated and at times even encouraged.

The second interwar decade proved to be a watershed of sorts for urban

Ukrainians. The events of the 1930s introduced a Ukrainian minority to most cities and the policy of Ukrainianization put a stop to assimilation. Still Ukrainian nationals remained underrepresented and the Ukrainian language under-used in the cities. At the time of the next all-union census in 1959 Ukrainian nationals constituted 62 per cent of the urban population, while Ukrainian speakers comprised 53 per cent.[30] However, ultimate control over the cities, investment, employment, education and media, rested with central, Russian, institutions. Thus the potential of the cities as instruments of assimilation persisted.

APPENDIX 1. RUSSIAN CONSTITUENT ASSEMBLY RETURNS IN MAJOR UKRAINIAN CITIES, 1917

City	Ukrainian Socialist	UPSR/ PSR Bloc	Minor Ukrainian	Bolshevik	Kadet	Jewish National	Other	Total
Kiev	46,764	–	1,860	32,576	18,742	15,922	69,487[a]	185,351
Odessa	28,525	12,510	–	45,281	28,131	47,784	21,300	183,531
Kharkiv	–	12,537	–	27,336	24,866	5,303	28,108	98,150
Dnipropetrovske	12,950	–	–	20,849	9,244	14,522	21,527	79,092
Mykolaiv	4,105	9,460	–	11,500	6,046	5,968	6,654	43,733
Poltava	3,896	5,564	762	4,304	4,824	4,404[b]	3,387	27,231
Kirovohrad	4,640	3,115	–	3,214	4,136	7,917	2,278	25,300
Kremenchuk	5,395	1,548	184	5,266	1,758	8,051[b]	2,789	24,991
Voroshylovhrad	2,122	–	–	11,345	3,300	?	6,884[c]	23,651
Kherson	1,783	4,090	–	4,082	3,170	5,524	3,452	22,101
Zhytomyr	3,389[d]	–	–	2,117	3,077	?	12,041[c]	20,264
Vinnytsia	2,848	–	–	3,058	1,420	3,227	3,708	14,261
Chernihiv[d]	1,148	–	411	492	1,724	2,134	2,299	8,208

(Continued on following page)

APPENDIX 1—*Continued*

Garrisons	Ukrainian Socialist	UPSR/ PSR Bloc	Bolsheviks	Kadet	Other Russian Socialist	Other	Total
Kiev	16,011	–	12,401	?	?	?	28,412[e]
Odessa	10,456	4,173	17,385	3,702	963	2,339	39,018
Kharkiv	–	5,795	8,623	829	436	459	16,142
Dnipropetrovske	3,770	–	1,756	301	1,701	1,478	9,006
Zhytomyr	1,786	–	656	931	1,076	457	4,906
Kirovohrad	1,000	2,097	1,470	417	74	175	5,233

SOURCE: City returns are compiled primarily from newspaper reports in late November-early December 1918; see especially *Vlast Naroda, Russkiia Vedomosti, Pravda, Robitnycha Hazeta*, and *Odesskiia Novosti*. For Poltava and Kremenchuk, see M. Sobolev, "Vybory do vserossiiskykh ta ukrainskykh ustanovchykh zboriv na Poltavshchyni," *Litopys revoliutsii*, no. 3 (48) (1931): 48–9; for Zhytomyr, Spirin, 48–9; and for Dnipropetrovske, *Bolshevistskie organizatsii Ukrainy v period ustanovleniia i ukrepleniia sovestkoi vlasti (noiabr 1917-aprel 1918 gg.)* (Kiev, 1962), 227. For garrison returns, see Spirin, 422–5; on Kiev, Oleh S. Pidhainy, *The Formation of the Ukrainian Republic* (New York, 1966), 211–12; for Odessa and Kirovohrad, *Odesskiia Novosti*, 17 and 21 November 1917.

[a]Includes List of Russian voters–36,602.

[b]Three Jewish Nationalist Lists.

[c]Includes Jewish vote.

[d]Does not include garrison vote; some figures calculated from reports in percentages.

[e]Garrison total for Kiev includes Ukrainian Bloc and Bolsheviks only. *Robitnycha hazeta*, 30 November 1917, indicates that these two lists captured 97 per cent of the 5,100 votes cast in the First and Second Military Precincts.

APPENDIX 2. POPULATION HISTORY OF MAJOR UKRAINIAN CITIES, 1910–39

City	Population in Thousands				
	1910	1920	1923	1926	1939
Odessa[a]	620.1	427.8	316.8	420.9	604.2
Kiev	527.3	366.4	413.1	513.6	846.3
Kharkiv	244.5	269.9	321.6	417.3	833.4
Dnipropetrovske	211.9	163.0	129.4	232.9	500.7
Mykolaiv	103.4	108.8	81.1	104.9	167.1
Kherson	91.9	74.5	41.3	58.8	97.2
Kremenchuk	88.4	66.4	55.0	58.8	89.6
Zhytomyr	88.4	56.4	68.3	76.7	95.1
Kirovohrad	75.8	77.1	50.3	66.5	100.3
Berdychiv	75.3	41.5	43.6	55.6	66.3
Bila Tserkva	69.9	22.9	37.9	43.0	47.4
Voroshylovhrad	60.3	52.1	44.2	71.8	213.0
Poltava	59.9	76.6	87.6	92.0	130.3
Nizhyn	51.9	29.6	34.5	38.0	39.3
Zhdanov	51.4	58.6	31.5	41.3	222.4
Kamianets-Podilskyi	49.6	26.6	29.5	32.1	34.8
Donetske	48.5	37.9	32.1	105.9	462.4
Sumy	48.2	37.2	36.9	44.2	63.9
Vinnytsia	47.8	38.0	51.3	58.0	92.9
Cherkasy	42.8	44.9	31.3	39.5	51.7
Uman	41.3	44.2	40.9	44.8	44.4
Khmelnytsky	40.6	18.6	21.9	32.0	37.5
Zaporizhzhia	38.1	49.7	43.9	55.7	289.2
Dniprodzerzhynske	35.5	16.9	?	34.2	147.8
Berdianske	34.2	37.0	22.0	26.4	51.7

SOURCE: For 1910: *Goroda Rossii v 1910 godu* (St. Petersburg, 1914); Odessa only, from Thomas S. Fedor, *Patterns of Urban Growth in the Russian Empire during the Nineteenth Century* (Chicago, 1975), 202, 215. 1920: *Statistika Ukrainy*, no. 28. 1923: *Statystyka Ukrainy*, no. 77. 1926: *1926 Census*, vols. 11–13, Tables 6 and 10. 1939: *Planovoe khoziaistvo*, no. 6 (1939): 14–17; and *Itogi vsesoiuznoi perepisi naseleniia 1959 goda, Ukrainskaia SSR*, Table 6 for cities with less than 50,000 population in 1939.

NOTE: List includes twenty-five largest cities in 1910.

[a]1911 figure.

Notes

1. *Pervaia vseobshchaia perepis naseleniia Rossiiskoi imperii 1897 goda* (St. Petersburg, 1897–1905) (hereafter *1897 Census*). The following volumes covering Ukrainian provinces were used: 8—Volhynia; 13—Katerynoslav; 16—Kiev; 32—Podillia; 33—Poltava; 41—Tavriia; 46—Kharkiv; 47—Kherson; and 48—Chernihiv. For the size of individual towns, see page one in each volume; for breakdown by native tongue, see Table 13. Throughout this paper data refers to the Ukrainian SSR in its 1926 borders and administrative divisions unless otherwise indicated. In terms of 1897 units the territory under consideration closely approximates all the provinces of Katerynoslav, Kiev, Podillia, Poltava, Kharkiv and Kherson; the continental portion of Tavriia; the eleven southernmost counties of Chernihiv; and the Volhynian counties of Zhytomyr, Ovruch, Novohrad-Volynskyi, Zaslav and Starokonstiantyniv.
2. *Statesman's Yearbook, 1917* (London, 1917), 1233–4; supplemented by entries for individual cities in *Istoriia mist i sil Ukrainskoi RSR*, 26 vols. (Kiev, 1967–74).
3. V. Shakhrai [V. Skorovstansky], *Revoliutsiia na Ukraine* (Saratov, 1919), 7–8, as quoted in H. R. Weinstein, "Land Hunger and Nationalism in the Ukraine, 1905–1917," *Journal of Economic History* 2 (May 1942): 31.
4. I. Tyshchenko, *Pershi naddniprianski ukrainski masovi politychni hazety* (New York, 1952), 2–6.
5. The most complete listing of pre-revolutionary Ukrainian periodicals is V. Ihnatiienko, *Bibliohrafiia ukrainskoi presy, 1816–1916* (reprint State College, Pa., 1968).
6. This decline continued a process in evidence since the last quarter of the nineteenth century when Kiev entered its phase of rapid growth. In 1874 Kiev was 30.3 per cent Ukrainian by native language compared to 22.2 per cent in 1897. See *Istoriia mist i sil Ukrainskoi RSR. Kyiv* (Kiev, 1968), 133.
7. At the time of the February Revolution Odessa had a garrison of over 50,000 troops; Kharkiv, over 40,000; Kiev and Mykolaiv, 35,000 each; Dnipropetrovske, 20,000; and Poltava, 15,000. Smaller garrisons were found in nearly every town. See S. M. Korolivsky, M. A. Rubach and N. I. Suprunenko, *Pobeda sovetskoi vlasti na Ukraine* (Moscow, 1967), 118.
8. The Third All-Ukrainian Military Congress in Kiev, held 21 October 1917, was notable for its aggressively nationalistic resolutions. The congress was attended by three thousand delegates, mainly Ukrainian SRs, who were elected by nearly three million soldiers at the front and in the garrisons. See *Kievskaia mysl*, 21 and 22 October 1917.

9. J. S. Reshetar, *The Ukrainian Revolution, 1917–1920* (Princeton, 1952), 136–8; also *Russkoe slovo*, 15 November 1917 and *Russkiia vedomosti*, 8 December 1917.
10. V. Andriievsky, *Z mynuloho (1917 rik na Poltavshchyni)*, 2 vols. (New York, 1963), 1: 110.
11. D. Doroshenko, *Istoriia Ukrainy, 1917–1923 rr.*, 2 vols. (New York, 1954), 1: 61–6; also *Volia naroda*, 6 June 1917.
12. Doroshenko, 2: 7.
13. In the eight predominantly Ukrainian provinces—Volhynia, Kiev, Podillia, Poltava, Chernihiv, Kharkiv, Katerynoslav and Kherson—the Ukrainian SRs and *Selianska spilka* [Peasant Union] captured about 55 per cent of the rural vote; another 18 per cent went to joint UPSR/PSR slates. For provincial returns to the Constituent Assembly election, see O. H. Radkey, *The Election to the Russian Constituent Assembly in 1917* (Cambridge, Mass., 1950), 78–80; and L. M. Spirin, *Klassy i partii v grazhdanskoi voine v Rossii (1917–1920 gg.)* (Moscow, 1968), 416–25. See Steven L. Guthier, "The Popular Base of Ukrainian Nationalism in 1917," *Slavic Review* 38, no. 1 (March 1979), 30–47, for an analysis of the regional and class base of the Ukrainian national movement in the light of the return to the Constituent Assembly election.
14. Coal output in 1922, after two years of steady improvement, stood at about one-third of prewar production; in the metal industry, production had regained only one-eighth of prewar levels by 1923. See M. Dobb, *Soviet Economic Development since 1917* (New York, 1966), 152–3, 161.
15. It should be noted that the tests for nationality in these three censuses did not correspond. The 1920 and 1923 enumerations questioned respondents on the national group, *natsionalnost*, with which they identified. By contrast the 1926 census employed the term *narodnost*. In 1926 census takers were instructed to ensure that respondents understood the nationality question in the sense of "ethnic origin," *plemennoe proiskhozhdenie*; the *narodnost* of their forebears was to be considered definitive. Religion, citizenship, residence in a national republic or identification with a nation were not to be substituted for *narodnost*. For a discussion of the instructions attached to census questions in 1897, 1920, 1923 and 1926, see N. Ia. Vorobev, *Vsesoiuznaia perepis naseleniia 1926 g.* (Moscow, 1957), especially 83–104. See also I. Sautin, "Naselenie strany sotsializma," *Bolshevik*, no. 10 (1940): 12–22, and R. M. Somerville, "Counting Noses in the Soviet Union: The 1939 Census," *American Quarterly on the Soviet Union* 3, nos. 2–3 (1940): 62–4.

    The effect of the change in census terms was to enumerate as Ukrainians by *narodnost* in 1926 those people who by virtue of assimilation or political expediency identified themselves as Russians by *natsionalnost* in 1920 and 1923. Thus the 1926 data tends to overstate the actual increase in the number of Ukrainian nationals vis-à-vis the earlier censuses. The improving climate in the cities for the Ukrainian language and culture in the early

1920s undoubtedly helped renationalize some assimilated Ukrainians, and may have offset distortions caused by the change in the census terms. To what extent this was the case cannot be determined. Thus while the figures in Table 7 demonstrate steady growth in the proportion of Ukrainians in the cities, one must have reservations about the magnitude of this growth.

16. *Vsesoiuznaia perepis naseleniia 1926 goda*, (Moscow, 1928–33), 11–23, Tables 6 and 10.
17. Native language was defined in the instructions as "that which the questionee speaks best of all or in which he usually speaks." Vorobev, *Vsesoiuznaia perepis*, 90.
18. The Ukrainian SRs and Ukrainian Peasants' Union took more than 80 per cent of the rural vote in the Constituent Assembly election in Kiev, Podillia and Poltava provinces. Compare Radkey, *Elections*, 78–80, with city returns presented above.
19. The level of assimilation in the Donets basin approached the high levels found among Belorussians, who have consistently demonstrated a low level of national consciousness. In 1926 49 per cent of urban Belorussians gave Russian as their native language. See S. L. Guthier, "The Belorussians: National Identification and Assimilation, 1897–1970," *Soviet Studies* 29, no. 1 (January 1977), 56.
20. A. G. Rashin, *Formirovanie rabochego klassa Rossii* (Moscow, 1977): 444–6. *1897 Census*, 13, Tables 21 and 22 show that workers in the Donets basin were two-thirds Russian and one-fourth Ukrainian.
21. *1926 Census*, 30, Table 1.
22. In the Constituent Assembly election Ukrainian socialists polled less than 5 per cent of the vote in the major Donets basin mines and under 10 per cent in the metallurgical city of Luhanske (Voroshylovhrad). See *Pravda*, 25 November and 1 December 1917.
23. See *Ukrainskaia zhizn*, no. 5 (1912): 99–102, and D. Doroshenko, *Moi spomyny pro davnie-mynule (1901–1914 roky)* (Winnipeg, 1949), 80–9.
24. *Izvestiia*, 2 June 1939.
25. See C. D. Harris, "The Cities of the Soviet Union," *Geographical Review* 35 (January 1945): 107–21. Soviet cities with over 50,000 inhabitants in 1939 are classified according to economic function on pages 114–20.
26. *Ukraine: A Concise Encyclopedia*, ed. V. Kubijovyč, 2 vols. (Toronto, 1963–71), 1: 811.
27. According to Mykola Skrypnyk, 1.3 million new workers arrived in the Donets basin in the first two years of the first Five Year Plan. Members of the CP(B)U who advocated Ukrainianization of the cities, including Skrypnyk, argued that this massive urban influx alone rendered unrealistic any attempt to Russify Ukrainians coming to the cities. See R. S. Sullivant, *Soviet Politics and the Ukraine, 1917–1957* (New York, 1962), 172–4, 364 n. 59.
28. I. V. Kuznetsov and E. M. Fingerit, *Gazetnyi mir Sovetskogo Soiuza, 1917–1970 gg.* (Moscow, 1976), 2: 200–37. Kiev already had a Ukrainian

newspaper as did most of the non-industrial cities of the Right- and Left-Bank regions. The press there had been Ukrainianized during earlier phases of Ukrainianzation between 1920 and 1925.

29. The campaign of press Ukrainianization was first terminated in those Donets basin cities where Russification had been most thoroughly imposed—Voroshylovhrad, Zhdanov, Makiivka and Horlivka. Here the Ukrainian papers were re-Russified in the mid-1930s. In contrast, the Ukrainianization of the press remained in force in the burgeoning cities of the Dnieper industrial area—Dnipropetrovske, Kryvyi Rih, Dniprodzerzhynske, Zaporizhzhia and Nikopol. As noted above the Ukrainian workers of these cities had demonstrated higher resistance to Russification than their counterparts in the Donets basin. The survival of the Ukrainian press here was both a reflection and reinforcement of this tendency. See Kuznetsov and Fingerit, *Gazetnyi mir*, 200–37, and *Ezhegodnik periodicheskikh izdanii v 1938 g.*, part 2 (Moscow, 1938).
30. *Itogi vsesoiuznoi perepisi naseleniia 1959 goda. Ukrainskaia SSR* (Moscow, 1963), Table 53.

Roman Szporluk

Urbanization in Ukraine since the Second World War

The Second World War marked a significant change not only in the history of the urbanization of Ukraine but in the history of the Ukrainian people as well. For the first time since the middle of the seventeenth century, all Ukrainian ethnic lands were united under a single political authority; Kiev and Lviv were no longer separated by an international boundary. The only period comparable in this regard was the period from 1569 to 1648, when most Ukrainian lands found themselves within the confines of the *Korona*, the Polish-dominated part of the *Rzeczpospolita*.

The Second World War also witnessed a profound ethno-demographic transformation in Ukraine. This subject is too complex to discuss here; suffice it to say that some five to seven million persons lost their lives in the war, and that those killed included no less than four million civilians. Proportionately, the most extensive were the losses suffered by the Jewish population, but in terms of absolute numbers they were equalled and even surpassed by the deaths of Ukrainian civilians and military personnel. Besides direct loss of life, the war and its aftermath witnessed mass population losses due to migration. Their overall, long-term effect was to cut drastically the number of Poles, Tatars, Germans, Czechs and other smaller groups living in the present boundaries of Ukraine and to establish conditions for the immigration into Ukraine of vast numbers of Russians.[1]

Perhaps the following very general data will convey something of the vastness of the population change brought about by the war and its aftermath. Since Ukraine did not exist in its present shape until 1939, let us first cite the data for the Ukrainian SSR in its boundaries prior to 17 September 1939 and then compare them with the figures for the same territory after the war. In 1939 the population of the Ukrainian SSR was

31,785,000, of which 73.5 per cent was Ukrainian by nationality (this should make the Ukrainian total 23,362,000), and 12.9 per cent Russian (4,100,000).[2] The balance of 13.6 per cent consisted primarily of Jews, Poles and Germans. In 1959, the year of the first postwar census, "Eastern Ukraine" had a population of 34,069,988. Ukrainians numbered 25,360,713 or 74.44 per cent, Russians 6,687,875 or 19.63 per cent and the remaining 5.93 per cent consisted of Jews, Bulgarians, Greeks and other minorities. Proportionately, the non-Ukrainians and non-Russians were reduced to less than half their prewar share. The number of Ukrainians increased by about 1 percentage point; and the Russian population increased by 6.7 points. Between 1939 and 1959 the number of Russians in Eastern Ukraine rose by over 60 per cent; the Ukrainians—by about 9 per cent. (In many ways, the history of the period between 1926 and 1939 was even more eventful: while the total population of Ukraine in those intercensal years rose by about 12 per cent, its Ukrainian component registered a growth of 1.9 per cent, as compared to the Russian element's 56.7 per cent.)[3]

The change in "Western Ukraine" was no less dramatic. On 1 January 1933 the Ukrainians formed about 66 per cent of the population of "Polish Ukraine," i.e., Galicia and Volhynia; 60.0 per cent in Bukovyna, and 61.2 per cent in Transcarpathia.[4] (In Western Ukraine, Poles, Jews, Czechs, Romanians and Hungarians were more numerous than Russians, who basically consisted of émigrés from the Soviet state.) In 1959 the demographic scene in Western Ukraine bore little resemblance to the prewar situation. The Ukrainians increased their share of the population in all parts of the historical region and constituted 87.2 per cent of Western Ukraine's population (6,797,780 Ukrainians out of a total population of 7,799,058). The "historic" nationalities of the region had been greatly reduced in size, and the Russians now made up the second largest group: numbering 402,938, they constituted over 5 per cent of the population.[5]

Before the Second World War Ukrainians were in a minority in the cities and towns of Ukraine. According to the 1926 Soviet census, they constituted 41.3 per cent of Ukraine's urban population. In the urban areas of Western Ukraine, they were similarly outnumbered by other nationalities, and the population of the unofficial capital of the region, Lviv, was only 16.2 per cent Ukrainian in 1931. To put the matter in another way, only one in ten Ukrainians lived in cities or towns in 1926; the proportion was also about the same in Western Ukraine.[6] By 1959 the situation had changed: for the first time in their modern history, Ukrainians made up the majority of the population in their own cities. In the republic as a whole, their share was 61.53 per cent; in Eastern Ukraine it fell slightly below to 60.34 per cent; in Western Ukraine it was much higher at 71.19 per cent. (However, Western Ukraine was much less urbanized than the East, and it had little influence on the republic average. Eastern Ukraine was 50 per cent urban in 1959, while the West was 27 per cent urban. The republic average was 46 per cent.)[7]

As an urban system, prewar Ukraine was characterized by the lack of a primate city. In 1897 Odessa was the largest city but also the least Ukrainian of the major cities located in Ukrainian territory. By 1939 Kiev was the largest city in Ukraine with a population of 851,000, followed by Kharkiv with 840,000 and Odessa with 599,000. The other principal cities were Dnipropetrovske (528,000), Donetske (474,000) and, across the Polish border, Lviv (340,000).[8] If one defines a primate city as one which is at least twice the size of the second largest, in accordance with what Mark Jefferson has called "the law of the primate city" ("a country's leading city is always disproportionately large and exceptionally expressive of national capacity and feeling"),[9] Ukraine clearly was not an integrated entity as late as 1939. If one counts the population of Kiev in 1939 as 100, the population of Kharkiv was 99 and that of Odessa, 70: this would place Ukraine at the bottom of a list of fifty-one cases illustrating the position of primate cities in relation to the second and third cities of their respective countries. (Italy in 1936 had a ranking of 100-96-75, and Spain, in 1934, a slightly higher one of 100–91–31.)[10]

In 1939 Ukraine was still a predominantly rural country (only 34 per cent of the population in the present boundaries of the Ukrainian SSR, and 37 per cent in the former boundaries, lived in urban locations; the urbanization level of Western Ukraine was lower).[11] Large-scale urbanization in Soviet Ukraine commenced only after 1945. Because the Ukrainians had historically been so closely identified with the village, their relationship with the Russians and Poles, the two nationalities most closely linked with Ukrainian history, had reflected itself in terms of an urban-rural dichotomy. In popular perception—and in sociological fact—Ukrainian ethnicity came to be identified with village ways of life, values and styles, and Poles and Russians in Ukraine became associated with the city and the world of high social, cultural and economic life. It was therefore of critical importance for the Ukrainian national movement in modern times to establish a Ukrainian presence in urban areas. To a considerable extent, the Ukrainians accomplished this goal in the Austrian part of their land, in that Ukrainians who were employed in the cities or who were otherwise occupied outside agriculture, forestry or fishing defined themselves politically and culturally as members of the Ukrainian nation. Under Austria and Poland the Ukrainians succeeded in establishing socially-mobilized but culturally-differentiated (from the Poles and to a lesser extent from the Romanians, Czechs and Hungarians) strata to provide leadership for the masses. By their example, these strata demonstrated that one could be urban, educated, high on the occupational ladder, in short, "modern"—*and* Ukrainian.

The development of analogous processes in Russian Ukraine proceeded more slowly and faced virtually insurmountable obstacles until 1917. The policy of Ukrainianization, which was proclaimed in the 1920s, aimed at the establishment of a Ukrainian presence (if not Ukrainian hegemony) in the modern urban environment. As is well known, this policy was not carried out as thoroughly as is portrayed in official decrees. Moreover, the whole concept was abandoned before the mid-1930s and the Russian language and culture were restored to their previous position of superiority in the cities of Ukraine. The Ukrainians were relegated to the role they had played in tsarist Russia: that of the ruling nation's "younger brothers," to use a term popularized by John A. Armstrong. (Armstrong stresses cultural proximity to the ruling nation as one of the characteristics of a "younger-brother" nation, the other being the latter's low level of social and economic development, in short, a predominantly rural habitat.)[12] In such a relationship, as Armstrong has noted, the cities in the younger-brother area were relatively small before the onset of mass industrialization, and they were also dominated linguistically by the ruling nation. (This included assimilated members of the dominated nationality.) In such a context:

> The cities are ... fortresses from which dominant ethnic forces sally forth to control the countryside economically and politically, and (through control of rural socialization and communication processes) to effect a measure of assimilation even there.[13]

When rapid industrialization (and thus urbanization) begins, large numbers of the younger-brother group enter the city and one of two possible results emerges: either this influx "swamps" the hitherto dominant group or the dominant group maintains its position by means of continuing in-migration from the outside.

Armstrong's scenario, which is inspired by the work of Karl Deutsch on nationalism and social communication, has to be amended in application to Ukraine. Stalin's treatment of Ukraine in the 1930s shows, in our opinion, that political violence on a mass scale can be used to regulate ethno-demographic processes in a period of rapid social change, urbanization and industrialization. It became quite clear in the late thirties that Ukraine was to become a modern region, but in the process the cities, industry, high culture and the world of science were to be Russified rather than Ukrainianized.

However, Stalin did not as yet control the western portions of Ukraine, in which, as we have already observed, the Ukrainians had succeeded, however modestly, in establishing their presence in the city. Moreover, their struggle for a place in the urban sun had been fought not against the Russians but against their western neighbours. The West Ukrainians were free, accordingly, of an inferiority complex toward Russia, and in general associated modernity with centres such as Warsaw, Vienna, Prague, perhaps Berlin or Paris, even New York, but certainly not tsarist or Stalinist Moscow or Leningrad.

This preliminary discussion may now be concluded and the principal concerns of this essay laid out. Urbanization being a complex, multi-faceted process, with wide ramifications, connections and consequences,[14] this paper is limiting itself to a discussion of two themes. First, we would like to examine the processes of population growth in postwar Ukraine with regard to ethnic change. Is urbanization accompanied by a change in the ethnic composition of the urban population? Are urban Ukrainians becoming assimilated to the Russian culture, or do they maintain their ethnic identity as city residents? Our examination of this problem will be conducted along with, and we hope will be illuminated by, a review of urbanization processes pertaining to the question of the primary city in Ukraine. Ukraine before 1939, we remember, lacked a really dominant urban centre. What changes have occurred since 1945? In the conclusion, we will attempt to tie these two themes—assimilation and urbanization, the rise of the primate city—together. What is the position of Ukrainians in the primate city—or its closest equivalent—of their land?

First of all, let us briefly characterize general population trends in Ukraine as revealed in data assembled in Table 1. Two southern regions of Ukraine, the South (proper) and the Dnieper, registered significantly higher population growth between 1959 and 1970. This trend (southward migration) was continued in 1970–7, when these two regions, especially the South, grew much faster than the republic as a whole. The North East and Central West on the other hand were increasing at a below-average rate. The growth rate of the Central West was about half the republican average, whereas the North East region grew slightly faster in 1959–70 but dropped behind the Central West in 1970–7. As will be seen later, both these regions owed their gains to the two main cities of their respective areas, Kiev and Kharkiv. Some oblasts located in these areas of Ukraine were actually declining in population. The West, on the other hand, appears to have stayed close to the republic average: it was very slightly behind it in 1959–70, but virtually level in 1970–7.

In the post–1959 period urban population (Table 2) has grown relatively slowly in the Donets basin, but one should take into account this region's already high degree of urbanization. The North East has also been relatively high on urbanization indices owing to the location in this area of the major city of Kharkiv. Moreover, there appears to have been a continual growth of urban population also in Poltava and Sumy oblasts. The urban population of the Dnieper region showed only a slight increase, but this region which includes Dnipropetrovske, Zaporizhzhia and Kryvyi Rih, remains the second most highly urbanized part of Ukraine.

The South has increased its urban population considerably throughout the postwar period, improving its share of Ukraine's urban population from 12.9 per cent in 1959 to 14.7 per cent in 1977. There has also been an above-average increase of urban population in the Central West (Kiev, Vinnytsia, Cherkasy and Chernihiv being among the fastest growing cities), and in the West, where the population of such oblast capitals as Rivne, Ternopil, Ivano-Frankivske and Lutske increased especially rapidly.[15] On the whole, however, Western Ukraine has remained a rural region and as late as 1977, less than 40 per cent of its population lived in the cities (Table 3). The figures for the Central West region were higher—50 per cent—due to the presence of Kiev in the region.

In the intercensal period of 1959 to 1970 the Ukrainian share in the population of the Ukrainian SSR declined from 76.8 to 74.9 per cent. In the republic as a whole the Ukrainians increased by 9.7 per cent while the overall population increased by 12.6 per cent; with a gain of 28.7 per cent, the Russians were maintaining a rate of growth three times higher than the Ukrainians. In the component regions, the rates of growth of Ukrainians and Russians varied, but the general trend was toward a decline of the Ukrainian majority (Table 4).

In view of these figures, brief comments on the ethnic scene may be in order. First, we note that in only one major region, the West, did the Ukrainians improve their relative strength; conversely, the Russian population declined, albeit very slightly. Secondly, Ukrainians seem to be facing the prospect of becoming a minority in two important areas: the Donets basin and the South (particularly the former). In relative terms, the Ukrainian population was growing in the South and Dnieper regions but the Russian population was increasing at an even faster rate. This illustrates our earlier comment about the southern migration of population. One should not exclude the possibility that the census of 1979 will reveal an improved Ukrainian standing in the Crimea or Kherson oblast, if not the South as a whole; such an outcome will depend on the intensity of

TABLE 1. POPULATION OF UKRAINE AND REGIONS, 1939–77

	1939	Percentage	1959	Percentage	1970	Percentage	1977	Percentage	Change 1959–70	Change 1970–7
Ukraine	40,469	100.0	41,869	100.0	47,127	100.0	49,300	100.0	12.6	4.6
Donets Basin	4,940	12.2	6,715	16.0	7,643	16.2	7,997	16.2	13.8	4.6
South	4,852	12.0	5,066	12.1	6,381	13.5	7,006	14.2	26.0	9.8
Dnieper	4,847	12.0	5,387	12.9	6,377	13.5	6,766	13.7	18.4	6.1
North East	6,159	15.2	5,632	13.5	6,037	12.8	6,154	12.5	7.2	1.9
Central West	11,622	28.7	11,228	26.8	11,935	25.3	12,221	24.8	6.3	2.4
West	8,049	19.9	7,800	18.6	8,754	18.6	9,156	18.6	12.2	4.6

SOURCE: *Itogi Vsesoiuznoi perepisi naseleniia 1959 goda. Ukrainskaia SSR* (Moscow, 1953), Table 5; *Itogi Vsesoiuznoi perepisi naseleniia 1970 goda* (Moscow, 1973), vol. 1, Table 2; *Narodnoe khoziaistvo SSSR za 60 let. Iubileinyi statisticheskii sbornik* (Moscow, 1977), 52. *Donets basin*: Voroshylovhrad and Donetske; *South*: Odessa, Crimea, Kherson, Mykolaiv; *Dnieper*: Dnipropetrovske, Zaporizhzhia, Kirovohrad; *North East*: Kharkiv, Poltava, Sumy; *Central West*: Kiev, Chernihiv, Cherkasy, Zhytomyr, Vinnytsia, Khmelnytsky; *West*: Lviv, Rivne, Volyn, Ternopil, Ivano-Frankivske, Transcarpathia, Chernivtsi.

NOTE: 1939 figures do not include Transcarpathia.

TABLE 2. URBAN POPULATION OF UKRAINE AND REGIONS, 1939–77

	1939	Percentage	1959	Percentage	1970	Percentage	1977	Percentage	Change 1959–70	Change 1970–7
Ukraine	13,569	100.0	19,147	100.0	25,689	100.0	29,844	100.0	34.2	16.2
Donets Basin	3,631	26.8	5,601	29.3	6,546	25.5	7,010	23.5	16.9	7.1
South	1,785	13.2	2,465	12.9	3,641	14.2	4,389	14.7	47.7	20.5
Dnieper	1,972	14.5	3,108	16.2	4,268	16.6	4,902	16.4	37.3	14.9
North East	2,044	15.1	2,539	13.3	3,293	12.8	3,792	12.7	29.7	15.2
Central West	2,386	17.6	3,327	17.4	4,932	19.2	6,119	20.5	52.8	24.1
West	1,751	12.9	2,107	11.0	3,009	11.7	3,632	12.2	42.8	20.7

SOURCE: *Itogi 1959*, Table 5; *Itogi 1970*, vol. 1, Table 2; *Nar. khoz. 1977*, 52.

NOTE: 1939 figures do not include Transcarpathia. Percentages may not add up to 100 because of rounding off.

Russification and the volume of Russian in-migration from other areas of Ukraine and the USSR. Finally, Ukrainian strength has declined in

TABLE 3. URBAN POPULATION AS PERCENTAGE OF TOTAL POPULATION OF UKRAINE AND REGIONS, 1939–77

	1939	1959	1970	1977
Ukraine	33.5	45.7	54.5	60.5
Donets Basin	73.5	83.4	85.6	87.7
South	36.8	48.7	57.1	62.6
Dnieper	40.7	57.7	66.9	72.5
North East	33.2	45.1	54.5	61.6
Central West	20.5	29.6	41.3	50.1
West	21.8	27.0	34.4	39.7

SOURCE: Tables 1 and 2.

NOTE: 1939 figures do not include Transcarpathia.

TABLE 4. ETHNIC COMPOSITION OF UKRAINE AND MAJOR REGIONS

	Ukrainians			Russians		
	1959	1970	Percentage change 1959-70	1959	1970	Percentage change 1959-70
Ukraine	76.8	74.9	9.7	16.9	19.4	28.7
Donbass	56.4	53.7	8.4	38.0	41.0	22.9
South	56.9	55.0	21.6	30.9	34.0	38.7
Dnieper	77.6	74.8	14.0	17.6	20.8	40.1
North-East	81.0	78.5	3.3	6.3	7.7	23.2
Central West	88.3	87.4	5.3	6.3	7.7	30.0
West	87.2	88.2	13.6	5.2	5.1	10.6

SOURCE: *Itogi 1959*, Table 54; *Itogi 1970*, vol. 4, Table 8.

NOTE: Percentage change 1959-70 is based on absolute figures; the figures for 1959 are taken as equal to zero.

traditional centres of Ukrainian life: the North East, which includes Poltava and Sumy oblasts (this may be due to Russian immigration to the cities of the region, Kharkiv, Poltava and others), and the Central West. The latter had a 30 per cent increase in Russian population from 1959 to 1970 due mainly to in-migration.

The 1959 census revealed that the cities and towns of Ukraine possessed Ukrainian majorities (Table 5). The overall majority was only 61.53 per cent, but significant nevertheless. The Russian population was virtually half the size of the Ukrainian (29.9 per cent), and the number of Russian-speakers was much higher. Other nationalities traditionally present in Ukrainian urban life were much reduced in size by 1959.

TABLE 5. ETHNIC COMPOSITION OF URBAN POPULATION: UKRAINE, WEST, CENTRAL WEST AND EAST AND SOUTH, 1959 AND 1970

	1959		1970		Percentage Change 1959–70
Ukraine	19,147,419	100.0	25,688,560	100.0	34.16
Ukrainians	11,781,750	61.53	16,164,254	62.92	37.20
unassimilated	9,973,430	(84.65)	13,388,207	(82.83)	34.24
assimilated	1,802,510	(15.30)	2,771,002	(17.14)	53.73
Russians	5,726,476	29.91	7,712,277	30.02	34.68
West	2,107,144	100.00	3,009,274	100.00	42.81
Ukrainians	1,500,102	71.19	2,329,350	77.41	55.28
unassimilated	1,437,853	(95.85)	2,261,887	(97.10)	57.31
assimilated	57,447	(3.83)	62,500	(2.68)	8.80
Russians	348,210	16.53	411,119	13.66	18.07
Central West	3,328,307	100.00	4,931,518	100.00	48.17
Ukrainians	2,340,673	70.33	3,668,765	74.39	65.74
unassimilated	2,049,511	(87.56)	3,304,330	(90.07)	61.23
assimilated	290,928	(12.43)	364,214	(9.93)	25.19
Russians	559,929	16.82	812,484	16.48	45.11
East and South[a]	13,711,968	100.00	17,747,768	100.00	29.43
Ukrainians	7,940,975	57.91	10,166,139	57.28	28.02
unassimilated	6,486,066	(81.68)	7,821,990	(76.94)	20.60
assimilated	1,454,135	(18.31)	2,344,288	(23.06)	61.22
Russians	4,818,337	35.14	6,488,674	36.56	34.67

SOURCE: *Itogi 1959*, Tables 53 and 54; *Itogi 1970*, vol. 4, Tables 7 and 8.
[a] East and South includes North East, Donets basin, Dnieper and South regions.

The distribution of Ukrainians in the cities was uneven. They were strongest in the West (a remarkable change from the pre-1939 era) and had a clear lead also in the Central West, where they constituted a majority in Kiev, but were much weaker in the cities of the East and South, traditionally more urban and more Russian. The regions of the South, Donets basin, Dnieper and North East together registered a Ukrainian majority of 57.9 per cent. Donetske oblast had a Ukrainian majority of 52 per cent in 1959, Voroshylovhrad one of 53 per cent. In Odessa oblast Ukrainians had a plurality of 44 per cent. In the Crimea, a new Ukrainian region (added to the Ukrainian SSR in 1954), 18 per cent of the urban population were Ukrainians. Ukrainians were particularly weak in the principal cities: Odessa (42 per cent), Kharkiv (47 per cent), Donetske (51 per cent) and Dnipropetrovske (59 per cent); they were better represented in the smaller towns, hence their regional totals were higher than those in the centres.[16] The population of the Central West had a Ukrainian share of 71.2 per cent, while Kiev itself reported 60.1 per cent (an impressive gain over the 1926 figure). In the West, there was a Ukrainian majority in Lviv (60 per cent), and an even higher one in the cities of Ternopil, Lutske, Rivne and Ivano-Frankivske, a plurality in Chernivtsi, and in Uzhhorod Ukrainians accounted for 50 per cent of the population.[17]

By 1970, the year of the next census, the Ukrainians had slightly increased their 1959 majority from 61.5 to 62.9 per cent. Considering that the urban population grew by more than one third, mostly through migration, one has to conclude that there was either an inordinately large inflow of Russians into Ukraine or widespread assimilation of Ukrainians into the Russian nationality. At any rate, the Ukrainian component of the urban population increased at a rate barely above the average and in the East and South fell somewhat below the average. (See Table 5.)

Focusing on the oblasts where regional centres are located, we note that Ukrainians suffered a relative decline in the cities of Donetske, Kharkiv and Dnipropetrovske; they improved their position in the oblast of Odessa, without, however, achieving a majority there; and they registered substantial growth in Kiev (city and oblast combined) and Lviv (Table 6). (The national composition of individual cities, revealed for 1959 by Naulko, has not been disclosed for 1970, except for Kiev.)

Perhaps more important and in the long run more threatening to Ukrainian survival in the cities was the disclosure that among the Ukrainians, the Russian speakers were increasing more rapidly than those who declared Ukrainian as their mother tongue. (Again, this suggests a high degree of linguistic assimilation which some scholars consider a transitional stage toward a change in ethnic self-identification.) From 1959 to 1970 the former increased by 53.4 per cent, the latter by 34.2 per cent. In the West (especially) and Central West the proportions were reversed. However, in the eastern and southern regions it was clear that urban Ukrainians were becoming Russified linguistically on a mass scale: those assimilated increased at a rate three times higher than those who retained the Ukrainian language. In the oblasts of Donetske and Voroshylovhrad (the Donets basin) there was actually an absolute, not merely a relative, decline in the number of Ukrainians who considered Ukrainian as their

TABLE 6. UKRAINIANS AND RUSSIANS IN URBAN POPULATION OF SIX OBLASTS (IN PERCENTAGES)

	Ukrainians			Russians		
Oblast	1959	1970	Percentage Change 1959-70	1959	1970	Percentage Change 1959-70
Kiev (city and oblast urban)	66.2	69.8	55.8	20.2	20.3	48.1
Kharkiv	60.8	59.8	22.4	32.0	34.1	32.9
Odessa	44.0	47.5	50.5	35.7	35.6	38.9
Dnipropetrovske	71.5	69.3	30.0	22.0	25.2	54.0
Donetske	52.0	49.9	12.4	41.5	43.9	22.8
Lviv	70.1	76.5	55.8	20.6	16.8	14.3
Ukraine	61.5	62.9	37.2	29.9	30.0	34.7

SOURCE: *Itogi 1959*, Table 54; *Itogi 1970*, vol. 4, Table 8.

TABLE 7. URBAN UKRAINIANS IN THE DONETS BASIN (BY NATIVE LANGUAGE), 1959–70

	1959	Percentage	1970	Percentage	Percentage Change 1959-70
Donetske	3,656,240		4,275,596		16.9
Ukrainians	1,902,583	100.0	2,137,010	100.0	12.3
unassimilated	1,425,590	74.9	1,398,651	65.4	-1.9
assimilated	476,817	25.1	738,182	34.5	54.8
Voroshylovhrad	1,944,633		2,270,884		16.8
Ukrainians	1,031,116	100.0	1,159,020	100.0	12.4
unassimilated	862,994	83.7	84,179	72.7	-2.3
assimilated	168,036	16.3	315,748	27.2	87.9

SOURCE: *Itogi 1959*, Table 54; *Itogi 1970*, vol. 4, Table 8.

native language; simultaneously the total urban population of the region increased by almost 17 per cent (Table 7).

A question arises: since the Donets basin is also the most highly urbanized region of Ukraine (see Table 3), will urbanization elsewhere in the republic be accompanied by a similarly intensive linguistic assimilation of Ukrainians? The answer, it seems, depends on which parts of Ukraine are involved. The rates registered for the oblasts of Kharkiv, Dnipropetrovske and Odessa in 1959–70 are presented in Table 8.

TABLE 8. UKRAINIAN URBAN POPULATION IN THE OBLASTS OF KHARKIV, ODESSA AND DNIPROPETROVSKE: PERCENTAGE RATES OF CHANGE 1959–70

	Kharkiv	Odessa	Dnipropetrovske
Urban Ukrainians	22.4	50.5	30.0
unassimilated	14.7	47.2	25.7
assimilated	54.7	58.0	66.1

SOURCE: Calculated by the author from sources in Table 7.

In Kharkiv, from 1959 to 1970, assimilated Ukrainians grew 3.7 times faster than those who considered Ukrainian their native language. In Dnipropetrovske, they increased 2.5 times as fast, but in Odessa the rate was much slower at 1.3, perhaps because of the rapid growth of the Ukrainian urban population in that oblast (50.5 per cent), compared with a 30 per cent increase in Dnipropetrovske, 22.4 per cent in Kharkiv and even lower rates in the Donets basin. One may further surmise that the migrants in Odessa were coming from less assimilated areas of Ukraine, such as the Central West or West. These figures confirm the strong assimilationist currents in the South and East, but they also suggest that the Donets basin represents an extreme case.

We have yet, however, to find data that would positively disprove the example of the Donets basin as a trend-setter in the urban development of the Ukrainians. The case of Lviv may provide such evidence (Table 9). In Lviv the situation was dramatically reversed: the increase in the numbers of non-assimilated urban Ukrainians exceeded that of Russified Ukrainians by twenty times. If official statistics are to be believed, the cities of Lviv oblast were less Russified linguistically in 1970 than they had been in 1959. In order to forecast the likely course of linguistic assimilation in those parts of Ukraine which lie outside the zone which we designated as "South and East," one should turn to Kiev. Let us look at the urban population of Kiev oblast together with that of the city itself. (As Kiev is the capital of the republic, information about the city is more

TABLE 9. URBAN UKRAINIANS IN LVIV OBLAST BY NATIVE LANGUAGE, 1959–70

	1959	Percentage	1970	Percentage	Percentage Change 1959-70
Lviv	821,338		1,148,649		39.9
Ukrainians	575,377	100.0	878,998	100.0	52.8
unassimilated	545,128	94.7	848,228	96.5	55.6
assimilated	29,742	5.2	30,505	3.5	2.6

SOURCE: See Table 7.

readily available than is the case with other cities of Ukraine.) We note that Ukrainians increased in Kiev and in the urban population of Kiev oblast at a higher rate than the total average; also, that those Ukrainians who declared Ukrainian as their native language increased twice as fast as those who preferred Russian. In consequence, by 1970, the proportion of Ukrainians, and among them those who declared Ukrainian as their mother tongue, was higher than in 1959. By disaggregating the data on Kiev oblast from the combined figures in Table 10, we discover that in the towns of the oblast the total population increased by 47.6 per cent, Ukrainians by 49.6, including Ukrainian-speakers by 50.0 and Russian speakers by 38.3 per cent. (The Russian urban population outside Kiev increased by 53.4 per cent, which exceeded the Ukrainian total.) Table 11 presents data for the city of Kiev itself. This summary also includes data on the Russian segment of Kiev's population in order to compare the position of both principal nationalities in the Ukrainian capital.

In the city of Kiev, the Ukrainians were more Russified linguistically in 1959 than the "provincials." This is not surprising: we saw in the South and East that the larger a city is, the greater is its Russian population, and the higher the proportion of assimilated Ukrainians. But by 1970 something rather unexpected had happened in Kiev: Ukrainian speakers emerged as the fastest growing segment of the city's population in the intercensal period. Those assimilated Ukrainians maintained a rate of growth somewhere near 40 per cent of that of the non-assimilated. Moreover, the Ukrainians increased faster than did the Russians and by 1970 Kiev had not only a Ukrainian majority—it had acquired this by 1959—but also a Ukrainian-speaking majority, or, to be more precise, a majority had declared to the census takers that they considered Ukrainian to be their first language. (Besides 77.4 per cent of the Ukrainians, self-declared Ukrainian speakers included nine thousand non-Ukrainians, mostly Russians, Poles and Jews.)

TABLE 10. URBAN UKRAINIANS IN KIEV OBLAST, INCLUDING THE CITY OF KIEV, 1959–70

	1959	Percentage	1970	Percentage	Rate of Growth
Kiev (city and urban portion of oblast)	1,547,907		2,286,725		47.7
Ukrainians	1,023,925	(66.0)[a]	1,595,564	(69.8)[a]	55.8
unassimilated	826,350	80.7	1,341,429	84.1	62.3
assimilated	197,575	19.3	254,135	15.9	28.6

SOURCE: See Table 7.

[a]As percent of total urban population.

How is one to explain this development which differs so significantly from the tendency prevailing in the East and South? Of the several

TABLE 11. UKRAINIANS AND RUSSIANS IN KIEV, 1959–70

	1959	Percentage	1970	Percentage	Percentage Change 1959-70
Total	1,104,334	100.0	1,631,908	100.0	47.8
Ukrainians	663,851	60.1	1,056,905	64.8	59.2
unassimilated	477,492	(71.9)[a]	818,315	(77.4)[a]	71.4
assimilated	186,276	(28.1)[a]	238,507	(22.6)[a]	28.0
Russians	254,269	23.0	373,569	22.9	46.9

SOURCE: See Table 7.
[a]As percentage of all Ukrainians.

explanations that come to mind, two appear most sound. One is that both Kiev and Lviv had experienced especially marked population displacement during the war and thus their population underwent a more fundamental change that the rates of growth would indicate (see Table 12). Lviv lost its Jewish and Polish citizens and although it had a Russian in-migration after 1944, this was not large enough to prevent the city adopting a definitely Ukrainian—new Ukrainian—appearance. Kiev also suffered heavy population losses in the war and seems to have drawn heavily on the Ukrainian countryside for its post-1945 growth. In this respect the situation after 1945, including the intercensal period of 1959–70, was very different from that before 1939, when the fastest growing cities were located in the East and when the population growth could not draw on migration from the western regions of Ukraine (at that time located in Poland, Romania and Czechoslovakia). Iu. I. Pitiurenko has compiled a statistical table estimating the volume of migration to the cities cited in Table 12.[18] We have adapted his data to produce Table 13.

Since 1945, in contrast to the prewar period when its growth rates were rivalled and even surpassed by Kharkiv and Donetske, Kiev has maintained a migration-based growth rate larger by far than any of its competitors for the status of the primate city in Ukraine. This may in turn have been due to such geopolitical factors as the westward expansion of the Ukrainian SSR, which opened up a densely populated hinterland, to the improved security after the establishment of socialist states in East-Central Europe and last but not least, to Kiev's role as Ukrainian capital. (We remember that Kiev did not become capital of the Ukrainian SSR until 1934. Had all those bureaucrats, apparatchiks, media people and so on, who customarily live and work in the capitals, not moved from Kharkiv to Kiev between

TABLE 12. POPULATION OF SUPRA-REGIONAL (INTER-OBLAST) CENTRES IN UKRAINE, 1939–77

Rank in 1939	City	1939 (000)		1959 (000)		1970 (000)		1977 (000)		Percentage Change 1939-59	1959-70	1970-77	1939-77
1.	Kiev	851	100	1110	100	1632	100	2079	100	130	147	127	244
2.	Kharkiv	840	99	953	86	1223	75	1405	68	113	128	115	167
3.	Odessa	599	70	664	60	892	55	1039	50	111	134	116	173
4.	Dnipropetrovske	528	62	661	60	862	53	995	48	125	130	115	188
5.	Donetske	474	56	708	64	879	54	984	47	149	124	112	208
6.	Lviv	340	40	411	37	553	34	642	31	121	135	116	189
7.	Zaporizhzhia[a]	(289)	34	(449)	40	658	40	772	37	155	147	117	267
...													
11.	Kryvyi Rih[b]	(192)	23	(401)	36	573	641	(641)	31	209	143	112	334

SOURCE: *Nar. khoz. 1977*, 61–3, 65 and 67.

[a]Zaporizhzhia is shown here because by 1959 it had outdistanced Lviv and improved its lead over Lviv in 1970 and 1977.

[b]In 1939, Kryvyi Rih was number 11 (after three cities in the Donets basin), in 1959–number 9, in 1970–number 7 (surging ahead of Lviv), but by 1977 it had dropped behind Lviv and became number 8, while Lviv regained seventh place.

1934 and 1939, Kharkiv would have been the largest city of Ukraine in 1939.)

TABLE 13. POPULATION INCREASE DUE TO IN-MIGRATION IN SELECTED UKRAINIAN CITIES, 1926–39 and 1959–70 (THOUSANDS)

	1926–39	Annual Increase	1959–70	Annual Increase
Dnipropetrovske	294	22.6	203	18.4
Donetske	360	27.7	180	14.5
Kharkiv	416	32.0	289	26.3
Kiev	333	25.6	528	48.0
Lviv	–	–	142	12.9
Odessa	181	13.9	225	20.5

SOURCE: Iu. I. Pitiurenko, *Rozvytok mist i miske rozselennia v Ukrainskii RSR* (Kiev, 1972), 121.

Besides the administrative aspect of city-building, one might distinguish a more clearly national contributory element in the rise of Kiev. V. V. Pokshishevsky has noted that certain cities of the Soviet Union have become "the centers of national culture and ethnic consciousness."[19] For Ukrainians, Kiev has been such a city: it houses the most important research institutes, publishing houses, libraries, editorial boards of journals and theatre companies. Such institutions are to be found also in Lviv (although on a smaller scale, especially in so far as the press and publishing are concerned), but much less so in Donetske or even Kharkiv. The cities in the East and South are mainly industrial and transportation centres, as well as seats of research and teaching in technology and science. For political reasons, work in the latter fields is carried out in the Russian language. Thus in contemporary Ukraine only two cities are both large and (relatively) Ukrainian: Kiev and Lviv. Of these two the more important is Kiev, since Lviv cannot aspire to national leadership. (In 1569, when Kiev and Lviv found themselves within one polity, Lviv appears to have been the more important; but it was also the larger then.) To what degree is Kiev the primate city of Ukraine in terms of urban hierarchy, not just as an administrative centre?

Table 14 applies Mark Jefferson's index of primacy—a ratio of population of the largest city to the combined population of the second and third cities in a given country or region—to Ukraine. The results suggest, first, that Kiev still does not possess a commanding lead over its immediate rivals, and second, that its relative position has nonetheless been improving throughout the entire period under discussion. (In 1939 four cities of

Ukraine were more than half Kiev's size; in 1977 only Kharkiv remained so, and Odessa was only half the size of Kiev.)

TABLE 14. PRIMACY INDEX FOR UKRAINE

	1939	1959	1970	1977
Kiev	100	100	100	100
Kharkiv and Odessa	169	150[a]	130	118

SOURCE: Table 12.
[a]Kharkiv and Donetske (Donetske was number 3 in 1959).

Some scholars believe that Kiev is too small to be the central city of Ukraine. Chauncy Harris believes that in 1959 Kiev was "only about a third as large as would be expected from the network of 301 cities and towns of more than 10,000 population in the Ukraine."[20] Peter Woroby, on different grounds, also concludes that Kiev is undersized.[21] Russell B. Adams, in a recent study, divides Ukraine into two major regions in his classification of the Soviet Union's regions: one centred in Kiev (including Odessa and Lviv), the other based in Kharkiv and consisting of the industrial eastern and southern parts of Ukraine.[22] On the basis of the 1959 census, Harris divided Ukraine into five urban-network regions (Kiev, Kharkiv, Donetske, Odessa and Dnipropetrovske).[23] David J. M. Hooson seems to have taken the most affirmative view of Kiev's rise to pre-eminence in Ukraine:

> The regaining of Kiev's capital function in 1934 has ensured a steady growth, in spite of its destruction during the War. It is a minor edition of Moscow in some ways .... Its industrial structure is well balanced .... Its historical significance in the Russian nationality, State and Church make it something more than a politico-regional centre for the Ukraine. Kharkov may conceivably grow larger, but cannot now challenge Kiev's preeminent position, anymore than Milan can supplant Rome as capital of the Italian State.[24]

Conclusions

This writer does not consider himself competent to evaluate the processes of urbanization in postwar Ukraine from the point of view of demography, geography, economics or urban studies. As a political historian, he is interested to discover that after 1945 the Ukrainians appeared in the cities of Ukraine in numbers large enough to make it possible to modify that old distinction between "Ukrainian village" and "Russian city," or "Ukrainian village West" and "Russian urban East."

The East has clearly remained Russian: but the West, including the "Central West," has become more urban and more Ukrainian in its urban component. This outcome has to be connected with the territorial unification of the Ukrainian nation during the Second World War. Secondly, a historian notes the rise of Kiev to a position of primacy (even if precise definitions of what constitutes primacy may be lacking) and he connects this with the westward shift of the Ukrainian SSR. He observes with interest the re-emergence of the Lviv-Kiev axis in Ukrainian life—after a three-hundred-year break. Finally, the example of Kiev and Lviv suggests that it may be possible even under the political conditions now prevailing in the USSR to emancipate the Ukrainians from the status of "younger brother" to the Russians: certain parts of Ukraine are both urbanized and remain loyal to the Ukrainian language. It might be argued that the contemporary phenomenon of dissent in Ukraine is a result of this fact. Our discussion suggests that behind the individual figures representing that phenomenon there may well exist a sizable constituency of socially mobilized (urbanized) but linguistically non-assimilated people.

Notes

1. See *Ukraine: A Concise Encyclopaedia*, ed. V. Kubijovyč, 2 vols. (Toronto, 1963–71), 1: 200–7; V. Kubiiovych [Kubijovyč], "Natsionalnyi sklad naselennia Radianskoi Ukrainy v svitli sovietskykh perepysiv naselennia z 17. 12. 1926 i 15. 1. 1959," offprint from *Zbirnyk prysviachenyi pamiati Z. Kuzeli* (Paris 1962) (*Zapysky NTSh* 169); and S. G. Prociuk, "Human Losses in the Ukraine in World War I and II," *The Annals of the Ukrainian Academy of Arts and Sciences in the United States* 13, no. 35–6 (1973–7): 23–50.
2. V. I. Kozlov, *Natsionalnosti SSSR (Etnodemograficheskii obzor)* (Moscow, 1975), 109. I am grateful to Bohdan Krawchenko, Canadian Institute of Ukrainian Studies, for drawing my attention to this item of information in Kozlov's book. According to Professor Krawchenko, this is the first published disclosure of the ethnic composition of the Ukrainian SSR in 1939.
3. *Itogi vsesoiuznoi perepisi naseleniia 1959 goda. Ukrainskaia SSR* (Moscow, 1963), Table 53; Kozlov, *Natsionalnosti*, 109; and Kubiiovych, "Natsionalnyi sklad," 6.
4. *Ukraine: Encyclopaedia*, 1: 212.
5. Calculated by this writer from *Itogi 1959*, Table 54; for a breakdown by historic regions (such as Volhynia and Galicia), see *Ukraine*, 1: 219. Ethnic composition of Western Ukraine by oblasts (in 1930 and 1970) is given by Y. Bilinsky, "The Incorporation of Western Ukraine," in R. Szporluk, ed.,

The Influence of East Europe and the Soviet West on the USSR (New York, 1975), 204.

6. Kubiiovych, "Natsionalnyi sklad," 6, and *Ukraine*, 1: 216. For the occupational breakdown of the Ukrainians, Russians, Jews and Poles in prewar Ukraine (Soviet and Western), see *Ukraine*, 1: 174–5.
7. Calculated by this writer from *Itogi 1959*.
8. *Itogi 1959*, Table 6; see also *Narodnoe khoziaistvo SSSR za 60 let. Iubileinyi statisticheskii sbornik* (Moscow, 1977), 59–68, for a listing of all Soviet cities with a population of 50,000 and above in 1939, 1959, 1970 and 1977. (This source will be cited later as *Nar. khoz. 1977*.)
9. M. Jefferson, "The Law of the Primate City," *Geographical Review* 29 (1939), 227 and 231.
10. *Ibid.*, 228.
11. *Itogi 1959*, Table 1.
12. J. A. Armstrong, "The Ethnic Scene in the Soviet Union," in E. Goldhagen, ed., *Ethnic Minorities in the Soviet Union* (New York, 1968), 14–15. See also my own discussion of Ukrainian-Russian relations in "Russians in Ukraine," in P. J. Potichnyj, ed., *Ukraine in the Seventies* (Oakville, Ontario, 1975), 195–217.
13. Armstrong, "Ethnic Scene," 15.
14. For a comprehensive treatment of urbanization in Ukraine, see P. Woroby, "Effects of Urbanization in the Ukraine," *The Annals of the Ukrainian Academy of Arts and Sciences in the United States* 13, no. 35–6 (1973–7): 51–115.
15. *Nar. khoz. 1977*, 59–68.
16. V. I. Naulko, *Karta suchasnoho etnichnoho skladu naselennia Ukrainskoi RSR* (Kiev, 1966).
17. Figures in Bilinsky, "Incorporation," 207.
18. Pitiurenko has an interesting classification of Ukrainian cities in terms of their functions. He places Kiev in a special category and then in the class of oblast centres, which he terms "multi-functional cities," he distinguishes a group of multi-functional centres of supra-regional importance. These supra-regional centres are Kharkiv, Dnipropetrovske, Odessa, Donetske and Lviv. See Iu. I. Pitiurenko, *Rozvytok mist i miske rozselennia v Ukrainskii RSR* (Kiev, 1972), 80–1.
19. V. V. Pokshishevsky, "Urbanization and Ethnodemographic Processes," *Soviet Geography* 13, no. 2 (February 1972): 116–19. More recently Pokshishevsky has written on the role of ethnic composition as a factor in the rise of the service sector in the cities. See "Differences in the Geography of Services and the Characteristics of Political Structure," *Soviet Geography* 16, no. 6 (June 1975): especially 359–64.
20. C. D. Harris, *Cities of the Soviet Union* (Chicago, 1970), 134–5.
21. P. Woroby, "Effects of Urbanization," 113. He notes, however, an improvement in the rank of Kiev between 1959 and 1970 (114).
22. R. B. Adams, "The Soviet Metropolitan Hierarchy: Regionalization and

Comparison with the United States," *Soviet Geography* 17, no. 5 (May 1977): 314–15 and ff.

23. Harris, *Cities*, 135.
24. D. J. M. Hooson, *The Soviet Union: People and Regions* (Belmont, Cal., 1966), 163. This was confirmed by the preliminary results of the 1979 census which were published when this work was in press. Kiev further strengthened its leading position among Ukrainian cities (it had 2.144 million inhabitants compared with Kharkiv's 1.444 million and Dnipropetrovske's 1.066 million), and the Ukrainian share in its population rose to 68.7 per cent even though in Ukraine as a whole Ukrainians dropped from 74.9 per cent in 1970 to 73.6 in 1979. See Roman Solchanyk's analyses: "The Ukraine and Ukrainians in the USSR: Nationality and Language Aspects of the Census of 1979," *Radio Liberty Research* no. 100/80, 11 March 1980, and "The Ukrainization of Kiev Continues: Partial Results of the 1979 Census," *Radio Liberty Research* no. 68/80, 15 February 1980.

Peter Woroby

The Role of the City in Ukrainian History

A. *Scope of the Problem*

The common feature of the three papers presented is the subject of *urbanization in Ukraine* with special emphasis on the role of the major urban centres. No clear-cut rules have been laid down for defining the minimal size of an urban area which in turn has contributed to different choices and interpretations. Thus, Patricia Herlihy selected five "typical" major centres (Kiev, Kharkiv, Lviv, Odessa and Luhanske) for the monographic study of their development, "set within varying geographic, economic and political surroundings." Except for a random remark in the introductory statement, she barely touches on the general aspects of urbanization in Ukraine. Steven L. Guthier is initially concerned with the functioning of a dozen major centres; the number is later increased to include more than thirty. His analysis, which is much more aggregate than that of the first paper, also refers to the small centres and stresses the regional effects of urbanization. Roman Szporluk, in turn, concentrates on the role of the principal city of Ukraine, Kiev, which is described within a framework of the widely discussed process of general urbanization.

The *role of the city* is highly diversified; it includes economic (commercial, industrial), cultural and administrative-political functions. Measured by this yardstick, Herlihy's paper is most satisfactory in its scope, though there is perhaps too much stress on the economic development and not enough on ethno-political activity. The latter criticism is particularly valid for the city of Lviv. Guthier and Szporluk focus on the political-national aspects of urbanization. Both writers support their findings with numerous demographical-statistical data and omit discussion of the economic and cultural performance.

The *historical periodization* of the analysed subject is quite acceptable. It deals with the question of urbanization in the nineteenth century, with the successive changes in the present century up to the Second World War, and finally with the present state of development. This may be considered a logical attempt at chronological classification; linkages between neighbouring periods are unavoidable, even desirable, although in the case of Professor Szporluk's paper they seem to be somewhat excessive.

B. *General Comments*

All three papers lack a *definition of urban centres*, which was the subject of significant variation throughout the analysed period. This statement is valid not only for the transition of pre-revolutionary Russia into the political structure of the USSR but also within both systems.

In the middle of the nineteenth century, the legal status of urban centres applied to settlements, "residents of which had a right to trade according to the urban privilege and which were inhabited by persons with urban occupation."[1] Here belonged cities (*mista*), towns (*mistechka*) and a few special settlements (*posady*) and suburbs (*peredmistia*). In 1858 the Russian territory of Ukraine possessed 113 cities, 547 towns and 12 other urban localities. Their combined population amounted to 2,564,000 which was equivalent to 21.4 per cent of the total population in 1863.[2] The urban population was evenly split between cities and towns.[3] By 1897, the year of the first imperial census, the urban population of Ukraine had almost doubled without altering its relative weight (21.3 per cent). This was caused by a significant decline in the number of towns (reduced to 463) which were administratively denied urban status; at the same time there were no actual additions to the category of cities (total number 114). Significant changes in reclassification, however, occurred in the period that followed. Thus in 1913 only cities were considered as urban centres, the number of which had increased to 139, while all remaining towns were thrown into the rural category. Consequently, the proportion of urban population, which numerically barely changed (4,902,000), was reduced to 15.1 per cent.[4]

The Soviet regime brought additional alterations to the urban concept, some of which were diametrically opposed to the previously existing scheme. Spread over a period of time and continuously modified, it classified the urban communities into cities and towns, the latter officially called "settlements with urban character." To become "urban" the community was required to have a minimum of five hundred persons (later raised to one thousand), half of whom should be employed in non-agricultural activities (later raised to 60 per cent). The city, in turn, had to have a higher minimum population (two thousand persons) and a higher percentage of non-agricultural occupations (75 per cent).[5] These changes were reflected in the 1926 census, which re-established 402 settlements as "urban," abrogated the privilege of cities to forty-seven centres and elevated seven settlements to the rank of city.[6]

It is obvious that administrative changes of urban status which are applicable to both periods must affect the material results—the number of urban centres and their population. This issue becomes further complicated when one considers the size of the comparable territory (Ukraine in imperial Russia, Ukraine in the USSR before 1939 and present-day Ukraine). The adjustment in urban definitions will still produce a general variation for each specific political constituency.

Similarly, one has to be careful in assessing the effects of urban growth. It includes not only the natural increase in the population of the existing urban centres but also the transfer into the urban category (upgrading) of some rural settlements. Depending on the circumstances of the general development and regional conditions, the share of the latter component could be quite significant. For example, in the period between 1959 and 1970, which was marked by the growth of already established urban centres, the increase of 6.5 million in urban population consisted of 2.5 million persons attributed to natural growth, 3.0 million rural-urban migrants and 1.0 million persons identified with the reclassification of the existing communities.[7]

Another aspect common to all three papers is the frequent reference to the *ethno-national composition of urban centres*. However, whereas the censuses of imperial Russia followed the line of linguistic delineation, the USSR widened this scope by incorporating the additional criterion of ethnic origin. It is obvious that these two classifications are not identical and are bound to produce numerical gaps which may vary significantly in time, community sizes and regions. Statistical results of the past and present reveal that the linguistic enumeration is less favourable to Ukrainians than the ethnic identification. This can easily lead to a certain misinterpretation and oversimplification of the complex ethno-national problem. One is naturally tempted to emphasize the use of the Ukrainian language and identify Ukrainian nationals with this group only. Persons of Ukrainian origin who speak Russian are often regarded as "assimilated" Ukrainians.[8]

Historical evidence and common sense suggest that this is a very dangerous inference which does not always hold true. Many

Russian-speaking Ukrainians joined the ranks of the nationally conscious Ukrainians and supported their goals. This was the case during the 1917–20 struggle for independence and in the successive Soviet period. If one considers mastering the Ukrainian language a dominant criterion of national identity, then one would have to strike out of this group some illustrious exponents of the Ukrainian political movement. It is no secret that Hetman Pavlo Skoropadsky and General Mykhailo Omelianovych-Pavlenko spoke with heavy Russian accents even in the late years of their exemplary lives. It is also known that prominent émigré Ukrainian scholars conversed in Russian among themselves to facilitate technical communication.

The third issue recurring in all three papers is that of the *Russification of Ukraine* and particularly of her urban centres. Before discussing this problem in detail one should consider its general magnitude and significance. The reference to the relatively high ratio of Ukrainians in the republic (74.9 per cent in 1970; 76.8 per cent in 1959 and 80.0 per cent in 1926) does not reflect the true effects of Russification since it applies to varying territorial dimensions and minority group compositions.[9] Focusing on the Russian ethnic group, one obtains entirely different results: a tremendous increase in the Russian population, from 2,978,000 persons in 1926 to 9,126,000 in 1970. These figures include the territories of Crimea and Western Ukraine. In terms of relative strength, the Russian population constituted 19.4 per cent of the total population in 1970. By excluding 446,000 Russians who settled in the West and concentrating on the core Ukrainian territory in the East the above figure reaches 22.6 per cent as compared with 10.0 per cent for the comparable territory in 1926. These results, which are highly significant, become more strongly pronounced when applied to the urban centres and the individual regions.

C. *Specific Aspects*

1) *Patricia Herlihy*

While one should not quarrel with the author's choice of a monographic method, which can be regarded as a suitable and powerful medium of presentation, one may have certain reservations regarding her *selection of analysed centres*. There is no dissension regarding the inclusion of such principal centres of Ukraine as Kiev, Kharkiv, Odessa and Lviv. One only wonders about the accidental or deliberate omission of Katerynoslav (Dnipropetrovske), which was the fourth ranking centre of Ukraine at the end of the nineteenth century with a population of 218,000 in 1912. It might also have been advisable to have substituted Iuzivka (Donetske) for Luhanske (Voroshylovhrad) in view of the contemporary size of this centre. Historically, both these places were resource-based—"one factory" towns—experiencing approximately the same pattern of economic development.

The other point that can be questioned is *the role of industry* as a city-building factor. Although its favourable effect cannot be denied, there is insufficient support for the thesis that "industry played a greater role than trade in the urbanization process." With the exception of the mining towns of Luhanske and Yuzivka, the remaining centres appear to have derived their primary strength from commercial, administrative and cultural activities. An above average contribution of industry was only evident in the growth of Katerynoslav. The majority of manufacturing in the major cities belonged to the category of food processing (sugar refineries, flour mills), which can be successfully performed in various plant sizes. Although they were larger than their "rural" counterparts and derived certain advantages from their "central" location, these conditions did not reach the proportions of the industries nor those realized during the Soviet period. Exemplified by metallurgical, chemical and machine establisments, they require a scale of operation that exclusively favours the larger urban centres.

The third problem requiring additional qualifications is that of *urban-rural migration* and closely related *Russification*. There is a widespread belief that the Ukrainians disliked the urban life and preferred the rural occupations (farming), and that this created a vacuum in urban development which has been filled by Russian immigrants. Although there might be a grain of truth in this generalization, the economic conditions in nineteenth-century cities were such that they could not absorb the surplus population from rural areas. This was simply a matter of the quantitative gap between supply and demand and the insufficient development of industries in urban centres, as a consequence of which the Ukrainian peasants had to look for agricultural employment in the virgin lands of Siberia or North America.

If there were "vacancies" in the urban sphere they were in occupations for which the rural residents were not adequately qualified (civil servants, clergy, educators and military men). There is no doubt that a significant number of people in this group, particularly in higher ranks, were transplanted Russians. In total, the urban-rural mobility, inclusive of non-autochthonous elements, was not very significant. The 1897 census reveals the following about the birthplace of urban residents. What is noteworthy in this tabulation is the relatively high level of "local"

TABLE 1. BIRTHPLACE OF URBAN RESIDENTS IN 1897

Area	Percentage
Own Administrative District (*povit*)	69.4
Other Districts of the Same Province (*guberniia*)	11.8
Other Provinces	17.2
Other Countries	1.6
Total	100.0

SOURCE: A. I. Dotsenko, "Heohrafichni osoblyvosti protsesiv urbanizatsii na Ukraini (xix-xx st.)," *Ukrainskyi istoryko-heohrafichnyi zbirnyk* 2 (Kiev, 1972), 47.

residents (the first two categories which comprise 81.2 per cent) and the low level of immigrants from other provinces (17.2 per cent). The latter figure is not identical with the inflow of Russians since it also includes urban newcomers from Ukrainian territory. Without minimizing the effect of Russification during the pre-revolutionary era, one should point to the magnitude of the changes that occurred thirty years later. Thus in the census year 1926 the number of urban dwellers born outside the boundaries of the Ukrainian republic assumed the enormous proportion of 40.9 per cent and in the mining region of Donetske (the Donets basin) it reached 57.3 per cent.[10]

2) *Steven L. Guthier*

This is a penetrating, analytical paper which focuses its attention on the ethno-political role of Ukrainian cities. It discusses the chosen subject within a framework of the general aspects of urbanization such as the regional development and the effect of community sizes. The economic development of the cities, however, has not been adequately stressed. The assessment of urban problems in the decade preceding the Second World War can also be criticized. It comprises less than one-fifth of the paper and does not reach the depth of presentation which applies to the period of the First World War and the succeeding years.

There is an interesting interpretation of the *decrease of Ukrainian population in cities during the Civil War*. The author attributes this to the general decline of urban population caused by "the food shortages, unemployment and political insecurity which plagued the cities from 1918 to 1921." He concludes that "hundreds of thousands of people sought relief in the countryside" and since the Ukrainians had "rural" roots in the surrounding area the "outflow was particularly heavy among Ukrainian nationals." Accepting this line of reasoning, one should understand why the percentage of Ukrainians in Kiev dropped from 16.4 in 1917 to 14.3 in

1920, since the general population declined from around 470,000 to approximately 365,000. The author also refers to the significant reduction of the Ukrainian proportion between 1897 and 1917 (from 22.2 to 16.4 per cent). He attributes it to "the dual effects of relatively small-scale Ukrainian influx to Kiev and the Russification of Ukrainians who did settle there." In other words the Ukrainians in Kiev were losers under both conditions of city growth and decline. In documenting statements of this kind with statistical figures, the author forgets to mention that there was also a decline between 1913, when the city reached a peak of 600,000 persons, and 1917. Had it been war-induced and characterized by a disproportionate exodus of Ukrainians into rural areas, then it would have started from a higher level of Ukrainian participation than 16.4 per cent. This, in turn, indicates that the Russification of Ukrainians during the urban growth was not as intense as the speaker suggests.

The paper contains a very revealing ethno-political *analysis of the municipal election* in Kiev in 1917. It shows that Ukrainian parties received 20.8 per cent of the total civil vote. This was, no doubt, a very favourable outcome when one recalls that the Ukrainian population in the city amounted only to 16.4 per cent, a quarter of which regarded themselves as "Little Russians." The author does not interpret further this very interesting phenomenon which reveals that there were numerous Russian-speaking Ukrainians who supported the aspirations of the "national" Ukrainians. In other words, the Ukrainian population by ethnic origin must have considerably exceeded the linguistic group and, contrary to the prevailing opinion, was not yet politically assimilated. At the time when it counted most, this group returned to the ethno-national fold. This conclusion appears to be very probable since it is doubtful that the Russian nationals, or other minority groups that identified their interests with those of the dominant Russian nation, voted for Ukrainian parties. Further, the above results do not take into account the fact that some Ukrainians must have also supported the rising Bolshevik movement, or other Russian parties.

In addition to the linguistic enumeration, the 1926 census introduced *the identification by ethnic origin.* This considerably increased the number of Ukrainians in urban centres (specifically, from 36.0 to 47.3 per cent). It also showed that out of four persons who regarded themselves as Ukrainian three had a full command of the Ukrainian language. In four principal centres, Kiev, Odessa, Kharkiv and Dnipropetrovske, which comprised 29.4 per cent of the total urban population, the share of the Ukrainian population was considerably lower (33.8 per cent) and so was the ratio of the Ukrainian-speaking nationals to their ethnic brothers who used Russian as a language of communication (approximately a 2:1 ratio).

Accepting the linguistic classification as a suitable basis for historical evaluation, the author reaches the conclusion that between 1897 and 1926 there was little change in the ethnic composition of urban centres. The corresponding figures for the urban Ukrainian population in 1926 and 1897 are virtually the same, 36.0 and 35.1 per cent. The results are not surprising; owing to the war, there was little urban growth over the thirty years. Although Soviet statistics show an apparent increase (5,359,000 versus 2,696,000 persons, equivalent to 18.5 versus 13.0 per cent), the results are not conclusive. One should recall the fact that the Soviets have considerably widened the definition of urban centres to include many rural communities (previously disregarded towns and newly industrializing villages). The Ukrainians recorded gains, however, in the centres that experienced the growth. Thus, the four principal cities mentioned above, which increased their population from 938,000 in 1897 to 1,578,000 in 1926, indicate a strengthening of the Ukrainian-speaking element from 16.6 to 21.0 per cent.

The significant changes in the ethnic composition of urban centres must have occurred in the 1930s, which were characterized by tremendous urban growth (33.5 per cent urban population in 1939) and in the postwar period (45.7 per cent in 1959). Unfortunately, the author does not discuss and document these effects thoroughly. Relating the 1926 to 1959 data the number of Ukrainians in urban centres increased from 47.3 to 61.5 per cent. This development was also accompanied by an improvement in the proportion of the Ukrainian-speaking population which moved from a 3:1 ratio (36.0 per cent) to a 6:1 relationship (52.1 per cent).

3) *Roman Szporluk*

The author presents a well-researched and documented paper. He differs from the others in that he deals with contemporary problems and is able to emphasize current trends and prognosticate future development. His generalizations, which are bold and thought-provoking, contain much subjective judgment. There are some shortcomings in the arrangement of the statistical material and in its evaluation. For example, the absolute numbers that supply the basis for the author's calculations are often omitted and the rates of change, based on actual growth, are listed in the tables that show the structural composition.

The paper shows the *ethno-political effects* of urbanization in the 1959–70 period. When the urban proportion of the population advanced to

54.5 per cent in 1970 the Ukrainian representation was 62.9 per cent, an increase of only 1.4 points over the eleven year period. Linguistically, it maintained the same relations as in the year 1959 (52.1 per cent). Obviously, the above figures are aggregate results subject to local variations. The author exemplifies this by the suitable choice of two contrasting regions, namely the oblasts of Kiev and Lviv on one hand, and Donetske and Voroshylovhrad on the other. They comprise urban and rural population. Table 2 consolidates and rearranges his findings.

TABLE 2. ASSIMILATION OF UKRAINIAN POPULATION IN SELECTED REGIONS OF UKRAINE (PERCENTAGES)

	Region	1959	1970	Difference
1.	**Voroshylovhrad and Donetske**:			
	Unassimilated Ukrainians	40.9	34.2	-6.7
	Assimilated Ukrainians	11.5	16.1	4.6
	All Ukrainians	52.4	50.3	-2.1
2.	**Kiev and Lviv:**			
	Unassimilated Ukrainians	57.9	63.7	5.8
	Assimilated Ukrainians	9.6	8.3	-1.3
	All Ukrainians	67.5	72.0	4.5

The above figures show the weakening of the Ukrainian element in the Donets basin and the growth of its strength in Western Ukraine. This overall trend was accelerated among Ukrainian-speaking nationals and decelerated in the Russian-speaking group (erroneously designated by the author as non-assimilated and assimilated Ukrainians).

Results of this kind cause the author to pose the question: which one of the two models of development will prevail in the future? He is optimistically excited about the positive changes in the West, particularly with the national rebirth of the capital city (an increase of the "unassimilated" Ukrainians from 43.2 per cent in 1959 to 50.1 per cent in 1970 and a decrease of "assimilated" Ukrainians from 16.9 per cent in 1959 to 14.6 per cent in 1970). This can be attributed, according to the author, to the westward expansion of the Ukrainian SSR with its ethnically homogeneous Ukrainian hinterland and to the role of Kiev as a political, cultural and educational centre.

While one can hardly disagree with the author's arguments and conclusions, the paper leaves out one important aspect of the urban analysis, i.e., direct *effects of Russification.* This problem contains more than the question of assimilation, it is concerned with the distribution and growth of Russian immigrants who were selectively directed into specific areas of Ukraine.

The heaviest concentration of Russians in 1970 was in the Donets basin, where they accounted for 41.0 per cent of the total population (the Ukrainian share was 53.7 per cent). It is also worthwhile to note that they experienced a very high gain in the 1926–70 period, from the original 26.1 per cent. Adjoining this area are the three industrial oblasts of Kharkiv, Dnipropetrovske and Zaporizhzhia. Their Russian population of 25.7 per cent exceeded the republic's average of 19.4 per cent; it approached 30.0 per cent in the Kharkiv and Zaporizhzhia oblasts and declined to some 20.0 per cent in the oblast of Dnipropetrovske. The salutary fact in this relationship is the relatively high number of Ukrainians in the three oblasts (69.7 per cent) although the Russian ethnic group experienced a significant growth from 16.0 per cent in 1926.

The third settlement zone of Russians is the Black Sea region which is anchored between two strongholds: the Crimean peninsula and the city of Odessa. In the Crimea in 1970 the Russians commanded an absolute majority of 67.3 per cent, a significant increase from 42.2 per cent in 1926. The Ukrainians, who amounted to 26.5 per cent, also showed a definite strengthening (from 10.8 per cent in 1926). Both groups were beneficiaries of the decline in the Tatar population which was expelled from the territory in the postwar years. The Russians in the urban and rural centres of Odessa oblast made up 24.2 per cent of the population whereas the Ukrainians were more than twice as strong (55.0 per cent). The latter started from a relatively strong basis in 1926 (17.0 per cent) with a more than adequate growth. The two oblasts, Kherson and Mykolaiv, positioned between the Crimea and Odessa regions, recorded 18.1 per cent and 16.1 per cent of Russians respectively, with relatively large Ukrainian populations (78.3 and 78.9 per cent). What is important, however, is the healthy increase of the Russian population (1926 basis being 11.4 and 9.0 per cent) in the sparsely settled region; the total population of these two oblasts barely exceeds two million.

Summarizing, one finds that in the specified area, which comprises slightly less than one-half of the republic's population (46.6 per cent), the proportion of Russians (urban and rural) is one-third (33.4 per cent). The remaining half of Ukraine (53.4 per cent), in turn, possesses only 7.1 per cent Russian settlers. Within this territory Kiev oblast records 14.0 per cent while Western Ukraine, which was annexed in 1939–45, has only 5.1 per cent.

This situation does not show any signs of improvement at the present. A careful examination of the data for the 1959–70 period reveals the intensive effort to Russify the population by increasing Russian immigration into the traditionally established areas. Thus, the increase in the republic's population, which amounted to 5,257,000, included 38.7 per cent Russians—which is twice as strong as their present status (19.4 per cent). Differentiating this inflow by spheres of influence, the Russians made up 49.2 per cent of the population increases in the Donets basin, industrial Dnieper and Black Sea regions and 17.9 per cent (less than one-half the ratio of the overall participation in the incremental growth) in the remaining areas. In the relatively neglected territories the highest proportion of Russians was in Kiev oblast (23.2 per cent) and the lowest in Western Ukraine (4.5 per cent).

One can conclude from this that the relative strengthening of the Ukrainian element in the West, although very positive in itself, was accompanied by a deliberate attempt to ease the pressure of Russification in these areas. This could well have been a temporary delay, caused, as some people argue, by the shortage of labour in other areas of the USSR. Whatever reasoning one may assume, one cannot deny that the emigration of Russians into Ukraine was carefully planned and directed into the strategically important territories. This trend, if continued, will have the effect of amputating and choking the traditional spheres of Ukrainian influence by depriving them of the resources in the Donets basin and denying access to the Black Sea.

Szporluk's paper brings forward another interesting subject, the strengthening of *Kiev as a primate centre* within a framework of urban hierarchy. This is an undeniable and welcome development. The economic reach of Kiev ranges between four and five hundred kilometres and can be circumscribed by the location of such cities as Minsk in Belorussia and Lviv, Odessa and Dnipropetrovske in Ukraine. In the East the corresponding counterpart could be found in the city of Kharkiv, which in the past was abnormally large and formed its own narrowly spaced system (two to three hundred kilometres wide) with the subordinate centres of Dnipropetrovske, Donetske and Voronezh. The latter city is located outside the ethnic and political boundaries of Ukraine. Thus, Ukraine inherited a twin hierarchy that persisted for some time and only started to diminish significantly in the years following the Second World War. Its traces are still visible and will likely remain, although this is not the author's opinion. The judgments here can vary considerably. What is important is that the full emergence of primacy might not be regarded as politically desirable. The accelerated growth of Kiev and the relative stagnation of Kharkiv would weaken the hierarchical ties in Eastern Ukraine. This could adversely affect the city of Donetske which, while maintaining its role as a secondary centre, would become appended to the capital city through the city of similar rank. The functioning of Dnipropetrovske would not be altered much because of its proximity to Kiev.

4) *Conclusion*

Critically appraising the last two papers, one has to mention some important omissions such as reference to the slower pace of urbanization in Ukraine when compared with the Russian republic, which is 7.8 percentage points ahead (54.5 versus 62.3 per cent in 1970); uneven distribution of urban centres in Ukraine that is characterized by a very strong concentration in the Donets basin and Dnieper regions and lack of urban development in Western Ukraine which can be delineated by a Kiev-Odessa axis; and the insufficient number and strength of two categories of the medium-sized centres, one with the population of 50,000–100,000 persons and the other with 20,000–50,000 persons.[11]

Most of the discussion (this is also to some extent true of the first paper) has been devoted to the ethno-political problems which were covered in considerable depth. One can hardly repudiate the well documented findings, although one may disagree with the authors' interpretations. The Russian-speaking Ukrainians are not "assimilated" Ukrainians yet, and their role as such has been quantitatively and qualitatively exaggerated.

All the papers have failed to stress the direct effect of Russification which, as pointed out above, represents a real danger to the Ukrainian nation. To illustrate the practical implication of this process one should step outside the USSR and refer to the political pronouncements of the anti-communist Russian exiles. Recently, in his third volume of *The Gulag Archipelago*, Aleksander Solzhenitsyn, donning the robe of magnanimity, suggests a local referendum regarding the separation of Ukraine from Russia.[12] Curiously enough he confines his proposal to the present political boundaries of Ukraine (excluding ethnic territories outside these limits), and moreover he advocates the tabulation of votes for individual oblasts. By following this procedure he expects and hopes that some of them, particularly those located east of the Dnieper, will decide to stay within Russia. Obviously, moral issues aside, he would not endorse such a project if he could not refer to the significant number of Russians in this area.

Notes

1. A. I. Dotsenko, "Heohrafichni osoblyvosti protsesiv urbanizatsii na Ukraini (XIX–XX st.)," in *Ukrainskyi istoryko-heohrafichnyi zbirnyk* 2 (Kiev 1972), 47.
2. *Ibid.*, 50.
3. According to Dotsenko (page 49), in 1858 the applicable proportions were as follows: inhabitants of cities 47.4 per cent, towns 50.3 per cent, other urban areas 2.3 per cent.
4. *Ibid.*, 50.
5. Akademiia Nauk UkRSR, *Ukrainska Radianska Entsyklopediia* (Kiev, 1959–65), 9: 238–40, 13: 33; *Entsykopediia narodnoho hospodarstva Ukrainskoi RSR* (Kiev, 1972), 4: 50.
6. Dotsenko, "Heohrafichni osoblyvosti," 57.
7. *Radianska Ukraina*, no. 94 (1971): 2.
8. See Szporluk's paper.
9. Present-day Ukraine with considerably reduced Polish, German and Jewish minorities and the Ukrainian republic in 1926 without the Crimea and Western Ukraine.
10. Dotsenko, "Heohrafichni osoblyvosti," 51.
11. For details, see P. Woroby, "Effects of Urbanization in the Ukraine," *The Annals of the Ukrainian Academy of Arts and Sciences in the United States* 13, no. 35–60 (1973–7): 51–115.
12. A. I. Solzhenitsyn, *The Gulag Archipelago 1918–1956: An Experiment in Literary Investigation*, trans. H. Willets, 3 vols. (New York, 1976), 3: 46.

George Y. Shevelov

Evolution of the Ukrainian Literary Language*

The question "When did the Ukrainian language arise?" is often asked and often answered with great assurance. It is, however, both unanswerable and unscholarly, for it ignores the difficulty of defining historically the term "Ukrainian language." The further back we trace the Ukrainian language, the fewer of its present-day characteristics are found until, sometime around the seventh or eighth century, it dissolves in Common Slavic. In the interval the gradual accumulation of specific characteristics which we now label Ukrainian occurred. But at what point a sufficient number of these characteristics is accumulated so that the language may be called Ukrainian remains open to question. The decision can only be arbitrary and, more often than not, it is politically motivated. What is undeniable is that a continuum has existed from the earliest local changes within Common Slavic to the present.

The emergence of a literary language in Ukraine (and by the same token, of the literary language *of* Ukraine) can, however, be dated with a considerable degree of precision. It coincides with the date of the Christianization of that area, or, more precisely, of its official Christianization, which occurred around 988 as indicated by the Primary Chronicle. This literary language was Church Slavonic, the vehicle of the new religion promoted as such by the church and by the state authority.[1]

Old Church Slavic, later Church Slavonic, was intended for all Christian Slavs. Although initially based on Macedonian, it was designed for and adapted to the idioms first of the Moravians, later of the Bulgarians and Serbs. Local variations of Church Slavonic inevitably appeared; admissible in principle, in practice they were due either to the

----

*At the behest of the author, the soft sign, transliterated by an apostrophe ('), is retained in this paper.

excessive zeal of local preachers who wanted to influence their flock as much as possible, or to the ignorance of users. No one, however, wanted to break the unity of the literary supralanguage and to cultivate the local tradition alone.

The Church Slavonic language came to Ukraine primarily in its Bulgarian adaptation. It is gratuitous to speak in terms of "ifs," but there certainly existed the necessary prerequisites for the creation of a single eastern version of Church Slavonic in the area from Lake Ladoga to the Byzantine frontier. The loss of political independence by Bulgaria in 972 and the demise of the Macedonian state after 1018 severed the contacts of Rus' with the areas south of the Danube. The newly introduced literary language found itself in the hands of the local clergy and scribes of rather recent vintage. It is no wonder that they were at first perplexed by the treasure to which they had become heirs. They could not cope with the great range of possibilities that Church Slavonic offered them in spelling, syntactic constructions and vocabulary. The copyist felt bewildered by the apparently excessive subtleties and either mixed them, helplessly losing control of the text he copied, or loyally and slavishly followed the original and betrayed his mother tongue only in occasional slips. The former attitude is represented, for example, by the text known under the Russian title *Trinadtsat' slov Grigoriia Bogoslova*, the latter largely by the *Izbornik* of 1073.

Yet, the *Izbornik* also attempts here and there to regulate the unwieldy imported language, at least in the inflection (instr. sg. of masc. subst. in *-m'* vs. Church Slavonic *-om'*, 3 pers sg. and pl. in *-t'* vs. Church Slavonic *-t*). This trend can be seen in a series of manuscripts, until in such texts as the *Vygoleksinskii sbornik* (late twelfth century), the *Hankenstein Manuscript* (thirteenth century) and others, a relative systematization was achieved.

In evaluating this evolution it should be kept in mind that it was not a result of any nationalistic attitude or desire to break with tradition and build the literary language on local foundations. The entire development proceeded inside the tradition and indeed strove to keep it alive and vigorous, while eliminating only those features which may have seemed "unnatural." What exactly was deemed unnatural depended on the social status and cultural level of the writer and, in the choice of vocabulary, on the thematic key of the passage in question (not on the genre of the work). The importance of thematic keys (which often influenced the language of the segments immediately following) can best be seen in various secular texts from the Chronicles or Vladimir Monomakh's *Testament* to the charters.

Thus the evolution of the literary language of Ukraine from its inception until the end of the fourteenth century was, broadly speaking, the result of its adaptation to local speech habits. This was achieved, however, not so much through the elimination of some Church Slavonic peculiarities as through a broadening of the range of variations within the literary language. Every *knizhnik* tried to use as much Church Slavonic in his language as his education, ability and the thematic key of the text permitted; but the extent of fulfillment of this goal varied widely. By the end of the fourteenth century, the unity of Church Slavonic lay more in the idea behind it than in actual usage, since it consisted of innumerable personal and local variations.

The evolution of the literary language in Ukraine was impeded by the political and demographic events of the thirteenth and fourteenth centuries. The Tatar invasion which resulted in the fall and destruction of Kiev in 1240, caused a mass flight of population from the Left-Bank and middle-Dnieper regions. The majority fled to the west and northwest, i.e., to Galicia and Polissia, but many intellectuals chose to move to the Russian lands. For several decades Galicia and Volhynia maintained the literature and literary language of Ukraine. In 1387, however, Ukraine was partitioned between Lithuania (which absorbed the greater part of the Ukrainain lands), Poland (Galicia, Kholm, now Chełm), Moldavia (Bukovyna) and Hungary (Transcarpathia). These powers had no interest in upholding the literary language of Ukraine. Further, the church, which might have been concerned with this task, was in a deplorable situation. After Metropolitan Peter left for the Russian lands in 1299, the metropolitan see of Kiev remained vacant until 1411. In the conditions of general instability, the decline of towns and of church authority, and the lack of educational institutions, it became impossible to preserve the standards of the literary language. Features of spoken, outright dialectal speech made inroads into Church Slavonic writings (e.g. in the *Kamianka-Buz'ka Gospel*, 1411, the second part of the *Chetia* of 1489, etc.).

From 1390 to 1550 a new type of Church Slavonic, the so-called Euthymian recension, was brought to Kiev from where it slowly expanded northward. The new trend tried to purify Church Slavonic and was hostile to any vernacularization of the church language. Without trying to restore the original Old Church Slavonic, the new trend fostered artificiality (at least in some features) as a device for keeping the written language above the everyday idiom. This trend emanated from the circle of clergymen and scholars centred around Euthymius, the patriarch of Trnovo in Bulgaria, and reached Ukraine via Mount Athos, Constantinople, the Moldavian monasteries and the Bulgarian refugees from the Turkish conquest of the Balkans.

Euthymian Church Slavonic was characterized by striking mannerisms in spelling, syntax and vocabulary. In Ukraine the most significant feature of the Euthymian language reforms was the reversal of the centuries-long evolution toward a synthesis of Church Slavonic with the vernacular. Such a synthesis was precluded now by the philosophical precepts of the trend: the literary language was considered the system of symbols reflecting the ultimate religious truth. Consequently, this "new" Church Slavonic could not admit elements of the vernacular, which could not absorb the former's esoteric rules. The literary language reached a fork between ecclesiastic and secular usage. The separation of the two led to diglossia.

This course of development was reinforced by the events which shaped the chancery language of the time. The Polish rule in Galicia put an end to the use of the local speech in court and administration records: in 1433 Władysław Jagiełło decreed the unification of the judiciary system (the Privilege of Cracow) which discontinued the use of *ius ruthenicale* and, by the same token, made Latin obligatory in court records. In the Lithuanian-occupied part of Ukraine, a new administrative language was introduced from the political centre of the country, Vilna (now Vilnius). This language which was called *rus'kyi* (not to be confused with modern Russian which was called Muscovite) will here be labelled Ruthenian. If one disregards the very few early records which had a Ukrainian tinge, the language was Belorussian based on the spoken language of the Vilna region.

When used by Ukrainians, Ruthenian, like Church Slavonic of the earlier period, occasionally manifested some Ukrainian features. However, in addition to these inadvertent Ukrainianisms, there arose a small set of almost obligatory substitutions reminiscent of the contemporary relationships between various branches of English like, for instance, British versus American. As an example one can take the treatment of *ě*. In the Belorussian version of Ruthenian, it freely alternated with *e*; in the Ukrainian recension this was not permitted and in the intermediary Polissia region this was allowed only in unstressed syllables. Many other substitutions were hidden behind the facade of conventional spelling. Such striking features of Belorussian pronunciation as *akanie, tsekanie* and *dzekanie* were in principle avoided, as were such Ukrainian features as the change of *o* into *u* (*kun'* "horse," traditionally spelled *kon'*, now *kin'*), but no doubt they were applied in reading the texts. Such substitutions, however, did not split the Ruthenian language into two or more branches, nor were they capable of changing its fundamentally Belorussian character.

In sum, the Ukrainians had to deal with two literary languages: a rather esoteric Church Slavonic, and Ruthenian, which was Belorussian-based although it tolerated a few Ukrainian features. The expansion and the prestige of Ruthenian as the language of administration can be measured by its use in some charters issued in Moldavia (which in the fourteenth and fifteenth centuries were predominantly Ukrainian with some admixture of Bulgarian and Romanian), in the diplomatic acts of the Cossacks, etc.

The philosophical premises of the Euthymian recension of Church Slavonic, if ever properly realized, did not have a lasting effect in Ukraine. Partly due to the Reformation, a desire arose to make the ecclesiastic language intelligible to the common reader. While preserving the orthographic attire of Euthymian Church Slavonic, attempts were made to synthesize the two literary languages, the most advanced being the vernacularized *Peresopnytsia Gospel* of 1556–61 and the numerous manuscripts of the Didactic Gospels of the following decades. But the Union of Lublin in 1569 eliminated the frontiers between Poland and Lithuania, and "Lithuanian" Ukraine, with the exception of the Berestia (now Brest) region, became part of Poland. The severance of ties with Lithuania made the fostering of Belorussian-based Ruthenian in Ukraine pointless and it simply withered away.

Further, after the partition, the social prerequisites for such a synthesis were no longer present. Within the Polish state there did not and could not exist any Ukrainian court. The Polish tax and legal system impeded the development and prosperity of the Ukrainian town dwellers and transformed the Ukrainian sections in towns into little more than ghettos. Other laws impeded the cultural development of the Ukrainian clergy. The majority of the nobility, the clergy and the townspeople either renounced their Ukrainian nationality or became second-class citizens. With the exception of the church, Ukrainian national institutions ceased to exist, and there were no social organizations capable of nurturing the literary language.

As the possibility of a synthesis of Ruthenian and Church Slavonic faded away, Polish and Latin began to spread into the country as the languages of the administration. The government started using it immediately after the Union of Lublin. The Ukrainian gentry protested in 1569, in 1571, in 1577 and several times more up to 1675, and the Polish government issued guarantees for the use of Ruthenian (privileges of 1569, 1591, 1638, 1681) but these were rarely enforced. As an example, of 172 Zhytomyr books of municipal and court records written between 1582 and 1776, 130 were in Polish, 25 in mixed Latin and Polish, 13 in mixed Ruthenian and Polish, 3 in Ruthenian and 1 in Latin. The basic law of the country, the Lithuanian Statute, was published for the last time in Ruthenian in 1588; the editions which followed, in 1614 and 1619, were in Polish. This trend was formally legalized by the resolution of the Warsaw Diet of 1696, which proscribed the use of Ruthenian in court records.

The depth of penetration of Polish into the literary language outside of the administration is shown by its use in the religious polemics which preceded and followed the Church Union of Berestia (1596). Although the Greek Orthodox writers used Church Slavonic and Ruthenian widely at the beginning of the conflict, the first Orthodox treatise in Polish appeared as early as 1597, and after 1628 Polish was the only language used.

The expansion of Polish outside of the administration proceeded primarily at the expense of Church Slavonic, which was gradually relegated to the status of a dead language of the liturgy. In turn, Ruthenian gradually lost its Belorussian components and adapted to the local dialects. Under the new name of *prostaia mova* (literally, the language of commoners), with a small Church Slavonic and substantial Polish admixture, it was used in private letters, secular songs, memoirs, fictional tales, some chronicles and also in the so-called Didactic Gospels. But its social status was low and its resistance to Polish intrusions feeble. The diglossia of former years was being replaced by the triglossia, with Polish playing the dominant role.

Under these conditions, the only viable intellectual force was the clergy. To oppose the Latin tradition championed by the Polish religious polemicists, the Orthodox clergy began turning to Church Slavonic and proclaimed it the legitimate heir to the glorious Greek tradition. An unprecedented revival of Church Slavonic began in the 1580s, initiated by the circle of Prince Konstantyn of Ostrih. It was taken up by the Lviv Fraternity after 1586, and brought to its acme in Kiev, first by the intellectuals of the Cave Monastery and later also by the Kiev Academy. The new trend appealed to the Greek and to the Orthodox Slav tradition without showing interest in a national Ukrainian foundation for the revived Church Slavonic. It is not fortuitous that the principal achievement of the Ostrih circle, the publication in 1581 of a Church Slavonic translation of the Bible, was based on a manuscript solicited from Russia in which very few adjustments were made. In turn, the grammars and dictionaries subsequently compiled by the Ukrainian students of Church Slavonic were based on this same book. These were virtually the first grammars and dictionaries of Church Slavonic: Lavrentii Zizanii (1596), Meletii Smotrytsky (1619), Pamva Berynda (1627), Iepyfanii Slavynetsky (1642), and Slavynetsky and Arsenii Koretsky (1649), to mention the most important.

Despite their "common Slavic" (excluding the Poles!) aspirations, the creators of the new version of Church Slavonic had no ambition or desire to restore Old Church Slavonic or Euthymian Church Slavonic to its original purity. Their Church Slavonic had no developed philological, philosophical or even theological orientation. It was first and foremost a practical tool in the struggle for the preservation of national and religious identity. The chief goal of their activity was to eliminate disorder in the church language by a rigid codification of language based chiefly on the patterns available in Ukraine, Belorussia and Russia, with some adaptation to the intricacies of Greek grammar and to the rules of Latin grammars current in Poland at the time.

The Meletian (from the name of Meletii Smotrytsky, one of the codifiers of the language) version of Church Slavonic was generally accepted in Ukraine, but adherence to it varied according to the training and zeal of the authors. Writers such as Tarasii Zemka rigidly limited Ukrainianisms in their works to the few accepted by Smotrytsky. Others allowed more licence so that in practice we find the whole gamut of shades and transitions between the Meletian Church Slavonic and the *prostaia mova* in the writings of the time, in perfect agreement with the requirements of the then predominant Baroque style.

The revived Church Slavonic superseded Polish as the literary language of those Ukrainians who did not undergo complete Polonization. The new diglossia was accepted by the society: Church Slavonic (*iazyk slavenorosskyi*) versus the vernacular (*prostaia mova*). In addition to liturgical books, the former was used in learned poetry, drama and theology; the latter in private documents, tales, etc., with a plethora of transitions.

The national revolution of 1648 produced an autonomous Cossack state east of the Dnieper as a Russian protectorate, whereas Right-Bank Ukraine remained under Poland after the second partition in 1667. This development enhanced the possibilities of the *prostaia mova* in the new *hetmanshchyna*, or Hetmanate, as the Cossack state was often called. It was widely used in the records of the central and local governments and became a strong contender for the status of the national literary language. Although it was not cut off from dialectal elements, it displayed a relatively high degree of standardization: essentially the same type of language appears in the documents compiled in Ukraine as well as in the non-Ukrainian parts of the country, e.g. in the records of Starodub. Clearly it was a kind of administrative koine in the making.

The disintegration of the Cossack state after Mazepa's defeat at Poltava in 1709, and the ensuing transformation of that part of the country into a

Russian colony affected the two literary languages of Ukraine in different ways. The high language, Church Slavonic, supranational by its character and intent, was replaced by Russian, an easy transition because of the important role Church Slavonic played in the structure of literary Russian. It was, in a sense, a switch from one type of Church Slavonic to another. This explains why, in the eighteenth and at the beginning of the nineteenth century, Russian was used by Ukrainian writers even in anti-Russian works, such as *Oda na rabstvo* by Vasilii Kapnist and *Istoriia Rusov*. The *prostaia mova* was in use as the language of administration in the provinces until the introduction of the Russian administrative system by Catherine II in 1780–4, after which it was restricted to private use, in songs, satires and other works not designed for printing. The linguistic dichotomy of the preceding period, Church Slavonic versus *prostaia mova*, continued in the contrast between Russian and *prostaia mova*, but the latter shrank substantially in the area of its usage. This is the situation which prevailed until the upsurge of Romanticism at the beginning of the nineteenth century.

Meriting special attention is the progressive replacement, in the literary usage, of the dialects of the north and west of Ukraine by those of the southeast. This development, though insignificant in itself because the vulgar style was not part of the literary language, is important in the evolution of modern Ukrainian. In the writings from the seventeenth century, and even in the greater part of those from the eighteenth, the dialects of the north and the west predominate, to the extent that dialect features are admitted at all. The dialects of the southeast assume importance only in the Romantic era in the works of Ivan Kotliarevsky (1769–1838), Petro Hulak-Artemovsky (1790–1865) and others, based on the dialects of Poltava, Kharkiv and the southern part of the province of Kiev. This change was probably due to the political dismemberment of Ukraine upon its third partition between Russia and Austro-Hungary (1793–5) and to the economic and cultural decline of its northern and western regions which turned Kiev, Poltava and, in particular, Kharkiv, after the founding of its university, into the principal cultural centres.

Romanticism began to penetrate Ukraine around 1820, superimposing its precepts on the old traditions and causing a modification of linguistic concepts. This movement was crowned by the works of Taras Shevchenko and Panteleimon Kulish, whose work eventually transcended the boundaries of Romanticism. The spirit of Romanticism, which is held responsible for the creation of the modern literary language of Ukraine and which, indeed, determined its nature, presented a striking contrast to the spirit of Classicism. The central concept of Classicism was a hierarchy or differentiation of what were called styles, actually genres; language was merely a tool in this programme. Romanticism, on the other hand, stressed what could be called the symbolic function of language: language became the banner, the platform, the slogan, and the measure of all things (see Appendix 1). Language was considered the expression of the nation's aspirations and soul and the sum of its historical experience. From this view sprang the search for the synthesis of national styles which was founded on the language spoken by the people and the language employed in its folklore. This synthesis is demonstrated in the works of Shevchenko and Kulish.

To turn the spoken language into a subtle expression of the "people's spirit" and of the nation's history, these writers had first of all to purge from it the "low" and vulgar elements which entered it during the whole of the preceding period (see Appendix 2). On the other hand, they had to impart to this language the heritage of former epochs. This led to a new injection of Slavonic elements, especially those used in the church. Shevchenko is closer than Kulish to the traditions of the former literary language of Kievan Rus' which tended to synthesize the popular language and Church Slavonic (but, of course, in quite different proportions). Kulish, on the other hand, is closer to the Baroque tradition of the seemingly chaotic mixture of heterogeneous elements although, in his theoretical manifestoes, he tended to neglect the usages of seventeenth-century Ukrainian.[2]

Briefly, the modern Ukrainian literary language, shaped above all by Shevchenko and Kulish, stems from the popular language (called "vulgar style" in the period of Classicism) which is based, in turn, on the dialect of the southeast (although Kulish himself was born and spent most of his life in northern Ukraine). This dialect was raised to the status of a language by the adoption of elements from folklore and of styles bequeathed by tradition. Despite all the differences between this language and the *prostaia mova* of the seventeenth century, the genetic ties between the two cannot be denied.

During the course of its development this literary language lost a considerable number of artificially introduced historical elements. Due to government restrictions and the influence of populism, the literary language began to lose its non-vernacular elements and even moved somewhat closer to the pre-romantic "vulgar style" (see Appendix 3). This development, however, was checked by the influences emanating from Western Ukraine, which had been incorporated into Austria, where there were no administrative (legal) obstacles to the development of the literary language.

Between 1860 and 1880 Western Ukraine adopted the literary language that the Romantics had elaborated. The regulations imposed by the Russian government in 1863, and in particular the 1876 prohibition of public use of written and spoken Ukrainian, led to the transfer of the majority of Ukrainian publications to Galicia. There many local elements penetrated the written language, especially those avenues of life which were closed off to Ukrainian in the Russian part of Ukraine: law, government, administration, technology, science, etc. The West Ukrainian influence involved not only the vocabulary but even, in a limited way, the phonology and morphology of Ukrainian.[3]

This "invasion" of "Galicianisms" provoked discontent and brought about two "linguistic discussions" (1891–3 and 1907–12) between the defenders of the original or "pure" language and those of the new, partly "westernized" idiom. The second of these discussions took place after the revolution of 1905, when Ukrainian publications were authorized again in the Russian part of Ukraine (see Appendix 4).

The reciprocal influence of the two variants of modern Ukrainian continued after the revolution of 1917 and the fourth partition of Ukraine among Russia, Poland, Czechoslovakia and Romania in 1919. The influence of the Galician characteristics increased in various ways especially during the twenties, the period of so-called Ukrainianization. Even at present, when Western Ukraine belongs to the same polity as the rest of the country and plays in it but a secondary role, a West Ukrainian linguistic influence is evident in books and periodicals published in Soviet Ukraine. The government, however, has been unfavourably disposed toward this influence since the early thirties.

The principal stages in the development of the literary languages of Ukraine may be presented in the (grossly simplified) table (page 226).

In the general typology of literary languages, the contemporary standard Ukrainian is not a literary language based on historical synthesis; it shows continuity only in part of its stages, it is not monodialectal in its foundation, and its geographical centres shifted. Contrary to Russian, Polish and Czech, but like Serbo-Croatian, Slovenian and Slovak, modern standard Ukrainian is essentially a product of Romanticism and bears an imprint of that period in the people's attitude toward their literary language.

The veneration of Ukrainian, rooted in a Romantic complex of ideas but continued during the post-Romantic era, placed the question of the Ukrainian language at the centre of the political conflicts of the late nineteenth and early twentieth centuries. Contrary to the opinion that literary languages, to assert themselves, require cultural centres created by

TABLE 1. PRINCIPAL STAGES IN THE DEVELOPMENT OF LITERARY LANGUAGES OF UKRAINE

Period	Approximate Date	Type(s) of Literary Language		
Old Ukrainian	988-1387	ChSl in Bulgarian recension adapted to Eastern Slavic with Ukrainian peculiarities		
Early Mid-Ukrainian	1387-1569	↓ ChSl (Euthymian)	Ruthenian (Belorussian with Ukrainian substitutions)	
Mid-Ukrainian	1569-1709	↓ ChSl (Meletian)	[Polish]	*prostaia mova* (since 1648 based on SE dialects)
Late Mid-Ukrainian	1709-1818	Russian [ChSl]		↓ *prostaia nova*
Modern Ukrainian	1818-present			↓ *prostaia mova* modified into the standard language (since 1876 with W. Ukrainian graft)

NOTE: Periods in the history of the literary language are very roughly marked off by the dates of important historical events. Arrows show continuity, the absence of arrows indicates lack of clear continuity. Brackets indicate that a given language played a secondary role in the development.

economic and political development, modern literary Ukrainian has been the work of a group of men of letters (primarily Shevchenko and Kulish) as a manifestation of the poetic spirit. There were practically no large towns in Ukraine; in those which did exist, the upper classes spoke and wrote in Russian. There were few intellectuals and the middle class was small. Generally, the use of Ukrainian was confined to the peasants and the lower clergy.

Once created, the literary language became a slogan, a banner, a goal. At the end of the nineteenth century, the Ukrainian national movement was concerned above all with questions of culture, education and literature viewed as political problems. In the twentieth century the linguistic controversy gradually lost its central position and purely political issues came to the fore (see Appendix 5).

Contrary to the conventional theories that a literary language develops as a result of political movements, the Ukrainian literary language offers the "miracle" of a linguistic development that has given birth to a political movement. The linguistic work of Shevchenko and Kulish prepared the way for the rise of political parties, states, armies, for wars, struggles and conflicts. Lovers of paradoxes may say that a poet created a language and that the language created a nation. Of course, the nation had its long historical tradition, but by the beginning of the nineteenth century this tradition had visibly reached the point of disintegration and extinction.

Appendix 1

In the works of Amvrosii Metlynsky the Ukrainian language is already considered a crystallization of the nation's history and the incarnation of the people's spirit:

Bulo shchastia, buly chvary,
Vse te het' sobi pishlo,
I, iak sontse iz-za khmary,
Ridne slovo iziishlo.
Pryinialo kozachi richi,
Rehit, zharty, plach, pechal':
Ozovet'sia iak iz Sichi,
Stane smikh i stane zhal'.

("Ridna mova," published for the first time in Metlynsky's *Dumky i pisni ta shche deshcho*, Kharkiv, 1839. Quoted from Amvrosii Metlynsky and Mykola Kostomarov, *Tvory*, Rus'ka pys'mennist', Lviv, 1914, 42.)

During the period of *Osnova* (1861–2) Kulish defined the role of the Ukrainian language in the following way: "The mother tongue alone is the strength of our people, the glory of our people, and it alone allows us to claim a place among other nations. ... The mother tongue, and nothing else, has given us the respect of other nations and has laid the new foundations of our historic life." ("Choho stoit' Shevchenko iako poet narodnii," *Osnova*, 1861, 3, quoted from Kulish, *Tvory*, Rus'ka pys'mennist', 6, Lviv, 1910, 486, 492.) The same theme appears in numerous poems by Kulish, especially in his collection *Dzvin* (Geneva, 1893). Take, for example, the poem "Do Marusi V":

Otechestvo sobi gruntuimo v ridnim slovi,
Vono, vono odno vid pahuby vteche,
Pidderzhyt' natsiiu na batkivs'kii osnovi ...

or the poem "Sum i rozvaha":

Slovo nam verne i sylu davneznu i voliu,
I ne odyn nam lavrovyi vinets' obivie kruh chola.

In Shevchenko's poetry the motif of the language (*slovo*) is especially important. With the help of a series of appositions and substitutions, Shevchenko identifies *slovo* with other concepts, such as soul, justice and vengeance. The poet views his historical mission as the resurrection of Ukraine by the *slovo*:

... Vozvelychu
Malykh otykh rabiv nimykh!
Ia na storozhi kolo ikh
Postavliu slovo ...
("Podrazhanyie XI psalmu," 1859).

The original psalm does not speak of the protection of oppressed peoples by their mother tongue. Psalm XI (XII) speaks only of preserving honourable men from wickedness: "Because the poor are despoiled, because the needy groan, I will now arise," says the Lord; "I will place them in the safety for which they long."

Shevchenko bases his faith in the future of Ukraine on the irrepressible power of the *slovo*:

I nesytyi ne vyore
Na dni moria pole,
Ne skuie dushi zhyvoi
I slova zhyvoho.
("Kavkaz," 1845).

For an analysis of Shevchenko's widely extended semantics of the *slovo*, see V. Samonenko, "Obraz Shevchenkovoi muzy," *Shevchenkivs'kyi zbirnyk* (Kiev: Sorabkop, 1924); B. Iakubsky, "Do sotsiolohii Shevchenkovoho epitetu," *Shevchenko*, richnyk 1 (Kharkiv, 1928); D. Chyzhevsky, *Istoriia ukrainskoi literatury* (New York, 1956), 441 ff. (In English: *A History of Ukrainian Literature*, Littleton, Colorado, 1975, 521 ff.)

In the appeal of the Fraternity of Cyril and Methodius to the Ukrainians (1846), which represents one of the first platforms of the Ukrainian national movement in the nineteenth century, the blossoming of the mother tongue has priority over social questions: "We declare that all the Slavs should unite .... But in such a way that each nation build its own republic and be governed separately so that each nation have its own language, literature and social order." (M. Kostomarov, *Knyhy bytiia ukrains'koho narodu*, Augsburg: Ukrains'kyi muzei-arkhiv pry UVAN, 1947, 25.)

Appendix 2

Shevchenko's struggle with the elements of the "low" genres of Classicism makes its appearance in his earliest works. The "vulgarisms" below destroy the style of the romantic poem. They disappear from this genre of Shevchenko's poetry after 1842, and are only retained in his satires.

Zarehotalys' nekhryshcheni ...
Hai obizvavsia, halas, **zyk'**
Orda mov rizhe. Mov skazheni,
Letiat' do duba ... **Ni chychyrk!**
("Prychynna," 1838),
Vychuniala *[Kateryna], ta v zapichku*
Dytynu kolyshe ...
("Kateryna," 1838),
Slipyi **vshkvaryv**. *Navprysiadky*
Pishly po bazaru.
("Haidamaky," 1841),

Appendix 3

The orientation toward a more "popular" style finds its expression in "Siohochasne literaturne priamuvannia" by Ivan Nechui-Levytsky: "The model of the literary language should be none other than the language of the peasant and its syntax," and, as far as vocabulary is concerned, "the Ukrainian literary language should develop on the basis of the living language of the peasantry by drawing on its terminology and suffixes: new words should not be sought in other Slavic languages, nor in Church Slavonic, but the vocabulary should be developed on the basis of popular Ukrainian variants." (*Pravda*, 1878, 26.) The language of Nechui-Levytsky's novels and novellas corresponds to a great extent to this programme.

Appendix 4

The first discussion opened with the article by Borys Hrinchenko (Chaichenko, "Halyts'ki virshi," *Pravda*, 1891, 9), which sharply attacked the Galician influence, and the reply by Ivan Franko ("Hovorymo na vovka, skazhimo i za vovka," *Zoria*, 1891, 18). Much less aggressive were the voices of M. Shkolychenko ("Chaichenko i Franko," *Zoria*, 1891, 23), I. Kokorudz ("Prychynok do sporu iazykovoho," *Zoria*, 1891, 24) and A. Krymsky (Khvanko, "Nasha iazykova skruta ta sposib zaradyty lykhovi," *Zoria*, 1891, 24). Hrinchenko entered the stage twice more in a conciliatory tone. The discussion ended in a compromise, with a tacit agreement to follow, to some extent, a *via media*. This is reflected in the subsequent works of Hrinchenko (his pamphlet *Tiazhkym shliakhom*, Kharkiv, 1907) and Franko ("Literaturna mova i diialekty," *Literaturno-naukovyi visnyk*, 1907, 2).

A new round of discussion was provoked by Nechui-Levytsky's pamphlets "Siohochasna chasopysna mova na Ukraini," *Ukraina*, 1907, 1–3, and *Kryve dzerkalo ukrains'koi movy* (Kiev, 1912). The distinctly anti-Galician position of Nechui-Levytsky, however, found no support. The responses it provoked (I. Steshenko, M. Zhuchenko, M. Levytsky, I. Verkhratsky *et al.*) championed the idea of compromise.

Appendix 5

The first appeal of the Central Rada of Ukraine, published on 22 March 1917, was vague in its formulations. Its only concrete demand concerned Ukrainian language rights. This document is typical and worth quoting at length.

> People of Ukraine! The chains that you have been wearing for centuries have fallen. Liberty has come to all the oppressed, to all the nations of Russia who were reduced to slavery. The time is ripe for your liberty and your awakening to a new, free and creative life. For the first time, you, the thirty million people of Ukraine, shall have the opportunity to express how you wish to live as a separate nation. Henceforth you shall forge with your own mighty hand a better destiny for yourselves in the friendly family of free nations. The government of the tsars has collapsed, and the provisional government has proclaimed that a constituent assembly will soon be convened, based on universal, equal and direct suffrage. It is there that your true voice, your real will shall be heard in the world for the first time. As we wait for this moment, we ask you to demand from the new government calmly, but resolutely, all the rights that belong to you by nature, and that you, the Great People, master of the land of Ukraine, should have; and for the immediate future you should demand the right to introduce your mother tongue in all the schools, from the most elementary to the most advanced, in the courts and in the administration of the country.

(Quoted from D. Doroshenko, *Istoriia Ukrainy 1917–1923 rr.*, 1, Uzhhorod, 1932, 43, where the text is reproduced in its entirety.)

Aside from a rather indefinite view on national autonomy, the First Universal (manifesto) of the Central Rada on 23 June 1917 demanded "that a certain proportion of the taxes levied on our people for the central treasury (in Petrograd) should be given to us, the representatives of this people, for the cultural needs of our nation." (The complete text is quoted by Doroshenko, *Istoriia*, 1, 88–92).

It was only in the Third Universal of 20 November 1917 that the democratic republic of Ukraine was proclaimed and that other demands were explicitly formulated over and above those relative to equality and the use of the Ukrainian language. For the complete text, see Doroshenko, 179–81. On the attitudes of the different political parties in Ukraine in 1917, see also J. S. Reshetar, *The Ukrainian Revolution, 1917–1920* (Princeton, 1952), 48 ff.

Notes

1. The Soviet claims of the 1930s and 1940s that an older or simultaneous literary language of purely native *drevnerusskii* character existed now appear politically motivated and do not deserve serious discussion. See Viktor Vinogradov, "Voprosy obrazovaniia russkogo natsionalnogo literaturnogo iazyka," *Voprosy iazykoznaniia* 1, (1956): 7–10, and Boris Unbegaun, "Some Recent Studies on the History of the Russian Language," *Oxford Slavonic Papers* 5 (1954): 119 ff.
2. See, e.g., Kulish's poem "Hryts'ko Skovoroda" in P. Kulish, *Sochineniia i pisma*, ed. I. M. Kamanin 3 (Kiev, 1909).

    Liakhy zh pys'menstvom popsuvaly
    Nam netiamni manastyri.
    Nauky nide bulo vziaty,
    Pryishlos' ii v Liakhiv shukaty,
    I my pol'shchyznoiu zhyly
    Todi, iak z neiu priu vely. (1, 15)

3. In phonology it was the matter of several characteristics in the pronunciation of loanwords. In morphology it was the exclusion of participles of the type *roblianyi, kladianyi*; the exclusion of the first person singular of the type *khodiu, nosiu* and of the third person singular of the type *khode, nose*; the predominance of the dative singular in *-ovi* for masculine nouns.

PROBLEMS OF TERMINOLOGY AND PERIODIZATION IN THE TEACHING OF UKRAINIAN HISTORY

Round Table Discussion at the Ukrainian Historical Conference
London, Ontario, 31 May 1978

MEMBERS OF THE PANEL:

Omeljan Pritsak (Harvard), Chairman
Taras Hunczak (Rutgers)
Ivan L. Rudnytsky (Alberta)
Orest Subtelny (Hamilton College)
Frank E. Sysyn (Harvard)
Lubomyr R. Wynar (Kent State)

DISCUSSANTS:

Marko Antonovych (Ukrainian Historical Association)
Alexander Baran (Manitoba)
Lubomyr Hajda (Harvard)
Patricia Herlihy (Wellesley College)
John-Paul Himka (Alberta)
Oleh S. Pidhainy (Symon Petliura Institute)
George Y. Shevelov (Columbia, emeritus)

OMELJAN PRITSAK:

Before we start the discussion, I would like to say a few prefatory words. University-level teaching of Ukrainian history is now becoming a reality both in the United States and Canada. It is time, therefore, to reflect on some of the basic problems connected with teaching Ukrainian history in this new framework.

The difficulties, both external and internal, are immense. The external ones include the very legitimacy and the place of Ukrainian history in the curricula of the departments of history at North American universities. On this continent, not the *universitas*, but the fragmented departmental structure is the basis of academic life.

There is no doubt that departments of history are suspicious of the need and right of Ukrainian history to enter their structure. There are two clear reasons for this. The first is the reluctance on the part of every establishment to give civil rights to a newcomer, unless he has proven his maturity. The other reason is deeply rooted in the intellectual background of the North American academy. Hegel's distinction between the historical and non-historical nations, later fully accepted by Karl Marx and Frederick Engels, is still the standard for assessing the right of any nation to have its own history. Since there was no Ukrainian state in the nineteenth century, Ukraine was neglected or relegated to the role of a so-called non-historical nation. It is worth noting that at the end of the eighteenth century, a representative body of continental and British historians decided to publish a corpus of universal history in monographic presentations, and an entire volume was devoted to Ukrainian history. The volume consisted of two parts: part one concerned the history of Ukraine and the Ukrainian Cossacks and part two dealt with the history of the Kingdom of Galicia and Volodymeria. The work in question appeared in Halle in 1796, and the author was the Austrian historian Johann Christian Engel. A few decades later, however, the scholars responsible for the Gotha Universal History (A. H. L. Heeren and F. A. Ukert), following Hegel, did not consider it necessary to devote a special volume to Ukrainian history. *Sic transit gloria mundi.* From this time Ukrainian history lost its legitimate place in universal history, and universal history and Ukrainian history have remained on non-speaking terms ever since.

Now it is time—and the duty of a body like the one gathered here—to start the dialogue again. No doubt, there are some discrepancies in theories, tools and methods between the more developed West European and American histories and, as it were, "underdeveloped" Ukrainian history. So it is necessary for representatives of Ukrainian historical scholarship to learn how to apply these methods to the study of Ukrainian history. Certainly, no North American university or any given department can be used to promote a "cause." Therefore, it is necessary for Ukrainian history to be presented in the same way as any other national history. In this endeavour we face a tremendous problem with definitions of various kinds.

What is Ukraine as a subject of history? Stefan Tomashivsky put the question as early as 1920. Is Ukrainian history the history of the Ukrainian people, that is, ethnic history? If we were to accept this definition, we would run into difficulty, for we would face a theoretical discrepancy: ethnic matters belong to social anthropology rather than to history, so they cannot be used as criteria for historical research. Is it the history of Ukraine as a state or nation-state? Here there are again problems because something is lacking—the continuity of the state. Is it possible to have a history of something which at times has been discontinued? Thus there are, indeed, many problems.

I don't pretend that I will present a solution. I would just like to stress that problems of this nature exist. Now as to the basic term: from time to time I hear from colleagues that to use the name Ukraine is probably unjustified. The name Ukraine is not historical, they say, since it only appeared in relation to the Ukrainian territory from the sixteenth or seventeenth century. The answer to this is very simple. I think there is no difficulty in applying the term "Ukrainian" to the history of that country in the same way as there is no difficulty in applying the term Spain or Spanish in dealing with what is called Spanish history. Everybody who studies Spanish history knows that the term *España* is not of Spanish but of Provencal origin and that it was a foreign word in Spanish. Even a monarch as great as Philip II was never styled the Emperor or King of Spain but bore the title "the Catholic King of Castile [because Castile was important], Leon, Aragon, Sicily, Jerusalem, Portugal, Navarre and the Indies." The term Spain had not yet appeared, but still Spanish history encompasses that period. I could give many other similar instances but this example must suffice. So we will agree that the term Ukraine applied historically makes sense.

We will encounter many other problems, of course. For example, what should be done about the Polovtsians or the Pechenegs or the Crimean Khanate? Where do these belong? Unfortunately, Professor Alan W. Fisher, a specialist in Crimean Tatar history, is not able to be with us. However, in conversation, we agreed that the history of Ukraine should be based on its contemporary territory. From that point of view, the history of the Bosporan Kingdom or the Pechenegs or Khazars or the Tatars is a part of Ukrainian history. This is one opinion, but we have here a round table so we can discuss the matter. I also invite everyone in the audience to participate when the panel's presentations are finished.

After agreeing that there is such a thing as the history of Ukraine and deciding what it means and includes, we can start discussing the next question—periodization. We must know the territory and then deal with the periodization, for unless we know the object, we cannot deal with the second question. Then we can turn to terminology which is connected with every aspect of our topic.

Enough words on my part. I ask Professor Rudnytsky to present his thoughts on periodization and terminology.

IVAN L. RUDNYTSKY:

A. Periodization

There exist two basic periodization schemes in respect to Ukrainian history: one is to be found in Soviet historical literature and the other is prevalent among pre- and non-Soviet Ukrainian historians. The Soviet periodization scheme is an application of the well-known Marxist theory of socio-economic "formations." Mankind allegedly advances through the stages of primeval communism, slave-owning society, feudalism, capitalism and socialism. This pattern of development is supposed to possess universal validity, although differences in the rate of progress among individual peoples are recognized. Accordingly, in their treatment of Ukrainian history Soviet scholars single out the epochs of feudalism (from the inception of Kievan Rus' to the middle of the nineteenth century), capitalism (from the 1860s to 1917) and socialism (since the October Revolution). In Soviet historiography this periodization framework enjoys the authority of an official dogma. It is imposed rigidly and no deviations are tolerated.

Ukrainian historians outside the USSR, on the other hand, following in the footsteps of their nineteenth-century, populist predecessors, commonly speak of "the princely era," "the Lithuanian-Polish era," "the Cossack era" and finally of an "era of national rebirth."

I do not find either of those two periodization schemes altogether satisfactory, although both may be partially valid. This is not the place to engage in a critique of the Marxist philosophy of history. It may suffice to say that for someone who is not convinced of the ontological priority of the economic factor in social and historical life, the basing of periodization exclusively on economic "formations" begs the question. It seems also extremely doubtful that a single, unilineal pattern of development can be devised for the entire human race. Leaving aside these objections of principle and keeping the debate on an empirical level, the obvious weak link in the Soviet-Marxist periodization scheme of Ukrainian and East Slavic history is the "feudal formation." It simply does not make historical sense to subsume a millennium, extending from Riurik to Nicholas I, under the label of feudalism. This does not imply that I deny the existence of feudalism, or at least of feudal-type tendencies, in the history of Ukraine. But to serve as a useful instrument of historical cognition, the concept ought to be applied much more restrictively. Medieval Rus' did not originally possess a feudal structure, and the process of feudalization in the Kievan state gained momentum only in the course of the eleventh century. One will concede that the Grand Duchy of Lithuania, to which the majority of Ukrainian lands belonged from the fourteenth through the sixteenth century, was essentially feudal. But it is preposterous to designate in this manner the Cossack body politic of the seventeenth and eighteenth centuries. Moreover, most Western students deny that imperial Russia up to the emancipation of the peasants and the "great reforms" of the 1860s may legitimately be considered feudal.

The rejection of the Marxist system of periodization does not necessarily imply a retention of the older scheme, evolved by pre-revolutionary Ukrainian historians of the populist school. Its chief deficiency is parochialism. Concepts such as "the princely era" and "the Cossack era," which cannot be extended to other countries, artificially isolate Ukrainian historical processes from a broader context. In addition, the populist periodization scheme suffers from conceptual looseness in the determination of the specific character of individual epochs. Let us take a look at the so-called "Cossack era," which was the favourite subject of populist historians. There is no doubt that Cossackdom was a most important phenomenon in the history of seventeenth-century Ukraine. But, prior to the Khmelnytsky revolution, the Cossacks were hardly central in the life of the Ukrainian people as a whole. Neither must we forget that at no time were the western Ukrainian territories deeply affected by the Cossack movement. Therefore, it is inaccurate to designate the whole epoch from the sixteenth through the eighteenth centuries as the Cossack Era.

What do I, then, propose in place of the two periodization schemes which have been found wanting? I think that there is no need to devise a special periodization for Ukrainian history, because the common European pattern can be well applied to Ukraine, with only minor adjustments. I am referring to the familiar great epochs of European history, namely Antiquity, the Middle Ages, and Modern Times, including such further subdivisions as the High and Late Middle Ages, Early Modern Times, etc. As a university teacher of Ukrainian history, I have divided the subject into the following four courses, arranged chronologically: Ancient and Medieval Ukraine, Ukraine in Early Modern Times, Nineteenth-Century Ukraine and Twentieth-Century Ukraine.

A full elaboration of the proposed periodization scheme cannot, of course, be attempted here. I would like, however, to add a few explanatory remarks. Owing to the establishment of a string of Greek settlements along the northern Black Sea littoral and to their impact on the hinterland, and owing to the later extension of the Roman protectorate over the Bosporan Kingdom, Ukraine became, at least marginally, a part of the world of ancient, Greek and Hellenistic-Roman civilization. The history of medieval

Ukraine can be easily divided into three sub-periods: the epoch preceding the emergence of Kievan Rus' (sixth-ninth centuries); the time of the united Kievan realm, of the so-called Kievan federation and of the Galician-Volhynian state (tenth to mid-fourteenth centuries); and finally the epoch of Lithuanian overlordship (from the middle of the fourteenth century to the Union of Lublin, 1569). It is evident that these divisions correspond to the European Early, High and Late Middle Ages. The one significant difference is that in Ukraine the medieval era lasted longer than in the West. It ended only with the Union of Lublin which radically altered the political status of Ukrainian lands, introduced a new social system based on the estates and opened the country to the influences of the Renaissance, Reformation and Counter Reformation. The early modern era in Ukraine lasted from the Union of Lublin to the late eighteenth century. The dominant social structure during those two centuries was that of the estates, of which Polish-type "gentry democracy" and the Cossack order were the two rival variants. The Baroque was the unifying theme in the cultural and intellectual life of that era.

In Ukraine, as in Western Europe, the *ancien régime* ended in the late eighteenth century. Among the events which marked the transition to a new historical epoch, the Nineteenth Century, the following were among the most significant: the abolition of Cossack autonomy; the Russian conquest of the Black Sea coastal areas and the closing of the steppe frontier; the partitions of Poland; and, in the cultural sphere, the impact of the Enlightenment and of Romanticism. As a period of Ukrainian history, the Nineteenth Century extended from approximately the 1780s-90s to 1914. I have analysed the characteristic features of that age in several previous articles, and I will not recapitulate my findings here. May it suffice to say that this was the era when, in the wake of profound social and cultural changes, the modern Ukrainian nation was beginning to emerge. This trend toward nation-building was, of course, not peculiarly Ukrainian but rather common to all the "submerged peoples" of Europe, from Ireland to the Balkans. The First World War and the resulting revolutionary upheaval were the opening of the recent and contemporary era, the Twentieth Century, which is still in progress today, in Ukraine as well as in Europe as a whole.

I think that the proposed periodization scheme offers three advantages. It is based on the actual structuring of the historical process itself; it organically integrates Ukrainian history into the course of general European developments; and, at the same time, it reveals the undeniable fact of Ukraine's relative backwardness and marginality in comparison with the geographical core of Western civilization. Ukraine experienced all the stages of Europe's evolution, but common European social and cultural trends usually reached Ukraine after some delay, and often in an attenuated form.

B. Terminology

It is legitimate, I believe, to apply retrospectively the modern national term, "Ukraine," to past epochs in the life of the country and the people, when the term did not yet exist or possessed different connotations. The case of Ukraine is not unique in this respect. French historians do not hesitate to include Celtic, Roman and Frankish Gaul into the history of France, in spite of the fact that the term "France" emerged only later and originally applied to the area of Paris alone, the Isle de France.

However, a conscientious student should be aware of the danger of anachronisms. Therefore, he will pay close attention to the actual content of terms at any given time and to their semantic evolution. For instance, in early nineteenth-century official usage "Ukraine" referred to the Slobozhanshchyna region. This explains why contemporary writers could contrast "Ukraine" (the Slobidska-Ukrainian province) with "Little Russia" (the provinces of Chernihiv and Poltava, corresponding with the former Hetmanate). Polish sources of the nineteenth century speak regularly of "Volhynia, Podillia and Ukraine," the latter meaning the Kiev region. Going further back in time, in the seventeenth century "Ukraine" meant the land under Cossack jurisdiction. Therefore, the name did not extend to Galicia, Volhynia and Transcarpathia. In those latter territories the term "Ukraine" prevailed only in the course of the present century, in the wake of the modern national-liberation movement and recent political changes.

A vexatious problem, with which we all are only too familiar, is that the Ukrainian people's older name, "Rus'," has been appropriated by the Russian nation and state. This nomenclature exercises a powerful hold on the minds of Western scholars who usually tie modern Russia to medieval Rus', which they refer to as "Kievan Russia." In this manner modern Ukraine has been deprived of its historical foundations and, so to say, left suspended in the air. Little wonder that Ukrainians react strongly against this spoliation of what they consider their legitimate historical inheritance.

I do not think that there is any need before this audience to advance arguments against the so-called "traditional scheme of Russian history." Instead of wasting time by proving the obvious, I will rather try to deal with the practical issue: what can be done to correct this situation? The question is of great urgency to those of us engaged in teaching Ukrainian and general East European history in a North American academic environment. My contention is that Ukrainian historians, and more so lay publicists, out of an understandable feeling of frustration, often react to the existing situation in a manner which is both faulty from the point of view of scholarship and self-defeating from the point of view of the desired practical result. By making dubious and unsubstantiated claims, we only weaken our own good case.

Among those exaggerated claims, I count the theory that medieval Kievan Rus' was exclusively Ukrainian and which denies the Russians and Belorussians any share in this inheritance. A corollary of this is another proposition which asserts that in the medieval, pre-Mongol era there already existed a clear-cut differentiation of the Eastern Slavs into three distinct national branches.

Limitations of time and space do not allow us to enter here into a detailed, substantive discussion of this complex problem. May I, however, mention a point of direct terminological relevance? Contrary to the statement frequently found in Ukrainian historical (and popular historical) literature, the old term "Rus'" was not simply coterminous with the modern term "Ukraine." During the pre-Mongol era, "Rus'" had two meanings. In the narrow sense, the name referred to the core of the Riurikid realm, comprising the principalities of Kiev, Chernihiv and Pereiaslav. In the broad sense, "Rus'" designated all the vast lands under the rule of the House of Riurik and the spiritual authority of the Kievan metropolitancy. Therefore, not all of modern Ukraine was included in Rus' in the narrow sense, while in the broad sense Rus' comprised also the whole of modern Belorussia and large sections of Russia as well.

Ukrainians object to the rendering of Rus' as Russia. But it cannot be denied that in medieval and early modern Latin, Rus' most frequently appeared as *Russia*. For instance, the Latin name for the *Rus'ke voievodstvo* (i.e., Galicia, a land which has never been politically a part of Muscovy and the Russian empire) was *palatinatus Russiae*. Occasionally Rus' was also rendered as *Rusia, Ruthenia, Rutenia, Ruzzia, Rugia*. One should not expect terminological consistency in the medieval and early modern sources. Following the usage of the papal curia, the East Slavic (Ukrainian and Belorussian) inhabitants of the Polish-Lithuanian Commonwealth were normally named, in Latin, *Rutheni*. But, contrary to a widespread opinion, sometimes we find this term applied also to the Muscovites. According to another erroneous allegation, the tsardom of Moscow became known under the name of "Russia" only in the reign of Peter I. However, the English Elizabethan traveller and diplomat Giles Fletcher wrote a classical account of contemporary Muscovy, entitled *Of the Russe Commonwealth,* first published in 1591.

What conclusions do I draw from the preceding observations? I suggest that it would be more profitable for Ukrainian historians to concentrate their efforts on issues of content and substance rather than on those of nomenclature. In dealing with medieval Rus', one ought to stress that not only was its geographical centre of gravity located in an area which today we call Ukrainian, but that also by its political institutions, social structure and cultural make-up the Kievan state is closer to the mainstream of the Ukrainian rather than the Russian historical tradition. It is possible to defend this reasonable and plausible position without denying that there were elements of the Old Rus' inheritance in the Russian nation and state. Only after having absorbed this substantive insight will Western scholars begin to feel the need to differentiate terminologically between Rus' and Russia. As long as this has not taken place, quixotic verbal polemics against the term "Kievan Russia" will serve to no avail, and are likely to be counterproductive. Issues of terminology are a subsidiary aspect of historical cognition and cannot serve as its substitute.

Careful reading of contemporary Western scholarly literature reveals that the authority of the "traditional scheme of Russian history" has already been seriously undermined. To bring about its radical revision, Ukrainian historians must produce works of high quality, capable of swaying independent, critical minds by the sheer strength and cogency of their arguments. The task ahead is admittedly difficult but not impossible. It also cannot be circumvented: there are no shortcuts in scholarship. Let us make a start by being honest with ourselves and let us recognize how little we have accomplished so far.

OREST SUBTELNY:

The problems of periodization are difficult in every type of history, but in the case of Ukrainian history this is especially true. We have talked about various characteristics of Ukrainian history such as the discontinuities. I have always seen Ukrainian history not so much as a matter of discontinuity, as a lack of definition. It is often difficult to know what exactly is meant by the term Cossack Ukraine, the Hetmanate or Kievan Rus'. Therefore, it is not so much a lack of continuity that disturbs me as the vagueness.

This being the case, how does one approach such a vague, sometimes amorphous body of knowledge? I have no well reasoned, systematic answer, just some definitions and considerations which I keep in mind when approaching a problem of this type. First of all, one must establish some basic parameters. They are time and space. One has to establish a certain time period when one speaks of Ukrainian history, and one must establish a certain area. When one speaks of Hetman Ukraine it involves a certain time and space. Seventeenth-century Ukraine, or as Professor Rudnytsky proposes "early modern Ukraine," gives me a time and a space, too. The only problem is that it doesn't tell us enough. I like to know exactly what I am talking about. That is why I hesitate to use the term "early modern period." I prefer to be more specific.

Establishing time and space in history is the easiest approach. It is a matter of description which is very easy to do. Sometimes one can do it almost arbitrarily. There are books on seventeenth-century France, and we know exactly the time and space. That is the easiest and safest approach; it is also the most broad. One doesn't have to argue about it or substantiate it. However, one may take that as a beginning and as the most general type of approach.

What if one wants to approach Ukrainian history and say something more with one's categories? One must then take the time and space and establish a certain organizing principle. This is a much more difficult approach and it's dangerous. There is usually considerable argument over whether the organizing principle should be based on political, economic or cultural criteria for that given time and space. One must ask: in what area are the most crucial changes occurring? If the answer is economics, the organizing principle might be industrialization or the agrarian system. If culture is considered the most significant factor in the given time and space, it could be Baroque. For politics, one might say the Hetmanate or Soviet Ukraine. The organizing principle tells us much more than does the time-and-space approach alone. It provides thematic as well as chronological and geographic parameters.

One final comment. There is discrepancy between the general and the unique. Professor Rudnytsky has pointed out that he prefers terms such as "antiquity" and "medieval." I think they are fine for general terms, but sometimes you want to point out the uniqueness of the Ukrainian case. A term like "Cossack Ukraine" gives a more precise definition than "early modern period." The time and space are there as well as the focus of interest, whereas "early modern" is very amorphous, with no organizing principle. I think the key is having an organizing principle that allows an arrangement of materials, so that the reader or listener knows where one is going from the start.

LUBOMYR R. WYNAR:

It is a truism that without clear-cut historical terminology and determination of historical periodization, no effective historical research is possible. According to Professor Rudnytsky, there exists at present only the Soviet and non-Soviet (Ukrainian) periodization of Ukrainian history. He thus omits the Russian imperial periodization which is accepted in many American historical textbooks and monographs. Therefore, I would add a third periodization, the American, which is based on the official pre-revolutionary Russian scheme as well as on the writings of émigré Russian historians.

Mykhailo Hrushevsky advocated the transfer of emphasis in historical investigation from the history of the organized state to the history of people and society. He rejected the official Russian historical scheme because of its artificial construction and stated that the most rational approach to studies of East European history is to present the history of each nationality separately in accordance with its genetic development from the beginning to the present.

It is interesting to note that the present trend in Western (West European and American) historiography follows a similar pattern, stressing the importance of "people" and "society" as key variables in the analysis of the historical process (this new trend was inaugurated by Lucien Febvre and Marc Bloch—founders of the *Annales* school in the 1930s). The emphasis on the study of social issues and the society as major "elements" of historical research constitutes the cornerstone of this "new history." Hrushevsky, at the beginning of the twentieth century, experienced views similar to those advanced today by many Western historians. Presently his major concepts are repeated in modified historical research models.

Now I wish to make a brief comment on another of Professor Rudnytsky's statements. He recommends that Ukrainian historians concentrate their efforts on problems of content and substance rather than terminology. In my opinion, historical terminology is directly related to the "content and substance" of historical research since one has to use clearly defined concepts and terms. Otherwise terminological confusion will occur in historical works.

Ukrainian history is a well-defined field of research, according to Hrushevsky's scheme and the Ukrainian state-oriented historiographical school, which accepted his historical periodization and terminology with few modifications. Thus, at present we do not have a "perfect periodization" and a "perfect historical terminology," but at the same time we are not starting from scratch. Professors Borys Krupnytsky, Dmytro Doroshenko, Oleksander Ohloblyn, Mykola Chubaty, Omeljan Pritsak and many other historians have contributed to this topic.

Regarding periodization, I fully agree with Professor Rudnytsky that we should follow in the steps of German and French historians and apply the name of Ukraine to *all* periods of Ukrainian history. I also accept his periodization terms: the ancient and medieval periods of Ukrainian history, the medieval period subdivided into Kievan State and Halych-Volhynian State, and the Lithuanian period. Some historians use the term "Lithuanian-Ruthenian" to designate the latter period. This is questionable. A more flexible categorization would be "Ukrainian lands under Lithuanian rule" or "Lithuanian period." In regard to the modern period, I recommend "Ukraine under the Polish Commonwealth and the development of Ukrainian Cossacks." There is no reference in Professor Rudnytsky's paper to the Ukrainian Cossack Hetman state. I think this period and term is essential, since it relates to political, social and cultural processes in Ukrainian historical development. This term and period is eliminated in Soviet historiography which follows Marxist periodization and official guidelines of the Communist party. I recommend reinstating the term "Ukrainian Cossack Hetman State" for the second half of the seventeenth century and the eighteenth century. (The end of this period is reflected in major political events—landmarks: liquidation of the office of hetman by Empress Catherine II in 1764; the destruction of the Zaporozhian Sich, 1775; the abolition of Ukrainian courts and transformation of Cossack regiments into regular Russian military formations, 1783.) This period is followed by the Russian and Austrian occupation of Ukrainian territory. The proper term for this era would be "Ukraine under Russia and Austria and the Ukrainian national rebirth in the nineteenth century." Finally, we have "Ukraine in the twentieth century and the restoration of Ukrainian statehood," with a number of sub-periods.

The above-mentioned periodization may serve as a basis for further analysis of this important subject. Professor Pritsak attempted to introduce the term "Rusians" (with a single "s") in order to designate Ukrainians in medieval times. This term is accepted in some publications and rejected in others. Some of my colleagues interpret this innovation as the term "Russia" (with a double "s"), only misspelled. I suggest that the terms "Rus' people" or "Ruthenians" should be considered.

At present we are faced with a terminological problem: confusion of the Ukrainian with the Russian and Belorussian historical processes. (E.g., the Harvard scholar Samuel Cross has stated that Russians, Ukrainians and Belorussians "are nonetheless parts of the same nation .... " Similar views are expressed by other scholars.) American and West European historians, in researching special topics in East European history, in many instances limit themselves to Russian historical literature and sources. Such an approach from a methodological and subject viewpoint is not justified and should, therefore, be critically re-examined.

I urgently recommend that in the future we form a special committee on East European historical terminology which would consist of historians, linguists, geographers and specialists in other relevant subject areas. The major objective of this proposed committee would be to clarify the terminological chaos in regard to various periods of Ukrainian, Russian and Belorussian history. This question has also been raised by Henryk Paszkiewicz in his monograph *The Origin of Russia*, in which he states that historical research would be facilitated if the relevant terminologies pertaining to East European history were internationally regulated.

TARAS HUNCZAK:

As I see it there are several problems. For Hegel it was enough to say that history is the unfolding of world reason. Everyone thought: here is a great man, he speaks wise words. Nobody knew exactly what it meant; I sometimes doubt that he could have defined it, but it sounds good. We try to put our particular stamp on that definition. That brings us to the next German luminary, Leopold von Ranke. He was slightly more disciplined, a professional historian. He said the objective is to find the content of that unfolding world reason and we can only do it if we discover how things actually happened in the past, *wie es eigentlich gewesen ist*.

We know that the past cannot be recovered completely. Think about this day since you got up in the morning. Try to remember everything in its complete content. Now if we have difficulty recreating our immediate past, how in the world—not to use any other word—can we presume to recall or recreate the entire past. Therefore I personally don't treat those things too seriously. I don't subscribe to the *magiia slova*—the magic of the word—that one simply applies the proper label and solves all the problems.

Admittedly, historians are a special breed of people. We create schemes to help us understand periods, but then we sometimes turn then into immutable categories. I think Professor Rudnytsky has a very good point. He says we should concentrate on the substance and not expend all of our efforts reaching for a verbal definition. By the time we are able to define something, we no longer have the energy to deal with the problem itself. While I essentially agree with what Professor Rudnytsky has to say about periodization, I disagree with certain aspects of his presentation.

In the West, periodization has been characterized by developments that were peculiar to the West European community—the Early Middle Ages, the High Middle Ages, etc. Authors and writers are developing all kinds of perspectives which we can use to put things together and match events with a particular era. However, developments in Eastern Europe are not characterized by the same experiences as found in the West. While we can always fill the categories with content, the periodization might be incorrect. As an example, one might agree there was a type of social interdependence in Ukraine that might suggest feudalism. My opinion, however, is that feudalism which entails contractual relationships with protection for both parties is not applicable to the East European experience.

I agree that one very useful term is the "early modern period." Since people like to attach characteristics to periods, I also will resort to this practice. What do I consider to be the early modern period? It starts around the time of the Union of Lublin. This is not because of the event itself, but rather because of some significant developments that coincide with it. The development of the Cossack organization and the church controversy are two of the many things that went into the making of a new consciousness, including political awareness. The latter eventually manifested itself when the Cossacks ceased to be mere adventurers and became a politically conscious force. The era ends with the reign of Catherine II. The second period extends from 1790 to 1917, with the final one lasting from 1917 to the present. This is probably as good a division as any.

As a teacher of history my problems are slightly different. Whereas some may teach primarily Ph.D. candidates, I teach undergraduates. The graduate student is forced to articulate the problems at a different level than a struggling undergraduate. My problems are practical ones, such as the shortage of textbooks in the English language. It may sound mundane, but it is a genuine problem. It is much easier for me to introduce my students to any number of historiographical concepts, since I was introduced to them by my professors. Sometimes I like to make excursions on my own. But such practical problems as finding textbooks are of a daily order.

The last point I want to make is about the terminology of Rusia or Russia. Looking at old maps of the seventeenth and early eighteenth century, we also find the term *Rusia Moscovitica*. On no old map did I find the designation *Rossiia*. In the seventeenth century the map-makers were still working from the old premise.

FRANK SYSYN:

I had hoped that one of the topics we could deal with here was the nuts-and-bolts of teaching courses in Ukrainian history: presentation, methodology, textbooks and reading material. Of course, questions of periodization and terminology are basic to these matters.

In planning university courses we must look into the reasons why students wish to study Ukrainian history. It is my impression that courses in Canada have a considerable segment of students who take the courses to find out about the country of their ancestors and to comprehend the Ukrainian cultural and political milieu that they participate in, without being sufficiently prepared to do so by formal education. A second segment is composed of students who specialize in Slavic regional studies and see that they need background on Ukraine to understand fully Russian and East European history and Slavic languages and literatures. Finally, a third segment consists of students of history who have chosen a course on Ukrainian history for the same reasons they might choose French or Japanese or Iranian history: curiosity, course distribution requirements, reputation of instructor (particularly his grading practices) or scheduling requirements. It is the high proportion of the first group of students that marks Ukrainian history courses off from most others at Canadian and American universities, although one presumes that German and Italian history courses may have a similar content and that courses in Canadian history in Canada or American history in the United States may at times be chosen for reasons similar to those that lead the Ukrainian Canadian or Ukrainian American to choose Ukrainian history. Yet given the small enrolments most Ukrainian history courses have, we face a very diverse student body with varied preparations and expectations. Our problems are to deal with an engineer of Ukrainian descent with no training in history, a student of Russian literature who is looking for a perspective differing from that offered in traditional courses in Russian history, and a history student who knows about medieval France, but has little idea where Ukraine is. We must construct syllabi, lectures and reading lists that can serve all constituencies without dropping to the lowest common denominator.

My courses in Ukrainian history at Harvard in the past two years have differed in their constituency from courses in Canada by their lack of students of Ukrainian descent. Yet my two years' teaching experience at Harvard was preceded by two years of teaching Saturday mornings at a local Ukrainian school. Hence, I have taught all segments.

In the Saturday schools my initial attempts to excite an audience of ten-to fifteen-year-olds about the intellectual problems in studying national history, the opportunities of understanding Latin and Byzantine, sedentary and nomadic, Islamic and Christian civilizations as they overlapped in the Ukrainian lands, and to face the challenges of tracing a Ukrainian culture, civilization and community evolving in a complex matrix of states and other cultures on the Ukrainian lands met with unmitigated disaster. At the end of the first year, Volodymyr the Great, Bohdan Khmelnytsky, Taras Shevchenko and Symon Petliura were jumbled in examination answers as contemporaries in an amorphous Ukrainian experience. My students wanted simple explanations that would tell them about their people through the ages and explain puzzling factors of their contemporary existence (why the press called them Russians, why people said they had no country because they had no independent state, why some Ukrainians are Orthodox and others Catholic). Their desires were neither to indulge in an intellectual exercise, nor to use data from Ukraine to study historical theories and methods, nor to approach East European or early modern history through a study of Ukraine, but rather to obtain a systematized body of knowledge that would place them in a historical community, the Ukrainian nation. I perhaps exaggerate their desires as opposed to their parents' earnest wishes, but I was struck by how little need there was to argue why one should study Ukrainian history. For even the most recalcitrant students, the answer was clear—they should know about Ukrainian history because they were in some way Ukrainian. They were frustrated in doing so because of their abominable level of study of general history and geography in American schools and because the complex political, cultural and social history of Ukraine and its people was not as easy to compartmentalize and present as that of the United States, their chief frame of reference. How can one explain Orthodoxy and Uniatism to a group that never heard of Byzantium? The second year I taught names and dates in a clearly structured chronological survey.

While I do not equate our university students of Ukrainian descent with my Saturday school students, I do believe they share some characteristics. What I hope is that we can use their desire to know "their" history, Ukrainian history, as a means to broaden their understanding of historical problems and surrounding cultures. Thus, the more students of segment two and three we attract, the better our courses and the general level of Ukrainian historical research in North America will become. But what do we have to offer these segments? For the second, the Slavic and East European specialists, the answer is clear: Ukraine and Ukrainians bulk large in the history and culture of the region. For the third segment, we can hardly argue that Ukraine and Ukrainians have played as great a role in the world and world civilization as France and the French. Yet we can justifiably argue that this people and land, so often a borderland and a transition zone, provide fruitful material for delving into a number of interesting problems (e.g., cultural continuity, relations of sedentary and nomadic peoples, contacts of Eastern and Western Christianity, modern nation-building). Our problems arise when we try to construct courses that allow for both an orderly presentation of systematized information and for a discussion of the problems, questions and controversies that each of us faces in our scholarly work on the Ukrainian past.

Our problems are greater than those of our colleagues in English or Italian history for two reasons. First, we work in a field that is underdeveloped, impacted by extra-scholarly, political struggles and stagnant in recent years. Every historian feels acutely that his area is somehow understudied and filled with unanswered questions. Historians of Ukraine know what it is to work in a field where frequently even the first stages of collecting sources and data have not been attempted. Second, we have woefully inadequate textbooks and very little auxiliary reading material. No anthologies of translated sources exist: suitable articles in English are few and still at times inaccessible. Some might question our very ability to offer courses at this juncture. I believe, however, that by offering courses we create a demand for the creation of the new textbooks and materials that we need. Hence, I see this conference and its discussion of questions of periodization and terminology as a positive step.

To me periodization and terminology are primarily conceptual tools for organizing and describing the past. They become counterproductive when they hinder rather than assist our understanding of people, events and processes. I support Professor Rudnytsky's proposals because they do not attempt to impose an all-encompassing theory for periodization. Hence, I also agree with Professor Hunczak that the desire for order should not lead us to distort the material. After all, even the subject of "Ukrainian history" is a controversial topic. I, for example, am uncomfortable with Professor Pritsak's argument that Ukraine is a well-defined territory and the subject of Ukrainian history encompasses all that took place within this area. I do not believe that we can forget that it is the Ukrainian people with their cultural traditions who constitute Ukrainian history, since for long periods Ukraine was neither a state nor a well-defined administrative unit and the borders of Ukrainian settlement frequently changed.

Terminology is, of course, an important issue because by the choice of terms we often express deeper conceptualizations. Specialists in East European history may well know that Kievan Rus', Muscovy and imperial Russia represent very different entities, but by referring to all these areas as "Russia" they do not convey this understanding to their students. We are, of course, torn between the desire to maintain terms as they were used in each period and the recognition that names should reflect our understanding of communities and events. The change of collective designations for Ukrainians from *rusyny* to *malorosiiany* to *ukraintsi* with regional variations in usage creates considerable tension. Yet the employment of so many terms for a people that was clearly demarcated and perceived as a historical community is cumbersome. Hence, we may well use "Ukraine" and "Ukrainian" as long as we make clear what names were used in various periods.

We may never agree on periodization and terms for our own teaching and writing. What is more important is that each of us produces the textbooks, source books and essays that will make the teaching of our history possible. It will not be through "correct" terms and periodizations that we shall succeed in teaching Ukrainian history, but by providing our students with the intellectual tools to grapple with the Ukrainian past.

PRITSAK:

Undoubtedly, introducing a periodization which is already somewhat familiar to the student has many advantages. There is a danger, however. I am not as pessimistic as my friend Professor Hunczak, who believes that we cannot reconstruct the past. Certainly, we cannot reconstruct millions of past events. Yet it is important to establish their distinctive features and to view the past using functional and structural models. Otherwise it would make no sense to have history as a scholarly discipline in the curriculum of a university. Probably it would be better to have history as a subdivision of fiction or something like that, where everyone could create his or her vision according to individual emotion and mood.

What is historically important? I suppose that, in answering this, linguistics has made better progress than historiography. It has isolated what it considers to be of central importance: the phonemical structure, i.e., some thirty to fifty distinctive phonemes out of thousands of sounds. Only this makes it possible for a language to function. The phonemes and not the *sounds* allow us to understand each other. History requires its own equivalent of a phonemical structure.

I agree with Professor Hunczak that to use the term "feudalism" in reference to Eastern Europe makes no sense. Certainly a distinctive feature here is the bilateral contract. If you don't have a contract, a juridical relationship, there is no feudalism. The fact that there are several principalities on one territory instead of *one* kingdom does not establish the existence of feudalism. This can be shown to have existed at different times in different parts of the world, even outside Western Europe; but this is not feudalism.

I would not suggest that we historians invite linguists, sociologists and representatives of other disciplines and ask them to participate in the establishment of our terminology. This would be very dangerous. Every discipline must have its own terminology based on the problems which the given discipline investigates. I have a spoon and a pencil. I cannot use the pencil to eat or the spoon to write. The bountiful terminology of linguistics or atomic physics is of no use to historians.

If we look at Ukrainian development and compare East European with West European development, we can see very clearly that beginning with the twelfth century there is a divergence. Something completely different is happening in the East and the West. In the twelfth century the West experienced a renaissance, followed by scholasticism, whereas in Ukraine scholasticism did not occur until the seventeenth century. What is very important is that in the West secular civilization developed, beginning with Humanism and the Reformation. These two movements did not have a pervasive influence in Eastern Europe. Secular development in Eastern Europe began in 1804–5 when Alexander I established the first secular universities at Kazan and Kharkiv and reorganized the University of Moscow. For the first time in Eastern Europe we had secular schools, and for the first time we had a secular civilization. I think this is of tremendous significance.

Then there is another issue. If we have feudalism in Western Europe, what do we have in Eastern Europe? We have the patrimonial system, and this system remains there still. Even today the ruler, the central committee of the Communist party, claims a monopoly on everything—on thinking, on political action, on economic decisions. Outside the party, no other body is allowed to participate in politics. This is something of great importance and we should take it into consideration. However, after 1848 in Galicia, for the first time one part of Ukraine was engaged in a societal development within a constitutional system, a state system which was no longer patrimonial. This is also of great importance.

I am also considering the very important event that occurred in 1848 in

Western Ukraine and in 1861 in Eastern Ukraine. Until these dates, the number of people who were regarded as human beings was about 100,000 in Galicia and about 150,000 in "Russian" Ukraine, altogether not much more than a quarter of a million. After these dates, millions of former serfs became human beings.

I would not agree with Professor Sysyn that territory should be ignored. Certainly, a territory alone without a society cannot be the subject of history. But a society has to be stationary on a territory, otherwise we do not have a higher society, we do not have a polity. Only a political human being is the subject of history. Here ethnos, religion and many other things are just part of what a *homo politicus* is.

SUBTELNY:

These kinds of things we could talk about for a long time. However, we are talking about labels. We want something practical. We want labels to tell us something about time, space and what is going on. Professor Rudnytsky's labels tell us about time—they don't go any further than that. They don't tell us anything about space, nor about what is going on. Because Ukraine has a very complicated history, the problem of space in Ukrainian history—whether it is Russia or the Habsburg empire or where the steppe ends—is very undefined.

What we should perhaps try to do is put down the most practical label and avoid philosophical discussions as much as possible. I realize that the two are related, but we are looking for something which establishes time, space and what is going on, not something that leads us into involved philosophical discussions.

JOHN-PAUL HIMKA:

I disagree. The question is the organizing principle versus the problematically neutral scheme of periodization which Professor Rudnytsky proposes. Each of these approaches has its own relevance in its own place. The whole virtue of the periodization scheme proposed by Professor Rudnytsky is that it is precisely a periodization scheme, almost a punctuation scheme. It is useful for dividing up courses, surveys, encyclopedia articles—providing a paragraphical way of thinking about history. The organizing principle, on the other hand, is something that will apply when one looks at certain problems. But to use it as a basis to divide history is, unfortunately, not only to bring up certain issues, but also to detract from other issues.

To call the nineteenth century "the Age of National Awakening" is to overdefine it. For example, the growth of industry in southern Ukraine is an important phenomenon and one that has been neglected in historical research, probably because we only see the national awakening. Also, at the same time as the *national* awakening, in Ukraine, as throughout much of Europe in the nineteenth century, there was a new *social* awakening. For Ukrainians most decisive was the growth of peasant consciousness. And wherever there were actual industrial workers, there was also a new kind of class consciousness emerging, of a different order than had existed in any previous era. The pristine neutrality of the scheme Professor Rudnytsky proposes seems to me to encourage openness to the multiplicity of historical problems. This periodization, moreover, has the special merit of putting Ukrainian history firmly within—to use Oscar Halecki's phrase—"the limits and divisions of European history."

HUNCZAK:

Just one word. I do not subscribe to the view that we have a holy confusion in the study of history; otherwise I would not be in this discipline. What I wish to say is that we cannot recover the past completely in every dimension. I do take history as a serious discipline, unlike Voltaire who said that history should be taught for entertainment rather than for instruction.

RUDNYTSKY:

This question was directed to me by Professor Wynar: What do I mean by saying that Ukrainian historians should concentrate on issues of content rather than on terminology? Obviously, we cannot write history without using terminologies, but I suggest that it is probably more fruitful to develop issues of terminology when dealing with problem of substance and not just tilt for words as so often historians, and especially pseudo-historians and journalists, do.

We should not get enraged when we hear the term "Kievan Russia," even if we don't like it. Instead, let us demonstrate that Kievan Rus' or Kievan Russia was more similar to Ukraine than to Muscovy. Then the question of labels will follow by itself.

Now, why did I omit the Russian imperial scheme of periodization? I did not include it for the very simple reason that in the traditional scheme, as still used in American texts, there is simply no place for Ukrainian history. Whatever we may say of our Soviet friends, we see textbooks of Ukrainian history appearing, so we know the subject is recognized after a fashion. The Kliuchevsky scheme, from which the American textbook historiography is derived, has no place for Ukrainian history as such. This is why I made no reference to that traditional scheme.

Here are some points which are of a more central nature. Either I do not fully understand Professor Pritsak's reasoning, or, if I understand him correctly, I would tend to disagree. This refers to my proposed periodization scheme. Can the common European scheme be applied to Eastern Europe, especially Ukraine? I will refer to the two strongest political and historical minds Ukraine has produced in the last hundred years, who stood at opposite poles but who agreed on this specific point. I refer to Drahomanov and Lypynsky. Both thought that what makes the distinction between Ukrainian history and Muscovite and Russian imperial history is that the basic framework of European history applies also to Ukraine, albeit in an imperfect form. For instance, there is a reflection of the Renaissance, or at least Humanism, in Ukraine; there is also a reflection of the sixteenth-century religious struggle. The European Reformation and Counter Reformation came to Ukraine two or three generations later, in the form of a religious crisis in the late sixteenth century. Drahomanov says specifically that Ukraine has passed through all the major stages of Europe's historical development, although with delays and breakdowns. This is the main difference between Ukraine and Russia, historically.

Obviously, this grid cannot be successfully applied for the interpretation of Russian history. For instance, Muscovy does not fit into the European Middle Ages nor into the pattern of early modern absolute monarchies. It is *sui generis*. Its frame of reference is different. It may be compared rather with the Near Eastern despotic monarchies, as Plekhanov has correctly stated in the "Introduction" to his *History of Russian Social Thought*.

Here is another point which is related: the concept of a patrimonial state, with which I am familiar and which derives from Max Weber. Do you think that pre-Mongol Kievan Rus' and the Lithuanian Grand Duchy were patrimonial states?

PRITSAK:

Yes, certainly.

RUDNYTSKY:

Well, I beg to disagree. If I think that the Byzantine empire or, later, Muscovy were patrimonial states, I perceive the so-called Kievan federation as something very different, because of its lack of bureaucracy and standing armies, its decentralization of power, considerable mobility and elements of popular participation.

PRITSAK:

Perhaps I can give you an example. Take the Kingdom of Galicia and Volodymeria in 1340. Only the king or prince or duke was representative of his state. The boyars had no say. When the king disappeared, the state disappeared, without any resistance. Hrushevsky and other historians could not understand how it could disappear completely without any trace. I am not talking about the Kievan period, because our sources might not be adequate; but I am talking about 1340. The prince and the state were identical. Prince Danylo could nominate his *koniukh* to be bishop one day, then dismiss him the next. Everywhere else in Europe the ecclesiastic and secular dignitaries could have a say. Think of the Magna Carta and the Golden Bull. At the beginning of the fourteenth century, it just happened that all of the old dynasties were dying out. The Piasts, Arpáds, Přemyslids. The same thing happened to the dynasty in Galicia and Volodymeria. However, these other states survived the dynastic crisis: Galicia did not.

RUDNYTSKY:

Here I am going to appeal to the rights of the estates against the crown in interrupting Professor Pritsak. I am struck by the fact that so many prominent historians who have dealt with that era ...

PRITSAK:

Drahomanov was an excellent specialist in ancient history but he was not a specialist in medieval history. He was a very good specialist in Roman history. He knew very little about medieval Ukrainian history. Lypynsky's field of research was the Khmelnytsky era.

RUDNYTSKY:

I think of scholars like Vernadsky, Dvornik and others who stress the individualistic, decentralized, libertarian character of pre-Mongol Rus', in quite clear contrast to later Muscovy. I feel that to move from twelfth-century Kiev to fifteenth-century Muscovy is to move to a very different world.

I do not want to continue this line of argument, but wish to make another point. I do agree with Professor Wynar that there is a very strong trend in contemporary Western historiography toward social history—interest in popular movements, popular revolts, outlaws. These topics have become very common in English, French, North American historical literature. Hrushevsky was a man of a different age, a genuine Ukrainian populist of the early twentieth century. But he happens to be in tune with this latest trend in Western historiography. Now we come to the right of the historian to select his own problems and approaches. I am not particularly interested in social history. I prefer pragmatic political history and the history of ideas. Of course, history may deal with anything that happened in human society. Biography, history of art, of music, of science, of fashions, of technology—everything can be treated historically. However, I would go along with Professor Pritsak that the centre of gravity, the centre of research is the history of organized political communities, and so I do not personally give preference to diffuse popular trends.

Now here is a question of one's philosophy. I believe that it is a misunderstanding to assume that philosophical questions arise because somebody looks into the blue and then begins to fantasize about it, has fanciful ideas. Philosophical problems arise from dealing with concrete issues. If you think about being, about the realities of human experience, then you deal with philosophical problems. Each discipline, without exception, has its philosophical dimension. Medicine, law, physics—any discipline—becomes philosophical once one begins to question the discipline's basic principles. Obviously, this also applies to our study. History is an empirical discipline; it deals with empirical realities. But to grasp empirical realities we have to go back to first principles and this means to think philosophically. I would not speak disparagingly about very great thinkers. For instance, the view of Professor Pritsak is the classical Hegelian view, namely, that history deals primarily with politically organized communities which we have commonly called states. So this is still a living concept today, after more than a century and a half. We can say that we do not accept it, but we should not treat it lightly.

One final comment, about chronological limits. This is how I try to introduce innocent undergraduates to chronological problems, how I try to make them think, at least to some extent, historically: on 31 December 475, people go to bed and say: "Well, here we are in Antiquity." Then they wake up on 1 January, on what is now the next year, and say: "Thank God! Now we have reached the Middle Ages." This is obviously not the way things happen. All history is a continuum, but one with changes. It is out of practical necessity, simply to divide books into chapters and to organize the subject matter, that we pick certain dates as dividing points. In a thousand years—assuming that mankind will survive—perhaps the first flight to the moon in 1969 will be considered the beginning of a new age in the history of mankind. But for those who have lived through this, it is part of one continuous life story of the people of that generation. These are very simple things which we should not forget.

SYSYN:

The time limit which Professor Rudnytsky has set down, 1569, is also the time Professor Pritsak sees as the first emergence of the state on Ukrainian territory. The next period is the early modern period, which Professor Rudnytsky wants to end around 1800. It is also the time which Professor Pritsak sees as the beginning of his centres of secular learning. So their conclusions, happily, are about the same.

MARKO ANTONOVYCH:

I have a small question about periodization in connection with what Professor Pritsak has said. Until 1340 we have one periodization for all of Ukraine. But afterward, there are separate developments in east and west. Maybe we should try to establish one periodization for the whole of Ukraine. This is a very important question, and I would appreciate some comments.

ALEXANDER BARAN:

I think that a common history for both east and west is a good idea, but I don't know how we can create complete periods for both sections. For the first period, we agree on ancient and medieval history, which ends with the fall of the Galician-Volhynian Kingdom. Then we have the early modern period which ends at the end of the eighteenth century. Thus we divide almost a thousand years into two parts. Then the next two periods are just two centuries—not even two complete centuries.

Why can't we divide the whole thing into four parts: namely ancient, medieval, early modern and modern? Certainly we have to divide the medieval period into two parts, the Kievan and Galician Rus' and then Lithuanian Rus'. The early modern period would be the Cossacks before the Hetman state and the Hetman state itself. The recent period could also be divided into two parts—the nineteenth century and the twentieth century. This would be much clearer.

OLEH S. PIDHAINY:

When I began teaching back in 1964 my main problem was how to treat the interplay between four active communities: Ukraine, Poland, Russia and Belorussia. Also, I was troubled by the fact that Ukraine was part of various states. Then I thought that perhaps one could develop an acceptable scheme on the basis of Hrushevsky's scheme for the Eastern Slavs, expanding it to include other major groups in Eastern Europe. So I suggest that a possible way to deal with Ukrainian periodization is to handle it within the larger framework of East European history. Basically,

East European history would become a special complement to West European history. I propose five major divisions. The first would be the era from the eighth century B.C. to the sixth century A.D. This would be the time from the Scythians to the period of the *Völkerwanderung*. The second era would be when Eastern Europe was under Byzantine influence, plus the great influence of Rome. That would be from the seventh century A.D. to the fall of Byzantium, in 1453. This would include the rise of Kiev and its disintegration, plus the period of Lithuanian rule. The third period would begin in 1453 at the time of the rise of Poland and end with the Battle of Poltava in 1709. At this time Poland was up for grabs and Catherine II liquidated it. The fourth period would encompass the rise of the Russian empire from 1709, which established the dominance of Russia in Eastern Europe, through to 1917, the date of the revolution. The fifth period would be since 1917. Basically, there is Greek influence in the first period; Byzantine influence including the Kievan state in the second; the third period is the rise of Poland; the fourth, the rise of Russia; and the fifth period is the disintegration of the Russian empire and the rise of the Soviet Union.

LUBOMYR HAJDA:

I have just one comment, and that is that the various periodizations which people have proposed conflict, I think, with a principle that everyone seems to agree with: that what constitutes the scope of Ukrainian history is the present territory of Ukraine. I am thinking particularly about my area of interest, Crimea and the southern steppe regions; I am afraid that these regions do not always fit into the periodizations that have been proposed by most discussants. We should be flexible enough in our periodization to take into account the different regional developments of the Ukrainian territories.

RUDNYTSKY:

I am always in favour of flexibility and I believe there is good cause for it in this case. On the one hand, we can say that all that happens on the territory of Ukraine is legitimately part of the Ukrainian historical process. But, on the other hand, one also has to insist on flexibility because the territory itself is not unchangeable. For instance, if you look at Soviet publications they take the present frontiers of the Ukrainian Soviet Socialist Republic as sacred limits. In dealing with prehistoric cultures, they show on a map only the territory of the Ukrainian SSR at the present time. What is beyond is left blank. This is the territorial principle pushed to the point of absurdity.

We must keep in mind that the territory of fifteenth- and sixteenth-century Ukraine was not identical with the Ukraine of today. As Professor Shevelov reminded us in his after-dinner address yesterday, the territory of Ukraine ended just south of Kiev. That was the end of settled land. Then there was no-man's land and then the Crimean Khanate. This does not mean that you should not be interested in the history of the Crimea. Still, I do not think that the history of the Crimean Khanate is an integral part of the history of Ukraine in the same way as that of the Galician-Volhynian state or Bohdan Khmelnytsky's state, which are central to Ukrainian history. In contrast, I would consider the Crimean Khanate only marginally a part of Ukrainian history. If you say you are the legitimate heir of the Crimean Khanate, you are referring to an uprooted people whose survivors are now dispersed in Kazakhstan and elsewhere. There are historical entities which have become extinct: for instance, the ancient Mayas. The Crimean Tatars have also become largely extinct. We sympathize with them, although our ancestors felt differently.

So let's be flexible about this. An ethnic community can be a carrier of history, but so can a political entity. You can write, for instance, a history of the Habsburg empire, which existed for hundreds of years and which was a political entity with a very definite identity. The peoples which composed that empire still live today, but the Habsburg empire no longer exists; it ended in 1918—nothing comes after that. On the other hand, you can write a history of the Czech people even at the time they were incorporated in the Habsburg empire. You can write history on different levels and from different perspectives. There is territorial, statist, ethnic history and so on. I think they are all legitimate and they can co-operate.

HUNCZAK:

You cannot deal at the same time with territorial and national history. I think that that is impossible. If I interpret you correctly, Professor Rudnytsky, you are suggesting that the history of Ukraine should deal with national Ukrainian history, and that only those elements that participated in this historical process to some degree would have to be defined as belonging to the Ukrainian nation.

The civilization that existed in medieval times is understandable to me when I deal with West European historiography. We can go to the fourteenth and the fifteenth centuries, the beginning of the Renaissance—we know what is happening at that time. One could go through in one's mind all the institutions and intellectual trends and all that would be totally inapplicable to Ukraine.

The point is that the Eastern spirit in the fifteenth century was altogether different. East European experience is taken not just from Ukraine; these experiences are totally different. For Ukrainian history, a terminology has to be devised that is appropriate to the development of that particular time.

SYSYN:

I think we have a problem with defining "spirit of the age." Savonarola, who came into the limelight well into the "Renaissance," didn't seem to know it and didn't act in an appropriate way for a Renaissance man. Living in a backward land, Iurii Drohobych, too, appeared in the wrong place at the wrong time, because he, as a man of the new learning, was very atypical for his society. But he did actually live in the fifteenth century. We forget that just being together in the same place around the same time doesn't necessarily mean that people live in similar ways at the same level of civilization.

I think that Ukrainians always had contact with what was going on among European peoples. In other words, Ukrainians cannot be separated from general European civilization. Of course, at many times in its evolution Ukraine was so different from what was going on in the rest of Europe that it cannot fit into general European categories, and it was certainly influenced by "non-European" peoples and societies. But it doesn't bother us at all to think of Norway as part of Europe. Norway was at a very different level than, say, Italy and at a very different level, obviously, than Greece. But all three—Norway, Italy and Greece—are European. Why shouldn't this be applicable also to Ukraine?

RUDNYTSKY:

May I continue with your line of thought and then maybe refer to some other things. What is European history? It is not simply a geographical concept. Think of Spain, or Iberia, under Moslem rule: Andalus. It is not that all European is good and all non-European is bad. Andalus was culturally much superior to contemporary Europe. But, obviously, Moslem Spain was not part of the European world, although it had a great cultural influence on it and Spain, Iberia, is geographically part of Europe. The Balkans were cut off from Europe by the Moslem conquest. Everything south of the Danube for a good four hundred years was lost to Europe. Now, I think, there is a good deal of agreement among historians, including Russian historians, as well as Westerners writing about Russia, that post-Mongol Muscovy—Muscovite Russia—does not belong in the European context socially or culturally. Muscovy was a world apart until Peter and even beyond. The Westernization of Russia by Peter and his successors was a problematic affair, as recognized by many Russian historians and social thinkers.

In contrast to this—and here I return to the point which Professor Pritsak and myself debated—I realize how delicate this problem is and that we should approach it with an open mind—if we think of Rus' of the eleventh or twelfth century, with all of the differences which existed between Kiev and Paris or Goslar, they were still parts of one world. Rus' accepted religion and higher culture from Byzantium and Bulgaria. But still, I would say, the political and social arrangements in Kievan Rus' were closer to the contemporary European pattern than to Byzantine theocracy. Byzantine theocracy was not transplanted to Kiev for the simple reason that the Caesar still existed in Constantinople. Byzantine theocracy could be transplanted to Moscow at a time when it had disappeared in Constantinople; but the grand dukes of Kiev, even Iaroslav, were unable to create a replica of Byzantium. I submit that the grand dukes of Kiev were not Byzantine *basileis*: they were something very different. I propose it not as a definite statement, but with a question mark. This refers to Professor Pritsak's concept of a patrimonial state. In the West, too, the state of Charlemagne was an attempt to imitate the Byzantine system. Obviously, Charlemagne wanted to revive the Late Roman-Byzantine system. The emperors of the Saxon and Salian dynasties tried the same thing and actually they continued to try this down to the Hohenstaufens. Also, the Hohenstaufens tried to continue the Byzantine patrimonial model, but they failed. Thus we can see that the difference between East and West was not absolute.

There is also the development of another system which we call, for simplicity's sake, feudal. I suggest that the process of decentralization in Rus' entailed the growth of a multiplicity of local centres. It was, of course, not exactly the same as Western feudalism, but was a parallel development, despite the absence of formal contractual relations between prince and boyar in Rus'. On this point we may perhaps agree with Soviet historians' stress on feudalism. On the other hand, Soviet historians tend to minimize the importance of the Mongol invasions. The Mongol invasion was a cataclysm which engulfed an Atlantis—Old Rus'. Subsequently, the emerging Muscovite state used some elements of the Kievan inheritance but basically was quite different.

BARAN:

The trouble is that we are mixing everything up. We cannot simply take over the divisions of Western civilization and apply them to Ukrainian history. Why? Because the two areas were divided from each other by cultural tendencies. In the West there was the medieval period, then the Renaissance, then the Baroque, Absolutism and the Enlightenment. These did not occur in Ukraine. Like the West, we experienced a Middle Ages, but it was considerably different. Our Renaissance came two hundred years later, at the time of the late Reformation. It was, as Professor Pritsak says, a Renaissance without humanism, without secularization. So we missed the most important influences on Western development. We must realize that Ukraine's development diverged from that of Western Europe. This is also true of the Balkan nations. They had the greatest divergence. For instance, they were not affected by the Renaissance, the Baroque, even by the Enlightenment, since under Turkish rule those trends couldn't penetrate.

I teach Balkan history and read the original Bulgarian and Serbian textbooks. They have complete and distinct periodization schemes of their history. It is interesting to note that the Bulgarian scheme and the Serbian scheme, even though they lived in the same situation and had very similar national developments, are completely different. I think that in Ukrainian history we have to find our own pattern of social and cultural trends which would reflect the development of our civilization. This is what our whole task is.

PRITSAK:

I would like to deal with Professor Rudnytsky's question about Kievan problems. I have devoted approximately forty years of my life to their study. I started to study all possible steppe peoples, not for the sake of the steppe peoples themselves, but to gain a better understanding of the problems of East European and especially Ukrainian history. There was some knowledge, certainly, which I was able to acquire.

First of all, if you take what we normally call the Kievan state, it was actually a blend of two systems. On the one hand, there was the traditional, or Khazar, system. We should not forget that Iaroslav was a *kagan* and that he was addressed as a *kagan* even by Ilarion. Byzantine, Oriental and other sources also refer to him as a *kagan*. On the other hand, there was the Byzantine system. Certainly, the system in Kiev was not a pure Byzantine system, for obvious reasons. One can say there were also Northern elements—Old Scandinavian and Old Germanic. It is not just a matter of accident that the ruler of Kiev was styled either *kagan* or *konung*. We are dealing with a kind of syncretism which was very complicated and certainly we cannot go into all the details now.

I can only stress that what existed in Kiev had nothing to do—very little to do, to be more careful—with the political ideas and structures in the West, especially after 1054, which was a very great divide. There was a profound difference between Kiev and Paris, or Kiev and Regensburg, or Kiev and any other place in the West; even Kiev and Cracow or Gniezno. Already in the twelfth century we can see this very clearly from a study of the Polish sources or, for that matter, by comparing the Kievan and the Hungarian courts. It would make no sense to try to westernize something which was quite different.

There is no doubt that the Kievan system was not identical to the later Muscovite system either. The Muscovite system was not just a replica of Byzantium. There were also other influences. But what is very important is this: everything which we had in Kiev—even, as I was able to prove, the Old Scandinavian system—was based on the Khazarian model. In the Kievan system we find two versions of the Khazarian system plus the Byzantine factor, all having roots in the patrimonial system, which allows for a myriad of variants.

If you have a species called dog, you can have a Saint Bernard, or a Pekinese, or poodle or any other breed. They look completely different, but there is still a common denominator which makes them dogs. So in this way we can also look at the patrimonial system.

WYNAR:

It is all very well to discuss these problems, but there is another one which is very critical. Frank Sysyn mentioned it. Several of us must face students and there are no general textbooks in Ukrainian history. What are we going to do about this problem of textbooks? What are we doing for the students?

PRITSAK:

We must realize that there are two levels of problems—scholarly historical research and history as a subject of instruction in university curricula—and we will not be able to settle everything. I might add that I have been working for a number of years on the preparation of a history of Ukraine in several volumes.

PATRICIA HERLIHY:

It is just a wee voice. I hope that when this history of Ukraine emerges and is in our hands, you will have made a definitive periodization of Ukrainian history which the rest of us can follow.
[*Laughter from audience*]

PRITSAK:

It is not so easy. It has never been easy to establish anything concerning the Ukrainian past that everyone will accept.

GEORGE SHEVELOV:

I am an observer here, no more than that. It seems to me, as an outsider, that you should first establish the basis of your periodization, because it sounds to me, to use the word that was used in other applications, like "confusion." But in this case it is a confusion of various criteria. Sometimes I hear that the criterion proposed is political, sometimes it is rather juridical or legal. The definition of feudalism which I heard is, to my ears, very juridical and not strictly political. There are also cultural considerations.

It would be advisable to agree first on what criterion you would base your periodization. Then also make it clear before you proceed any further—after selecting one criterion—whether you intend to elaborate a periodization which would also cover other criteria; that is, a periodization based on, say, the political criterion, but which would also apply to cultural developments, to developments in language, in arts. Or you could base your periodization on one criterion to the exclusion of all others, with the understanding that others can elaborate their own periodization.

From my own experience, I can say that I frequently faced the problem of periodization in my book on Ukrainian phonological history. I based it on external criteria, that is, I just followed the stages in the development of the literary language. There is not much room for controversy here. The division between—to use conventional terms—Kievan Rus' and Lithuanian Rus' is obvious. So is the distinction between the Lithuanian and the Polish periods. So is the distinction between the time before 1720 and the time after 1720. Thus I take 1720 as an orientation date.

Only in the conclusion to my book do I suggest, as a kind of preliminary hypothesis, a periodization on the basis of the internal phonological development. That is what I reported briefly and in a very simplified way yesterday. But ideally the phonology, the history of literature and political history should each have their own periodization. Then the possibility, or lack of possibility, of finding any common denominators should be explored. As long as you do not make clear for what purpose and on which criterion you base your periodization, you will not arrive at anything but a "Babylonian confusion of tongues."

PIDHAINY:

May I say that Professor Shevelov's idea appeals to me very much and I think that culture should be the basis for such a periodization. Culture would be a very useful concept, because it would also bring to light the linguistic ties of the various Slavic nations. In other words, I am suggesting that we view Ukraine as part of the East European civilization, based upon the closeness of language of the Western Slavs and the Eastern Slavs. This is based upon the common cultural background of being the battlefield between the Latin influence and the Greek influence. Only in this way will we be able to develop a periodization of Ukrainian history.

WYNAR:

My only suggestion is that in the future a special task force be formed to deal with the problem, and then probably some results could emerge. It is not manageable to come to conclusions concerning periodization or terminology here. We have made a good start and we should continue in the future as a special committee or task force.

RUDNYTSKY:

May I comment on this. I think that our profession is both a co-operative and a very individualistic one. It is impossible to visualize some high authority which would decree that from a certain date on we must all follow the same terminology. Each one of us should apply our ideas to the best of our ability. The final responsibility belongs to the individual scholar who has to write according to his lights, his understanding. I don't see the possibility of an authoritative academy which declares: "This is the rule." It cannot be done that way, at least not in a free society. But what is needed is more discussion, more exchange, more clarification.

To return to the first point which Professor Wynar directed at me. The reason that the so-called traditional scheme of Russian history was accepted was not that in the United States some holy synod or some central committee told American scholars to use it. It happened simply because there were these highly respected historians—classical nineteenth-century Russian historians—who exercised such an impact that other people followed in their footsteps. I think this is the only way we can hope to have an effect, not in a prescriptive way, but by producing works of lasting value which will then be able to convince people.

WYNAR:

May I add to this. The reason, in my opinion, that the Russian scheme was adopted by many American historians is that in the 1930s-40s we had a number of Russian historians at major American universities: Michael Florinsky at Columbia, Nicholas Riasanovsky at Berkeley, Leonid Strakhovsky at Georgetown, Michael Karpovich at Harvard, Anatole Mazour at Stanford and George Vernadsky at Yale. In the 1930s they didn't have access to primary sources and thus concentrated on writing historical textbooks.

There is an interesting monograph by Elizabeth Beyerly on Russian historians in exile, published in Holland (*The Europocentric Historiography of Russia: An Analysis of the Contribution of Russian Emigre Historians in the U.S.A.*, 1973). The author illustrates the intense influence of émigré historiography on American historical writing and university curricula. I see a direct relationship between American historical studies and the influence exercised by Russian émigré historians.

PRITSAK:

Now as we conclude our session I would like to stress that, although we have not solved our problem of periodization or terminology, I still believe that this exchange was very beneficial. I agree with Professor Wynar and Professor Shevelov that a seminar or working group, rather than a holy synod, be established to do something about this problem.

At the beginning of this session I stressed that at present we are facing a new situation and that we should do something about it. Of course, Ukrainian history is not the first national history to be presented. There are, fortunately, histories of the United States, Canada and single European and Asian nations. There are principles expressed in them. There also exist theoretical works. I suppose it would be very useful to divide the task among four or five members of the panel: to establish how many theories there are about what constitutes a national history. Then they might apply these various theories to Ukrainian history and see how well they fit.

Also, as Professor Shevelov has pointed out, first we could try to work with an external criterion. This is why I am concerned about the concepts of patrimonialism and secularization. Until 1800 not a single secular book was printed in Ukraine. After 1800 we had secular books. Of course, I am not saying we must use this periodization—pre-secular, secular—but it might be useful as an external reference. After this has been established, we might apply "phonological" and other criteria, using linguistic terminology. Finally, having prepared the external and internal criteria, we could probably find a common denominator. But this has to be studied; it will not come from nothing. The Holy Ghost will not help us. It demands very serious work.

Fortunately, models do exist. Let us study them, and let us start the experiment. As you know, we have to reach a level of abstraction. Every scholarly discipline, including history, can only be pursued on the level of abstraction. The subject of history is not Napoleon as a human being, but his historical function—i.e., the function of Napoleon's actions. We cannot get to Napoleon and weigh him or smell him; that will not help us and it makes no sense. In this way, as we bring everything to the level of abstraction, we may reach agreement. As long as you have two apples and four oranges, it is very hard to find a common denominator; but if you have the numbers 2 and 4 and 5, you can find a common denominator. Two apples is not an abstraction, but 2 is an abstraction. In this way I hope we will find what we need.

Finally, it only remains for me to express my gratitude to everyone, panelists and non-panelists, for sharing wonderful suggestions and ideas, for sharing our troubles and hopes.